TO
DENY OUR
NOTHINGNESS

CONTEMPORARY IMAGES OF MAN

With a new Preface and Appendix
by the author

MAURICE FRIEDMAN

THE UNIVERSITY OF CHICAGO PRESS
Chicago and London

TO THE MEMORY OF

ALBERT CAMUS · CARL JUNG

HERMANN HESSE · ALDOUS HUXLEY · T. S. ELIOT

MARTIN BUBER · PAUL TILLICH

GABRIEL MARCEL · ANDRÉ MALRAUX · JOHN STEINBECK

"The greatest mystery is not that we have been flung at random among the profusion of the earth and the galaxy of the stars, but that in this prison we can fashion images of ourselves sufficiently powerful to deny our nothingness."

ANDRÉ MALRAUX

The excerpts from the poems and plays of T. S. Eliot are reprinted from his volumes *Collected Poems 1909–1962, The Cocktail Party* and *Murder in the Cathedral*, Copyright, 1935, 1936 by Harcourt, Brace & World, Inc.; Copyright © 1950, 1963, 1964 by T. S. Eliot by permission of Harcourt, Brace & World, Inc., and Faber and Faber, Ltd.

THE UNIVERSITY OF CHICAGO PRESS, CHICAGO 60637
The University of Chicago Press, Ltd., London

*Copyright © 1967, 1978 by Maurice Friedman
All rights reserved. First published 1967
Phoenix Edition 1978
Printed in the United States of America*

82 81 80 79 78 5 4 3 2 1

ISBN 0–226–26337–1
LCN 77–92748

This Phoenix Edition of *To Deny Our Nothingness*
is published by arrangement
with the author.

CONTENTS

CONTENTS

PREFACE TO THE
PHOENIX EDITION

T HIS publication of *To Deny Our Nothingness* insures that the book will continue to be available to the large readership it has found through previous printings and, in particular, to those college and university teachers who have used it in a variety of departmental and interdisciplinary courses. It also makes available to the reader a necessary link in my series of books on the "image of man," or, as I now call it, "the human image."

The first of these books, *Problematic Rebel*, was originally written and organized as an intensive study of Melville, Dostoevsky, and Kafka. Then, following the suggestion of an editor, I reorganized the book according to thematic types, such as the Modern Exile, the Modern Promethean, the Modern Job, and the Problematic of Modern Man. It was in this form that I first published the book. Five years later, when I used *Problematic Rebel* in a graduate seminar on religion and literature, I realized that I had to take a third step and restore the integrity of the literary interpretations by grouping together the material concerning each novelist while retaining the thematic types as subheads within the discussion of each writer. These types were then brought together with still greater cogency in the "depth-image of modern man" at the end. Thus evolved the second, radically reorganized and somewhat enlarged edition of *Problematic Rebel*, which had the new subtitle *Melville, Dostoievsky, Kafka, Camus*.[1] Because it is the foundation of my work on the human image, I have a number of times quoted or cited material from *Problematic Rebel* in *To Deny Our Nothingness*. Al-

[1] Maurice Friedman, *Problematic Rebel: Melville, Dostoievsky, Kafka, Camus* (Chicago: University of Chicago Press, Phoenix Books, 1970).

though these citations are to the original edition of *Problematic Rebel,* the reader can easily find the corresponding chapters or parts of chapters in the new edition by consulting its table of contents.

Seven years after the publication of *To Deny Our Nothingness* I published my third and last book on the image of man, *The Hidden Human Image.*[2] In *The Hidden Human Image* I apply the conclusions of *The Worlds of Existentialism, Problematic Rebel,* and *To Deny Our Nothingness* to such fields as values, education, science, psychotherapy, literature and religion, and social change. *The Hidden Human Image* devotes one chapter to Elie Wiesel and one to Martin Luther King. Other chapters cover topics ranging from anxiety, death, sex and love, and women's liberation, to psychologism, encounter groups, the power of violence and nonviolence, and "the community of otherness and the covenant of peace." The last chapter, "The Modern Promethean and the Modern Job," is a conclusion not only to *The Hidden Human Image* but also, in a very real sense, to the whole series of books on the human image that began with *Problematic Rebel* and continued with *To Deny Our Nothingness.*

After the publication of *To Deny Our Nothingness* I discovered to my astonishment that Coccioli had written a sequel to *Heaven and Earth,* entitled *The White Stone.* Don Ardito Piccardi, we learn, was blindfolded and heard the guns fire but was not, after all, executed—a deception which deprived him of his faith. The sequel follows his story by means of the narration of those who were with him in prison camp, in hiding in the forest, and in France and Mexico after the war, and it assesses his impact upon them. *The White Stone* develops further the character of Ardito Piccardi, but it does not leave him any less problematic nor does it remove him from that special category of sainthood that makes him of central importance to other men but—with the exception of the young priest Augustin Nevers—not a direction-giving image of man for them.[3]

I am grateful to Professor Hazel Barnes of the University of Colorado for bringing to my attention the relevance of Aldous Huxley's *Island* and Sartre's *Drole D'Amitié* for *To Deny Our Nothingness.* In contrast to *The White Stone,* each of these novels represents a decisive new development in the author's image of man. Therefore I have devoted a short Appendix in this new edition to a discussion of them. Professor Barnes also takes me to task for twice speaking "of Sartre's taking the Cartesian reflective *cogito* as his point of departure whereas the essential novelty of Sartre's psychology rests on his postulate of the pre-

[2] Maurice Friedman, *The Hidden Human Image* (New York: Dell Publishing Co., Delacorte Press and Delta Books, 1974).
[3] Carlo Coccioli, *The White Stone,* trans. Elizabeth Sutherland and Vera Bleuer (New York: Simon and Schuster, 1960).

reflective *cogito*."[4] She is, of course, correct as far as *Being and Nothingness* is concerned, as I myself recognize in *The Worlds of Existentialism*. Therefore I have changed the first reference from "Descartes' *cogito*" to "the prereflective *cogito*, or consciousness." My second reference I cannot change because it is Sartre's own language in his little book *Existentialism* and because I use it as he did, in the context of his progression beyond Descartes to the recognition of a "world of intersubjectivity."

While I still believe that my criticism of Jung in *To Deny Our Nothingness* is sound, I am distressed by my failure in this chapter to give a dramatic sense of what Jung meant and still means to me. The reader can only understand aright the point of view which animates this chapter if he recognizes that I was a thoroughgoing Jungian before I became a "Buberian." In 1944 when the remarkable English Quaker, Irene Pickard, came to visit our unit of conscientious objectors at the institute for the feebleminded where I was working as part of my three and a half years in Civilian Public Service camps and units, she introduced me to T. S. Eliot's *Four Quartets* and to the writings of C. G. Jung. When, following her advice, I began writing my dreams down every morning, I found that I dreamed in a more and more Jungian manner, replete with "archetypes" of the "collective unconscious" accompanied by great intensity of affect. The emptier my waking life in the wards of imbeciles or the special diet kitchen, the richer and more charged my dreams: blue flowers and golden weddings, levitations and figures of the Great Mother. At this point in my life, Jung was my "touchstone of reality."

What has remained to me of the influence of Jung is his emphasis upon dreams as genuine symbols of an ineffable reality, rather than as disguised signs of external reality, as Freud sees them. Also important to me is his concept of the "shadow"—that which disturbs us in others because they manifest openly what we have repressed and allowed to turn malignant in ourselves. Along with this there has remained the belief in the reality of an intense archetypal dimension that enters into our dreams and at times into our waking life. In my Jungianism of thirty years ago, however, I also found encouragement for the contrast between what I liked to call my "small, petty, false, outer self" and my "great, true, heroic, inner self." In two of the autobiographical chapters

[4] Hazel E. Barnes, "Philosophical Criticism," *Contemporary Literature*, Vol. IX, No. 3 (1968), pp. 427–30. At the end of this article Professor Barnes writes: "It is in his unwavering attempt to develop the human that Friedman himself comes out best. Seeking a balance between the purely logical rational and the irrational, between selflessness and self-deification, between isolation from the social and submersion in it, Friedman admirably obeys his most fundamental principle: to hold steadily to the sense of self-direction while keeping oneself open to those possibilities of inner change and growth which come to us from the world outside."

of my book *Touchstones of Reality*, I have described the disastrous consequences of this attitude when brought into the "group dance" of the "Creative House."[5] It was these experiences and the tendency of many Jungians to view others in the first instance as functions of one's own individuation (as one's "anima" or "animus") that led to the critical counteremphasis that finds expression in the chapter on Jung in *To Deny Our Nothingness*.

On the other hand, I should like to testify here to the deeper understanding of Jung that I have gained through friends, colleagues, and students who are Jungian therapists and students of Jung's thought, and to my keen awareness of how very much of a live option Jung remains for many as a contemporary human image. Once while working with a group of non-statistical-track doctoral students at the California School of Professional Psychology, I referred to Alfred North Whitehead's statement, "Aristotle was concerned with the procession of forms. We are concerned with the forms of process." After I had quoted this statement, its relevance to Jung suddenly struck me. Jung's understanding of archetypes is closer to that of Whitehead than to that of either Aristotle or Plato. The person who is going through the journey of individuation is in process, and the archetype that the person may embody or dream of at any given time is only a form of that process, not some fixed, eternal form that can be known in itself, as are Plato's *eidos*, or "ideal forms." This conforms to Jung's own statement that an archetype can never be known in itself. This insight has revealed Jung to be more existential in his thinking than I had given him credit for.

An interesting confirmation of my subsuming Simone Weil under "The Modern Gnostic" has been the recent publication of a biography of her by her closest friend, Simone Petrement, author of a distinguished and highly sympathetic study of Gnosticism.

For a full-scale interpretation of the writings of Elie Wiesel, I refer the reader to my book *The Hidden Human Image*.[6]

I have added to my dedication the names of Gabriel Marcel, André Malraux, and John Steinbeck, who have died since the publication of the first edition of *To Deny Our Nothingness* in 1967.[7]

MAURICE FRIEDMAN

[5] Maurice Friedman, *Touchstones of Reality: Existential Trust and the Community of Peace* (New York: E. P. Dutton, 1972; Dutton Books, 1974), Chaps. 4 and 5.
[6] Chap. 7, "Elie Wiesel: The Job of Auschwitz," pp. 106–34.
[7] Among the books referred to in the footnotes of *To Deny Our Nothingness*, the following have been published or printed in new editions since 1967: *The Worlds of Existentialism: A Critical Reader*, edited with Introductions and a Conclusion by Maurice Friedman (Chicago: The University of Chicago Press, Phoenix Books, 1973); Maurice Friedman, *Martin Buber: The Life of Dia-*

logue, 3rd edition, with a new Preface and additions to the Bibliography (Chicago: The University of Chicago Press, Phoenix Books, 1976); Paul Arthur Schilpp and Maurice Friedman, editors, *The Philosophy of Martin Buber,* The Library of Living Philosophers, Vol. 12 (LaSalle, Illinois: Open Court Publishing Co., 1967); Martin Buber, *Pointing the Way,* ed. and trans. Maurice Friedman (New York: Schocken Books, 1973); Martin Buber, *For the Sake of Heaven,* trans. Ludwig Lewisohn (New York: Atheneum Books, 1969); Martin Buber, *The Legend of the Baal Shem,* trans. Maurice Friedman (New York: Schocken Books, 1969); Paul Ricoeur, *Freud and Philosophy: An Essay in Interpretation,* trans. Denis Savage (New Haven: Yale University Press, 1970); Leslie H. Farber, *Lying, Despair, Jealousy, Envy, Sex, Suicide, Drugs, and the Good Life* (including most of the essays in Farber's *The Ways of the Will,* now out of print) (New York: Basic Books, 1976). Elie Wiesel's books *Night, Dawn, The Accident, The Town Beyond the Wall,* and *The Gates of the Forest* are all published by Avon Books.

PREFACE

WHEN I first taught "The Image of Man in Modern Literature" at Sarah Lawrence College in 1953, the "image of man" was an uncommon term. Even as late as 1957, when I suggested "Images of Man in Current Culture" as the theme for the five-year national conference of the Religious Education Association, the sociologist Philip Rieff said "You mean 'concepts of men.'" "No," I replied, "*images* of *man*." I was pleased when some months later an article by Philip Rieff appeared on the front page of *The New York Times Book Review* under the title, "Freud Gives Us a New Image of Man." Even now, when the term is more common, few use it as I do—not as purely descriptive or as an ideal, but as a direction of movement which shapes the raw material of the given into authentic personal and human existence.

When I began work on this book in 1959, I organized it in terms of subject matter—literature, philosophy, psychotherapy, religious thought. I have since found a more organic and precise form, namely, the organization according to types, such as the Modern Socialist, the Modern Mystic, the Existentialist. I did not begin with the image of man and then apply it in a critical and detached way to the various types of authors dealt with here. Rather, I immersed myself in these writers, and only in the course of this immersion developed the image of man as both a unifying focus and a critical approach. Much of what I have presented here, at times fairly critically, I have lived through at various stages of my life: the socialism of my Harvard days; the Jungianism, comparative mysticism, and concern with saintliness of my years in camps for conscientious objectors; my subsequent enthusiasm for Hasidism as a joyous communal mysticism; my response, at first simply affirmative, later somewhat more critical, to the works of Erich Fromm; my gradual shift of focus from mysticism to existentialism, culminating in my book, *The Worlds of Existentialism;* my search for the meeting point of the image of man and psychotherapy during my years as a member of the faculty of the Washington School of Psychiatry, a guest lecturer at the William Alanson White Institute of Psychology, Psychoanalysis and Psychiatry, and a member of the Council of the Association of Existential Psychology and Psychiatry.

Even those phases which are past, such as my Jungianism, are still of value to me both as insights and building blocks. Others, such as my admiration for Eliot's *Four Quartets* and my years of work on Martin Buber, are fully present. Within the general critical approach offered by the image of man, there also exist specific personal responses informed by what I have made more fully and lastingly my own. In many essential respects, nonetheless, this book goes decisively beyond my work on Buber—the approach of the image of man, the use of types, the concept of "the dialogue with the absurd," the concluding chapter on "The Image of Man and Moral Philosophy," to name a few.

The relation between this book and my 1963 work, *Problematic Rebel: An Image of Modern Man,*[1] is somewhat different, however. *Problematic Rebel* is an intensive study of Melville, Dostoyevsky, and Kafka set in the context of the "death of God," the alienation of modern man, the Modern Exile, and two types of modern rebels—"the Modern Promethean" and "the Modern Job." I see these two books as complementary expressions of my years of concern with the image of man. *Problematic Rebel* is intensive, *To Deny Our Nothingness* extensive. *Problematic Rebel* begins with Biblical, Greek, and Renaissance images of man before focusing on the nineteenth and twentieth centuries; *To Deny Our Nothingness* is almost entirely contemporary. *Problematic Rebel* is largely based on literature; *To Deny Our Nothingness* makes use, in almost equal measure, of literature, philosophy, psychology, and religious thought. *Problematic Rebel* is, in the first instance, descriptive—an image of modern man; *To Deny Our Nothingness* points from the outset toward a modern image of man. On the other hand, though they proceed from quite different starting points and by quite different methods, they meet in a common concern with "the dialogue with the absurd." This does not mean that these two books cannot stand alone: each in itself is an organic whole. At the same time, there is, I believe, a rich interrelationship between

[1] New York: Random House.

them which can add a further dimension to the reader's understanding. On a number of occasions, I have quoted from *Problematic Rebel* to illustrate and enhance the meaning of what was being said.

This book would never have become a reality had it not been for the initiative, patience, and friendly criticism of my editor, Richard Huett. It was he who suggested that I cast into book form my course on "Contemporary Images of Man" at the New School for Social Research. He believed in this book before I did, and if it has become a book which seems significant to me, too, I owe this in large part to him. I want also to express my gratitude to Pendle Hill, the Quaker Center for Study and Contemplation, for the 1965 teaching position which has given me the comparative leisure necessary to revise this book.

Writing the preface, I was struck by the number of significant figures in this book who have died since I began writing it in 1959. Nothing brings home so clearly our debt to the generation that is now passing. Albert Camus, Carl Jung, Hermann Hesse, Aldous Huxley, T. S. Eliot, Martin Buber, Paul Tillich—how many giants have been taken from us in so short a time, and how great our gratitude for what they have left us! It is to these men—pioneers and pathfinders in the contemporary image of man—that I dedicate this book.

MAURICE FRIEDMAN

Bronxville, New York
December 1965

I

INTRODUCTION

1

CONTEMPORARY
IMAGES OF MAN

THE "image of man" is often used as a sociological or literary category of a purely descriptive nature—the image of man of Renaissance England or of the nineteenth-century Russian novel. The full depth of the term, however, is more closely approximated by the way in which André Malraux uses it—not only an image of what man *is*, but also "an exemplary image of man" that helps him discover, in each age anew, what he may and can become, an image that helps modern man rediscover his humanity. "The greatest mystery," writes Malraux in *The Walnut Trees of Altenberg*, "is not that we have been flung at random among the profusion of the earth and the galaxy of the stars, but that in this prison we can fashion images of ourselves sufficiently powerful to deny our nothingness."

The image of man, as we shall use the term here, is an integral part of man's search to understand himself in order to become himself, of his search for an image of authentic personal existence. "Authentic personal existence" does not mean some moral standard imposed from without, or some universal "ought" that need only be applied. It implies a meaningful, personal direction, a response from within to what one meets in each new situation, standing one's ground and meeting the world with the attitude that is rooted in this ground. Man cannot live without searching for authentic existence, for man, as Nietzsche said, is a valuing animal. However a man may think *qua* scientist, technician, and observer, as a *person* he must be concerned again and again with potentiality, choice, and decision, with the better and the worse, with discovering an authentic response to each situation he faces. "I should like to ring true," says Bernard in André Gide's novel *The Counterfeiters.* Such "ringing true" is no abstract possession of truth, but the ever-new authentication of one's truth in one's concrete daily life. Here, the pole of the unique and the pole of the human stand in fruitful tension with each other: in each situation, I must be concerned with what is authentic *human* existence and what is authentic existence for me in particular. These two can never be divided from each other, nor can they be identified. What we mean by "man," by "human," is at once something we take for granted and something we do not know and must constantly discover and rediscover. That we are all "men" is the commonest presupposition of social intercourse. What man is, can be, and ought to become is continually changing, however, not only with each new culture and period of history, but also with each new individual. It is precisely in his uniqueness, and not in what he has in common with others, that each man realizes what *man* can become in him. Although no member of the French Resistance could tell whether or not he would "squeal" when tortured by the Nazis, says Jean-Paul Sartre, every time one person stood the test, *man* was invented anew.

Man comes to awareness of himself as a self not just through his individuality and not just through his differences from others but in dialogue with other selves—in their response to him and in the way they call him into being. Because man lives as a separate self, yet in relation to other persons and to society, present, past, and to come, he needs an image of man to aid him in finding a meaningful way of life, in choosing between conflicting sets of values, in realizing his own unique potentialities. Our human existence itself is at once tradition and unexplored future, acceptance and rebellion. The image of man is an embodiment of an attitude and a response. Whether it is an image shared by only one man or by a society as a whole, the individual stands in a unique personal relation to it. His image of man is not some objective, universal Saint Francis, but the Saint Francis who emerges from his own meeting with this historical and legendary figure.

The image of man does not mean some fully formed, conscious model of what one should become—certainly not anything simply imposed on man by the culture, or any mere conformity with society through identification with its goals. For each one of us, it is made up of many images and half-formed images, and it is itself constantly changing and evolving. It proceeds and develops through every type of personal encounter we have: a friend stands by us in a crisis; a poet speaks to us through his poems; a great historical figure affects us through the impact he had on those among whom he lived; the characters of novels and plays seize our imaginations and enter into our lives through a dialogue we carry on with them in the wordless depths of our being.

Even when it occurs through ideal types, such as the knight, the courtier, the Roman citizen, the Spartan, and the saint, the image of man implies a more concrete representation of what man is and should be than the abstract and conceptual descriptions of the human condition that are customary in philosophical anthropology. Alyosha, in *The Brothers Karamazov,* is believable just because he is a particular person rather than a generalized type, yet that very particularity at first glance seems to stand in the way of his representing authentic, human existence in general. The key to this dilemma is that there is no such thing as human existence in general. If *man* is to be recognized in men, as Saint Exupéry stresses in *Flight to Arras,* it cannot be through some abstract essence of man, some general conception of human nature, but again and again through the concrete uniqueness of single persons who realize their humanity by becoming what only they can become. The universality of Ecclesiastes is not yet an image of man, only a description of the human condition—the movement of time, the alternation of seasons and activities, the vanity of human effort, nothing being new under the sun. But the hero of the Book of Job *is* an image of man just in his uniqueness. Dostoyevsky makes this explicit in a comment on Alyosha in his Foreword to *The Brothers Karamazov:*

> Not only is an eccentric "not always" a particularity and a separate element, but, on the contrary, it happens sometimes that such a person . . . carries within himself the very heart of the universal, and the rest of the men of his epoch have for some reason been temporarily torn from it, as if by a gust of wind.

If an image of man is not a mere photographic representation of the factual, neither is it a mere ideal. A cartoon in *The New Yorker* pictures a couple in a midtown Manhattan apartment drinking martinis while the man says to the woman: "So what if Albert Schweitzer did escape the rat-race? Name three others!" Here, Albert Schweitzer is no longer an image of man; he is merely the exception that proves that the rest of us are rats in a maze, the rare example of personal fulfillment and human greatness that gives us some vicarious satisfaction and a chance to forget our own futile existences, but no guidance and direction as to how we too can authenticate our lives. *Our* only alternatives seem to be shallow conformity and sterile rebellion. The very universality of our age makes us all too aware of the conditioned, culturally limited, and relative nature of all our modern images: we look on them as merely pragmatic means of fulfilling already established values. Our age, rich in everything else, is remarkably poor in providing sources for discovering personal direction and authentic human existence.

In the fall of 1959, an exhibition was held at the Museum of Modern Art, in New York City entitled "New Images of Man." In an article on this exhibition in *The New York Times Magazine,* the well-known art critic, Aline B. Saarinen, raises one of the most significant questions that will concern us in our assessment of the contemporary images of man. The title of this exhibition might lead some to expect a return to the idealized or naturalist figure, she writes. Instead,

> the new images of man that will confront the spectator in this exhibition are disturbing, disquieting, even unhinging. Here are human figures with bodies distorted, misshapen, mutilated. Sometimes their flesh is decayed and corrupt, sometimes corroded or charred. Here are faceless figures—or figures that seem to have death's heads—looming, leering out of nightmarish nothingness. Here are giant effigies and huge heads . . . some of them savagely present, others existing enigmatically in life and death. Here are figures possessed by animal and erotic frenzies. Here are figures that seem imprisoned in cagelike spaces and others incarcerated in spaces "measureless to man."[1]

This exhibition is concerned with the human predicament in our time, states Mrs. Saarinen. "It is disquieting and unsettling precisely because it ruthlessly invades our inner privacy and inexorably lays bare modern man's fears and anxieties, his bestiality and his loneliness." Old and young, European and American, famous and obscure—the artists in this show share "a curiously common kind of horror image" —a common vision of "a world for which Freud, Einstein, Kierkegaard, Kafka, Sartre, Camus, Beckett, Faulkner, Robert Penn Warren, Tennessee Williams and Charles Addams are typical spokesmen." This common horror image is at once the product of Freud and the age of depth psychology and of the holocaust of Buchenwald and Hiroshima which revealed man's bestiality, unleashed his violence, and abandoned him to the isolation and bewilderment of an atomic age and a dehumanized world of automation and electronic brains.

There is no question but that a contemporary image of man, to be truly so, must embody within itself some of the contradictions and paradoxes of modern existence. No modern man is excluded from a relationship to the images of man of past ages—Jesus, the Buddha, Saint Francis, Socrates, Lao-tzu, Job—but he must relate to them just as the modern man that he is, bringing the whole complexity and

[1] *The New York Times Magazine,* September 28, 1959, p. 18.

perplexity of his modern existence into that relationship, or they will not be genuine images of man for him. During a conversation about Dostoyevsky's Alyosha, I once asked Martin Buber whether he thought there could be such a thing as a "modern saint." "There can be a saint living now," Buber replied, "but he will not be a modern man—a man who bears in himself the contradictions of modern existence." Buber's judgment on this point might seem an arbitrary qualification of "sainthood" until we recall that the very conception of the saint grew out of another age and implied a social integument very different from our own. The man who remains in vital relation to the contemporary age will, for better or worse, share in the tension and problematics of that age. Such a man is excluded from a simple personal sanctity or a self-sufficient, spiritual perfection because the very wholeness of his personal existence includes his relationship to people and situations shot through with contradiction and absurdity. One of the finest and most moving of Kierkegaard's devotional writings is *Purity of Heart Is To Will One Thing*, but anyone who knows the other side of Kierkegaard—the problematic and dialectical, pseudonymous author whose "leap of faith" was based on paradox and the absurd—will recognize that he was a complex, modern man, not a simple and purehearted saint.

We cannot deny, therefore, that no matter how monstrous, misshapen, irrational, and distorted the images of man presented to us by contemporary literature and art may be, they do mirror "significant aspects of the human condition in our time." This does not mean, however, that we must confine ourselves to just the violent and "monstrous" representations of man, or that, taken in themselves, these representations offer us a complete image of man in our sense of the term. The common horror images portray the "is" of contemporary man—not even the whole "is," but only that part of man which, neglected and overlooked, has come into prominence through the events of our century. Such images are raw material, given us to be shaped, if possible, into meaningful form, resistant clay which may perhaps be molded into a figure of authentic existence.

In the end, of course, we must each decide through our unique personal response what contemporary images of man possess the right tension between the raw material of the absurd and the shaping force of a new direction toward authentic existence. Particularly important here is our own experience of social violence and psychological demonry. How we have responded to this experience and let it enter into our basic attitudes will affect our judgment as to what minimum amount of "horror" is necessary before we can begin to ask whether a given writer presents a realistic image of authentic personal existence.

The literature of contemporary man reflects the absence of an image of man in an astonishingly rich documentation of inauthentic existence. By far the largest part of the literature of the nineteenth and twentieth centuries presents us not with a positive image of man but with the lack of one. Indeed, it finds its integrity precisely by limiting itself to that task. Ibsen in *The Wild Duck* pits Gregers Werle and the "claim of the ideal" against Dr. Relling and the "life-lie," only to leave us with the conclusion that both have contributed alike to the catastrophe, that neither is a possible image of man. In Chekov's *The Sea Gull*, this is still clearer. In a comedy or tragicomedy in which the author stands outside both sets of characters, Treplev and Nina are more sympathetic than Trigorin and Madame Arkady, but they are the ones who get crushed by the less sensitive. What happens to Blanche in Tennessee Williams' *Streetcar Named Desire* is determined before the beginning of the play, not by Fate but by psychological and social conditioning. We can neither identify with her nor experience catharsis through her downfall. The final mood of the play, like that of most so-called modern tragedies, is one of irony rather than reconciliation with the order of things. The same holds true of Arthur Miller's *Death of a Salesman*. Although we sympathize with Willy Loman, we see him, like Blanche, from the outside. His downfall is an ironic commentary on American goals and values rather than any kind of tragic catharsis and reconciliation. Eugene O'Neill's *Mourning Becomes Electra* translates Greek fate into an equally inexorable Freudian determinism which, because it is psychological and internal, allows no possibility either of significant understanding with others within an order or of any reconciliation with the order. At the same time, O'Neill omits Freud's own optimism—his faith in reason, in the conscious, in therapy—in favor of a world of unrelieved darkness.

These writers illuminate the starting point of our concern with the image of man—the sense that the novelist and the playwright gives us *from within* of the inauthenticity of the existences that he portrays. José Ortega y Gasset, in his brilliant essay, "In Search of Goethe from Within," takes us a decisive step further toward the positive meaning of an image of man. "We must get over the error," writes Ortega y Gasset, "which makes us think that a man's life takes place inside himself and that, consequently, it can be reduced to pure psychology. . . . Life is as far as possible from a subjective phenomenon. It is the most objective of all realities. It is a man's *I* finding itself submerged in precisely what is not himself, in the pure *other* which is his environment. To live is to be outside oneself, to realize oneself. The vital program which each one of us irremediably is, overpowers environment to lodge itself there." Our "I," Ortega y Gasset stresses, is not our subjective feelings, but our movement forward in relation to the world. Each individual life *makes* itself, not according to any general principles, but in terms of its own particular design, its program or vocation—what it is called to become. This design is no conscious idea, freely chosen, but, anterior to all ideas and choices of the will, it is "that single programmatic personage who must be realized." "Life is essentially a drama, because it is a desperate struggle—with things and even with our character—to succeed in being in fact that which we are in design." This concrete sense of the encounter between self and world precludes the notion that two men are ever in the same situation. "I am a certain absolutely individual pressure upon the world: the world is the no less definite and individual resistance to that pressure." The original meaning of "vocation" is "calling," what one is called to become. In this sense of the term, "our I is our vocation" to which we can be true "in greater or lesser degree and thus have a life which is authentic to a greater or lesser degree."

Ortega y Gasset takes care to distinguish this inner calling from any kind of general and abstract conception of what man "ought" to be or of the moral destiny of man, "which is merely a concept by which man tries to justify his existence."

> Let there be no confounding the *ought to be* of morality, which inhabits man's intellectual region, with the vital imperative, the *has to be* of personal vocation, situated in the most profound and primary region of our being.

The distinction which he is making here is an important one. One's personal vocation is unique. It can never be deduced from any general conception of man or any universal morality. It is also existential, not merely conscious or rational. Yet the "ought" must enter into a vocation, not just the "has to be," or it is no true calling to authentic existence—only a mere conditioned reaction. In reacting against the abstract and the rational, Ortega y Gasset is in danger of turning too simply to the emotional and irrational, injuring the wholeness of man in so doing. This tendency is no doubt caused, in part, by his clear realization of how reason may lead one away from one's true vocation and of the inauthenticity of whatever one attempts to substitute for it.

> A man can have but *one* authentic life, the life which his vocation demands of him. When his freedom induces him to deny his irrevocable *I* and arbitrarily substitute some other for it—arbitrarily, even though in accordance with the most respectable "reason"—he leads a spectral, unsatisfied life between . . . "poetry and reality."

Even more important, for our purposes, is Ortega y Gasset's recognition that one's vocation is *not* identical with realizing one's potentialities, as is assumed almost as a matter of course today. "Potentialities" are invariably thought of in terms of function, use, or application outside the person. "Vocation," as he uses it, is first of all *personal*: its meaning is always that of calling the person into authentic personal existence.

> It would be a fundamental error to believe that a man's vocation coincides with his most indisputable gifts . . . sometimes it runs contrary to them. There are cases—such as Goethe's—in which the multiplicity of gifts troubles and disorients the vocation, or at least the man who is its axis.

Not only may a multiplicity of gifts trouble a personal calling; it may also delude its possessor into believing that for him authentic existence consists in never limiting or committing himself, in devoting his life to the cultivation of ever-fresh potentialities without the necessity of choosing which he will actualize and which leave undeveloped. Such a person, genius though he may be, remains a perpetual adolescent. Only an adolescent can claim the privilege of enjoying all possibility and experience without that limiting commitment which brings us into vital relation with the world of the other. Like Kierkegaard's "aesthetic man," he lives in a world of multiple riches yet never tastes real existence.

> Life consists in giving up the state of availability. Mere availability is the characteristic of youth faced with maturity. The youth, because he is not yet anything determinate and irrevocable, is everything potentially. Herein lies his charm and his insolence. Feeling that he is everything potentially he supposes that he is everything actually.[2]

The problem Ortega y Gasset leaves us with and, so far as I can see, sheds no light on in this essay is *how* one becomes aware of one's vocation, how one tells one's true vocation from a false one. He seems to suppose a sort of intuitive certainty, or even romantic sense of inner destiny, which in no wise corresponds to the actual situation of the man who must discover and rediscover his vocation by listening to the call of each new situation in which he finds himself. Is one's vocation *in* one as a preformed design, like a sort of fate, providence, or Platonic idea, or is it something that emerges from one's meeting with the world and with one's fellowmen in the world? If the former, there arises the impossible prospect of a vocation that has no essential connection with one's life in the world, however much it may be concerned with superimposing itself on the world. If the latter, then

[2] José Ortega y Gasset, "In Search of Goethe from Within," translated by Willard Trask, in William Phillips and Philip Rahv, editors. *The New Partisan Reader, 1945–1953* (N. Y.: Andre Deutsch, 1953), pp. 289–313.

one's vocation cannot be quite so certain, inexorable, or independent of the intellect and will as Ortega y Gasset claims: it must rather be a response to the call that comes to one from the concrete persons and situations that one meets. The response comes from within, but the call does not.

The image of man distinguishes between man's potentiality and the direction he gives to his potentiality. Such terms as self-fulfillment, self-expression, and self-realization are comforting to many in our age who vaguely feel that they are living without expressing themselves; yet they offer little real help toward an image of man, for they leave unanswered the question of what direction one must take in order to "realize" or meaningfully "express" the self. If we had only one set of potentialities, then the question could be simplified to one of realizing them or not realizing them. But our potentialities are, in fact, legion, and until we bring them under the guidance of a personal direction, they are likely to conduct themselves as the demons who named themselves thus before Jesus, rather than as the angelic bearers of abundant life. To give our potentialities direction means to decide —not consciously, but again and again through the response of one's whole being—what is the more and what is the less authentic choice in a particular situation, what is the more and what is the less authentic attitude and response, what way is *ours* because it is true for us and we have committed ourselves to be true to it. Albert Schweitzer had to choose not only among being an organist, a theologian, or a missionary doctor in Africa, but also, and more significantly, between becoming one sort of person and another. We become ourselves through each particular action; we choose ourselves in each act of becoming. Actually, we cannot know our real potentialities in the abstract at all. All we can know are generalizations about ourselves from past situations in which we have had other and different resources. Our actual resources are inseparably bound up with what we are as *persons*, with our direction as persons, and with what calls us out in the concrete situation. We cannot foresee these. Potentiality is not in us as an already existing objective reality. We know it only as it becomes actuality in our response to each new situation.

In this book, we shall discuss a number of contemporary images of man, selected, first, because they are significant in themselves and, second, because they give us insight into important types of contemporary images, such as the Modern Mystic, the Modern Gnostic, Psychological Man, and the Existentialist. Of these specific images and types, we shall ask: Are they sufficiently concrete to be believable, sufficiently human, even in their uniqueness, to be significant? Do they include enough of the tensions of modern man to speak to us today, and do they at the same time speak to us of man as man? Do they offer us direction as well as "self-realization," concrete image as well as abstract "authenticity"? To answer these questions we shall have need not only of objective analysis, comparison, and contrast, but also of a real meeting with the image in its uniqueness—a dialogue which includes the possibility of withstanding and denying as well as of accepting and affirming.

Since the image of man is no mere ideal, no modern image of man can ignore the new knowledge that psychotherapy offers as to what man *is*. But since the image of man is also not a mere photographic representation of the factual, it is equally necessary to recognize that psychotherapy cannot in itself *qua* science give us an image of man. Each school of psychotherapy has, with varying degrees of clarity, its own image of man. That image stands in fruitful dialectic with the therapeutic practice of the members of the school, but it is not, for all that, a scientific product of that school. On the contrary, the far-reaching differences between the many schools of psychotherapy derive in part from the fact that implied in the positive goals they enunciate are different images of man. Such central therapeutic terms as "health," "integration," "maturity," "creativity," and "self-realization" not only imply an image of man, but also usually essentially different ones for different schools and even different members of the same school. "The critical battles between approaches to psychology and psychoanalysis in our culture in the next decades, as always," writes Rollo May, "will be on the battle ground of the image of man."[8]

Man's nature is often taken by schools of psychotherapy to be itself the norm. Man should live according to his "nature," according to his "real self," and the like. However, it is also in man's nature to become ill. The very meaning of "health," therefore, implies some sense of what is authentic direction for man, for this person—in short, an image of man. As Helen Merrell Lynd points out, the "real" or "spontaneous" self is not a given that need only be freed from its social encrustations. It is the product of a lifelong dialogue with our image of man.

> Horney, Fromm, and even Sullivan at times, seem to assume that there is an already existent real or true or spontaneous self which can be evoked into active existence almost at will. There is a tacit assumption that somehow we know the dictates of the real self, and that we should live in terms of these rather than of a romanticized self-image or of the pseudo-self of others' expectations. But . . . such *a real self*

[8] Rollo May, "Some Comments on Existential Psychotherapy," an essay written for *The Worlds of Existentialism: A Critical Reader*, edited with Introductions and a Conclusion by Maurice Friedman (N. Y.: Random House, 1964), p. 447.

is something to be discovered and created, not a given, but a lifelong endeavor.[4]

Literature is the real homeland of the image of man, for it retains the concrete uniqueness of individual men. At the same time, it allows us a relationship with these men sufficiently close for them to speak to us as bearers of the human. Yet in its very particularity literature defies the easy generalizing and universalizing that holds good in other branches of human culture and, unlike other fields, forces us to remember the varieties of man and the varieties of culture. Literature is art, not life, yet art that remains more closely bound to life than most forms of art and certainly than most forms of knowledge about man.

No novel can present an image of man if its author merely stands in objective relation to his character; none can present such an image if the author merely identifies with his character in a subjective way that destroys the aesthetic and personal distance between author and character. It is the dialogue between author and character that produces the image of man; this image is never a direct expression of the author's views, but a genuine product of this dialogue. Conversely, the image produced never takes on the fixed quality of a visual image, but retains the open, unfinished quality of living dialogue. The dialogue between author and character also makes possible a dialogue between character and reader—the personal response of the reader that is, in the end, the most important element of any character's becoming an image of man for him. He does not take over this character as an image through some sort of visual impression, but through a personal, even, in a sense, reciprocal relationship with him.

By approaching the novels with which we deal in this way, we can come to understand our contemporary image of man more directly and concretely than by examining any other expression of human culture. Through considering together both literary and nonliterary works, we can gain a deeper understanding of the image of man as the hidden ground in which literature, philosophy, psychotherapy, religion, and social thought all meet. Finally, through constructing a typology of contemporary images of man, we can throw fresh light on many of the figures and works with which we deal, while recognizing the interrelation and overlapping of types. Many of these thinkers, as we shall see, belong to more than one type; each has a uniqueness that cannot be captured by any type.

[4] Helen Merrell Lynd, *On Shame and the Search for Identity* (N. Y.: Science Editions, 1961), p. 203. (Italics added.)

2

IMAGES OF
INAUTHENTICITY

THE most effective approach to contemporary images of man is to examine those images of inauthentic, human existence that throw light on what writers feel is lacking in our age and that point, however indirectly, toward the direction in which they feel we should move. By images of inauthenticity we do not mean the innumerable works which illustrate the absence of a modern image of man, but those which are *explicitly* concerned with human values that are inauthentic—either because they are truncated or twisted, hypocritical or "seeming," or reflect a desire to escape from the human condition, from the necessity of taking responsibility for the values one creates in order to be in any true sense a man. Three such explicit portrayals of the varieties of inauthentic man in our time, each of which is a classic in its own right, are André Gide's novel, *The Counterfeiters*, T. S. Eliot's early poems through *The Waste Land*, and André Malraux's novel, *Man's Fate*.

GIDE'S COUNTERFEITERS

The Counterfeiters combines a virtuoso display of types of inauthenticity with a single, groping attempt at a positive image of man.

The images of inauthentic life with which *The Counterfeiters* abounds are best understood as a series of concentric circles of which the outermost and most obvious circle—that of the actual counterfeiters led by Strouvilhou—is also the most superficial. Moving progressively inward, we come to the circle of the group of boys who distribute the counterfeit money and who, under the leadership of

Ghéridanisol, Strouvilhou's nephew, try to ape the actions of Strou-vilhou and his world. A circle still closer to the center is that of the bourgeois families in Paris—the families of Olivier and Bernard, the two young heroes of the book—behind whose respectability of office and wealth the author discloses the hypocrisy of sordid extramarital affairs and double standards of justice in which the sons of judges are not punished for fear of creating scandal. The density of hypocrisy increases with the next, tighter circles. Passavant, Lady Lilian, and Vincent constitute one of these. Count Passavant is the literary counter-feiter, the man of pseudo-culture, who knows how to ride the crest of literary fashion by borrowing from the ideas, inventions, and even conversation of others. Lady Lilian, unlike Passavant, has some stan-dards and some sense of a way of life, but not enough to build a life of any reality. Unable to relate to other people in a meaningful way, she holds it a point of honor to cut herself off from them in a clean fashion, as, during a shipwreck in her youth, the sailors chopped off the fingers of passengers drowning in the water who clung to the sides of the overfull lifeboat. Vincent, on the other hand, thrives on self-deception. A thoroughly bourgeois, moral young man, preparing to be a doctor, he is sent to a sanitarium with what seems to be in-curable tuberculosis. He has an affair there with the similarly afflicted Laura, a relationship which is not so much illicit (despite Laura's being married) as it is removed from any social context. When both unexpectedly return healed to the social world they have left and Laura becomes pregnant, the world of bourgeois values from which Vincent has sprung reasserts itself. On the one hand, he finds himself in the unhappy dilemma of wishing to be rid of this impediment to his career as a medical student, but on the other feels guilt and re-sponsibility toward Laura. Finally, he takes the five thousand francs his parents have saved to set him up in an office and decides to spend it on Laura. Only, he further decides, it is not enough; so he stakes it all gambling and loses the lot. Lady Lilian lends him another five thousand francs; this time he wins, but now he does not want to give Laura anything, until Lady Lilian persuades him to chop off the fingers neatly. In the course of this triumph, Vincent develops an "ethic of immanence," which Gide ascribes to the "devil" in his "Journal to the Counterfeiters." This ethic enables him to shed his sense of guilt by the convenient rationalization that each moment is its own justification and needs nothing beyond itself. Lilian and Vincent go off together in Passavant's yacht, presumably to further Vincent's research; finally, on the coast of Africa, their mutual attraction is revealed as purest hate. Vincent murders Lilian and goes mad himself.

A still more concentrated degree of inauthenticity is represented by the family of pastor Vedel, to which Laura belongs. The old music teacher always talks of shooting himself, but in the end is too cowardly to do so, while his little grandson, Boris, actually kills himself with his grandfather's gun. The pastor is a puritanical hypocrite who neglects his family for his parishioners, imposes a false piety on his household, and records secret sins in his diary. Rachel, the eldest daughter, is the responsible but bitter woman who tries to make up for the irresponsibility of her father and the frivolity of her brother and sisters. Sarah, Laura's younger sister, wants nothing but to break away from all this. She sleeps with Bernard after the Argonaut's literary banquet, while Armand, her brother, first locks the two of them in the bedroom, in brotherly encouragement, and then tells Rachel on them and has Bernard thrown out of the house. Armand ends up by taking over the editorship of Passavant's fake review. Of the whole family, only Laura comes close to being a real human being, and she is hopelessly mixed up between her marriage to an Englishman, her affair with Vincent, and her unreciprocated love for the novelist and central consciousness of the novel, Edouard.

The final tests of inauthenticity, however, come in the central characters—Olivier, Edouard, and Bernard. Olivier goes through a period of complete artificiality under the tutelage of Passavant and becomes the first editor of his journal. Not only his activities, but also his clothes, his taste, his manner of speaking have all become so unreal that they evoke nothing but ridicule from his friend Bernard when they meet again. Olivier is unable to stand up to his friend's censure, goes through a crisis, a near duel, drunkenness, and finally happiness in the arms of his Uncle Edouard—a happiness so unbearable that he immediately tries to commit suicide. Gide, of course, is not suggesting that Olivier's life is inauthentic *because* he is a homosexual, but his homosexuality seems intimately connected with that weakness of the ego that makes it necessary for him to depend on one person or another. We leave him under better tutelage but hardly more advanced toward an independent development.

The problem of inauthenticity becomes most complex in the novelist, Edouard, the most subtle character of the novel and the one with whom Gide, to some extent, obviously identified. Edouard is writing a novel about a novelist—a mirror-within-mirror effect—and the theme of his novel is to be "the counterfeiters." If he is unable to reciprocate Laura's love with anything but kindness, it is not only because he is a homosexual, but also because he can never really give himself to anyone. He is first and foremost an observer, and his involvement in life always takes place under the aegis of his observation. Laura and Bernard both rightly doubt that he will ever finish his novel, on the basis of his own theory of it. He desires complete realism, but he is unable to accept reality in its otherness and ends by rejecting little Boris' shooting himself as too improbable and accidental to have any meaning. When Bernard consults him about what direction to take in life, Edouard can only advise being true to himself and expressing himself. When this still does not satisfy Bernard, he says that one may know the way by the fact that it is uphill. Like the Modern Gnostic, the novelist-observer sees nothing in the world of value in itself, since all is there for eventual transformation into art. He can accept everything with equal tolerance, therefore, and does not have the problem of choice and decision that confronts the man who attempts to live as a whole human being.

Bernard makes such an attempt. Young and unfinished as he is, Bernard comes nearest of all Gide's characters to a positive image of man, not only in *The Counterfeiters*, but, so far as I can see, in all of Gide's works. Bernard's predecessors—Michel in *The Immoralist* and Lafcadio in *The Adventures of Lafcadio*—are mainly concerned with throwing off the shackles of a life-denying morality and finding the freedom either in direct, sensual living or the completely unmotivated, gratuitious act.

For Bernard, freedom is insufficient. He must also find a goal which would give meaning to his freedom, a direction through which he can authenticate his existence. He runs away from home when he discovers that he is a bastard, works as secretary for Edouard, returns to Paris and wrestles with his angel, overcoming the temptation to join the Action Française and find "meaning" in action for action's sake. Finally, he agrees to return to his father, for he now understands that his father needs him; he can go back to him as an adult and not as a child. Bernard's dissatisfaction with the formulae that Edouard offers him in their last conversation shows that he will still have to develop in order to find his own way. He is not an image of man, but we can at least say that this young man, in contrast to everyone else in the novel, "rings true."

ELIOT'S WASTE-LAND WORLD

In the decade following World War I, T. S. Eliot was the very voice of the "lost generation" wandering and groping in the modern waste land. In his early poetry, Eliot splits mankind, in almost Freudian fashion, into Sweeney, an embodiment of pure "id," and Prufrock, a man entirely dominated by "superego." Sweeney is hardly human, while Prufrock has lost touch with his vital forces almost entirely. The Sweeney poems are full of animal images; for even though he stands erect, Sweeney is not in fact a man. Even the murder of Sweeney is not tragic, as Eliot brings out through ironic contrast with the murder of Agamemnon—a scene from classical Greek tragedy with its essentially human meaning born of suffering and reconciliation.

Prufrock, on the other hand, is a man who lives, or subsists, like some dessicated embodiment of pure consciousness turned back on itself. He is not an isolated individual; he is intensely social—the wrong way around. He cannot move a step without thinking of what others are going to think of him. Yet he never really sees anything from the point of view of the other person. For him, other persons exist only in order that they might say, "But how his arms and legs are thin!" "The Lovesong of J. Alfred Prufrock" opens with a confession in hell, and hell for Prufrock, as for Sartre, is "other people," people to whom one cannot relate in any meaningful fashion and yet must join with in "the taking of a toast and tea." Even though he possesses a self-relationship that Sweeney entirely lacks, Prufrock, like Sweeney, is no tragic figure.

The sense of futility pervading "Prufrock" is based on the movement of time, which Eliot portrays, in the language of Ecclesiastes, as an endless cycle that never attains a meaning. Ecclesiastes' tone is that of a grand pessimism, however, while Eliot's is one of ironic triviality. The mood of Ecclesiastes is sad and stoic acceptance, that of Prufrock pathetic indecisiveness. "In a minute there is time / For decisions and revisions which a minute will reverse." In this sort of time, there is no possibility of a real present and, by the same token, of real presentness with others. There will be time "to prepare a face to meet the faces that you meet," but no time really to meet others as person to person. The complement of Prufrock's isolation in the midst of many is the empty sociality of the chorus of culture-seekers: "In the room the women come and go / Talking of Michelangelo." Such pseudo-culture means no real contact, and Prufrock, who knows how to move in an aristocratic, Boston society, knows also that he is never so alone as when he does so:

> And I have known the eyes already, known them all—
> The eyes that fix you in a formulated phrase,
> And when I am formulated, sprawling on a pin,
> When I am pinned and wriggling on the wall,
> Then how should I begin
> To spit out all the butt-ends of my days and ways?
> And how should I presume?

Prufrock sees himself as a butterfly fixed on a pin, an object for others' analysis. He cannot really talk with others, even in confrontation or opposition. Even his failure is insignificant, therefore, and his end, when it comes, not tragic.

> But though I have wept and fasted, wept and prayed,
> Though I have seen my head (grown slightly bald)
>   brought in upon a platter,
> I am no prophet—and here's no great matter.

Because he cannot really address another, Prufrock cannot really enter into life. He is thrown back upon himself—not in the lofty meditations of a Hamlet, the Renaissance man who could preserve dignity even in his indecisiveness, but as an undignified Polonius— "At times, indeed, almost ridiculous— / Almost, at times, the Fool." What is ridiculous about Prufrock is his own self-relationship. He cannot summon up passion; for in the moment of giving himself to another, he is afraid that a chilling response from the other will suddenly make his action seem inappropriate, leaving him ludicrous and exposed. In the discovery that there is no understanding between him and the woman he is approaching, his "overwhelming question" would suddenly become trivial. Hence, he is cut off equally from the lust of Sweeney and from the personal relationship of which Sweeney is incapable. Sweeney does not have the self to be a person, but Prufrock's self is expended in self-consciousness and so brings him no nearer to real personal existence. Consciousness to him, as to Dostoyevsky's Underground Man, is a continual self-torment.

The conclusion is already at hand: growing old without ever having really lived, aping the young but knowing himself forever excluded from the music of life.

> I have heard the mermaids singing, each to each.
> I do not think that they will sing to me.

He has *heard* the orchestra of existence, but he cannot play in it himself, or even respond to it by listening so that, in the words of *The Four Quartets*, "You are the music while the music lasts." He has no share and stake in it, nor does modern man in general. In the end, the portrayal of inauthentic existence is broadened from the isolated, unusual man into "all of us," and the subjective confession of Prufrock becomes a general and objective "confession in hell."

> We have lingered in the chambers of the sea
> By sea-girls wreathed with seaweed red and brown
> Till human voices wake us, and we drown.

Each of us lives in his private dream world, a world which can offer us no real satisfaction, no real life. When we wake, we wake into a reality for which we have left no room—the world of the inter-human that is common to all. When the voices of others call us back to an existence other than our own fantasy life, we awaken and drown. "We are all . . . so unused to real life that we cannot breathe in it," says Dostoyevsky's Underground Man. In Rilke's phrase, we die of "unlived life."

Prufrock and Sweeney are two complementary opposites. They do not add up to man, however, but to the absence of man, the absence of any genuine human existence. Together they make up the world of *The Waste Land*—consciousness without life, and lust without love. Both preclude any real relationship between men. The immediate prelude to *The Waste Land* is Eliot's poem "Gerontion." "Gerontion" is the reflections of an old man on an empty life. His life, in the words of Psalm XC, has been "a tale that is told," but it has not taught him "to number his days so as to grow a heart of wisdom," for it is a tale "signifying nothing." He has had no real existence, so his being old is also without meaning. "Thou hast nor youth nor age," Eliot quotes at the top of this poem, "but as it were an after-dinner sleep, dreaming of both." He was neither at the hot gates, nor did he fight in the warm rain. He belongs, like the people in *The Waste Land*, to Dante's Limbo where those are sent who have not really existed because they have done neither good nor evil. Even more clearly than Prufrock, he speaks not only for himself but for all of us—for modern Western man after World War I.

The word of revelation which might give a meaning to personal life and to history is lost in the welter of grasping hands which snatch at life in order to devour it. Our communion is a backward one—a cannibal orgy or a homosexual debauch, sitting at the "last supper" and already planning our betrayal:

> In depraved May, dogwood and chestnut, flowering judas,
> To be eaten, to be divided, to be drunk
> Among whispers; by Mr. Silvero
> With caressing hands, at Limoges . . .

Our betrayal is the old magic in new form: instead of hallowing the life that has been given us, we profane it. We do not share in existence, we pervert it, treating the means as the end, "living to eat." Our age puts every present moment to work for some future end, turns every-thing genuine into account and everything precious into calculable assets. "After such knowledge, what forgiveness?"

This knowledge is the knowledge of history, too, the history that has broken in on the self-satisfied progress of Western man with a holocaustal judgment. Yet it is a judgment from which we do not learn. Our heroism fathers unnatural vices, while virtues are forced on us by our impudent crimes. "These tears are shaken from the wrath-bearing tree." Christ the tiger, whom we have betrayed, eaten, divided turns from passive victim into active destroyer: "The tiger springs in the new year. Us he devours." We must ourselves be sacrificed in order that a real communion can come about which will usher us from death in life to death and rebirth. But if we have not lived, the judgment will come upon us as the judgment of our own nonexistence, like the sinners in Psalm I who are as chaff blown by the wind, men without roots in real ground beside living waters.

This judgment is merely death and no rebirth, and the death is without meaning, tragic or sacrificial. "Think at last / We have not reached conclusion, when I / Stiffen in a rented house." "I have not made this show purposelessly," he adds, "I would meet you upon this honestly." But the only meeting ground is the ground of no meeting, the only honest communication the impossibility of any communication.

> I have lost my passion: why should I need to keep it
> Since what is kept must be adulterated?
> I have lost my sight, smell, hearing, taste and touch:
> How should I use them for your closer contact?

I cannot use my passion in any pure way, for my existence adulterates it even as I use it. I have lost my five senses, the means whereby I came near your heart, but I could not have any real contact with you even if I had not lost them. All that is left to me is the decadence of pure sensation.

> Protract the profit of their chilled delirium,
> Excite the membrane, when the sense has cooled,
> With pungent sauces, multiply variety
> In a wilderness of mirrors.

As the existential psychiatrist von Gebsattel says of the addict, in terms of existentially immanent time this life moves nowhere. "Tenants of the house. Thoughts of a dry brain in a dry season."

The dryness of the ending of "Gerontion" points us to *The Waste Land,* the central theme of which is the absence of water, the sterility of the land. Building on the ancient associations of water and life, Eliot creates a modern myth in which fertility cults, the hanged and drowned gods of ancient religions, and the Tarot cards all work together to establish a universal statement with particular application to the inauthenticity of modern man. In this way, Eliot reenergizes the ancient myths and at the same time gives a depth dimension to his statement about the modern waste land. The deliberate, musical interplay of literary allusion of every sort creates a total ricocheting effect, more powerfully expressing the complexity of modern existence than any direct statement.

The waste land is the land on which the curse has come, as we are told from the ancient Grail stories in which the court of the Fisher King is hidden from the view of mankind when the virgins of the shrine are raped. The cause of the curse, then, is violation, the rape which produces sterility. In the fertility cults, the relationship between human sex and the fertility of nature was basic. But what Eliot is talking about here is the sterility of modern life; this sterility grows out of the modern violation of sex, the rape of lust without love. The waste land is not only the world of the animal lust of Sweeney, but also of the frustrated and trivialized passion of Prufrock, who in his way is no more capable of love than Sweeney.

> April is the cruellest month, breeding
> Lilacs out of the dead land, mixing
> Memory and desire, stirring
> Dull roots with spring rain.

Spring awakens us into a reality we do not want to face—the reality of our death-in-life.

The modern waste land is an amoral one. It knows no real decision, for good or evil. It knows no holiness, nor blasphemy, for there is nothing sacred to profane. The Hebrew exiles in Babylon, complaining in passionate song, become the bored expatriates in Geneva—"By the waters of Leman I sat down and wept." The sound of horns in the spring heralds not Diana of Acteon, the goddess of chastity, but our old friend Sweeney going to Mrs. Porter, the woman who runs a house of prostitution. The ancient initiation by the hierophant into the mystery rites of the hanged god is replaced by Mr. Eugenides, the Smyrna merchant, who invites the speaker to a homosexual weekend at the Metropole.

In "Death by Water," the next to the last section of *The Waste Land*, the way to a new life is indicated through a different kind of death—the death of the self, the death of lust and craving that overcomes sterility and leads to a rebirth in spirit. This coming to life is magnificently portrayed in the final section, "What the Thunder Said," in which the thunder comes at last bringing rain. The garden of Gethsemane and the Crucifixion are coupled with the death of the fertility god to create a common expectation of resurrection. "He who was living is now dead." Our life, in contrast, is simply a living death, a long, drawn-out process of dying. "We who were living are now dying / With a little patience." Thus, the breakdown of our civilization is coupled with the coming of a new theophany. The meaning of this breakthrough from sterile into fertile existence is couched in Sanskrit terms—*datta, dayadhvam, damyata:* give, sympathize, control. "What have we given?"

> The awful daring of a moment's surrender
> Which an age of prudence can never retract
> By this, and this only, we have existed

Prufrock could never muster the daring for a moment's surrender; never giving himself to another, he know no real life. Prufrock and Sweeney alike are cut off from sympathy, from real participation in the lives of others.

> *Dayadhvam:* I have heard the key
> Turn in the door once and turn once only
> We think of the key, each in his prison
> Thinking of the key, each confirms a prison

There is no communication between us. Each of us is imprisoned in his own consciousness. Only sympathy, Eliot implies, can begin to overcome the isolation of modern man. And with it control, discipline, direction, bringing oneself into the focus of a single intent.

The force of this poetic myth is the suggestion of its universality. Yet if we look at it more carefully, we see that it is not, in fact, universal. Not only is it Eliot's own personal synthesis, rather than the myth of a people, but also it is a myth of and for modern man, a sophisticated mosaic with eight pages of footnotes in five languages. The assent that it claims is not that of immediate experience and response, but of the interrelationships of meaning suggested by multifarious allusions and ironic contrasts. Hence, it is the exact opposite of what myth has always been to those among whom it has arisen—an immediate, dramatic presentation of a unique event. It belongs, rather, to that modern myth-mongering—to coin a phrase—which substitutes the secondary meaning derived from the similarity of myths in different times and places for the direct meaning of the myth taken by itself that was available to ancient man. The myth-monger asks us to accept a rich sense of everything having significant relation to everything else in place of any immediate insight into any particular event or reality. The modern myth that is created in this way is a confession of the absence of meaning: in the end, it betrays its own nihilism.

The central paradox in Eliot's waste-land myth is that the myth itself, the evocation of history and tradition, and the depiction of modern civilization all depend for their force on a sense of community, of common destiny and common suffering. Yet the solution offered is one which leads the individual off to his own private purgation, to set his own lands in order, leaving the universal statement with only a negative meaning. In "What the Thunder Said," the breaking through of rain seems a primeval, universal event, just as all the previous sections have seemed. Yet at the end of the poem, no rain has fallen, the plain is still arid, the waste land is as sterile as before, and only the "I" of the story has experienced any transformation. There has been no general rebirth, only an individual one. We are still in the waste-land world. I can seek some meaningful life for myself, but our civilization itself is decadent and crumbling.

MALRAUX AND THE ESCAPE FROM MAN'S FATE

The original, French title of André Malraux's novel, *Man's Fate*, is *La Condition Humaine*.

The human condition for Malraux is, above all, isolation and suffering. This painful human condition is one from which men would like to escape. Yet through his hero, Kyo, Malraux makes the claim that it is possible not only to accept the human condition, but also to justify it by giving it dignity.

Kyo is a man of action. He is the leader of the communist uprising in Shanghai in 1927 which unsuccessfully tried to overthrow the domination of Chiang Kai-shek and the nationalists. In contrast, Kyo's father, Gisors, is an eminent, Marxist theoretician who supplies the rationale for the actions of his son and the other communists. Kyo is the hero, but it is old Gisors who voices the author's point of view and his observations on the characters. It is Gisors who recognizes how rare it is "for a man to be able to endure . . . his condition, his fate as a man" and who makes the desire to escape from this fate the explicit source of the failure to live authentically as a man. While he speaks in general of opium, hashish, and women as the way that China, Islam, and the West try to free themselves from man's fate, he thinks in particular of the characters of the novel itself:

> Under his words flowed an obscure and hidden countercurrent of figures: Ch'en and murder, Clappique and his madness, Katov and the Revolution, May and love, himself and opium.[1]

This reflection is the key to the series of brilliant images of inauthenticity with which *Man's Fate* provides us.

The probing character of Gisors' consciousness gives us a deeper sense

[1] André Malraux, *Man's Fate*, translated by Haakon M. Chevalier (N. Y.: Modern Library, 1934), p. 241.

of the fate which man tries to escape. Gisors sees the deepest, most imperishable part of himself as a "furious subterranean imagination" existing in paranoiac isolation. "With his intruding consciousness he was anxiously treading a forbidden solitude where no one would ever join him," a solitude which owed nothing to the senses or to contact with others, a total solitude from which even his love for Kyo did not free him. One can never *know* another human being, and the attempt to do so "with one's intelligence is the futile attempt to dispense with time . . ." The best one can do, as in the case of Kyo, is to cease to feel that one does not know another. "The knowledge of a person is a negative feeling," Gisors says. "The positive feeling, the reality, is the torment of being always a stranger to what one loves." Gisors cannot escape from himself into another being, but he can find relief from his torment—through opium.

Ch'en's escape from the human condition is of a more active and intense nature than Gisors'. Ch'en, the former disciple of a Christian missionary, has turned to communism not for the sake of brotherhood and solidarity, but for the solitary madness of violence and murder. *Man's Fate* opens with Ch'en's assassination of a sleeping man—a task assigned him by the Party, yet one which isolates him from all his comrades. The act of murder itself is described not as that of a fighter for the Revolution, but as that of a sacrificial priest. It can only be consummated, in fact, when Ch'en presses the point of the dagger into his own arm; this blood communion is repeated after he has plunged the dagger into the man's heart:

> A current of unbearable anguish passed between the corpse and himself, through the dagger, his stiffened arm, his aching shoulder, to the very depth of his chest, to his own convulsive heart. . . . He was utterly motionless; the blood that continued to flow from his left arm seemed to be that of the man on the bed.[2]

This communion might seem to free Ch'en from his isolation, but in fact it only completes it. "Cut off from the world of the living, he clung to his dagger," overcome with religious dread: "He was alone with death, alone in a place without men, limply crushed by horror and by the taste of blood." The millions of lives of the men in the city all now reject his. He is held by the world of murder "with a kind of warmth," and even when he returns to his comrades, he can pass on information, but cannot convey what he feels.

Both Gisors and Ch'en recognize man's solitude, even while trying to find relief from it. In contrast, the French financier, Ferral, has the illusion of escaping from himself through the domination of others.

2 *Ibid.*, p. 12.

Whether concerned with his factories or with his mistresses, Ferral
has only one real passion—to possess. He defines intelligence as "the
means of coercing things or men," but he means by this only his own
intelligence, since only he should dominate. Ferral sees understanding
possible between man and woman only when the woman gives herself
and the man possesses her. Possession to him means not merely the
sensual enjoyment of Valerie's body, but the pleasure that he derives
from the sensual transformation of her features. For this reason, he
keeps turning on the light switch when she turns it off and enjoys a
temporary victory through witnessing her domination by sexual feelings, an event which occurs "only at the beginning of an affair, or when
she was taken by surprise":

> A familiar warmth seized her, mounted along her body to the tips
> of her breasts, to her lips, which she guessed by Ferral's look were
> imperceptibly swelling. She gave herself up to this warmth and, press-
> ing him against her with her thighs and her arms, plunged with long
> pulsations far from a shore upon which she knew she would presently
> be thrown back, but bringing with her the resolve not to forgive him.[3]

This scene is a perfect illustration of Jean-Paul Sartre's thesis that
the lover does not want to possess the beloved as an object, but as a
freedom subject to his own freedom. The way in which such possession
takes place is through seducing the other's freedom into becoming
incarnated in her flesh. But it is also a perfect illustration of the inherent
instability of such love when the other reasserts himself as a subject
whose look may reduce the sadistic lover to an object. When Ferral
next comes to see Valerie, she stands him up together with another
caller. He is handed a letter which says, "You will probably die without
its ever having occurred to you that a woman is also a human being."
Valerie is a "love object," but she is also a person. "I refuse to be regarded as a body," she writes Ferral, "just as you refuse to be regarded
as a check-book."

No repulse could have been more explicit, but it has not the least
effect on the basic pattern of Ferral's life—regarding others as existing
only for the sake of shoring up his self and at the same time enabling
him to escape it.

> In reality he never went to bed with anyone but himself, but he
> could do this only if he were not alone. . . . His will to power never
> achieved its object, lived only by renewing it; . . . he would possess
> through this Chinese woman who was awaiting him, the only thing
> he was eager for: himself. He needed the eyes of others to see himself,
> the senses of another to feel himself.[4]

[3] *Ibid.*, p. 126–7.
[4] *Ibid.*, p. 245.

Like Prufrock, Ferral is utterly isolated, yet his self-relationship in this isolation is mediated to him by "the look" of others!

The most obvious and frightening attempt to escape from the human condition in *Man's Fate* is by Baron Clappique, the "mythomaniac." A colorful, but utterly empty poseur, Clappique is pictured by Gisors as someone who "could cease to exist, disappear in a vice, in a monomania," but who "could not become a man." "A heart of gold, but hollow." Clappique seems not so much to have tried to escape man's fate as to stand outside it by his very existence: "Gisors perceived that at the base of Clappique there was neither affliction nor solitude, as in other men, but sensation." This does not make Clappique an exception to Malraux's image of man, however, for his very "existence" is revealed to be a nonexistence. The police chief gives Clappique a tip that will save Kyo's life if Clappique reaches him in time. Yet instead of going directly to Kyo, he stops at a roulette table. The fact that Kyo is wholly unaware that his life is being played away in this fashion gives "to the ball . . . the living reality of conjunctions of planets, of chronic diseases, of everything by which men believe their destinies to be governed." Clappique is giving over his responsibility to a total chance which becomes cosmic destiny. It enables him to be at once nothing and everything and to escape thereby from that limited freedom which is man.

> That ball which was slowing down was a destiny—*his* destiny. He was not struggling with a creature, but with a kind of god; and this god, at the same time, was himself.[5]

Clappique has "managed to escape almost everything upon which men base their lives—love, family, work; but not fear," and fear "rose in him, like an acute consciousness of his solitude."

The escape from man's fate implies the desire not to be powerful but to be all-powerful, Gisors says to Ferral. Man wants "to be more than a man, in a world of men. To escape man's fate. . . . The visionary disease, of which the will to power is only the intellectual justification, is the will to god-head: every man dreams of being god." Pascal recognized that man is a finite middle between the infinite and the infinitesimal, that he is neither all nor nothing. But the mistrust of existence has grown so since Pascal's day that typically modern man can no longer bear this middle position and prefers escape either into selflessness or self-deification. What the "Modern Promethean" cannot tolerate is precisely his existence as a self with a ground of his own, yet facing a reality which he must recognize as other than his self. For Malraux, however, it is not the unusual man but all men, not modern

[5] *Ibid.*, p. 257.

man alone but man in every age who is so cut off from meaningful
relationship to other men and the world that solitude becomes the
inevitable human condition whether or not one seeks to escape it.
Malraux goes beyond the fact that every man dies and, to some extent,
lives alone and posits an ultimate solitude and an ultimate absence of
communication as the norm. Actually, his images of inauthenticity reflect an inauthentic situation of modern man which cannot legitimately
be posited of man as man.

POINTERS TO THE AUTHENTIC

If the "seeming" of Gide's counterfeiters is inauthentic, then an
existence which "rings true" would be authentic, even if Bernard had
not made this his explicit aim. If the imprisonment in solitude prevents
Eliot's characters from communicating with each other and the split
between consciousness and life force joins with this isolation to
prevent the possibility of a real, full life, then unity of consciousness
and life energy, communication, sympathy, dedication are all implied
as positive values. Similarly, if escaping from the human condition of
suffering and solitude means an inauthentic life, whether it takes place
through opium, violence, mythomania, or revolution, then accepting
and justifying man's fate is implied as the positive image of man.
What is more, despite the basic difference in their themes, the three
writers join in the deprecation of a life that has no personal commitment, no personal direction, no real personal center, no real communication with others.

A life may be inauthentic, even judged from within, however, without its necessarily following that the man in question has the real
possibility of authenticating his life. There are tragedies of situation,
of contradiction, of limited resources, of limited confirmation, of insufficient grace in which the inauthentic must be recognized at the
same time as the hopelessly exiled. These tragic limitations are also
a part of our image of man, as Melville recognizes when he adds to
the employer's sigh over the forlorn Bartleby the further sigh "Ah,
Humanity!" [6]

[6] For an explicit discussion of this agonizing question in the detail and depth that
it deserves, I must refer the reader to my *Problematic Rebel: An Image of Modern
Man* (N. Y.: Random House, 1963). See in particular Part II, "The Death of God
and the Alienation of Modern Man"; Part III, "The Modern Exile"; and Part V,
"The Problematic of Modern Man." The discussion is particularly in terms of
Melville, Dostoyevsky, Kafka, and Camus, but also of Hardy, Kierkegaard, Nietzsche, and others.

II

THE
MODERN SOCIALIST

3

MALRAUX, KOESTLER, STEINBECK, SILONE, AND CARLO LEVI

A**N IMAGE** of man is essentially an attitude, a certain type of response, and one cannot fix a response in a formula—whether it be that of rebel or revolutionary—abstracted from the concrete and ever-changing social reality to which one must respond. For this very same reason, however, one may say that one of the significant, basic responses of *our* time has been that of the socialist and the social revolutionary. We live in an era of basic and widespread social change, and it is inevitable that again and again the test of our authenticity should be the way in which we respond to this historical situation.

For many, communism has seemed to be the ideal answer to the question of how to restore man to his alienated humanity. Karl Marx's essay, "The Alienation of Labor" (1844), shows man alienated from his work, from nature, from other men, and from himself. From this it follows that the establishment of a new society which would no longer reduce the worker to a commodity, but would give him back his dignity as a man, is the urgent task of this historical hour. Those who take this task on themselves authenticate their existence as men.

In *Man's Fate*, as we have seen, Malraux gives us a number of different communists with quite different images of man, and he distinguishes between those who are ultimately inauthentic—Gisors, Ch'en, and Katov—and Kyo, who is authentic. It is not in Kyo's communism alone that his authenticity lies, therefore, but in the use he makes of it—to accept man's fate and to justify it by giving it dignity.

Kyo has a heroic sense that makes his life simple and disciplined. "Individual problems existed for Kyo only in his private life." When it came to the meaning of his life per se, it was a public, general, even impersonal meaning, although one that was at the same time intensely personal.

> His life had a meaning, and he knew what it was: to give to each of these men whom famine, at this very moment, was killing off like a slow plague, the sense of his own dignity. He belonged with them: they had the same enemies. A half-breed, an outcast, despised by the white men and even more by the white women, Kyo had not tried to win them: he had sought and had found his own kind. "There is no possible dignity, no real life for a man who works twelve hours a day without knowing why he works." That work would have to take on a meaning, become a faith.[1]

What Malraux fails to point out is that the man who finds a meaning in his life through giving meaning to the lives of others has no immediate meaning of his own. He has tied his personal existence to his social cause in such a way that the failure of that cause can rob his own life of all meaning. Even its success does not assure him of meaning, as Kyo and his creator think, for it would still be *their* meaning and not his.

"All that men are willing to die for, beyond self-interest," Kyo holds, "tends more or less obscurely to justify that fate by giving it a foundation in dignity: Christianity for the slave, the nation for the citizen, Communism for the worker." This is the age of communism, and even in its "death-stroke," the concentration of defeated fighters awaiting their execution is seen by Kyo as the object of an almost religious devotion "wherever men labor in pain, in absurdity, in humiliation." Kyo can join these men in their murmur of complaint, and he can die with them an active, "virile" death of brotherly solidarity.

> He had fought for what in his time was charged with the deepest meaning and the greatest hope; he was dying among those with whom he would have wanted to live; he was dying, like each of these men, because he had given a meaning to his life. . . . It is easy to die when one does not die alone. A death saturated with this brotherly quavering, an assembly of the vanquished in which multitudes would recognize their martyrs, a bloody legend of which the golden legends are made! . . . No, dying could be an exalted act, the supreme expression of a life which this death so much resembled.[2]

Kyo dies with a *sentiment* of brotherhood and solidarity, but without the reality. Though he lies beside his friend Katov on the floor, he says no word of farewell to him before swallowing the poison and leaving

[1] André Malraux, *op. cit.*, p. 70.
[2] *Ibid.*, p. 323.

him "thrown back into a solitude which was all the stronger and more painful."

In the end we must conclude that Kyo's authenticity is not really *shown* by Malraux; it is *deduced*. Gisors believes that Kyo alone resists the category of men who seek to escape from the isolation and anguish of the human condition. Yet it is not the events of the novel which support this view, but merely the author's repeated assertion that Kyo has given meaning to his life by trying to give dignity to the worker. An image of man cannot be derived from a general idea. It must be pointed to in all concreteness if it is to have value as a reality to which we can respond.

In *Darkness at Noon*, Arthur Koestler draws an illuminating picture of the socialist revolutionary who becomes aware of the inauthenticity of deducing an image of man in this way. Its hero, Rubashov, is one of the old guard of the Russian revolution, on trial for his life in the great Soviet purge of the nineteen thirties. His cause is not unsuccessful, like Kyo's, but so successful that it becomes an institution, the preservation of which justifies the destruction both of the men who built it and of the very principles on which it was built. The drama of the book is outwardly the imprisonment, questioning, public hearing, and execution of Rubashov—first by men like himself and later by the new "Neanderthal" generation of realists who have transformed the doctrine of the idealistic end justifying the opportunistic and inhuman means into an acceptance of those means as themselves the end. But the inward and more important drama is the dialectic that takes place in Rubashov himself.

As Rubashov paces up and down in his cell, he thinks back over his past life; for the first time, he experiences a sense of guilt for having, at different times, sacrificed a young German communist, the leader of a dock strike in Belgium, and his secretary, in each case for an abstract cause. He had felt that the Party was more important than any individual, that as the embodiment of the revolutionary idea in history, it could never be mistaken. But now he realizes that the inexorable logic of the Party had made him and the other Communist leaders inhuman.

> When and where in history had there ever been such defective saints? Whenever had a good cause been worse represented? If the Party embodied the will of history, then history itself was defective. . . . All our principles were right, but our results were wrong. . . . We diagnosed the disease and its causes with microscopic exactness, but wherever we applied the healing knife a new sore appeared. . . .

Our will was hard and pure, we should have been loved by the people. But they hate us. Why are we so odious and detested?[3]

The events and mental debates of the rest of the book serve one central purpose—to answer this question. One part of the answer is Rubashov's discovery of "the grammatical fiction"—a silent partner within himself, the real "I" which he had ignored for the past forty years in favor of the external, nonpersonal "I," the rational Party member. He had used his logic as a means of suppressing his more human feelings. "But the realm of the 'grammatical fiction' seemed to begin just where the 'thinking to a conclusion' ended." This grammatical fiction shows Rubashov his real guilt—not unfaithfulness to the logic of history, but the denial of the person and of the infinite. And again, this guilt is connected with the defectiveness of an image of man whose validity is deduced from abstract love of humanity:

> The infinite was a politically suspect quantity, the "I" a suspect quality. . . . The definition of an individual was: a multitude of one million divided by one million. The Party denied the free will of the individual—and at the same time it exacted his willing self-sacrifice. It denied his capacity to choose between two alternatives—and at the same time it demanded that he should constantly choose the right one. It denied his power to distinguish good and evil—and at the same time it spoke pathetically of guilt and treachery.[4]

Rubashov has recognized the inadequacy of an image of man based on pure logic and on the doctrine that the end justifies the means. But neither he nor his author has found a positive image of man to put in its place. At best, there is only a hint of a vague, intellectualized mysticism and of a time centuries later when party members "will wear monks' cowls and preach that only purity of means can justify the ends."

A much more positive and significant foil to *Man's Fate* is John Steinbeck's *The Grapes of Wrath*. In this novel, Steinbeck allows his hero, Tom Joad, to grow and develop in response to real situations. The Joad family is uprooted from Oklahoma because of dust storms and because the bank in Tulsa forecloses the mortgage on their home. Along with other "Okies," they make the long and painful journey west to California, only to find themselves chased by vigilantes and ruthlessly exploited by the orange and cotton growers in whose migrant

[3] Arthur Koestler, *Darkness at Noon*, translated by Daphne Hardy (N. Y.: Modern Library, 1946), p. 58.
[4] *Ibid.*, p. 257.

camps they live and work. A former revivalist preacher, Jim Casy, who has journeyed with them, shows them a practical, if entirely immanent, Christianity which stands its ground and witnesses for brotherhood in the face of injustice and violence. The source of his strength is his belief that everyone is part of one big soul—that the holy spirit is the human spirit—"all men an' all women we love."

The experience of the Joad family plus the murder of Casy by the vigilantes lead Tom Joad step by step to the point where he is ready to devote his life to fight for justice through organization and strike, the only weapons of the migrant workers. Tom Joad arrives at conclusions not so different from those of Kyo. The real impact of the novel does not lie in such conclusions abstracted from the story, however, but in the image of Tom Joad himself. Tom has become a true man by faithfully answering the cruel demands of an ever-changing situation. We feel him grow, and we grow with him, and when we put the book aside, we take him with us, not just his ideas. When Tom leaves his family because he has killed the man who killed Casy, he tells his mother—the strong and human Ma Joad—that she need not worry about what will happen to him because,

> maybe like Casy says, a fella ain't got a soul of his own, but on'y a piece of a big one—an' then . . . Then it don' matter. . . . Wherever they's a fight so hungry people can eat, I'll be there. Wherever they's a cop beatin' up a guy, I'll be there. If Casy knowed, why, I'll be in the way guys yell when they're mad an'—I'll be in the way kids laugh when they're hungry an' they know supper's ready. An' when our folks eat the stuff they raise an' live in the houses they build— why, I'll be there.[5]

When I was an undergraduate at Harvard, a Radcliffe friend, for whose integrity and spirit I had great admiration, told me that she had joined the Young Communist League because of a debt that she owed to Tom Joad! Here was a dramatic testimony to the influence of an image of man in a work of fiction. She did not speak of Tom Joad's ideology's being correct, as most communists would, but of a personal responsibility to him. To suggest that that responsibility was unreal because Tom Joad is a character in fiction would be shallow. Tom Joad is a product of Steinbeck's encounter with the world of his time, and our meeting with Tom Joad is a part of that same encounter. To relate that my friend withdrew from the Young Communist League a short time later because she could not reconcile its methods with

[5] John Steinbeck, *The Grapes of Wrath* (N. Y.: The Viking Press, Compass Books, 1958), p. 572.

her own integrity is a humorous commentary on her political naïveté, but it in no way diminishes the significance of her response to Tom Joad as an image of man.

In *The Yogi and the Commissar*, Arthur Koestler says that the need of the present age is for a man who is a combination of the saint and and the revolutionary. Ignazio Silone has portrayed such a man in Pietro Spina, the hero of *Bread and Wine*, but Spina's character does not include either the saint or the revolutionary in its full intensity. It is just this fact which makes him so convincing an image of man. Through his loyalty to truth and his courage in accepting suffering, he gradually moves from the revolutionary who is abstracted from society and who works with propaganda and political action, to the Christian socialist living in harmony with nature and the poor and affecting the attitudes of others by a sincere and nonattached way of life. But he does not trade the fanatic intensity of the revolutionary for the inhuman holiness of the medieval saint. He remains a modern man and, what is more, a unique person with very human foibles, personal quirks, and shortcomings. Despite a decided tendency to verbalize, he emerges irreducibly concrete and unique, and in this lies his significance for us.

The setting of *Bread and Wine* is Fascist Italy in the middle 1930's, around the time of the Italian campaign against Ethiopia. The slavery that the dictatorship imposes on the people consists essentially of the substitution of falsehood for truth in all spheres of life. "The scourge of our time . . . is insincerity between man and man, lack of faith between man and man, the pestilential Judas Iscariot spirit that poisons public and private life!"

At the beginning of *Bread and Wine*, Pietro Spina has just returned from exile abroad. By treating his face with iodine, he has given himself the appearance of an old man and has succeeded in reaching his native countryside without detection by the authorities. Spina is ill and is forced to convalesce in the disguise of a priest, Don Paolo Spada. Don Paolo becomes aware of a split in his character between the religious adolescent and the revolutionary who has been superimposed on it. And his meditations from then on take the form of an altercation between his two selves.

> He knew that it was impossible to revert to his adolescence and the mythological tenets of religion, and hand his problems over to a transcendent God. He could not, even if he wanted to, retire into private life, shut his mind to the inhuman fate of the poor, and accept the dictatorship. And it seemed impossible now to go on with his party life,

accept its rules and customs, intrigue, lie, consider the interests of the party as the supreme good, and judge moral values as petty-bourgeois prejudices.[6]

This altercation is also given expression in dialogues with Cristina, an unusually spiritual girl of Pietrasecca who is preparing to take the veil. In these dialogues, he tries to convince her that morality cannot be purely contemplative and that one's spiritual riches should be expended in a life with one's fellowmen. Don Paolo continues these dialogues in private in a diary. Cristina is of the opinion that the man of faith is not alone even in a monastery, but that the atheist is alone even in the most crowded city.

> The soul that does not know God is a leaf detached from the tree, a single, solitary leaf, that falls to the ground, dries up, and rots. But the soul that is given to God is like a leaf attached to the tree. By means of the vital sap that nourishes it, it communicates with the branches, the trunk, the roots, and the whole earth.[7]

Pietro's whole life is a denial of Cristina's statement that there is an irreconcilable conflict between spirit and matter and that "to search for a compromise means to sacrifice spirit to matter." He complains to Cristina that the custom of keeping religion and life separate has resulted in a bestial society on the one hand and secluded religious communities on the other.

> If a peasant ever succeeds in overcoming his animal instincts, he becomes a Franciscan friar; if a girl ever succeeds in freeing herself from bondage to her own body, she becomes a nun. . . . Do you not think that this divorce between a spirituality which retires into contemplation and a mass of people dominated by animal instincts is the source of all our ills?[8]

Through these dialogues, Pietro becomes aware that his original reason for joining the socialists was his disgust at the abyss between the practical actions of the Church and the words which it preached. But he found the same cleavage, the same opportunism in the party with its "party truth" and "party justice." This gap between words and actions is true of almost all men in the false society of a dictatorship. Insincerity reaches such great proportions that it may be spoken of as a disintegration.

The peasants are susceptible neither to government nor to socialist

[6] Ignazio Silone, *Bread and Wine,* translated by Gwenda David and Erich Mossbacher (N. Y.: Penguin Books, 1946), p. 88.
[7] *Ibid.,* p. 82.
[8] *Ibid.,* p. 81f.

propaganda. What is called for is not the political agitator talking at the top of his voice to a crowd, but genuine, personal dialogue. "To establish relations between man and man, to inspire confidence and have confidence, to exchange ideas and not words, two men must be alone together, talk softly and with many pauses, the better to be able to reflect." One could not deal with the peasants as a group and build on them, for the relations among the peasants themselves were unstable, frail, and fugitive. The peasants were not susceptible to words but only to facts. Underlying the class struggle is "man, a poor, weak, terrified animal." What is needed to help this man is a living image of what man can be.

> There are malcontents and there are perpetrators of violence, but Men are lacking. . . . It would be a waste of time to show a people of intimidated slaves a different manner of speaking, a different manner of gesticulating; but perhaps it would be worth while to show them a different way of living. No word and no gesture can be more persuasive than the life, and, if necessary, the death, of a man who strives to be free, loyal, just, sincere, disinterested; a man who shows what a man can be.[9]

Pietro Spina is deeply influenced by his old teacher, Don Benedetto —a priest who shows what an uncompromising Christianity can be in the face of social injustice and Church opportunism. As a result of this experience, all that remained alive and indestructible of Christianity in Pietro was revived:

> a Christianity denuded of all mythology, of all theology, of all Church control; a Christianity that neither abdicates in the face of Mammon, nor proposes concordates with Pontius Pilate, nor offers easy careers to the ambitious, but rather leads to prison, seeing that crucifixion is no longer practiced.[10]

But Pietro Spina is not simply an uncompromising Christian. He is a Christian *socialist*. He redefines the concept and method of revolution.

> It is . . . a matter of a new way of living. It is a matter of becoming a new man. Perhaps it is sufficient to say that it is a matter of becoming a man, in the real sense of the word. . . . At heart every revolution puts this elementary question afresh: What, it asks, is man? . . . You cannot conceive what it would mean to a country like ours . . . if there were a hundred youths ready to renounce all safety, defy all corruption, free themselves from obsession with private property, sex, and their careers, and unite on the basis of absolute sincerity and

9 *Ibid.*, p. 256.
10 *Ibid.*, p. 289.

absolute brotherliness: a hundred youths, who would live among the people, in contact with the workers and the peasants, and refuse to be parted from them; a hundred converted youths, who would speak the truth on every question and on every occasion, nothing but the truth, and live according to the truth.[11]

"In a society like ours a spiritual life can only be a revolutionary life," Pietro tells Cristina, but he looks to this revolutionary life to produce in the first instance a new type of saint, a new type of martyr, a new type of man. Such a spiritual life is one that struggles and takes risks. "Spiritual life and secure life do not go together," not even the security of one's own virtue.

In removing from his Christian socialism the whole transcendent meaning of Christianity as founded on the incursion of divine grace into human history, Spina takes for granted both the source of moral values and the resources to live by them. His basic humor and confidence in man might have been shaken by the example, not so many years hence, of the depths of evil to which humanity could sink in the dictatorship of the Nazis, one that made Mussolini seem a comic buffoon in contrast to the terrifyingly demonic. Yet in the person of Pietro Spina, Silone's confidence in man carries a certain persuasiveness, not as religious doctrine or abstract theory of human nature, but as trust, courage, and hope.

When Pietro Spina learns that he is in danger of being arrested, he sends Cristina the dialogues which he has written, and then he runs up the mountainside toward the one path by means of which he might escape. Deeply moved by the dialogues, Cristina tries to intercept Spina on the mountainside with clothes and food, only to be answered by the howl of wolves who come galloping through the snow to devour her. Here is both the real and the symbolic consequence of that dualistic separation between the spiritual and the material life which Pietro Spina earlier told Cristina was the source of all evils. Cristina was seeking spiritual security. She turned her back on the vicissitudes of human existence and human relations to be the bride of Christ. Though this appeared to be a total commitment and a total dedication, it was actually a dualism in which she offered her spiritual essence to God and denied God the social reality in which she lived. She had renounced everything for herself personally and was only waiting to enter the nunnery until her family's affairs were in better order. Yet she objected on the grounds of tradition to Pietro Spina's suggestion that some of the vast lands that belonged to her family should be used to house the poor peasants. Her death exemplifies the fate of

[11] *Ibid.*, p. 291f.

detached spirituality when it goes out into the world, at the mercy of the evil which it has hitherto avoided.

In *The Seed Beneath the Snow*, the sequel to *Bread and Wine*, we learn that Spina did not try to make the mountain pass; he instead doubled back and took refuge in a small cave in which one of the local farmers kept his donkey. This cave is the spiritual center of the two novels. All the spiritual changes in Spina in *Bread and Wine* lead up to the cave, and all his thoughts and actions in *The Seed Beneath the Snow* proceed from it. In it, Pietro feels his last attachments slip away, and he becomes again a child, full of wonder at the world around him, experiencing all things as ever-present and all creation as renewed in every moment. Through this experience, love of the poor, friendship, simplicity, mature knowledge of suffering, and sadness at man's fate become the very foundations of his being. His whole past life seems to him to consist of a gradual stripping of gross pretenses leading up to the cave, and the cave seems as familiar to him when he reaches it as if he had carried its image inside him.

> When we really see beneath the surface of this world of ours, . . . we find plain traces of the fragility, the vain show and the essentially temporary character of a theater curtain. . . . I have come to think that the quiet, the peace, the happiness, the well-being, the hominess, the companionship which I found in that stable derived from a contact with simple, true, difficult, painful forms of life, immune from the plague of rhetoric.[12]

Pietro feels that his life belongs with all those things that are completely real and vital. He constantly endeavors to reduce his life to reality and is passionately opposed to intellectuals and intellectualism. He is gentle and affectionate toward animals; he values the emotions of the heart above the thoughts of the mind; and he has faith that nothing can destroy pure, simple, and true words. Above all, the crowning fruit of his new life is friendship. Although he knew thousands of people in the party, in fifteen years he never had one real friend. Now he forms real friendships, friendships which give meaning to the rest of life. " 'There are moments of harmony and plenitude between friends that cancel out years of hardship and aridity.' "

Two other related motifs that enter into Pietro's new way of life are the need for spiritual self-realization and the necessity of accepting suffering. He used to think looking after his soul, i.e., trying to know himself and find the meaning of his life, "a sign of bourgeois decadence." Now he sees it as the *sine qua non* without which no

---

[12] Ignazio Silone, *The Seed Beneath the Snow*, translated by Frances Frenaye (N. Y.: Harper & Bros., 1942), p. 170.

man can help another. "'Before we can give something of ourselves
to others, we must first possess ourselves. A man who is spiritually a
slave cannot work for true freedom.'" This applies particularly to
the man he now recognizes himself to have been in his politically
active days, a man marked by "arrogant party fanaticism," "the cocki-
ness of the self-educated man," "the vanity of the petty bourgeois who
turns to the people out of personal resentments," "the unhealthy joy
of commanding," the desire to enjoy "revolutionary glory and popularity." He was that man because of his fear of real suffering, just as
he has become a new man through his acceptance of suffering. "Every
mask and every pretense can be reduced to one great evasion: the
desire to overcome the sorrows of life with palliatives and tricks of
the imagination rather than with sincerity and a manly impulsion."
He recognizes, of course, that there is sorrow caused by wounded
vanity and frustrated ambition.

> But there is a sorrow inherent in our human fate which we must
> learn how to face and make into our friend. We must not fear even
> despair . . . as long as it is serious and sincere and has some funda-
> mental reason. We must not fear to ask ourselves: Who am I?[13]

Pietro has chosen a way of life that implies the readiness to sacrifice
comfort and convenience whenever friendship or truth demands it. At
the end of The Seed Beneath the Snow, it is friendship that claims
him. To protect Infante, the deaf-mute with whom he shared his cave
and whom he has befriended since, Spina claims that it was he and
not Infante who killed the latter's father when the father beat him.
In so doing, he sacrifices not only himself but also his newfound love
for Faustina, a girl with whom he has fled from his grandmother's
town. Yet he gives himself up to the police as the most natural thing
in the world. He has remained a highly conscious man, expressing
himself with a great many words, given to theories and abstractions.
Even his exaggerated enthusiasm for the "real" and the "natural"
testifies to his failure to attain to the completely simple way of life to
which he aspires. Yet he shows us in his unique way what it means
to authenticate one's humanity. To this extent, he can be for us a contemporary image of man as Kyo and Rubashov cannot.

Pietro Spina's movement away from party theorizing toward concern with the concrete relations between man and man is a gain both
for socialism and for the image of man. Yet Silone has made it sound
as if one could turn from political concern to concern about oneself
and that true socialism and true revolution would follow from this.
Actually, even for Pietro Spina, this is not the true picture. He does

[13] Ibid., p. 299.

not begin by discovering who he is and then go out to help others. On the contrary, he begins by trying to help others and in the course of his failures changes himself, his approach to social action, and his understanding of what is effective socialism both as method and goal. In other words, he never once puts aside his concern for others for the sake of finding himself, nor is his finding of himself ever really his goal. If it were, he would be no whit different from Cristina.

What is really at issue here is the contrast between what Martin Buber calls "the political principle" of domination and control and the "social principle" of fellowship and social spontaneity.[14] But Silone seems to reject the former for the latter, whereas Buber recognizes that the political is always necessary even though it must be reduced again and again to the minimum essential to maintain order, thereby allowing the social principle the freedom to develop. For Buber, too, as the German educator Heinz-Joachim Heydorn has pointed out, socialist renewal begins with the question about man.

> But this question remains closely bound to reality; it is concerned with man in his present-day form, with man in our time. The reality in which this man lives, the reality of his technical greatness, has barred him in growing measure from the true road to himself. We shall not be able to reopen this road for him if we wish to redeem him through purely political means without restoring to him the immediacy of his existence.[15]

The immediacy of man's existence means here the immediacy of the dialogue between man and man and the immediacy of community. It does not mean beginning with man as an individual taken by himself. Similarly, the recognition that man cannot be redeemed through purely political means does not imply dismissing those means in favor of the social, but giving them meaning through informing them with the spirit of the social. The same applies to the problem of specialization and the technical complexity of modern work, so far removed from the simple life of Pietro Spina's peasants. In a discussion of Gandhi and politics, Buber wrote:

> One should, I believe, neither seek politics nor avoid it, one should be neither political nor nonpolitical on principle. Public life is a sphere of life; in its laws and forms it is, in our time, just as deformed as our

[14] See Martin Buber, *Pointing the Way*, edited and translated with an Introduction by Maurice Friedman (N. Y.: Harper Torchbooks, 1963), "Society and the State"; Martin Buber, *Paths in Utopia* (Boston: Beacon Paperbacks, 1957); and Maurice Friedman, *Martin Buber: The Life of Dialogue* (N. Y.: Harper Torchbooks, 1960), Chap. XXIII, "Social Philosophy."

[15] Heinz-Joachim Heydorn, "Martin Buber und der Sozialismus," *Gewerkschaftliche Monatshefte*, Vol. IV, No. 12 (December, 1953), p. 709 (my translation).

civilization in general; today one calls that deformity politics as one calls the deformity of working life technique. But neither is deformed in its essence; public life, like work, is redeemable.[16]

Both Silone and the contemporary Italian writer Carlo Levi would agree with Buber's valuation of the social principle over the political and its corollary—a social restructuring directed toward a federalistic communal socialism. Levi's autobiographical "story of a year," *Christ Stopped at Eboli*, is more realistic than Silone's novels in its understanding of the complexities of the interrelation between the political and the social. This book, too, is set in Mussolini's fascist Italy, and Levi, like Silone, becomes the person he is in opposition to it. Eboli, according to legend, was the farthest outpost of Christian conversion, and the village south of Eboli to which Levi is exiled by the government is a peasant society untouched by Christian culture, i.e., outside of both history and civilization. Levi is the central figure of his book, but he does not portray himself as a hero. In contrast to Pietro Spina, he does not think that there is much that he can do for these poor and underprivileged people that would not upset them without helping them. His role rather is that of doctor, painter, and sympathetic observer, living in friendly relations with these people, but finding neither motive nor occasion for sacrificing himself to them. Instead, he returns to Rome and writes of his experience in a powerful, humane, and persuasive book that has helped in the growing movement of concern about Sicily. To this extent, Levi is a forerunner of Danilo Dolci and his *Report from Palermo*, although Dolci, like Pietro Spina, lives and works among the people.

Carlo Levi returns with a new understanding of Sicily and the southern Italian peasant who cares nothing about what form of government is in power. This is not just because the peasant is "backward." It is also because the politicians are "all unconscious worshippers of the State."

> Whether it was tyrannical or paternalistic, dictatorial or democratic, it remained to them monolithic, centralized, and remote. This was why the political leaders and my peasants could never understand one another. The politicians oversimplified things, even while they clothed them in philosophical expressions. Their solutions were abstract and far removed from reality; they were schematic halfway measures, which were already out of date.[17]

The problem of the South cannot be solved by changing the political labels, but by creating "a new kind of State which will belong also

---

[16] Martin Buber, *Pointing the Way, op. cit.*, p. 136.
[17] Carlo Levi, *Christ Stopped at Eboli*, translated by Frances Frenaye (N. Y.: Farrar, Straus & Co., 1947), p. 249.

to the peasants and draw them away from their inevitable anarchy and indifference." This new kind of state must be one in which the "social principle" will predominate, to use Buber's phrase. In order for this to take place, a new, more realistic concept of the individual which "will do away with the now unbridgeable gulf between the individual and the State" is needed.

> The individual is not a separate unit, but a link, a meeting place of relationships of every kind. This concept of relationship, without which the individual has no life, is at the same time the basis of the State. The individual and the State coincide in theory and they must be made to coincide in practice as well, if they are to survive.[18]

Thus, Carlo Levi's experience in the South of Italy gave him a new and more concrete image of man. The concreteness of the image lies in the fact that it puts aside the tendency to isolate and abstract the individual from his relations with others in favor of an understanding of the existence of the person as inseparable from the relations between man and man, between man and his community, and between community and community. If Levi were to rest with the statement that "the individual and the State coincide in theory," he would not have brought us much further along. "The State" is a huge abstraction to which the individual seldom has any direct relation. But Levi goes beyond this and identifies himself with that important, but inadequately recognized, movement of socialism that aims at a federation of free and organic communities rather than a monolithic state that will impose socialism on the people from above.

> This reversal of the concept of political life, which is gradually and unconsciously ripening among us, is implicit in the peasant civilization. And it is the only path which will lead us out of the vicious circle of Fascism and anti-Fascism. The name of this way out is autonomy. The State can only be a group of autonomies, an organic federation. The unit or cell through which the peasants can take part in the complex life of the nation must be the autonomous or self-governing rural community. This is the only form of government which . . . can assure the peasants a life of their own, for the benefit of all. But the autonomy or self-government of the community cannot exist without the autonomy of the factory, the school, and the city, of every form of social life. This is what I learned from a year of life underground.[19]

Like the early Marx, Levi is concerned with the gestation of the new society in the womb of the old rather than the emphasis on political action per se that became the concern of the later Marx and

[18] *Ibid.*, p. 253.
[19] *Ibid.*, p. 253f.

still more of those who followed him. Unlike Marx, however, he sees the economic problem as only a part of the larger problem of the absence of community in modern times. He recognizes that aiming at a certain type of political government, if one has not first been concerned with the creation of real community, is of no use. At the same time, he avoids the danger that Silone sometimes falls into of swinging all the way from political action in relation to the crowd to the opposite extreme of concern for the meaning of one's individual existence. One wonders, however, whether Levi, with a more detached perspective, has understood as well as Silone that a new type of community means not only a more adequate concept of what man *is*, but also a new man, a new image of what man can and should be.

This double difference between Silone and Levi brings us to the heart of a problem not only of the Modern Socialist, but also of any contemporary image of man. An image of a man in abstraction from an imperfect social situation in need of change is unthinkable in our day. What is more, this process of change does not always produce heroes or saints. On the other hand, it is equally unthinkable that one could concentrate on political movements without concern for the sort of person the leaders and followers of those movements are becoming. Then one would run into the contradiction that stands at the heart of *Darkness at Noon*: the résults that one would obtain both individually and socially would be much more likely to resemble the means that one uses than the end one has in mind.

In *Darkness at Noon*, Rubashov's friend, Ivanov, says to him that there are only two ethics, one a collective ethic, in which the end justifies the means, and the other an individualistic Christian ethic, in which only pure means are used: "Humbugs and dilettantes have always tried to mix the two conceptions; in practice, it is impossible."[20] That there is an ethical issue here which a merely pragmatic approach cannot solve is true enough. But the polarization of the choice into that of pure extremes only serves to darken the issue. In any actual situation, the real choice is not between these opposites—so startlingly similar in their tendency toward ruthlessly abstract action which disregards the concrete reality of the present and of other people's views. Rather, the choice again and again is between responding to the demands of the situation with the resources that are available to one, and failing to do so. If one does respond, one does so for the sake of the situation—the social change that is demanded and in which one feels called to participate. One does not respond for the sake of one's own becoming. This means that one does not aim directly at

[20] Arthur Koestler, *op. cit.*, p. 152f.

becoming a certain sort of man, or even at finding and realizing an image of man. It means, too, that we can never allow the heroic figure —Kyo, or Tom Joad, or Pietro Spina—to obscure the sober reality that an imperfect society must produce imperfect men. Even when these men respond with greatness and become great in responding, they still bring with them something of the very violence, injustice, and inequality that drove them to action.

In considering other types of contemporary images of man, therefore, we must remember that when social milieu and social responsibility are not stressed, they are not, for all that, absent. They are only bracketed for the sake of focusing on the types of *response* to the situations of our time which have been pointed to as most necessary, most meaningful, and most hopeful.

III

THE
MODERN VITALIST

4

BERGSON
AND KAZANTZAKIS

GIVING the name of Idea to a certain settling down into easy intelligibility," writes the French philosopher Henri Bergson in *An Introduction to Metaphysics*, "and that of Soul to a certain longing after the restlessness of life, . . . an invisible current causes modern philosophy to place the Soul above the Idea." The high valuation that our culture places on such terms as "dynamic," "creative," and "evolving" is ample testimony to the truth of Bergson's statement. Nietzsche, William James, pragmatism, *Lebensphilosophie*, and even existentialism are among the foremost representatives of that "restlessness" that leads much, though by no means all, of modern philosophy to see the dynamic as more real than the static, time as more real than space, the unique as more real than the universal. Far beyond the boundaries of philosophy per se, vitalism has entered the mainstream of modern culture and left a decisive imprint on many contemporary images of man. Very often, this imprint is a partial one, coupled with other elements; for the celebration of life and life energies, like the words "dynamic" and "creative" themselves, evokes enthusiasm more easily than it lends direction.

Friedrich Nietzsche's poetic classic, *Thus Spake Zarathustra* celebrates "evil" and chaos as the very source of those creative energies that are needed for the fullness of living:

> I tell you: one must still have chaos in one, to give birth to a dancing star. I tell you: ye have still chaos in you.

> When your heart overfloweth broad and full like the river, a blessing and a danger to the lowlanders: there is the origin of your virtue.

Since humanity came into being, man hath enjoyed himself too little: that alone, my brethren, is our original sin!

—For there is a salt which uniteth good with evil; and even the evilest is worthy, as spicing and as final over-foaming:—[1]

This attitude can easily lead, as in Goethe's *Faust*, to a celebration of the dynamic per se, valuing it because of its energy and assuming that it is only the suppression of this energy which leaves it evil. So long as man lives and his desires stir, "he cannot choose but err." Yet "a good man through obscurest aspiration has still the instinct of the one true way." "He who ever strives—him can we save," *Faust* concludes. This same valuation of the active, creative energy as good and passive suppression as evil informs both the positive affirmation and the negative critique in the novels of D. H. Lawrence—*Sons and Lovers, Women in Love, Lady Chatterley's Lover,* and even such a late, quasimystical work as *The Plumed Serpent.* One must now distinguish between the "evil" to which society is hostile, but which is really an indispensable part of the good, and what is really evil— that which kills or suppresses energy and prevents it from expressing itself.

The corollary of this view of energy as evil only when suppressed is the high, positive valuation of creativity as the one true goal of life. In its name, Nietzsche attacks all half-willing, all comfortable virtue that calls its mediocrity moderation, all those "last men" who "have their little pleasures for the day, and their little pleasures for the night, but they have a regard for health." Where one cannot long and will with one's whole being, "where one can no longer love, there should one—*pass by!*" It is because men cannot love in this way that women are no longer women: "Only he who is man enough, will—save the woman in woman." There could be no more exact anticipation of Lawrence's novel, *Lady Chatterley's Lover,* in which the decadent, essentially unmanly lord, paralyzed from the waist down, is deserted by his wife for the rough and manly gamekeeper.

It is Henri Bergson who has made vitalism into a comprehensive philosophy. In his central work, *Creative Evolution,* Bergson identifies reality and value with a vital force, or *élan vital,* which is at once physical and biological energy, extending from the repetitive energy of matter to the highest reaches of the human spirit. Bergson compares the total world process to a fountain: the streams of water ever pressing upward symbolize the ceaseless evolution of vital forces, the water falling back to the ground symbolizes matter which

[1] Friedrich Nietzsche, *Thus Spake Zarathustra,* translated by Thomas Commons (N. Y.: Modern Library, n. d.), pp. 11, 80, 94, and 259.

is itself energy that has lost its creative *élan* and suffered a diminution into crystalized patterns. Bergson's view of time is essentially different from the mechanistic understanding of Darwin and much nineteenth-century thought. Time is not a matter of discrete moments, of causes followed by effects, but an unbroken organic continuum. Time is experienced not as a measured entity, therefore, but as a flowing "duration." "Intuition" is the apprehension of that duration, first within ourselves and then in other beings. Evolution has gone farthest in man, on the one hand, and in insects, on the other. In insects, the *élan vital* has taken the form of instinct, in man typically the form of intelligence. But man also has access to intuition as no animal or insect does. Man's intellect represents an abstraction from the stream of life which gains freedom at the cost of isolation; the insect's instinct represents an immersion in that stream and the loss of all freedom; intuition represents a middle sphere of evolution between the two which combines the organic connection of instinct with the freedom of intelligence. On this basis, Bergson distinguishes, in his *Introduction to Metaphysics*, between "two profoundly different ways of knowing a thing." The first is the analytical intelligence, which perceives objects from without and reduces them to elements already known that are common to it and other objects. The second is intuition, which is "the kind of *intellectual sympathy* by which one places oneself within an object in order to coincide with what is unique in it and consequently inexpressible."

To recover authentic existence we must move from the world of spatialized, quantitative, successive time to the organic flow of time. Like Kierkegaard, Bergson distinguishes between the becoming, or processes, of the inner soul and the tendency to fix these processes into objects, categories, and words in the outer world. His attack on *"homo loquax,"* who thinks he knows everything already and is ready to reduce all new and unique fact to old and general categories, is indeed welcome. But he falls into the unnecessary trap of treating all words and language as merely functional, by the same token reducing the sphere of the social to a purely secondary, utilitarian dimension of human existence. Bergson protests "against the substitution of concepts for things, and against . . . the socialization of truth," thus depreciating the social and equating it with the "outer" and the "physical." In doing this, he has denied the real wholeness of man's life. If there is such a thing as a "truth" which points us back to immediacy and reality, is not that truth already social in that it is shared and communicated between us? Are not Bergson's hundreds of thousands of words, his precise definitions, his passionate and vivid affirmations socialized truths of just this sort?

Even in talking of the soul, Bergson distinguishes between outer and inner in the form of surface and depth and equates the wholeness of the soul with its depth. Provided that they go deep enough, each of one's feelings "make up the whole soul, since the whole content of the soul is reflected in each of them." On the very next pages, however, Bergson distinguishes between "a fundamental self," which seems to be naturally there, and "a parasitic self," the product of education, "which continually encroaches upon the other." "It is the whole soul, in fact, which gives rise to the free decisions and the act will be so much the freer the more the dynamic series with which it is connected tends to be the fundamental self." But how can one's "fundamental self" be a real self at all when it is *not* connected with one's dynamic series of actions?

Sometimes Bergson uses *"élan vital"* as a purely descriptive term, synonymous with all that is, and then one wonders how he escapes his own strictures against philosophical terms which, at the point where they designate everything that exists, mean no more than existence itself and hence are tautologies which add nothing to our knowledge. At other times, Bergson identifies the creative with the good, the essential, and the real, and then one wonders at the absence of some second principle to explain the relation of the creative to all that is not creative, of the inner to the outer, the things to words, the individual to the social, time to space.

Like Alfred North Whitehead, Bergson stresses "the continuous creation of unforeseeable novelty." In opposition to the Platonic Whitehead, however, Bergson denies that the possible precedes the real and claims rather that the possible grows out of the fullness of the real. The moving precedes the inert in this view. Time is pure indetermination, not because it is empty of determinants, but because it is immediately given. The creation of unforeseeable novelty means an organic flow in which each new moment of time gives a different meaning to the whole of the past. "Disorder is simply the order that we are not looking for."

Philosophy offers us, as a result, a new image of man, "a preparation for the art of living." We shall have greater joy through perceiving "the ever-recurring novelty, the moving originality of things," and "we shall have greater strength, for we shall feel we are participating, creators of ourselves, in the great work of creation which is the origin of all things, and which goes on before our eyes."

> Thanks to philosophy, all things acquire depth. . . . Reality . . . affirms itself dynamically, in the continuity and variability of its tendency. What was immobile and frozen in our perception is warmed and set in motion. Everything comes to life around us, everything is

revivified in us. A great impulse carries beings and things along. We feel ourselves uplifted, carried away, borne along by it. We are more fully alive and this increase of life brings with it the conviction that grave philosophical enigmas . . . arise from a frozen vision of the real and are only the translation, in terms of thought, of a certain artificial weakening of our vitality.[2]

There could be no finer and more inspiring statement of the Modern Vitalist image of man than this. To Bergson goes the credit of having stated it with a force, a precision, and a purity that no one else has matched. Yet there remains the question of whether the "creation" in which we participate as "creators of ourselves" is only our inner life, dualistically separated from the creation as the Bible understood that term. Not only does Bergson depreciate space, the outer and the social, as we have seen, but he also explicitly defines personality in *The Creative Mind* as "the continuous melody of our inner life." To equate the personality as a whole with the inner life is to suggest that one's relations to nature and to other men are either impersonal or antithetical to personality or, at best, a watered-down expression in the outer world of the reality of the inner. If words per se falsify, then true "self-expression" is all but impossible. If, on the other hand, the meeting with the other is a more than functional reality, as we would hold, then what takes place in that meeting is not "self-expression" at all, i.e., the transference of something that is inside the self to something outside it, but communication—sharing in a common relationship and a common situation.

In his last great work, *The Two Sources of Morality and Religion*, Bergson goes a decisive step beyond the mere valuation of creativity toward a more concrete image of man—a fusion of "creative evolution" and the example of the Christian saints. In this work, Bergson attempts to construct a philosophy based on an interpretation and synthesis of modern science, a philosophy that will serve as a rationale for an image of man taken from a world far removed from contemporary man.

The two perfect types of association, writes Bergson, are "a society of insects and a human society, the one immutable, the other subject to change; the one instinctive, the other intelligent." An insect society is like an organism "whose elements exist only in the interest of the whole," while a human society leaves "so wide a margin to the individual that we cannot tell whether the organism was made for them or they for the organism." In human society, the inventive effort of evolution is continued through the activity of individuals

[2] Henri Bergson, *The Creative Mind: A Study in Metaphysics*, translated by Mabelle L. Andison (N. Y.: The Wisdom Library, 1946), p. 157.

who possess initiative, independence, and liberty along with intelligence. But these qualities threaten to break up social cohesion and therefore necessitate a counterpoise to intelligence which is found in the myth-making faculty. This myth-making faculty gives rise to religion whose function is to uphold the customs of the group. Religion is a defensive reaction against the representation by intelligence of the inevitability of death, of "the depressing margin of the unexpected between the initiative taken and the effect desired," and of the reality of individual aims and interests as opposed to those of the organic group.

This identity of religion with the survival interests of the group Bergson calls "static religion," and the morality of custom that grows out of it he calls "closed morality." In opposition to it, he sets a "dynamic religion" and an "open morality" which represent the continuation of the upward thrust of evolution in higher individuals in contrast to its stagnation in groups. It is here, in dynamic religion, that Bergson presents us with his own image of what man can and ought to be. It is neither possible today to accept Bergson's picture of primitive religion, based on Levy-Brühl's notions of a *participation mystique*," nor to accept his conception of discursive intelligence as *preceding* and necessitating myth, rather than, as Cassirer has shown, following it as a quite different stage of thinking and of consciousness. Nor can we accept Bergson's simple contrast between "static" and "dynamic" religion, since even a primitive religion is not without individuality, and no great religion is ever an affair of the individual alone. For all this, we may still assess in its own terms the image of man that Bergson presents us in his discussion of "dynamic religion."

This image is that of the man who has deepened the intuition common to all men to a mysticism known to only a few. However, this mysticism is still to be understood, as Bergson understands intuition, as a continuation and upward movement of the *élan vital*: "The ultimate end of mysticism is the establishment of a contact, consequently of a partial coincidence, with the creative effort which life itself manifests." This creative effort so embodies all reality and value for Bergson that he identifies it with the divine action. "This effort is of God, if it is not God himself." Pervaded by this mighty power, without losing his own personality, the mystic cares little, says Bergson, whether this be the transcendent cause or merely its earthly delegate. What matters are the effects of the experience on the mystic himself. Detachment from each particular thing becomes attachment to life in general. Bergson's mystic has the best of both worlds: his mysticism lifts him to another plane, yet "ensures for the soul, to a preeminent degree, the security and the serenity which it is the function of static religion to provide." The mystic is more than a man, he is the man-God, the human bearer of the divine principle who continues and extends the divine action. From this "standpoint, which shows us the divinity of all men, it matters little whether or no Christ be called a man. It does not even matter that he be called Christ." Bergson found in the Christian mystics and, before them, in the Biblical prophets that active love which represents to him the highest upward surge of the creative force.

On one page, Bergson speaks of God as the creative energy itself and love as the definition of this energy; on another, he speaks in the language of the Old Testament of a God who needs us as we need him and of creation "as God undertaking to create creators, that He may have, besides Himself, beings worthy of His love." In the first passage, love is identical with an almost impersonal flow of spiritualized energy; in the second, love is brought back to its original meaning of a personal relation between persons. Again, though Bergson sees God as a "creative effort," he asserts that "religion, be it static or dynamic, regards Him, above all, as a Being who can hold communication with us," which is "just what the God of Aristotle, adopted with a few modifications by most of his successors, is incapable of doing." Bergson was not aware of these contradictions because he possessed simultaneously a conception of God based on his philosophy and an image of God derived from the prophets and the Christian mystics. His intellectual acceptance of the former enabled him to give an emotional allegiance to the latter, but it is no less a contradiction. In his image of a loving God who creates creators that he may love and be loved, God, world, and man are separate—separate and in relationship. Yet in his philosophy, Bergson has eliminated the separate reality of the transcendent, the world, and man in favor of a monism of creative "energy"—a metaphor which enables him to include the farthest reaches of matter and spirit in one dynamic process. *Although he begins with the dynamic, he leaves the ground of the concrete—reality seen from within the standpoint of actual human existence, which is always personal, separate, and in relation and never merely a flowing totality.*

In Bergson's image of man, as in his image of God, we find an uneasy marriage between a *conception* of man derived from his philosophy and an *image* of man taken from tradition. Like Aldous Huxley, Bergson seeks a "perennial philosophy" to be justified by the appeal to the unanimity throughout all times and cultures of those who share "a singular privileged experience." "Mystics generally agree among themselves," "the path followed is the same," and "they have in any case the same terminal point," writes Bergson in support of this thesis. Bergson is unaware of, or ignores, the essential differences between the mystics. Like William James, he is concerned more with the effects of the mystical experience than with the experience itself. The mystic realizes at once his unity with the all and his personal uniqueness: "The individual then becomes one with the emotion; and yet he was never so thoroughly himself; he is simplified, unified, intensified." But he does not simply rest in this unity and wholeness. In the complete mysticism of the Christian mystics, the mystic passes through the mystical state only to burst a dam and be "swept back into a vast current of life." From the increased vitality of these mystics, "there radiated an extraordinary energy, daring, power of conception and realization." "Henceforth for the soul there is a super-abundance of life. There is a boundless impetus. There is an irresistible impulse which hurls it into vast enterprises." Through the mystic the love of God for all men pours into the world. He is a link in the chain of divine, creative energy. "Through God, in the strength of God, he loves all mankind with a divine love." Here, the Christian *agape* and the Bergsonian energy come closest to fusing. But the love of God is not enough for Bergson. Like the true modern and the true pragmatist, he wants *results*. "Just think," he writes, "of what was accomplished in the field of action by a St. Paul, a St. Teresa, a St. Catherine of Siena, a St. Francis, a Joan of Arc, and how many others besides!"

The saints and mystics, then, are the images of man that Bergson offers to the contemporary world. In order to show their relevance for modern man, he makes their relation to their own religions a fairly external one that borrows from it on the one hand and intensifies it on the other, but possesses "an original content, drawn straight from the very wellspring of religion, independent of all that religion owes to tradition, to theology, to the Churches." Whereas most mystics see the meaning and goal of mysticism either in the reciprocal love of the human "I" and the divine "Thou," in union with the Godhead, or realization of the already existing identity of Self and Absolute, Bergson turns the creative process itself into the sum and substance of the mystical experience, thus calling into serious question the divinity of what in itself never reaches the transcendent and unconditioned.

To understand the inner working of the vital impetus, the philosopher turns his intuition inward to apprehend the flow of duration within himself. In its first intensification, this makes "us realize the continuity of our inner life." A deeper intensification, however, carries "it to the roots of our being, and thus to the very principle of life in general." "Now is not this precisely the privilege of the mystic soul?" Bergson concludes. Instead of apprehending God, the mystic now apprehends "the principle of life in general." He is a sort of super-philosopher, or philosopher-king, who shows the way to the ordinary philosophers, like Bergson, who can go only part of the way but not the whole way. "The mystics . . . have blazed a trail along which other men may pass. They have, by this very act, shown to the philosopher the whence and whither of life." But Bergson judges this to be the case not through his own mystical experience, primarily, but through a philosophical criterion. The high valuation he places on the mystic turns out in the end to be an extrinsic one. He sees their experience in terms that they could neither recognize nor acknowledge. Every one of the saints whom he cites believed in and prayed to a transcendent God who could never be identified with the creative activity present in the soul. Nor were any of these men convinced of the truth of their experience because of its pragmatic effects. What Bergson really values is not so much the experience itself of the mystic, but the philosophy which he believes finds support in that experience and which, in fact, he reads into it through his interpretation of it. In order to achieve the consonance between his philosophy and the mystical experience that he assumes, he has to convert personal devotion into impersonal process.

To what extent, we must now ask, has Bergson bequeathed to us a contemporary image of man? Insofar as he has pointed to the lives of concrete and unique individuals and from there has pointed to the more general image of the Christian mystic and saint, we may say that he has given us an image of man. Taken in themselves, however, they are not and cannot be contemporary images of man, for the very meaning of their lives and activities stems from a medieval world that does not share the problems and tensions of modern man and in large part cannot speak to it. Even when a figure such as St. Francis does project beyond his own world and speak to ours, there is no sense in which we can say that *Bergson* has offered him to us as an image of man, since he does not deal with him in his own terms, but in terms quite extrinsic to him.

The marriage between the particular images of man that Bergson points to and his more general conception of man is in constant danger of annulment, therefore, or even divorce. If we follow Bergson in emphasizing not the figures he offers as illustrations, but the generalized image of the mystic as the man who pushes intuition to its farthest depths and becomes part of the divine creative effort, then we must say that this image of man is defective in its very generality. More important still, it offers no real direction for one's potentialities, no guidance in the response to particular situations and in the movement toward authentic, personal existence. Bergson's worship of evolution, energy, and "creativity" has led him into the fatal error of assuming that any movement onward is also upward. He sets the mystic in relation to the stream of divine energy, but he does not see the concrete, existing individual in relation to other men and to the world of things. He does not bear in mind the real man who must again and again make real decisions as to what is better and what is worse and who cannot simply rely on "creativity" or the outpouring of love. Understandable as a reaction against the sterile abstractions of philosophical idealism and rationalism, Bergson's vitalism falls into the trap of an identification of energy with ultimate reality and of a relativism in which all movement, of whatever nature, is equally good so long as its flow is not staunched. That Bergson himself would have been the first to be horrified by the Nazi conversion of vitalism into unlimited demonry only shows that he had other values that found no explicit place in his philosophy.

The problem of the Modern Vitalist may be grasped with more subtlety if we examine the powerful novel, *Zorba the Greek*, by Nikos Kazantzakis. This novel comes as close as almost any contemporary one to presenting a really positive image of man in the figure of Zorba, the sixty-year-old "Sinbad the Sailor" who goes to work for the narrator of the story as the foreman of his lignite mine in Crete and at the same time tries to teach the "boss" about the meaning of a life lived in fullness and immediacy. For all his lack of education, the many-sided Zorba is a Modern Vitalist hero, if ever there was one. Yet it is impossible to understand the image of man that Kazantzakis presents us in this novel by looking at Zorba alone. The portrait of Zorba is the central theme and subject matter of the book, but the central concern is with the boss' relation to Zorba and what he learns and does not learn from him. In other words, here the familiar split between actor and observer is complicated because the "boss," too, is an actor in his way—not enough of one to be an image of man in his own right, but too much of one for us to be able to focus on Zorba alone. Rather, we must listen to the counterpoint between these two men—one man indirect and the other direct, one reserved and the other passionate, one bookish and the other a man of the people, one a lover of Buddhist contemplation and the other the lover of countless women. We cannot capture this counterpoint directly, however, for we see Zorba only through the eyes of the "I"—eyes of longing, envy, and detachment, eyes of admiration and amusement—so that statements about Zorba almost always betray the boss' relation to him.

Zorba was the man I had sought so long in vain. A living heart, a large voracious mouth, a great brute soul, not yet severed from mother earth.

The meaning of the words, art, love, beauty, purity, passion, all this was made clear to me by the simplest of human words uttered by this workman.[3]

To Zorba, to be a man means to be free—to play his stringed *santuri* only when the spirit moves him. To the boss, it means freedom from attachment, "a Buddhist compassion, as cold as the conclusion of a metaphysical syllogism." To Zorba, it means cutting off his finger with a hatchet when it gets in the way of his work as a potter; to the boss, it means the avoidance of pain. But the contact with Zorba makes the boss ashamed of his delicate hands, his pale face, and his life which "had not been bespattered with mud and blood." This does not mean that Zorba is a simple, unthinking man, unacquainted with the sadness of man's fate. On the contrary, he sees his compulsion to run after women as the fault that will kill him; along with his enjoyment of life, he sets up a constant cry of revolt: Why has God made women, death, injustice, suffering? The boss, in contrast, accepts everything as fate, or sees its harmony with the universal pattern of things. He is incapable, as a result, of either grief or anger. The paradox is that Zorba despises men and thinks they are brutes, yet lives and works with them, while the boss "believes" in men, but only when they have been abstracted into ideas for his writings. Under the impetus of his admiration for Zorba, the boss wants to free himself from his metaphysical speculations and "make direct and firm contact with men." Yet the only way he can do it is through the exorcizing task of writing his Buddha book.

One of the most important questions concerning vitalism is raised by Zorba's "confession of faith"—when he finally answers the boss' insistent question as to whether he does not believe in anything:

> I don't believe in anything or anyone; only in Zorba. Not because Zorba is better than the others; not at all, not a little bit! He's a brute like the rest! But I believe in Zorba because he's the only being I have in my power, the only one I know. All the rest are ghosts. I see with these eyes, I hear with these ears, I digest with these guts. All the rest are ghosts, I tell you. When I die, everything'll die. The whole Zorbatic world will go to the bottom![4]

Most of the novel suggests that Zorba does believe in and care about people and that it is to the boss—the sympathetic observer and de-

[3] Nikos Kazantzakis, *Zorba the Greek*, translated by Carl Wildman (N. Y.: Simon and Schuster, 1959), p. 13.
[4] *Ibid.*, p. 54.

tached actor—that people are really ghosts. When Zorba dies, he so little believes "the whole Zorbatic world" has gone to the bottom that he sends a message to the boss and leaves him his beloved *santuri*. Nonetheless, coupled with the almost tiresome paean of praise that the "I" is always singing about Zorba is a blatant note of self-celebration trumpeted by Zorba himself. Zorba is, in fact, his own myth; to this extent, he is neither so simple nor so immediate as both he and the boss make out.

If Zorba shares Lawrence's celebration of the vitality of sex, he also shares the Vitalist's closeness to the earth and to the Great Mother—the earth goddess of old. Educated people are seen, in contrast, as "empty-headed birds of the air," because they lack this contact with the earth. Zorba is the natural man whose mind has not been perverted by school. (We recall Bergson's contrast between the "fundamental self" and the "parasitic self" produced by education.) His mind is open and his heart bigger without his having lost one ounce of his primitive boldness. One would think that Zorba was the one man living without any self-relationship or reflective consciousness, that he was authentic by virtue of being completely natural, completely Zorba!

> "Have you got confidence in me, boss?" he asked, anxiously looking me in the eyes.
> "Yes, Zorba," I replied. "Whatever you do, you can't go wrong. Even if you wanted to, you couldn't. You're like a lion, shall we say, or a wolf. That kind of beast never behaves as if it were a sheep or a donkey; it is never untrue to its nature. And you, you're Zorba to the tips of your fingers."[5]

If this statement were entirely true, Zorba undoubtedly would not have asked his question, nor would the boss have answered it. But the boss is consistently ambivalent in his relationship to Zorba since he admires him and yet persists in stressing the contrast between the two of them. Zorba's road is the right one; he has the truth, the boss reflects. If I could go to his school, I would throw myself into life—"fill my soul with flesh, . . . fill my flesh with soul." "In other, more primitive and creative ages, Zorba would have been the chief of a tribe," but now he "sinks into becoming some pen-pusher's buffoon." Zorba is not after all a man, a free man. He does not play his *santuri* whenever the boss wants, but otherwise he is there to talk, to tell stories, to amuse, entertain, enlighten, instruct, chide, and laugh at the boss while the latter listens, observes, learns, laughs, enjoys, or is amused!

[5] *Ibid.*, p. 69.

Zorba follows Dylan Thomas' cry to the old: he, too, "will not go gently into that goodnight"; he too rages "against the dying of the light." "The longer I live, the more I rebel," Zorba says to the boss. "I'm not going to give in; I want to conquer the world!" The boss reflects at one point that the only way to human deliverance, however pitiable, is "to say 'yes' to necessity and change the inevitable into something done of their own free will?" But Zorba leads him to ask whether there is not a place for revolt—"the proud, quixotic reaction of mankind to conquer Necessity and make external laws conform to the internal laws of the soul, to deny all that is and create a new world according to the laws of one's own heart, which are contrary to the inhuman laws of nature." What he does not reflect on is that these two opposite attitudes, which he and Zorba respectively embody, are startlingly similar in that neither of them takes seriously the encounter between man and the world. The one removes the demands of man in favor of the world, the other removes the world in favor of the demands of man. Confronted with a lusty widow, the boss wants to avoid her because he does not want any trouble. To Zorba, in contrast, "life is trouble" and to live means "to undo your belt and look for trouble!"

> I knew Zorba was right, I knew it, but I did not dare. My life had got on the wrong track, and my contact with men had become now a mere soliloquy. I had fallen so low that, if I had had to choose between falling in love with a woman and reading a book about love, I should have chosen the book.[6]

Like Nietzsche, who defines original sin as not enjoying ourselves, Zorba quotes a saying, that he who can sleep with a woman and does not, commits a great sin. The boss himself thinks that "being a man" would mean running after the widow, taking her by the waist, and dragging her to her large widow's bed. But he sees himself as Zorba sees him—someone who weighs things up, reflects, and calculates, someone who lets reading and writing about life take the place of living. The Buddha came too soon, he concludes. "We have neither eaten, drunk, nor loved enough; we have not yet lived."

Zorba is set before us as a modern primitive for whom the universe "was a weighty, intense vision," a man who "lived the earth, water, the animals and God, without the distorting intervention of reason." He is the man who cracks "life's shell—logic, morality, honesty—" and goes "straight to its very substance." "The cry came from the depth of Zorba's being, and the whole thin crust of what we call civilization cracked and let out the immortal beast, the hairy god,

6 *Ibid.*, p. 101.

the terrifying gorilla." He is at the same time the perfect Nietzschean man. Lacking all the little virtues of moderation, he has an "uncomfortable, dangerous virtue which is hard to satisfy and which urges him continually and irresistibly towards the utmost limits, towards the abyss."

Zorba is the finest example in contemporary literature of what the Jewish mystic and philosopher, Abraham J. Heschel, calls the quality of "radical amazement." He sees everything each day in its pristine freshness, as if for the first time.

> He is forever astonished and wonders why and wherefore. Everything seems miraculous to him, and each morning when he opens his eyes he sees trees, sea, stones and birds, and is amazed.
> "What is this miracle?" he cries. "What are these mysteries called: trees, sea, stones, birds?"[7]

Perhaps because Zorba is less of a poet than Heschel, it is hard after a while not to feel Zorba's "radical amazement" as too conscious to be quite real.

> "What is that?" he asked stupefied. "That miracle over there, boss, that moving blue, what do they call it? Sea? And what's that wearing a flowered green apron? Earth? Who was the artist who did it? It's the first time I've seen that, boss, I swear!"[8]

In Zorba himself, in the observer boss, and still more in Kazantzakis, such passages raise the question of the extent to which the modern search for the natural and the primitive is not really a hothouse plant, to what extent the *cultivation* of spontaneity is anything but spontaneous. If Zorba is his own myth, he is still more the myth of the boss and of the author. He uses his myth as a way of living, but they use it as a way of consoling themselves for not living, by deriving from him a second-hand feeling of being alive.

The latter is a way of living without genuine seriousness. For all the difference in their ages and experience, one never quite has the feeling that the boss sees Zorba as a real person. Zorba sees God as someone created in his own image—someone who breaks all the commandments with impunity, and he insists again and again that God and the devil are the same. Similarly, the boss sees Zorba as a god—the god who enables him to exorcize the Buddha.

> He had lived with his flesh and blood—fighting, killing, kissing—all that I had tried to learn through pen and ink alone. All the problems I was trying to solve point by point in my solitude and glued to

[7] *Ibid.*, p. 151.
[8] *Ibid.*, p. 228.

my chair, this man had solved up in the pure air of the mountains with his sword.[9]

But they were not the same problems or the same answers! Zorba had killed till he was revolted against killing and could no longer accept the patriotism that urged him to murder, rape, and arson. The boss had theorized about mankind as a whole.

The boss is finally able to respond to the image of man he has found in Zorba to the extent that he sleeps with the widow. But when bloodthirsty villagers leap upon the widow because a young boy drowned himself for love of her, the boss is completely ineffectual in his attempts to reason with them. Zorba, on the other hand, calls shame down on the villagers and fights like a tiger to save her. But before Zorba can lead her to safety, the widow is beheaded by the father of the young boy. Zorba's reaction to this incident is a Job-like protest that goes far beyond the merely romantic revolt that denies reality in favor of the heart's desire. "I tell you, boss, everything that happens in this world is unjust, unjust, unjust! I won't be a party to it!" The boss, in contrast, wants to put everything right as usual by laying it before destiny's door. He turns the woman to whom he had made love shortly before into an abstract symbol:

> The terrible events of that one day broadened, extended into time and space, and became one with great past civilizations; the civilizations became one with the earth's destiny; the earth with the destiny of the universe—and thus, returning to the widow, I found her subject to the great laws of existence, reconciled with her murderers, immobile and serene.[10]

The boss is ashamed before Zorba's sorrow, the sorrow of a real man who lets real tears run down his cheeks, and the reader is ashamed of the boss too, as no doubt Kazantzakis wanted him to be.

Zorba dies in true Zorba style, saying, "I've done heaps and heaps of things in my life, but I still did not do enough. Men like me ought to live a thousand years." But even before his death, he has become a legend to be talked over by the boss and his friends:

> We admired the proud and confident bearing, deeper than reason, of this untutored man. Spiritual heights, which took us years of painful effort to attain, were attained by Zorba in one bound. And we said: "Zorba is a great soul!" Or else he leapt beyond those heights, and then we said: "Zorba is mad!"[11]

[9] *Ibid.*, p. 227.
[10] *Ibid.*, p. 249.
[11] *Ibid.*, p. 306.

There is no question that Zorba comes off well as an image of man, particularly in contrast to the "I" of the story. Although he is a vitalist who celebrates himself and equates God and the devil, he has worked through to a living sense of values and shows tenderness, care, and sympathy for others as well as a marvelous sense of humor. Perhaps the real secret of his impact on the boss and on the reader is that he is all there in whatever he does. He attains that moment-by-moment wholeness which comes to those who are really present:

> "I've stopped thinking all the time of what happened yesterday. And stopped asking myself what's going to happen tomorrow. What's happening today, this minute, that's what I care about. I say: 'What are you doing at this moment, Zorba?' 'I'm sleeping.' 'Well, sleep well.' 'What are you doing at this moment, Zorba?' 'I'm working.' 'Well, work well.' 'What are you doing at this moment, Zorba?' 'I'm kissing a woman.' 'Well, kiss her well, Zorba! And forget all the rest while you're doing it; there's nothing else on earth, only you and her!' "[12]

A Western afficionado of Zen might say that Zorba had attained "every-minute Zen." All Zorba claims is that he gave his old mistress greater pleasure than any of the admirals that used to make love to her. While they were kissing her, they kept thinking about their fleets, or the king, or their wives. "But I used to forget everything else, and she knew that, the old trollop."

If Zorba is not one-hundred percent believable as the natural, primitive man that the boss wants to make him out to be, he is a good deal more believable than the boss himself. Although the latter admires Zorba, turns him into a legend, and takes one or two hesitating steps in his direction, he seems content in the end to use Zorba for a sort of aesthetic satisfaction, an enjoyment of vitality from the safe position of the observer and the semiparticipant. He not only recognizes that he cannot burn his books and relearn life at Zorba's school, he does not really want to. And this is what, in the end, prevents Zorba from being a full-dimensional image of man to contemporary man. Kazantzakis has used Zorba as a commentary on contemporary man, but he identifies the latter with the "I" who cannot and will not be like him. The boss finds Zorba such a revelation because he had not expected to find such vitality, wisdom, humanity, and humor in an uneducated man. But he and his friends are less than honest when they pretend that Zorba attained at one bound the spiritual heights they toiled for. Zorba wanted no "spiritual heights" at all. There lies the difference!

The Modern Vitalist offers us no help with the problem of what

[12] *Ibid.*, p. 273.

we ought to do to become fully human other than the minimal, and by itself meaningless, demand for the full use of human energy. Along with its indispensable message of more abundant life, vitalism bequeaths to contemporary man the problem of how to direct that life, of what value decisions, if any, may make that life worth living. This problem is particularly acute because of the tendency of Modern Vitalists to form their doctrine in reaction against those forces in society which deny and suppress life. This reaction leads them to assume that energy, vitality, and even the irrational are good things in themselves and need only be liberated to transform and fulfill our life.

IV

THE
MODERN MYSTIC

5

ALDOUS HUXLEY

MYSTICS differ in essential respects as to the way of man and the image of man that follow from their experience. To some, mysticism means chastity, isolation, and contemplation; to others, it is best expressed in marriage, community, and work. And even where both of these trends are affirmed, some say the one is higher, some the other.

It is customary, and not inaccurate, to say that the mystic realizes the paradox of God's being both immanent and transcendent. We may put this more concretely by saying that mysticism is immediacy and presentness *plus* presence—a strong sense of the immanence of God not as doctrine but as immersion in a directly experienced reality of divine presence. Mysticism includes not only person-to-person contact with God but also the presence of the spirit of God. This is the Brahma *vihāra*, or living in Brahman, of Hinduism, the flowing with the Tao of Taoism, the sudden illumination of the thousand and one things of Zen Buddhism, the testimony of Saint Paul that in God "we live and move and have our being." To the mystic, our existence is not only God's address and our answering response, but also discovering ourselves in the presence of God, knowing ourselves as known by him.

Aldous Huxley follows the modern Vedantists of the Ramakrishna Society in asserting that the identity of Brahman and Atman, the Absolute and the innermost Self, is the essence of all religions. To him, as to W. T. Stace in *Time and Eternity,* God and the mystic are identical within the mystical experience of the infinite and eternal which intersects time, but is not in time. Not only are all mystical experiences identical for him, but also all mystics are identical within this experience.

Although Aldous Huxley is the author of many novels with a contemporary setting, some of which are of a specifically mystical cast, his greatest contribution to the presentation of the Modern Mystic as a contemporary image of man is his powerful historical novel, *The Devils of Loudun*. The setting of this novel is early-seventeenth-century provincial France. The plot is the witch trial of Urbain Grandier, a talented man whose enemies are finally able to undo him through the testimony of hysterical nuns that he is a sorcerer who has caused them to be possessed by devils. The backdrop of the novel, however, is Huxley's "perennial philosophy," already expounded in a book of that title.

The first principle of Huxley's perennial philosophy is that the ground of individual being and knowing in time is identical with the ground of divine Being in eternity. The practical corollary of this principle is that the authentic way of man is to die to or transcend the self. Only thus will the essential Self be free to realize, in terms of finite consciousness, the fact of its own eternity and the fact that every particular in the world of experience shares in this eternity. Enlightenment, consequently, means to see things as they are "in themselves" and not in relation to a craving and abhorring ego. This leads Huxley to a contrast between "the world"—"man's experience as it appears to and is molded by the ego"—and the "other world"—the mystic Kingdom of God within. This contrast is represented in the book by the ambitious and worldly Urbain Grandier and the mystical and unworldly Jean-Joseph Surin, the Jesuit who is sent to help in the exorcism of Loudun's devils.

> "The world" . . . is that less abundant life, which is lived according to the dictates of the insulated self. It is nature denatured by the distorting spectacles of our appetites and revulsions. It is the finite divorced from the Eternal. It is multiplicity in isolation from its nondual Ground. It is time apprehended as one damned thing after another. It is a system of verbal categories taking the place of the fathomlessly beautiful and mysterious particulars which constitute reality. It is a notion labeled "God." It is the Universe equated with the words of our utilitarian vocabulary.[1]

The essentially Hindu cast of Huxley's earlier presentation of his perennial philosophy is modified in *The Devils of Loudun* by an attempt to recast this philosophy in Christian terms. Complete en-

---

[1] Aldous Huxley, *The Devils of Loudun* (N. Y.: Harper & Bros., 1952; Harper Torchbooks, 1959), p. 65.

lightenment, Huxley tells us, can only be attained through union with all three persons of the Christian Trinity—the Father as the transcendent ground, the Son as the human world, and the Holy Spirit as the link between them. Union only with the Father leads to the danger of quietism—falling into contemplation and refusing to take active part in life. Union with the Son alone leads to the danger of historicism—making the events of history the sole criteria of reality. Union only with the spirit leads to the danger of occultism—leaving both the ground of being and the reality of the concrete human world for the explorations of astral spheres, reincarnation, astrology, or the like.

The Devils of Loudun illustrates several important obstacles to enlightenment, which Huxley does not fail to bring to the reader's attention. The first is that moral teaching induces its opposite. Good actions are not really good, because the intention behind them is not really pure. The intention is not pure, surprisingly enough, not because the man in question is not singleminded, pure in heart, or a whole person, but (as Huxley also maintains in *The Grey Eminence*, the biography of Father Joseph, the unseen power behind the Thirty Years' War) because action is not balanced by contemplation. Contemplation here means, of course, not thinking about things, but the mystical prayer of silent regard, "unitive knowledge" of God.

The second obstacle to enlightenment arises from the fact that the ugliest passions are given free reign under the cloak of virtue because of the absolutizing of dogmas and institutions. All of the evils of religion can flourish without the belief in the supernatural, Huxley reminds the contemporary man who self-righteously wishes to blame religion for all the wars and hatred of the past. Through the absolutizing of political bosses or positivistic, scientific, or political theories, modern man is able to treat those who disagree with him as incarnate devils. For us, says Huxley, radical evil has ceased to be metaphysical and has become political or economic, incorporating itself in representatives of the hated class, race, or nation.

> Today it is everywhere self-evident that *we* are on the side of Light, *they* on the side of Darkness. And being on the side of Darkness, *they* deserve to be punished and must be liquidated (since *our* divinity justifies everything) by the most fiendish means at our disposal. By idolatrously worshiping ourselves as Ormudz, and by regarding the other fellow as Ahriman, the Principle of Evil, we of the twentieth century are doing our best to guarantee the triumph of diabolism in our time.[2]

[2] *Ibid.*, p. 175.

Urbain Grandier, with his worldliness and sensuality, represents one danger. But Surin goes to the opposite extreme and mortifies not only his craving ego in its attachment to the world, but also nature itself, thus cutting himself off from contact with the world. Surin proceeds from a dogma of nature—of the human and nonhuman as radically corrupt. To Huxley, in contrast, God must also be realized in nature and the world. "It is only through the *datum* of nature that we can hope to receive the *donum* of Grace. The Fact must be approached through facts." We need to mortify not our nature but our catalogue of likes and dislikes and our verbal patterns to which we expect reality to conform. Surin's struggle in the end was between the realist and the verbalist, the man who commutes words into hideous pseudo-realities. With greater subtlety than Bergson, Huxley suggests that words are at once indispensable and fatal, depending on whether they are treated as working hypotheses and useful frames of reference or as dogmas, idols, and absolute truths. This notion of the working hypothesis might liberate mankind from its collective insanities and compulsion to mass murder, suggests Huxley.

The total framework of *The Devils of Loudun* is that of "self-transcendence." The desire for self-transcendence is as great as the desire for self-assertion, Huxley claims. True self-transcendence is upward, toward union with the Divine Ground; this is what Surin achieved at the end of his life and, to a lesser extent, Grandier when he is tortured and then burned alive. In most cases, however, self-transcendence is either sideward or downward into animality, derangement, or dispersion in art, science, and politics. Downward self-transcendence is the most common Grace substitute. One form of it is intoxicants—alcohol, narcotics, drugs (apparently Huxley would exclude here mescalin and LSD, about which he wrote so enthusiastically during the last years of his life!). Another is elementary sexuality without love. The third, crowd delirium, is worst of all, says Huxley, because it can be indulged in with good conscience. This temporary dehumanization of individuals is used to consolidate the religious and political powers that be.

Most people choose to go sideward. Without sideward transcendence, there would be no civilization and culture, but there would also be no war, saturation bombing, and extermination of political and religious heretics. If sideward self-transcendence is not accompanied by a conscious and consistent effort to achieve upward self-transcendence into the life of the Spirit, the goods achieved will always be mingled with counterbalancing evils. "Every idol, however exalted, turns out in the long run to be a Moloch, hungry for human sacrifice," concludes Huxley in the last sentence of this book.

One of the problems which *The Devils of Loudun* raises is whether Huxley has presented us with a *concept* or an *image* of man. The torture and execution of Grandier is the real climax of the story, but it is not the culmination of its ideas. The most powerful section of the book, for which the first two hundred pages have successfully prepared us, it moves us to real indignation and raises Grandier to a hitherto impossible heroic and tragic stature, inducing in us an identification which makes these scenes profoundly sickening. The illustrations of the great spiritual heights attained by Surin, in contrast, are of far less dramatic interest. Similarly, Surin himself is more vivid to us for his mental illness and loss of contact with the world than for his spiritual attainments.

To what extent has Huxley himself conceptualized and dogmatized in a fashion similar to that for which he criticizes Surin? He quotes the Third Zen Patriarch about the importance of seeing immediate facts, but does he not see the particulars of this story through the universal framework of the perennial philosophy, proceeding from the abstract to the concrete rather than vice versa? Huxley is particularly effective in his effort to distinguish between the genuinely mystical and the occult. He recognizes the dangers of psychological aberration and of inspiration from other than divine sources. Yet he is always looking for evidence to support his thesis, assuming that this evidence can only be interpreted in one way. To begin with, he derives his perennial philosophy through abstracting from the particulars—the real differences in attitude and the real historical contexts of the various religions.

A still more important question is whether Huxley's explanations of Grandier and Surin are the only convincing ones. Cannot Grandier be equally well explained as a person who failed to achieve personal unification and give direction to his energies without assuming that he had to become a mystic and attain upward self-transcendence? Cannot Surin be explained as a person who has lost contact with the world, not only in the sense that Huxley points out of seeing dogmas instead of facts, but also in the sense of being cut off from real relationship with other people? Is not insanity itself often a form of self-isolation from the necessary, real relationship with others, thus producing the split person as the "other" in the self?

These questions suggest a criticism of Huxley's scheme of horizontal and upward self-transcendence. Is upward self-transcendence really the only cure for absolutizing the relative? Can there not be a distinction between two types of horizontal self-transcendence—that which is really open to the facts and hence treats persons as real in themselves and that which sees only what fits into its categories and hence treats persons as objects for use or according to an authoritarian scale of prestige and social position, race, class, or religion? Does not Huxley fall into the very danger he points out—that suspension of the ethical in which it is possible to sacrifice humanity to Moloch, in this case just *because* the relation to God is essential and that to man secondary? In *The Devils of Loudun* human existence is not seen and related to in itself. It is seen as the finite manifestation of an infinite Ground and is used as a means to the end of union with the infinite. If God is in the world, as Huxley stresses, then it would follow that he can be reached not by upward self-transcendence alone, but also by a different relation to the world in which each person and thing is seen as of value in itself. It is not contemplation of the Divine Ground, but the acceptance of the concrete, particular man in his otherness and uniqueness which protects us from human sacrifice to our false absolutes.

Arthur Miller, in his play *The Crucible,* has also used the witch trials (this time American) of the seventeenth century as a commentary on the polarization of good and evil in the modern political scene. No trace of mysticism enters into Miller's play, to be sure, but he does show a possibility which Huxley fails to consider: that a man may choose sideward self-transcendence as the path to authenticity in opposition both to downward *and* upward self-transcendence. John Proctor becomes embroiled in the witch trial through sexuality, by making love to a girl who later envies and wants to ruin him. He admits that part of his guilt, but he refuses to make a martyr of himself and give his life for some ideal of saintliness or holiness. Yet he finally does give his life when he realizes that what is in question is not being a saint, but being a man. "Being a man" means here to recognize his solidarity with the men and women of integrity in his community who are also being put to death and whom he would be betraying if he signed a false confession. Miller's attempts to bring out the current political significance of his play (which grew out of his own experience during the McCarthy period) are far cruder and less intellectually sophisticated than Huxley's, yet John Proctor is a much more convincing image of man than either Grandier or Surin, or even both taken together.

6

T. S. ELIOT
AND MARTIN BUBER

ALDOUS HUXLEY has responded to the absence of a contemporary image of man by advancing a "universal" mysticism that transcends confessional boundaries. T. S. Eliot, in contrast, is a *Christian* mystic, speaking out of the heart of Christian orthodoxy. Yet he, too, as we have seen, begins with the inauthenticity of modern existence, and he, too, like Huxley and Bergson, wishes to present an image of man to contemporary man. His dogmatic formulations are informed by Christian theology, but his starting point and his ultimate concern are the life experience of modern, Western man.

In *The Four Quartets*, Eliot sets himself one central task—to point to that immediacy of realization of the spirit which all of us glimpse as children and which the mystic experiences in the fullness of ecstasy, and to remind us that we are cut off from this immediacy by original sin, by the inauthenticity of our individual and collective existence. To return to it, we must go the long, painful road of discipline, prayer, observance, and ritual. This way is not only an individual one, but also a way of religious community, even religious socialism, although of a strongly hierarchical and traditionalist nature. Now there is no longer just the individual man setting his lands in order. There is the community of the saints and martyrs, who through purgation, the "dark night of the soul," recover the immediacy that we have lost. And there is the larger community of the ordinary men who by their more limited dedication and devotion provide the significant soil in which these exceptional men can take root. The dualism of Prufrock and Sweeney, contrasting inauthentic types of the waste-land world, is now replaced by a dualism within the blessed community itself.

The first quartet, "Burnt Norton," begins with two Greek aphorisms from Heraclitus—"The way up is the way down" and "Each acts as if he were a law unto himself"—implying at the outset a truth to be realized through paradox, but a truth which is common to all men. This paradoxical common truth is presented by Eliot, first of all, in the statement that time past and time future point us to time present. One cannot expect any future moment to compensate for the meaninglessness of the present moment, for each moment is *the* moment, each moment is the *now* in which real existence is centered. The past is memory, the future anticipation, as Augustine pointed out in his *Confessions*. Our real existence takes place in the present. Time does not move through space like a typewriter ribbon through the section where the keys strike; rather, we move through ever-present time like the typewriter keys which always strike the same center. Therefore, time itself points us to the rose garden, the door we never opened, those moments in childhood when we lived simply in the present and had a direct ecstatic perception that the anxious movement of time past and time future has long since obscured.

In our first world, the world of birds and children, immediacy is always possible. This is the immediacy of direct, mutual response, bringing to mind the *Duino Elegies* of Rainer Maria Rilke, in which the star is waiting for us to see it, the violin playing because we are going by. But it is also the immediacy of the hyacinth girl and the hyacinth garden, the death-in-life of love and the still deeper dying of mystical ecstasy.

> And the pool was filled with water out of sunlight,
> And the lotos rose, quietly, quietly,
> The surface glittered out of heart of light.

Thus, the ecstasy of the rose garden expresses on different levels of intensity the experience of the child, the lover, the poet, the mystic.

In the second section of "Burnt Norton," Eliot provides us with one of the finest descriptions of mystic ecstasy in literature:

> At the still point of the turning world. Neither flesh
>   nor fleshless;
> Neither from nor towards; at the still point, there
>   the dance is,
> But neither arrest nor movement. And do not call it fixity,
> Where past and future are gathered.

The still point is still and moving at the same time, like the hub of a wheel which remains perfectly centered as the wheel goes round, or like a dancer in the symmetry of the dance—at once entirely moving and yet at rest because in perfect balance of movement, or like the whole universe thought of not from the standpoint of any one place, but all moving together in the dance of the atoms and of the stars. "Except for the point, the still point, / There would be no dance, and there is only the dance." This inner point, this immediacy is the reality from which the whole whirlpool of time derives its meaning when it remains in connection with it. We are no longer limited to the option of Ecclesiastes, the futile passage of time. Instead of being part of an endless and meaningless procession, each moment of time can be linked to the center around which the wheel is moving. Or we can imagine a sphere in which each point on the surface is a moment in time. If one keeps to the surface of the sphere, one moves from moment to moment and never reaches a meaning. But by going inward to the center, one can attain a connection between time and the eternal at every moment, for each moment is as close to eternity as every other. The eternally new, present moment is our one access to an eternity which underlies time yet stands outside it.

The figure of reaching the still point by moving inward to the center of the sphere corresponds to the experience of the mystic who ventures inward to discover another self or perhaps even a level of consciousness transcending self in whatever form he has ever known it. Through purgation of the attachments and cravings that have made up his existence till now, he attains, "The inner freedom from the practical desire, / The release from action and suffering, release from the inner / And the outer compulsion" which leads him to the experience of ecstasy:

> . . . surrounded
> By a grace of sense, a white light still and moving,
> *Erhebung* without motion, concentration
> Without elimination,

a state of being not only self-evident in its own sublimity, but also casting meaning backward in time like a searchlight illuminating the dark places of personal and human history:

> . . . both a new world
> And the old made explicit, understood
> In the completion of its partial ecstasy,
> The resolution of its partial horror.

By moving from where we are to a wholly different relationship with the moment in time, we do not simply put the past away, but redeem it into the deeper meaning we have attained.

Yet we cannot apprehend this still point at all times. The conditions

and limitations of human existence itself preclude it. "Human kind
cannot bear very much reality." Past and future "woven in the weakness of the changing body" protect us "from heaven and damnation /
Which flesh cannot endure." To be conscious is not to be in time,
writes Eliot, implying that the reality of existence is found in consciousness itself. We can only get beyond time by remaining in the
present—"Time past and time future allow but a little consciousness."
But we live in past and future, and the moment in the rose garden
must be involved in past and future if our life in time is to be redeemed from meaninglessness. This can be done only in time itself:
"only through time time is conquered." The still point must be brought
back into history in order that history itself may become the dance.
This is no acosmic mysticism, therefore. History itself is meaningful
as the eternally new place in which the timeless moment is woven
into temporary existence.

The third section of "Burnt Norton" describes the modern waste
land, the place of disaffection in which there is

> Neither plenitude nor vacancy. Only a flicker
> Over the strained time-ridden faces
> Distracted from distraction by distraction
> Filled with fancies and empty of meaning
> Tumid apathy with no concentration.

"Distracted from distraction by distraction"—a perfect picture of
modern existence, from the advertisement in the subways to the TV
shows, to the crackle and cackle of conversation at a cocktail party!
"Not here the darkness, in this twittering world."

One must descend into the darkness to attain that purgation which
will "purify the soul / Emptying the sensual with deprivation /
Cleansing affection from the temporal." This purgation means a putting
off of everything the self has been attached to, all that, in fact, which
seemed to confirm its existence as a self:

> Internal darkness, deprivation
> And destitution of all property,
> Desiccation of the world of sense,
> Evacuation of the world of fancy,
> Inoperancy of the world of spirit.

The mystic moves through the dark night of the senses of St. John
of the Cross, abstaining from movement until his movement may become real, "while the world moves / In appetency, on its metalled
ways / Of time past and time future." The world thinks it is being
active, but is in fact merely conditioned, a vast mass of inertia that

helplessly rolls around. "He who sees the action that is in inaction, the inaction that is in action is wise indeed," says Krishna in the *Bhagavad Gita.*

"Burnt Norton" indicates the long ascent back to the immediacy. The other three quartets show how this ascent must be prepared for and achieved in human life and history. To the themes of time, consciousness, and lust that we found in Eliot's early poems and of the timeless moment that we found in "Burnt Norton," the last three quartets add the themes of history, humility, suffering, and love.

"East Coker," the second quartet, is another type of meditation on time—not the waste past and future in relation to the timeless moment of the present, rather the succession, movement, and rhythm of time, the succession of the generations. The succession is not only endless, but also futile. The natural rhythm of life is also the rhythm that carries man's life away without its ever having reached a purpose or meaning. There is "only a limited value in the knowledge derived from experience." The great myth of modern times, the worship of experience, carries with it the assumption that the more experience one has, the greater knowledge one has. But as we do not learn from history ("Gerontion"), so we do not learn from personal experience either.

> The knowledge imposes a pattern, and falsifies,
> For the pattern is new in every moment
> And every moment is a new and shocking
> Valuation of all we have been.

The knowledge derived from experience does not itself possess the immediacy of experience. It is rather a category or pattern of inter-relationship that we use to "explain" experience. Such generalization from past experience is often used as a form of immunity against the uniqueness of each new present moment and the meanings that moment may open up to us in retrospect about all the moments that have gone before. "Experience" is either lost in time or an abstraction from it. Neither way does it bring meaning. "The only wisdom we can hope to acquire / Is the wisdom of humility: Humility is endless." Only humility can stand back from the stream of time and yet relate to each new moment in such a way as to be open to its uniqueness. Therefore, only humility can find the depth in the moment and the depth in the relation between moment and moment—the wisdom that the knowledge by experience misses.

In the third section of "East Coker," we have again the double darkness of "Burnt Norton"—the contrast between the darkness of the waste-land world, with its emptiness of mind and spirit, and the internal darkness into which the mystic descends to find the still point. The former is the darkness of the underground train, the subway, when the train "stops too long between stations / And the conversation rises and slowly fades into silence / And you see behind every face the mental emptiness deepen / Leaving only the growing terror of nothing to think about." But there is also the consciousness which is conscious of nothing, as under ether, and this points us to that other darkness, "the darkness of God."

This darkness must be reached, as we have seen, through putting aside the distractions of the world and the attachments of the senses, which means the way of purgation—waiting without hope, love, faith, or thought since you are not ready for them. Any move you would make toward them now would be the wrong move with the wrong motivation. In the waiting itself, there is faith, hope, and love—the glimmer of the still point: "So the darkness shall be the light, and the stillness the dancing." Only in the stillness can we find a real movement which is not automatic and mechanical. Only in the darkness can we recover the laughter in the rose garden, not heard since our childhood yet never entirely removed from us: "Echoed ecstasy / Not lost, but requiring, pointing to the agony / Of death and birth." We must die to the self that leeches on time past and time future, if we are to recover the immediacy we have lost.

> To arrive where you are, to get from where you are not,
>   You must go by a way wherein there is no ecstasy.
> In order to arrive at what you do not know
>   You must go by a way which is the way of ignorance.
> In order to possess what you do not possess
>   You must go by the way of dispossession.

In the paradox of the surgeon who cuts in order to heal, of the fever which must rise before we can get better, Eliot finds an analogue of human existence itself. Our disease is the original sin which cuts us off from the "rose garden," from access to immediate reality. The way to authentic existence, therefore, must be the paradoxical one of denial, of putting off, of submitting to Christ's way of the cross, "the sharp compassion of the healer's art." The "dying nurse," the church, is concerned not to please us, but to remind us "of our and Adam's curse," and God leads and guides us (the seventeenth-century meaning of "prevent") by an "absolute paternal care / That will not leave us, but prevents us everywhere." This leads us to the central paradox of the Crucifixion itself:—"If to be warmed, then I must freeze / And quake in frigid purgatorial fires / Of which the flame is

roses and the smoke is briars." Only through the briars of the Crucifixion can we attain the mystic rose of Dante's "Paradiso."

It is not our purgation alone that makes this possible. It is the Incarnation through which the transcendent and the immanent are
paradoxically united and the Crucifixion through which we ourselves
are able to share in this unification:

> The dripping blood our only drink,
> The bloody flesh our only food:
> In spite of which we like to think
> That we are sound, substantial flesh and blood—
> Again, in spite of that, we call this Friday good.

Only through the dripping blood and bloody flesh of Communion
do we attain any real existence. Good Friday is the day of the Crucifixion. It is "good" only in a perspective that inverts our ordinary
way of looking at life. We depend for our very existence not on
what we held to be most reliable—our using what we come in contact with to add to ourselves—but on what we have most dreaded
and avoided—giving up ourselves, making ourselves the sacrificial
offering, taking up our cross and following Christ.

This is an ever new task. "What there is to conquer / By strength
and submission, has already been discovered / Once or twice, or
several times, by men whom one cannot hope / To emulate." These
men are the saints: they remind us of our task, but they are too far
beyond us to be images of man for us. Our task, "now, under conditions that seem unpropitious," is to recover what has been lost. Eliot
is fully aware of the difficulties that beset modern man, yet only in
this direction lies real existence. "For us, there is only the trying. The
rest is not our business."

"The Dry Salvages," the third quartet, also centers on the movement of time and the lack of human purpose. "Where is there an end
of it, the soundless wailing, / The silent withering of autumn
flowers . . . ?" Time means change, the perishing of life. "Behold all
flesh is as the grass," says Isaiah, "and all the goodliness of man is as
the flower thereof; the grass withereth, the flower fadeth." There is
no end to the drifting wreckage of existence, only further addition.
We have not quite got over the eighteenth-century notion of progress,
which makes us assume that as we go onward we also go upward. If we
face existence squarely, all we see is progression, not progress, the
endless addition of new moments which never reach a goal, a meaning,
or a purpose so long as we stay on the surface of the sphere of time.

To Melville, life means constant risk: man is out at sea in an open boat with harpoon lines whizzing around his head, threatening at any moment to carry him overboard to his death. To Eliot, the boat itself without the harpoon lines suffices, for death is certain in any case: "In a drifting boat with a slow leakage" man listens silently "to the undeniable / Clamour of the bell of the last annunciation." Every moment of our lives is a gradual submergence into death. Yet neither in our own lives, which have a beginning and end, nor in the beginningless, endless movement of time itself can we find a meaning:

> We cannot think of a time that is oceanless
> Or of an ocean not littered with wastage
> Or of a future that is not liable
> Like the past, to have no destination.

This is the thought man cannot face. To live as a person, man has to have a sense of meaning in his personal life and in history. Yet there is nowhere in time itself that that meaning can be found. We are forever setting out on "a trip that will be unpayable / For a haul that will not bear examination." There is no end to "the drifting wreckage, / The bone's prayer to Death its God." Yet there is another annunciation that stands in contrast to the undeniable annunciation of death—"the hardly, barely prayable / Prayer of the one Annunciation." The Incarnation of God in Christ, the intersection of the timeless with time, is the one possibility of our finding a meaning in the endless succession of time.

Superficial notions of evolution have become to the popular mind a means of disowning the past, says Eliot. Evolution does not explain the reality of events themselves, nor does it prove that the latest in a series of happenings is necessarily the most meaningful. The past remains present and, in one sense, unredeemable, for it is carried along by the present moment as a part of its meaning. "Time the destroyer is time the preserver, / Like the river with its cargo of dead Negroes, cows and chicken coops, / The bitter apple and the bite in the apple." Lynchings, original sin, natural catastrophes, these are carried along in the flood of time and become part of the reality with which we work, whether we know it or not.

We do not stand on the shore of time watching the past recede and the future approach, but we are ourselves borne along by the ocean of time and ourselves change with it. Lamartine complains in "Le Lac" because, "toujours poussés vers les nouveaux rivages," we cannot cast anchor even for one day. But Eliot points out that we are not even the same people who saw the harbor receding or who will dis-

embark at some foreign port. Realizing this, we can consider past
and future with equal mind. We can understand now, says Eliot, that
emphasis on the reality of the present that leads the *Bhagavad Gita*
to say that one's future incarnation is determined by "whatever sphere
of being the mind of a man may be intent [on] at the time of death."
The time of death is every moment, interprets Eliot, and our spiritual
state of being at this moment is the one "action" "which shall fructify
in the lives of others: And do not think of the fruit of action." The
Gita's central emphasis upon *karma yoga*, selfless action without
attachment to the fruit of action, merges here with Eliot's Dantesque
prayer in *Ash Wednesday*: "Teach us to care and not to care / Teach
us to sit still / Even among these rocks / Our peace in His will."

In the final section of "The Dry Salvages," Eliot contrasts the
occultist, whose fear of man's fate leads him to "search past and
future and cling to that dimension," with the true mystic, whose self-
denial includes putting aside all attempts to map out the astral spheres:

> To communicate with Mars, converse with spirits, . . .
> Describe the horoscope, haruspicate or scry,
> Observe disease in signatures, evoke
> Biography from the wrinkles of the palm
> And tragedy from fingers; release omens
> By sortilege, or tea leaves, . . . or dissect
> The recurrent image into pre-conscious terrors—
> To explore the womb, or tomb, or dreams

—all these will always concern men since our human condition is one
of uncertainty, perplexity, and danger.

> But to apprehend
> The point of intersection of the timeless
> With time, is an occupation for the saint—
> No occupation either, but something given
> And taken, in a lifetime's death in love,
> Ardour and selflessness and self-surrender.

Only the saint is able to find authentic existence; he alone is able
to find the point at which the timeless intersects the line of time
that otherwise moves meaninglessly around the surface of the sphere.
Most of us are not saints and cannot dedicate and devote our lives
as they do. "For most of us, there is only the unattended / Moment
. . . in and out of time, . . . music heard so deeply / That it is not
heard at all, but you are the music / While the music lasts." Most
of us have only hints and guesses of the timeless, "and the rest" is
the long, painful road of "prayer, observance, discipline, thought and

action." There is no simple way to surrender oneself to mystic immediacy. On the contrary, we must live and move in time, in history, in the complexities of our personal existence, and attain what can be attained in this dimension.

That we can attain anything at all is due to the Incarnation, "the hint half guessed, the gift half understood," for here, where God becomes man, transcendence unites with immanence, infinite with finite, eternity with suffering man; "the impossible union of spheres of existence" otherwise sundered "is actual." Here is the only possible conquering and reconciling of past and future. Otherwise, time has no real source of movement and is "driven by daemonic, chthonic powers," the undesirable movement of desire, the metalled appetency. For true movement, we must descend to the still point of the turning world, yet this point is cut off from us, or we from it. Unlike Bergson or Aldous Huxley, Eliot does not believe that the divine is fully accessible in the immanent. "Quick now—here now—always" is true of the moment of ecstasy in the rose garden only because the Incarnation and the Crucifixion have given us contact with transcendent grace that otherwise would be denied us.

Even the saint and the martyr find the intersection of the timeless and time through the grace of Christ. We come into contact with this moment of intersection largely through the saint while we provide for him in turn the community that makes his life of devotion possible:

> For most of us, this is the aim
> Never here to be realised;
> Who are only undefeated
> Because we have gone on trying;
> We, content at the last
> If our temporal reversion nourish
> (Not too far from the yew-tree)
> The life of significant soil.

The yew tree, in contrast to the moment of the rose, stands for duration in time. It grows in the churchyard, the graveyard. Although we live and die in this time without ourselves attaining what the mystic, martyr, and saint may attain, we find through them a link to real existence. Thus, here, the two dimensions come together—on the one hand, the community and social order, and, on the other, the exceptional individual who stands at the center of that community and reaches upward beyond the temporal order to the intersection of the timeless with time. Here, the dualism between the two kinds of members of the religious community is now made fully explicit. It only awaits embodiment in *Murder in the Cathedral* and *The Cocktail Party*.

The central theme of "Little Gidding," the fourth quartet, is the relation of suffering and love, the fire of purgation and the mystic rose of ecstasy and fulfillment. Eliot begins with a meditation on history. The unique meaning of each new present can never be determined by the fact that one has attempted to circumscribe it in the past by positing an aim or goal. "Either you had no purpose / Or the purpose is beyond the end you figured / And is altered in the fulfilment." One does not find the timeless moment by leaving the moment in time or by renouncing history, but only by including all past history in your own moment in time and finding there, in this time and place, the intersection of the timeless with time. It is not thought but prayer that enables us to apprehend this intersection, for prayer is the wholest expression of our being, the total consciousness that grows out of what we are and what we are becoming.

During the night-long air-raid watch for "the dark dove with the flickering tongue," which sprays its machine-gun fire and drops its load of bombs, the poet looks back with bitterness on a lifetime's effort crowned by "the cold friction of expiring sense / Without enchantment, offering no promise / But bitter tastelessness of shadow fruit / As body and soul begin to fall asunder." Rage at human folly, too, but worst of all

> the rending pain of re-enactment
> Of all that you have done, and been; the shame
> Of motives late revealed, and the awareness
> Of things ill done and done to others' harm
> Which once you took for exercise of virtue.

Now the material for purgation is not the present but the past, which must be relived, seen in a new and unbearable light in which "fools' approval stings and honour stains."

> From wrong to wrong the exasperated spirit
> Proceeds, unless restored by that refining fire
> Where you must move in measure, like a dancer.

The state to which Eliot points is neither attachment nor indifference but "caring and not caring," action without attachment to the fruits of action—the use of memory for liberation from the future as well as the past by the expanding of love beyond desire. "History may be servitude, history may be freedom." History must be brought within that broader sphere in which our own field of action becomes of little importance, but never unimportant. In this sphere, one understands that there is, after all, a redemption of time through time.

> See, now they vanish,
> The faces and places, with the self which, as it could, loved them,
> To become renewed, transfigured, in another pattern. . . .

> All shall be well and
> All manner of thing shall be well
> By the purification of the motive
> In the ground of our beseeching.

Not success, good fortune, or victory, but purification of our own relationship to history is the source which promises to give redemptive meaning to individual and communal life in time.

This purification means suffering—not just suffering voluntarily embraced, but the suffering which history itself brings to us. This is the somber revelation in which the Holy Spirit of Jesus' baptism and the murderous airplane of World War II fuse into one inescapable reality:

> The dove descending breaks the air
> With flame of incandescent terror
> Of which the tongues declare
> The one discharge from sin and error.
> The only hope, or else despair
>   Lies in the choice of pyre or pyre—
>   To be redeemed from fire by fire.

Our choice is between the fire of lust which will destroy us ("The Fire Sermon") or the "refining fire" of purgation which will lead us to death and new birth. But this latter fire is even more terrible in its cruel and compassionate reality than the former. It is love itself that devised this torment, perhaps the all too real torment of a flyer trapped in a burning plane.

> Love is the unfamiliar Name
> Behind the hands that wove
> The intolerable shirt of flame
> Which human power cannot remove.

Our choice is between fire and fire. There is no neutral ground or limbo in between, not even the decadent waste-land world of the "Lost Generation." The history of our times has brought with it its own dreadful apocalypse which "stabs us broad awake" into the

reality of life-and-death and of how far we fall short of the demand
that the new historical moment places upon us.

We do not find the meaning of our lives by going backward to the
beginning any more than we find it by going forward to some
imaginary notion of a progressively better future. In the meeting of
time with the timeless moment, the death of time is overcome, trans-
figured into a meaning extending over history and transcending it.
"The moment of the rose and the moment of the yew-tree"—the
timeless moment of the still point and the everlasting extension of
time in history—"are of equal duration." Not by fleeing into an
ahistorical timelessness, but by living in sufficient depth this moment
when the Nazi planes are flying over London can we redeem the
past and future and recover the timeless moment of the wild straw-
berry and the winter lightning:

> A people without history
> Is not redeemed from time, for history is a pattern
> Of timeless moments. So, while the light fails
> On a winter's afternoon, in a secluded chapel
> History is now and England.

History becomes not a futile succession of moments and of generations,
but an organic tradition, a succession in which the timeless moments
apprehended in the lives of the saints and martyrs are inwoven, a
movement of individuals and communities drawn by that unmoving
love which is itself the source of all movement: "With the drawing
of this Love and the voice of this Calling."

At the end we find ourselves where we started from, but we know
it for the first time—not with the simple immediacy of the child, but
with that immediacy of fulfillment that includes and redeems the
moments that have led up to it, completing the partial ecstasy and
resolving the partial horror. It is all there, in each of the elements,
"the hidden waterfall" and "the children in the apple tree"—"not
known, because not looked for," but still waiting, calling to us,

> half-heard, in the stillness
> Between two waves of the sea.
> Quick now, here, now, always—
> A condition of complete simplicity
> (Costing not less than everything)

It is simple but total, no less than loving God with the whole of one's
existence. This means, to Eliot, dying to the self as we have known it
and walking in the long, painful path of personal life and history.
Through this way, all those ordeals and illuminations—the suffering,

love, and humility, the purgation of self and the mystic ecstasy, the terrible trial of history and the laughter of children in the foliage— in the end become one:

> And all shall be well and
> All manner of thing shall be well
> When the tongues of flame are in-folded
> Into the crowned knot of fire
> And the fire and the rose are one.

The fire of purgation and the thousand-petalled rose of Dante's "Paradiso" unite here into the high vision not only of the individual mystic way, but also of "the love which moves the sun and the other stars," the union of personal fulfillment with the total order of the universe. When the tongues of flame are in-folded into the rose, then suffering and love become really identical—two aspects of one reality—and we no longer have to ask whether existence or history has a meaning, for that meaning is an inseparable aspect of existence itself.

No one can demand of a writer that he construct a model which will apply alike to all men. Yet Eliot, on principle, always seems to have excluded a large part of mankind from the possibility of authentic existence. The Sweeney of the early poems is not really human; he is more of an animal in the form of man. In *The Four Quartets*, "Shall I now at least set my lands in order?" no longer refers just to the individual, but to the organic, traditional community building the historical pattern of timeless moments. Yet this community is set in conscious contrast to the nonorganic, nontraditional waste-land world, which Eliot never allows us to forget. When Eliot wrote in "After Strange Gods" (1934) that Virginia should not allow "too many free-thinking Jews," it was not anti-Semitism which he was expressing, but the feeling that he later developed in *Notes Toward a Definition of Culture* (1951) that organic continuity must be put ahead of individual freedom. One wonders whether Eliot's religious community would be broad enough to have a place for Franz Kafka!

The second form of Eliot's dualism, as we have seen, is his clear division between the saint, the martyrs, and the mystics, on the one hand, and "the rest of us" who must be content if our temporal reversion nourishes "the life of significant soil." Eliot has no image of man for man as such, but only for classes of men, one of which receives its meaning only in secondary fashion from the other. Not that the image of man must offer a self-sufficient wholeness to every man; yet the question of modern man is precisely whether he can find a meaningful direction to his own unique life and not whether he can *deduce* a meaning from his position in an organic community and his relation to the central figures of that community.

A third and very different type of dualism derives from the fact that reality, for Eliot, is *not* accessible in the "lived concrete." To find a real or authentic existence, according to Eliot, we must put off the senses, deny the self, overcome our attachments and all that has made us the self that we are. Creation is now, as it were, divided into two parts. Creation in its simple givenness becomes a trap if we give way to it, for our original sin prevents us from finding that other immediacy of the still point. Creation here is not so much to be hallowed as to be put aside in favor of the inner spiritual realization, the mystic consciousness. "Art is not to express personality but to overcome it," Eliot wrote in criticism of the romantics in "Tradition and the Individual Talent." "But only those who have personality will know what I mean." This statement reflects more than snobbishness: it reflects the desire to put off personality, to plow under the person in his wholeness and uniqueness in favor of the essential consciousness through the development of which life can find a meaning.

In *The Cocktail Party,* Sir Henry Harcourt-Reilly offers two ways to the troubled people who come to him. One is the way taken by Celia, who comes to Sir Henry burdened not by the guilt she should feel for an adulterous affair with Edward, but by her failure to respond to some call that she felt to be hers. Celia chooses the way of the saint and the martyr. She goes as a missionary to an island where the natives crucify her, where she is eaten alive by ants. Edward and Lavinia have only the choice between the inauthentic existence they have been leading and an authentic existence, whose form is so similar to their former one that both may be symbolized by "the cocktail party." In the inauthentic world, people simply make use of each other. Lavinia is convinced that she is unlovable; Edward, her husband, believes himself incapable of love. As a result, they turn from each other to love affairs that leave each more lonely than before. The way that Reilly opens to them he describes to Celia as a reconciliation with the human condition:

> Learn to avoid excessive expectation,
> Become tolerant of themselves and others,
> Giving and taking, in the usual actions . . .
> Two people who know they do not understand each other,
> Breeding children whom they do not understand
> And who will never understand them.

When Celia asks Reilly which way is better, he replies that neither is better; it is only necessary to make a choice between them. Yet it is clear from *The Cocktail Party* itself, even if it were not already abundantly clear from *The Four Quartets*, that for those who can do so, Celia's way, the way of the saint who apprehends the intersection of the timeless with time, is by far the better. The other is a good life, only because it is an alternative to the unrelievedly bad life that otherwise opens before the average man. "In a world of lunacy, / Violence, stupidity, greed . . . it is a good life," says Reilly. It is "making the best of a bad bargain," as Reilly also says, a compromise arrangement that leaves the waste land unredeemed, relationships between man and man only a little less meaningless and mutually isolating than before.

Murder in the Cathedral is at once poem, play, and modern Mass, all three working together to create that sense of historical tradition and organic religious community that shows forth history as a pattern of timeless moments. The dualism of saint and ordinary man is even clearer in *Murder in the Cathedral* than in *The Cocktail Party*, through the contrast between the martyr and future saint Thomas à Becket, and the Greek-type chorus of the women of Canterbury in twelfth-century England. In the first act of the play, Thomas appears the tragic hero, tempted to "the greatest treason: To do the right deed for the wrong reason." "Seek the way of martyrdom," the Fourth Tempter says to Thomas, "make yourself the lowest / On earth, to be high in heaven." And Thomas acknowledges his own "sinful pride," his "soul's sickness." By the end of Part One, however, Thomas, and apparently Eliot, too, believe that he has overcome this temptation and that it will not come again. Yet both the Sermon in the Interlude and Part II leave us with real doubt as to whether this is so, precisely because he is so sure he has overcome it and because his view of his own action attains an objectivity which invites self-deception in its very selflessness.

Thomas' opening speech (which the Fourth Tempter later recites back to him) already sets the whole of the dramatic action within the framework of an objective, divine design, bringing to mind Reilly's statement that Celia's crucifixion is "part of the design":

> They know and do not know, that acting is suffering
> And suffering is action. Neither does the actor suffer
> Nor the patient act. But both are fixed
> In an eternal action, an eternal patience
> To which all must consent that it may be willed

And which all must suffer that they may will it,
That the pattern may subsist, for the pattern is the action
And the suffering, that the wheel may turn and still
Be forever still.

This passage, recalling to us "the still point of the turning world," shows in the present context the exact link between the timeless moment and the community, namely the suffering and action of the martyr and the saint. It shows it, moreover, in the framework of an extra dimension that was not present, or at least not explicit, in *The Four Quartets*, namely an objective heavenly hierarchy in which each of the saints and martyrs has a destined place to which he is called.

Thomas' sense of his destined place in this hierarchy is expressed with utmost clarity in his Christmas Sermon in the Interlude between Part I and Part II. A Christian martyr is no accident, he says, and still less is it "the effect of a man's will to become a Saint."

> A martyr, a saint, is always made by the design of God, for His love to men, to warn them and to lead them, to bring them back to His ways. A martyrdom is never the design of man; for the true martyr is he who has become the instrument of God, who has lost his will in the will of God, not lost it but found it, for he has found freedom in submission to God. The martyr no longer desires anything for himself, not even the glory of martyrdom. . . . So in Heaven the Saints are most high, having made themselves most low.

Thomas here repeats the invitation of the Fourth Tempter to "make yourself the lowest / On earth, to be high in heaven."

The most troublesome part of this passage, dramatically speaking, is Thomas' statement that the martyr does not even desire the glory of martyrdom. This statement is unconvincing in Thomas' case because the sermon is centered around Thomas' own expectation of becoming a martyr; "I do not think I shall ever preach to you again; . . . it is possible that in a short time you may have yet another martyr." Nor does Eliot find any dramatic way of confirming Thomas' judgment of his own motivation in the remainder of the play.

Thomas insists, against the protests of the priests, that the knights who have come to kill him be admitted to the cathedral. In so doing, he puts his action once again within a heavenly framework and one, moreover, that neither priests nor knights nor any common man can understand:

It is not in time that my death shall be known;
It is out of time that my decision is taken
If you call that decision
To which my whole being gives entire consent.

I give my life
To the Law of God above the Law of Man.
Those who do not the same
How should they know what I do?
How should you know what I do? . . . .
We are not here . . . to fight with beasts as men. We have fought the
　beast
And have conquered. We have only to conquer
Now by suffering.

Thomas' pride and his sense of superiority to all the other actors in
this drama is as clear in these final speeches as it was at the beginning.

The chorus of the women of Canterbury leaves no doubt that
Thomas' view of his own death is also that of Eliot and that which
Eliot wishes the reader to accept, too.

> We thank Thee for Thy mercies of blood, for Thy redemption
> 　by blood. For the blood of Thy martyrs and saints
> Shall enrich the earth, shall create the holy places.
> For wherever a saint has dwelt, wherever a martyr has
> 　given his blood for the blood of Christ,
> There is holy ground, and the sanctity shall not depart
> 　from it . . .
> From such ground springs that which forever renews the earth
> Though it is forever denied. Therefore, O God, we thank Thee
> Who has given such blessing to Canterbury.

At the end, therefore, the chorus bursts the bounds of Greek tragedy,
and Thomas the role of tragic hero with a tragic flaw, in favor of the
glorification by the common people of the saint and martyr.

The appeal of Eliot's poetry has always been to the subjective experience of modern man; he has been at his best in finding the "objective correlatives" to communicate such experience. In *Murder in the
Cathedral*, however, he imposes on his audience an objective, universal,
and sacred design which they must accept, as the women of Canterbury accept the death of Thomas, and he makes of his central figure
the main spokesman for that design. In so doing, he forces us to ask
how a man whose motivation has just been in question from a modern,
psychological point of view is suddenly to be taken at face value
when, without any evidence that he has changed either in his actions
or his attitudes, he tells us that the problem that only now racked
him is no more.

We are forced to question still more deeply by Thomas' explanation
of why this problem is no more, namely, his claim that he now has no
will of his own, that he has become entirely an instrument of God to

carry out His objective design. Even if we accepted his statement that he has overcome the ambition to be a martyr, we might still accuse him of a still greater sin of pride: that of the man who identifies himself with objective reality. Such a man thinks that he is acting in complete humility precisely at the point where he has projected his own point of view onto the universe at large. Eliot's Thomas never really listens to others; he knows in advance the whole meaning of the drama that is to be played, he knows himself to be the center and focus of meaning of this drama, and he feels himself superior to all the other actors, since none of them knows or understands as he does. When man reaches the place where he thinks, like Thomas, that he no longer has a will of his own, then he is denying the self-evident ground on which he stands—the inescapable reality of his own particular existence and his own point of view. The pseudo-objectivity of Eliot's Thomas stands in marked contrast to the great religious figures of the world's history—Job contending with God, St. Francis receiving the stigmata in passionate love for Christ, the Buddha stubbornly persevering until he attains his own enlightenment in his own way, and Jesus himself in the Garden of Gethsemane praying, "Father if it be Thy will, may this cup be taken from me. Nevertheless, not my will but Thine be done." There is no question in each of these cases that there is a real self, a genuine existential subject over against the divine. What is more, each of these relationships is unique. Jesus in the Garden is not thinking of some category he will fit into through his death, but of his concrete situation and his direct relation to God.

The imposition of a divine scheme on men in the name of objective truth easily, and almost invariably, leads to an imposition of a social hierarchy in the name of that same truth. This is what happens in *Murder in the Cathedral*, as in the rest of Eliot's mature works. The Chorus of the women of Canterbury are "ignorant women" who know what they must expect and not expect, waste-land creatures, "living and partly living." They are the contact with the physical and irrational world, as Thomas is with the spiritual and rational one. In them, as in Sweeney, man goes over into the animal, "I have seen rings of light coiling downwards," says the Chorus, "Leading to the horror of the ape." These women pray to Thomas out of their shame.

> now is too late
> For action, too soon for contrition.
> Nothing is possible but the shamed swoon
> Of those consenting to the last humiliation.

The martyrdom of Thomas calls forth a Te Deum of glory from these women, but it is far from narrowing the abyss between blessed Thomas and themselves. Their final chorus, the last lines of the play itself, is an acknowledgment by them of their essential, almost natural inferiority to the saints and martyrs through whom they find salvation:

Forgive us, O Lord, we acknowledge ourselves as type of the
common man,
Of the men and women who shut the door and sit by the fire;
Who fear the blessing of God, the loneliness of the night of
God, the surrender required, the deprivation inflicted;
Who fear the injustice of men less than the justice of God;
Who fear the hand at the window, the fire in the thatch,
the fist in the tavern, the push into the canal,
Less than we fear the love of God.
We acknowledge our trespass, our weakness, our fault; we
acknowledge
That the sin of the world is upon our heads; that the blood
of the martyrs and the agony of the saints
Is upon our heads. . . .
Blessed Thomas, pray for us.

That mysticism does not necessarily imply these kinds of dualism can be seen by contrasting T. S. Eliot's mystical image of man with Martin Buber's. In a lifetime of work, Martin Buber re-created the legends and teachings of Hasidism—the popular communal mysticism of East European Jewry during the eighteenth and nineteenth centuries. He advanced this unique strain of Jewish mysticism as an image of man and a live option for contemporary man. Buber's interpretation of Hasidism speaks in compelling accents of a wholehearted service to God that does not entail turning away from one's fellowmen and from the world. What is asked is not the denial of self and the extirpation of the passions, but the fulfillment of self and the direction of passion in a communal mysticism of humility, love, prayer, and joy. In the *zaddik*, or leader of the Hasidic community, Buber found a new image of man—he who is the humble man, the loving man, and the helper:

Mixing with all and untouched by all, devoted to the multitude and collected in his uniqueness, fulfilling on the rocky summits of solitude the bond with the infinite and in the valley of life the bond with the earthly, . . . he knows that all is in God and greets His messengers as trusted friends.[1]

[1] Martin Buber, *The Legend of the Baal-Shem,* translated by Maurice Friedman (N. Y.: Harper & Bros., 1956), "The Life of the Hasidim," p. 50. "The Life of the Hasidim" is reprinted in Buber's *Hasidism and Modern Man.*

One could perhaps say of Buber what he himself says of the founder of Hasidism, namely, that he espouses

> a realistic and active mysticism, i.e., a mysticism for which the world is not an illusion from which man must turn away in order to reach true being, but the reality between God and him in which reciprocity manifests itself, the subject of his answering service of creation, destined to be redeemed through the meeting of divine and human need; a mysticism, hence, without the intermixture of principles and without the weakening of the lived multiplicity of all for the sake of a unity of all that is to be experienced.[2]

But one would then have to add, with Buber himself, that "a 'mysticism' that may be called such because it preserves the immediacy of the relation, guards the concreteness of the absolute and demands the involvement of the whole being" may be called "religion" for just the same reason. "Its true English name is, perhaps: presentness."

According to his own testimony, Buber has brought Hasidism into the Western world against its will and because of the need of the hour. This need he sees in the form of the crisis of Western man recognized a century ago by Kierkegaard "as an unprecedented shaking of the foundations of man as man." What particularly marks this crisis is the dualism which separates ideas, ideals, and culture from ordinary life. The spirit is hedged off so that one's ideas and ideals may make no claim on personal existence. "No false piety has ever attained this concentrated degree of inauthenticity." Hasidism points the way to the overcoming of this dualism through the hallowing of the everyday:

> The wretchedness of our world is grounded in its resistance to the entrance of the holy into lived life. The spirit was not spun in the brain; it has been from all eternity, and life can receive it into human reality. A life that does not seek to realize what the living person, in the ground of his self-awareness, understands or glimpses as the right is not merely unworthy of the spirit; it is also unworthy of life.[3]

To open life to the spirit does not mean to trade in the material for the spiritual or to attain spiritual perfection. It means to bring one's life to wholeness in the sight of God, to become holy in the measure and manner of one's personal ability:

---

2 Martin Buber, *Hasidism and Modern Man*, edited and translated, with an editor's introduction, by Maurice Friedman (N. Y.: Harper Torchbooks, 1966), p. 180f. This book has been reprinted as a paperback, together with Martin Buber, *The Origin and Meaning of Hasidism*, edited and translated, with an introduction, by Maurice Friedman (N. Y.: Harper Torchbooks, 1966).

3 *Ibid.*, p. 40.

Man cannot approach the divine by reaching beyond the human; he can approach Him through becoming human. To become human is what he, this individual man, has been created for. This, so it seems to me, is the eternal core of Hasidic life and of Hasidic teaching.[4]

It is in his chronicle-novel *For the Sake of Heaven* that Buber has made his most profound and concrete contribution to the Modern Mystic as a contemporary image of man. Although it is set in the time of the Napoleonic wars and centers in the internal struggles of obscure Hasidic communities, it was only during World War II that Buber, according to his own testimony, was finally able to write it. What made the novel "write itself" and what is reflected in the novel was that war's "atmosphere of a tellurian crisis, the frightful waging of power, and the signs here and there of a false Messianic."

The Seer of Lublin wishes to hasten the coming of redemption through magical, mystical intentions and prayers which will strengthen Napoleon, whom he identifies with the apocryphal Gog of the land of Magog, and thus force God to send the Messiah. His disciple, the holy Yehudi, in contrast, stays clear of magic and teaches that redemption can come only through our turning back to God. It is in him that Buber achieves an image of a mystic of great goodness *and* great strength—a rare accomplishment in literature. The Yehudi is a man of great sincerity, unusual in his combination of deep study and fervent ecstatic prayer. He is marked by an intense concern for the truth as something to live and fight for. The Yehudi tells the Rabbi that he does not believe in miraculous happenings which contradict the course of nature: the miracle is "our receptivity to the eternal revelation." Similarly, the coming of redemption depends not on our power or on the practice of magic incantation over mysterious forces, but on our repentance and our return to God.

At the Seer's suggestion, the Yehudi leaves him and founds a congregation of his own. He remains a loyal disciple of the Seer, however, despite the latter's growing hatred and distrust of him. Through his emphasis on the divine power of the *zaddik* and through the awe of his disciples, the Seer holds the place of an oriental potentate in his congregation. The Yehudi, in contrast, preserves an informal and democratic relation with his disciples. The Seer uses his disciples for magic purposes, the Yehudi helps his disciples find the path they seek to pursue of and for themselves. He teaches his disciples that man's turning is not for the sake of individual redemption alone; it is also for the sake of the Shekinah, God's indwelling glory which is in exile. Redemption takes place not in isolation, moreover, but in a communal life of justice, love, and consecration.

[4] *Ibid.*, p. 43.

Of the legends that surround the Yehudi's death, Buber has chosen the one in which the Seer asks the Yehudi to die so that the Seer might find out from the upper world what next step to take in the great Messianic enterprise. The Yehudi obeys, though he knows that all the conflicts of Gog and Magog arise out of the evil forces that have not been overcome in our hearts. The method of the Yehudi's death is itself mystical. He falls into a great ecstasy of prayer, such as he has experienced from his youth on, not without danger of death. This time he does not return. The moments before his death are given up entirely to the thought of the Shekinah, for whom he has suffered and endeavored during his life. Repeating the words of Deutero-Isaiah about the suffering servant, the lamb who is led to slaughter, he dies with the phrase, "The only one to declare Thy oneness," on his lips.[5] Of all the holy men who work "for the sake of heaven" in this novel, only the Yehudi has refused to work for redemption with external means or to accept a division of the world between God and the devil or a redemption that is anything less than the redemption of all evil. His struggle with the Seer is a part of this affirmation of the oneness of God. It prevents us from seeing the conflict of the story as one between good and evil. Rather it is tragedy in that special sense in which Buber defines it, as the "cruel antitheticalness" of existence itself, the fact that each is as he is and that there are not sufficient resources in the relationship to bring the opposition into genuine dialogue and to prevent it from crystalizing into oppositeness.

The Yehudi is a charismatic figure, like Thomas à Becket; he, too, is the center of a religious community. But he is not so through appointment, like Thomas, but because he is the man that he is. His charisma is personal and not official. In this sense Thomas stands closer to the Seer, who receives a special reverence and credence from his disciples and stands at the head of a structured, authoritarian community. The Yehudi is a mystic and is given to mystical ecstasy, as Eliot's religious figures are. But his mysticism is one that puts off neither creation nor community, neither the life of the senses nor the relation between man and man. Rather, it brings all of these into his relation with God, hallows them through his relation to them, liberates the spark of the divine in each thing through his everyday contact with it.

The Yehudi, too, is a martyr. From the Seer's point of view his martyrdom might resemble that of Thomas à Becket, since the Seer hopes that it will help in his magical-apocalyptic actions to bring the coming of the Messiah. But from the point of view of the Yehudi, his

[5] For a full-scale treatment of *For the Sake of Heaven*, see Maurice Friedman, *Martin Buber: The Life of Dialogue* (N. Y.: Harper Torchbooks, 1960), Chap. XVIII, pp. 149–58, parts of which are used here.

dying is not part of any predestined design or of any spiritual hierarchy, and he accomplishes no purpose by his death in the sense of a means that can lead to some end. He is simply an image of a man who takes suffering on himself. He stands, Buber suggests, in the succession of figures who, in every generation, become Deutero-Isaiah's "suffering servant of the Lord." But he is also and equally the image of a man who refuses to allow the tragic contradiction of existence to cut him off from faithful relationship with the teacher whom he acknowledges even while he opposes him. The Yehudi does not speak of his enemies as beast and madman, as does Eliot's Thomas. "You are not to think that those who persecute me do so out of an evil heart," he says to a disciple. "The fundamental motive of their persecution of me is to serve Heaven." He does not leave the evil of the world unredeemed; he brings the tragic contradiction into his relationship with God. Redemption in Eliot, in contrast, begins by cutting off a part of the world as in principle unredeemable—the world of Sweeney, of the waste land, of the cocktail party. This world cannot be redeemed in and of itself; it can at best be transformed through contact with a reality deep within it or far above it, but never simply present in everyday existence:

> Against the Word the unstilled world still whirled
> About the centre of the silent Word.[6]

To Eliot, reality is found in two places—in the transcendent and in the still point reached by entering the center of mystical consciousness. The meeting of these two realities, as we have seen, comes about primarily through the incarnation of God in Christ and secondarily through the death to self of the saints, martyrs, and mystics. For the Yehudi, in contrast, reality is found in the everyday itself. One reunites God with his Shekinah, his exiled immanence, only through the way in which one responds to what one meets on the road of life.

> The road of the world . . . is the road upon which we all fare onward to meet the death of the body. And the places in which we meet the *Shechinah* are those in which good and evil are blended, whether without us or within us. In the anguish of the exile which it suffers, the *Shechinah* looks at us and its glance beseeches us to set free good from evil.[7]

In a vision the Shekinah says to the Yehudi:

> One cannot love me and abandon the created being. I am in truth

[6] T. S. Eliot, *Ash Wednesday*, V.
[7] Martin Buber, *For the Sake of Heaven*, translated from the German by Ludwig Lewisohn (N. Y.: Meridian Books, 1958), p. 25.

with you. Dream not that my forehead radiates heavenly beams. The glory has remained above. My face is that of the created being.[8]

When Celia tells Reilly that her love for Edward was not a real mutuality but a dream in which each loves only what he has created in his imagination, Reilly says to her, "Compassion may be already a clue / Towards finding your own way out of the forest." One wonders whether Eliot might not have found a clue to a less dualistic image of man if he had been able to have compassion for Sweeney as he had for Prufrock.

The Modern Mystic goes back to the great mystics to find a contemporary image of man, but reinterprets them in some modern way. Mysticism itself is a modern category which tries to find common elements in religious phenomena that remain irreducibly particular. It is of value as a typology for the phenomenological study of the history of religions. But it is of little value as a method of distilling a pure mystical core out of the encrustation of church and creed. The attempts of modern interpreters of mysticism to define mysticism in terms of some doctrinal content or philosophy will always be misguided.

Still more questionable is the tendency of Bergson, Huxley, and T. S. Eliot to make a distinction between "higher" and "lower" mystical experience, that which is nearer God or the "full self-realization of God" and that which is not. This value hierarchy depends for its truth on an articulation of stages and degrees of mystic experience. Yet all of these men make a point of saying that they themselves have not reached the highest stage! Thus, we have once again the question as to whether the criterion of higher and lower is a philosophical one imposed from without. Certainly, it does not derive from the testimonies of the mystics themselves, for they are by no means in agreement as to which experiences, symbols, and philosophies are the highest, nor can we divorce their statements from the immersion in particular cultures and religious traditions that leads them to interpret their mystical experiences in terms of one symbol or philosophy rather than another.

This split between the actual mystics and the modern thinkers who present mysticism to us as a contemporary image of man leads us to the question of the extent to which the Modern Mystic looks to the "similarity" of all mysticisms as a secondary, derived meaning to take the place of the immediacy that the great mystics themselves experienced. This does not mean that he has had no mystical experience of his own, only that he has gone far beyond that experience in the direction of an intellectual synthesizing which he has mistaken for

[8] *Ibid.*, p. 229.

reality itself. He has tended to substitute the *concept* of a nonconceptual Absolute for the reality of the meeting with that Absolute! As a famous Zen saying puts it, he takes the finger pointing at the moon for the moon itself.

In putting forward mysticism as the goal and essence of human existence, the Modern Mystic is often concerned with the mystic only in terms of his individual "experience," extracting him from the context of his religion, his culture, and his own set of personal meanings and relationships. As such, mysticism is not only uprooted from the concrete particular contexts in which it flowers; it is also transformed and distorted by that modern valuation of experience for experience's sake which would have been so utterly unthinkable to any of the great mystics of the past. It is, in fact, a part of that modern *psychologizing* of reality that leads contemporary man to convert the meaning of the events which he lives through in common with others into inner psychic experiences—enriching, interesting, or even terrifying. The current fascination with mind-transforming drugs as a source of "religious experience" is an excellent example of this trend. One's personal existence in relation to what is *not* oneself—nature, other men, the world, God—is now reduced to what is *within* one. One thing that the Modern Vitalist, the Modern Mystic, and the Modern Gnostic have in common is their tendency to divide existence into the "inner" and the "outer" and to place a higher value on the "inner" as the real and essential.

The heart of vitalism lies in dynamic movement itself, the pulsation of creative energy, the upward thrust. The heart of mysticism, in contrast, lies in the immediacy of spiritual apprehension of the "ineffable within" and the "ineffable beyond," to use the language of Abraham J. Heschel. The highest vision of the former is creative energy. The highest vision of the latter is the Eternal—the ultimate spiritual reality transcending and including both time and space, the finite and the infinite, the moving and the static, life and death, coming to be and passing away.

V

THE
MODERN "SAINT"

7

COCCIOLI,
BERNANOS, AND GREENE

M
UCH that we have already considered has prepared us for the problem of the Modern "Saint." This is an important type of contemporary image of man, yet it is one in which "saint" must be left in quotation marks. It means the juxtaposition of a category derived from traditional religions of the past, and in particular from early and medieval Christianity, with a category derived from existence as a modern man. This raises the question whether it is possible to be a saint today and still bear within oneself the paradoxes and contradictions that characterize modern man. In Silone, the saint no longer implies the isolated, dualistic life of a Cristina, but the refusal to compromise with the social injustice of Don Benedetto and Pietro Spina and the new type of man who will be socially effective through sincerity, truth, nonattachment, poverty, and friendship. In Buber, the traditional meaning of "saint" is replaced by the conception of being "humanly holy"—of serving God by becoming fully a man. Even the Hasidic saints of *For the Sake of Heaven* learn that they deny the Creator when they turn away from ordinary human life as the Yehudi turned away from his first wife. The Hasidic message of being "humanly holy" is more compatible with the modern temper than the superhuman, spiritual and moral perfection of the medieval saint. The Yehudi is a powerful figure to whom it is difficult not to respond, but in what makes him most attractive—the wholeheartedness with which he wrestles with the evil urge in himself and turns to God—he lacks the problematic of modern man. We may be helped in finding our way by the Yehudi, but we cannot *be* the Yehudi.

Prince Myshkin, the hero of *The Idiot*, is a complex figure—at once

epileptic and saint; wiser than other men and far more naïve; intellectually unaware of evil and intuitively attuned to the deepest horror;
meek, forgiving, and loving, yet careless of the one he loves while
fascinated by the demonic beauty and suffering of her rival. He is
what one might expect if one set out, as Dostoyevsky clearly did, to
create a modern saint—a man of unusual moral and spiritual qualities
who, nonetheless, bears within himself the tensions and contradictions
of modern existence. Myshkin's suffering points us to the dreadful
question whether a man can find the highest meaning in a lonely suffering in which he is not only abandoned but unconfirmed. Can one
continue to exist *as a person* without the grace received from others
that enables him to be human? Some will say, following the traditional
conception of the saint, that Myshkin knew grace from God; he did
not need the grace of human confirmation. But lacking it, Myshkin was
unable to descend into the abyss of horror into which he was drawn
without succumbing to the terror himself and experiencing, as a result,
the most dreadful engulfment of his spiritual and physical self.[1]

Another, more contemporary, but hardly less problematic, attempt
to create a Modern "Saint" is Carlo Coccioli's Italian novel *Heaven and
Earth*. The very first paragraphs of the book set the question that is
repeated on almost every page: the question of understanding Don
Ardito "just as he was, in his disconcerting character as a man and
perhaps a saint, and as a bridge between heaven and earth." Many
characters witness that he is the only saint they have ever known, and
many others are quick to worship him and pray to him in the traditional Catholic manner. Others speak of him as the most real man they
have ever known. His friend, the atheist schoolmaster whom he converted, speaks of Don Ardito as "the holiest and most tortured soul I
ever met in my life" and adds that his memory will cheer him for the
rest of his days and be upon his lips when he is dying. Many do not
like him, and many even hate him, but no one is capable of ignoring
him. He is again and again spoken of as the hub around which the
whole wheel moves, and a number of the important figures in this
drama testify that they were created solely for the sake of making his
saintliness manifest.

Don Ardito is aptly characterized by his superior as a man who is
not at all lovable because he does not inspire the least pity. He is a
proud man, a man severe with himself and others, a man cold on the

---

[1] For a full-scale treatment of *The Idiot,* see Maurice Friedman, *Problematic
Rebel: An Image of Modern Man* (N. Y.: Random House, 1963), pp. 267–76,
and the still more complete version in Maurice Friedman, "Prince Myshkin—
Idiot Saint," *Cross Currents,* Vol. XIII, No. 3 (Summer, 1963), pp. 372–82.

outside and impassioned within, a man who keeps everything to himself and suffers in silence. His voice is frightening, repressed, and burning, like that of a madman. "It seemed as if his heart were on fire and he was spending most of his time trying to beat down the flames." He sees tolerance toward himself and others, and even kindness, as a way of giving in to the temptations of Satan. He cannot live the comfortable life that most priests do, for the power of killing God and sharing his body with the communicants places the priest on the side of heaven and in necessary hostility to everything earthly. When he celebrates the Mass, even the unbelievers feel that something real is happening and are revolted by the sense of blood sacrifice.

There is much about his character, especially as a younger man, that is revolting. His goal is to become a saint, and though he does not believe, as Gerald Heard once wrote, that one can achieve this goal in a fixed number of years through a prescribed method, he does think it can be attained through sheer strength of will. He gives away all his money, insists on leaving his comfortable, first parish, mortifies his body with a whip with nails on it, and, in the mountain parish of Chiarotorre, lives a completely ascetic life. Although he recognizes that his ideal of sainthood is a temptation, he is constantly preoccupied with his soul, his sainthood, his temptations, and his destiny. If he questions such self-preoccupation, it is only that he feels he is unworthy to dare to imitate Christ, to suffer from the mortification of his body, to live on earth the life of a saint when the place of sainthood is heaven. Except for rare hours teaching the children or with nature, he never knows a moment of joy, ease, or peace. His iron will rejects all peace in the world as temptation.

In Chiarotorre, there is a twenty-three-year-old boy whose mother has recently died. The boy confesses to Don Ardito his homosexuality, and Don Ardito guesses his even deeper grief concerning his mother. Don Ardito not only tries to drive Satan out of the boy's soul by direct, almost violent means, but also tells the boy he must give up caring so much for his mother. The result is that the boy becomes convinced that he has no justification for existence and commits suicide, to the everlasting grief of Don Ardito.

Don Ardito is a split man. He confesses to his superior that he wants more than anything else in the world to be loved. Yet he feels that to let himself be loved for what he is not would be a betrayal of truth. Therefore, he refuses to put up with the sins and weaknesses of his parish and is quite generally disliked. Even his "spiritual life is frigid and changeless." In prayer, he knocks in vain at a door which will not open and which leaves him dying on the outside. Even the miracle of healing that he performs at Chiarotorre is embittered by the boy's suicide, and he gives up his parish to be director of an elegant city club.

In the course of repeated crises, Don Ardito comes to understand that he has loved men in God rather than God in men. He learns that God is not only in heaven but on earth and that since we stand on this side of the bridge between earth and heaven, for us to love means to love God in men. He returns to Chiarotorre with a new understanding. Instead of attacking Satan with severity and self-torture, he now wishes to destroy him by the only way in which he can be overcome—with love. He knows that this love will arouse hatred. Men feel they are under the power of anyone who loves them and try to throw off that power with hate. The only answer is to love them in return, but that is very difficult. Yet it is just this difficult thing that Don Ardito attempts when he persuades a Nazi captain to allow him to be shot in place of four boys from his parish who are to be executed in reprisal for a partisan raid. He goes to his death stooping and miserable. "I think he must have been afraid, for . . . he seemed very small, almost puny, and beaten." Yet no doubt is left in our minds that this is the last act of a sacred drama that gives meaning not only to Don Ardito's life, but to the lives of all associated with him.

Is Don Ardito Piccardi a saint? His author certainly intends us to see him as one. If he is a saint, does he become one only during the last part of his life, when he learns that he must love God in men and not men in God, or is he one in the midst of all his aspirations to sainthood, his severity with others, and his self-mortifications and worship of Satan? There is a very strong suggestion throughout this book that being a saint is a dimension of holiness that produces a majestic awe quite divorced from moral or even human considerations. There is also a suggestion that what he learns through the terrible solitude and frightful torments of his life is also a part of his saintliness. What is more, not unlike Eliot's *Murder in the Cathedral*, his life and death have a collective meaning as part of a drama in which each scene and each character "is directed toward a certain end, wherein lies its justification." The characters are compared to a chorus, like Eliot's Women of Canterbury. They see him as at the center of the wheel, pulled around by the workings of his destiny, "fated to play out the game." Don Ardito goes even further than Thomas in saying explicitly to the boy who commits suicide and others that they "have significance only because of me" and that the responsibility for them is completely his. At the end, he turns back to the love of others and gives himself to them, but even then he

sees what is happening as a drama centering around himself. The Te
Deum that arises at his death is subtler than that of the Women of
Canterbury at the death of Thomas, but it is no less certain.

No book could better illustrate the problem of the Modern "Saint."
It is a deeply affecting book, yet one does not know to what extent
the impact of the book depends on an acceptance of a traditional
framework for the "saint" that would be impossible for the non-
Catholic and for many modern Catholics as well. The opening sentence of the book refers to Franz Werfel and by implication to his
moving book, *The Song of Bernadette*. Don Ardito's "sainthood" constantly sets him apart without making him, until the end, inspiring
or even sympathetic. He is indeed "disconcerting" and for no other
reason than that he is at once a traditional saint and a modern man,
but in such a way that one cannot put them together into one figure
and speak of him as a Modern Saint. By the same token it is very
difficult to see him as a contemporary image of man. His progression from loving men in God to loving God in men is impressive as
a growth in humility, in love, in concern for others. Yet one feels
that what is important is that *he*—this man endowed with supernatural holiness—made this progression and not that we can make
it, too! This is nowhere so clearly expressed as by the schoolmaster,
looking back on Don Ardito's life:

> His greatest sorrow was the necessity of reining in his generous im-
> pulses and the hot flowing blood in his veins. He, who by divine grace
> and his own will was a saint, was afraid to be one. . . .
>
> He was a saint.
>
> But what is a saint and what does a saint mean to us? . . . I have
> known one man whose saintliness was more real to me than the fact
> of my own existence—Don Ardito Piccardi. But who and what was
> he? . . . He moved over the earth like a giant walking across the
> frozen plains of the ice age, standing erect and tall, and holding a
> globe of fire in his outstretched hands.
>
> But look in the creases of the plains which he traverses, search un-
> der the ice-bound stones. For when these are dug up, lo, there is the
> whole of suffering humanity, prostrate and waiting. This is its only
> hope of surviving its frozen state. *The expectation of his coming.* The
> expectation that he will scatter on the earth the fire which he alone
> has preserved, that he will strew it over the hard ground like seed on
> the autumn fields, and that the fire will spring up, and the ice melt
> away, and that we ourselves may be born again through his virtue.[2]

Don Ardito Piccardi is a saint. But he is clearly no contemporary
image of man. Even more than Eliot's Thomas à Becket, he *takes*

[2] Carlo Coccioli, *Heaven and Earth*, translated from the Italian by Frances Frenaye
(N. Y.: Prentice-Hall, Inc., 1952), p. 80.

the place of the image of man. Through his sacred drama, he relieves us of the responsibility of our becoming what we are called to become in the uniqueness of the personal vocation that we find through our response to our images of man.

In *Diary of a Country Priest,* by the French novelist Georges Bernanos, we find another contemporary presentation of a Modern "Saint." The country priest is the prisoner of Gethsemane, the Garden of Christ's final agony. To his lot falls the torment and despair of wrestling with the spirit of the Lord through the long night of earthly pain and defeat. He is a young priest whose first parish is in a village made up of peasants and small townspeople. He is plagued in his work by a sensitive, poetic nature, a natural shrinking from pain, a habit of constrained silence, and an utter inability to order anyone around. He is constantly embarrassed and defeated by his clumsiness and impracticality. Although he easily wins friends, he cannot handle people without offending them. Despite his almost occult insights into people when under pressure, he is a poor judge of character and is constantly being disappointed in his expectations.

The little priest's clumsiness and impracticality have left him with little confidence in himself. Even in prayer, he is not so apt to find peace as agonized struggle, and when the spirit of prayer leaves him, he is cast into a terrible void of darkness and despair. These spiritual struggles are accompanied by constant physical suffering. He is troubled with recurrent pains in the stomach, which get worse as the book proceeds, leaving him unable to eat anything except bread soaked in wine. Finally, he goes to see a doctor and learns that he has a cancer from which he must soon die.

From a background of extreme poverty, the little priest has inherited a burning concern for the sufferings of the poor and a strong sense of justice. Although he believes that ultimately it is not social reform but Christ alone that can bring real peace to the poor, deep within him is still smoldering an indignation and rebellion connected with his childhood poverty. In the inn where his mother worked, he saw poverty invariably coupled with lust, and he is plagued throughout by a terror of lust because he was forced to witness it too early in life.

> Lust is a mysterious wound in the side of humanity; or rather at the very source of its life! To confound this lust in man with that desire which unites the sexes is like confusing a tumour with the very organ which it devours, a tumour whose very deformity horribly reproduces the shape.

. . . .

We priests are sneered at and always shall be—the accusation is such an easy one—as deeply envious, hypocritical haters of virility. Yet whosoever has experienced sin, with its parasitic growth, must know that lust is forever threatening to stifle virility as well as intelligence. Impotent to create, it can only contaminate in the germ the frail promise of humanity.[3]

Unlike Zorba, the little priest does not identify virility or vitality with sleeping with a woman whenever the opportunity offers itself. He is as concerned as Zorba with unlived life, but he recognizes lust as something that prevents a full life. He sees sin not only as a cause, but also as a product of failing to live fully. To him, living fully means an awareness "of the huge risk that salvation entails" and that it is this risk which "gives to human life all its divinity."

Many men never give out the whole of themselves, their deepest truth. They live on the surface, and yet, so rich is the soil of humanity that even this thin outer layer is able to yield a kind of meagre harvest which gives the illusion of real living. . . . How many men will never have the least idea of what is meant by supernatural heroism, without which there can be no inner life! Yet by that very same inner life shall they be judged. . . . Therefore when death has bereft them of all the artificial props with which society provides such people, they will find themselves as they really are, as they were without even knowing it— horrible undeveloped monsters, the stumps of men.[4]

Evil is the product of unlived life, but to the priest it is ultimately impersonal, vast, and mysterious—a vague, miasmal force below the depths of life.

The world of evil is . . . nothing . . . but a half-formed shape, the hideous shape of an abortion, a stunted thing on the very verge of all existence. I think of sullied translucent patches on the sea. Does the Monster care that there should be one criminal more or less? Immediately he sucks down the crime into himself, makes it one with his own horrible substance, digests without once rousing from his terrifying eternal lethargy.[5]

Essential evil is a "vast yearning for the void, for emptiness." If ever mankind perishes, it will be of boredom and stale disgust. The repeated imagery of abortion, the stunted, and the monstrous shows that evil is for the priest a positive malignant force—the spiritual equivalent of the cancer which he later discovers is eating away his

[3] Georges Bernanos, *Diary of a Country Priest*, translated by Pamela Morris (N. Y.: The Macmillan Co., 1937), pp. 123; 125-6.
[4] *Ibid.*, p. 108f.
[5] *Ibid.*, p. 144.

own substance. But there is also, closely related, a negative evil, the leprosy of boredom (the medieval *acedia*, or sloth)—the petrification of unlived life. The little priest contrasts "the fierce inquisitiveness of devils, their horrible solicitude for humanity" with "that shifty fear of the Divine, that oblique flight through life."

It is disgust and despair which the little priest must face in the hours of prayer when he faces the inner depths of his cankered self. His face is described by one of the characters of the novel as "worn by prayer"—by "a continual anxiety with regard to prayer, a fight, a struggle." His greatest crisis in the book takes the form of a long period when the spirit of prayer has left him. He is dry and empty before the void—unable either to pray or to pity.

> Never have I made such efforts to pray, at first calmly and steadily, then with a kind of savage, concentrated violence, till at last, having struggled back into calm with a huge effort, I persisted, almost desperately . . . in a sheer transport of will which set me shuddering with anguish. Yet—nothing. . . . At that moment I needed prayer as much as I needed air to draw my breath or oxygen to fill my blood. What lay behind me was no longer any normal, familiar life, that everyday life out of which the impulse to pray raises us, with still at the back of our minds the certainty that whensoever we wish we can return. A void was behind me. And in front a wall, a wall of darkness.
>
> . . . .
>
> The saints experienced these hours of failure and loss. But most certainly never this dull revolt, this spiteful silence of the spirit which almost brings to hate. . . . The same solitude, the same silence. And no hope this time of forcing away the obstacle. Besides there isn't any obstacle. Nothing. God! I breathe, I inhale the night, the night is entering into me by some inconceivable, unimaginable gap in my soul. I, myself, am the night.[6]

The spiritual desolation which the little priest experiences is similar to the "dark night" of Saint John of the Cross. Saint John speaks of the "dark night" as a period of inner desolation, emptiness, and aridity which the soul must go through in order to purify itself of its attachments to the senses—"the dark night of the senses"—or, at later stages, to the imagination and the images of the mind—"the dark night of the soul." But the little priest's inner emptiness cannot be subsumed entirely under Saint John's mystical stages. The saints knew hours of failure and loss, according to the priest, but never the dull revolt of the spirit which he is now experiencing. He is less "all of a piece" than the saints. One of his main problems lies in the inner restlessness and conflict, the hatred of self and re-

6 *Ibid.*, pp. 103; 105.

bellion against the world which he has never been able to conquer. His unlived life has turned malignant, adding to the power of the void, and his terror before lust has helped to sour his natural joy and canker his spirit.

For all his own pain, he is constantly taking upon himself the burden of those with whom he lives and works. He tries to love and make his own the pain of other men. He "communes" with the pain of the other, and he claims that it is prayer that enables him to do so. Instead of turning him from others, it unites the individual with mankind in the spirit of universal charity. "The unanimous testimony of saints is . . . that this kind of deepening of the spirit . . . , instead of showing us more and more of our own complexity," "ends in sudden total illumination." As in Pietro Spina, this illumination is turned toward men; the priest thinks of this suffering as the spirit of God suffering in mankind. "Man's fate" is still a tragic one, but the sadness in it is bound up with the exile of the Spirit:

> What we call sadness, anguish, despair, as though to persuade ourselves that these are only states of the Spirit, are the Spirit itself. I believe that ever since his fall, man's condition is such that neither around him nor within him can he perceive anything, except in the form of agony.[7]

The little priest sees himself as sharing man's fate, but as occupying a special, eternal place in it—"the prisoner of His Agony in the Garden."

Yet even though he takes upon himself the pain of others and has only good intentions toward all with whom he deals, he meets hostility on every side. He is not judged by his intentions, but by his clumsiness and the fact that his simplicity and directness make people uncomfortable and offend their sense of propriety. But the country priest does not blame others for his defeats, nor does he judge them. Indeed, his great problem is that he is too severe in judging himself. He sees his whole life as an oscillation between ignorance and despair. "I've only to set pen to paper to awaken in me the knowledge of my deep, inexplicable incompetence, superhuman clumsiness."

The priest's humility does not prevent him from exercising his inner spiritual authority, even though it stands in the way of his taking advantage of his authority of office. In conversations with the daughter and the wife of the local Count, he acts on impulse, speaks with the stern voice of a prophet, discovers in himself the power to read the deepest thoughts of the person to whom he is talking, and

[7] *Ibid.*, p. 199.

is submitted to by people who have nothing but contempt for him as a person. In both cases, he becomes aghast at his own temerity and in the deepest anguish experiences the return of the spirit of prayer and inner peace.

In trying to persuade the daughter not to run away, and the mother to prevent her, he discovers that the Countess hates her daughter, her husband, and God for the loss of her baby son. The priest tells her that we are bound to one another in good and evil, that hell is not to love any more, that she will never be reunited with her son if she does not love. With almost unbelievable spiritual violence mixed with complete humility and deep sadness, he tells her that she must face God, resign herself to Him unconditionally, give her life to Him as it is. But the Countess is hard and proud. She surrenders to the priest and not to God. Her act of submission is one of deliberate self-hatred—she flings the medallion with the hair of the infant into the fire. The priest thrusts his own arm into the fire, badly burning it, and pulls it out, too late to save the lock of hair.

> "What madness," I stammered, "how could you dare? . . . Do you take God for an executioner? God wants us to be merciful with ourselves. And besides, our sorrows are not our own. He takes them on Himself, into His heart. We have no right to seek them there, mock them, outrage them. . . . My daughter, you must be at peace," I said. And then I blessed her. . . . We exchanged no words. The peace I had invoked for her had descended also upon me; and it was so ordinary, so simple, that no outsider could ever have shaken it.[8]

The Countess dies that same night of a heart attack. The priest's first reaction is one of dumb rebellion, for he does not understand. But later, he accepts the fact that God granted him the power to give to the Countess a peace which he did not possess himself, and he ceases to torment himself over the possibility that his emotional violence hastened her death. His conversation with her was overheard, however, and as a result, the Count requests of the bishop that the priest be removed from his position.

From that time on, the priest's main concern, perforce, is his own illness. He has several fainting spells accompanied by internal hemorrhages. He finds during this period that the quality of his prayer changes from insistence to weightlessness—symbolic of a profound inner change. He realizes now that he was wrong to hide his youth, and that his doubt of himself was "the most hysterical form of pride" which robbed him "of confidence, of life, and the hope of doing better." When he learns that he is going to die, he cries and

8 Ibid., p. 173f.

is surprised to find how much he loves life. At first, he feels a deep shame of his body and a horror of his death. He is terrified by the realization that his death will be no fine martyrdom, but a mediocre, commonplace affair exactly like his life. This shame does not last, however. He soon becomes reconciled to himself and his death, and he no longer reproaches himself for his follies. On the contrary, he knows now that he was wrong to underestimate the gift of youth. That he is going to die young makes it clear to him that he was meant to be just what he is—youthful, clumsy, eager, and humble.

In his final entry in his diary, just before his death, he states the great lesson that life has taught him: *one must love oneself*.

> I am reconciled to myself, to the poor, poor shell of me. How easy it is to hate oneself! True grace is to forget. Yet if pride could die in us, the supreme grace would be to love oneself in all simplicity—as one would love any one of those who themselves have suffered and loved in Christ.[9]

That he dies too soon to receive Extreme Unction does not even disturb his new peace. "Does it matter?" he cries. "Grace is everywhere."

Bernanos' little priest is a mystic and a man of the spirit, but he is not a saint in the traditional sense of the term. His inner restlessness and his rebellion prevent him, until the end, from binding up his life into one piece to offer at the altar of God. Yet he may, in some ways, show us the lineaments of the Modern "Saint." He gives a new, existential depth to the traditional concerns of piety, prayer, evil. Justice to him is a flowering of charity rather than a formal impartiality. Lust is not a surface sin, but something which eats at the roots of our life. Sin is a product of our unlived inner life, and it is accompanied by the boredom of leprosy which spreads defeat and despair. There is no reason to doubt that the dull revolt he experiences was not experienced by the saints of old, as we know them. But for this very reason, he may offer us moderns an image of man as they do not. We share in his divisions and conflicts, in his self-hate and self-torment. How can we fail to be impressed by his honesty and his humility?

The most difficult problem in assessing the country priest is the spiritual violence which precipitated the Countess' death. Not only was it impulsive rather than calculated: he experienced it as something that happened *through* him rather than *by* him. Here, we have none of the pride of Eliot's Thomas à Becket, who proclaims himself the selfless instrument of the will of God. Rather we have an overpowering inner force that masters the priest and then the Coun-

9 *Ibid.*, p. 296.

tess. It horrifies the priest both in itself and in its effects, and only after a struggle is he able to accept it as the will of God. Nonetheless, this upsurge of spiritual power is in part a product of the priest's inner division. It would be hard to go further than the little priest in the direction of depreciating oneself. At the same time, he was a man who constantly practiced mystical prayer. Is it not likely that a concentrated spiritual power built up within him which was able, in this crisis, to compel the Countess to obey him without he himself being aware of this power? Does not his extreme humility lead him to a danger related to that of Thomas à Becket, namely, an unawareness of the extent to which his deep inner self is acting and a tendency to lay the whole responsibility for his actions on God? He could not have willed otherwise to be sure, but is not even this a product of his own inner division as much as of the workings of divine spirit within him?

If these questions have any import, it is to suggest that the country priest is a problematic modern man, that he is perhaps a Modern "Saint," but that his very sainthood is inseparable from his problematic personal existence.

Another, very different type of Modern "Saint" is the man who is not only unconcerned with his own salvation and sainthood, but deliberately takes on damnation for the sake of others. This is the theme which the English novelist, Graham Greene, elaborates in *The Power and the Glory*. Here, it is not a question of a rich priest giving up his money for the poor or of an educated priest trying to become one with the poor, but of a simple "whisky priest" who *is* one of the poor and who, as the last remaining fugitive priest in Mexico after the revolution, has nothing to sustain him but the belief that the priest carries God to the people whatever his own moral character may be.

> It doesn't matter so much my being a coward—and all the rest. I can put God into a man's mouth just the same—and I can give him God's pardon. It wouldn't make any difference to that if every priest in the Church was like me.

> He remembered the gift he had been given which nobody could take away. That was what made him worthy of damnation—the power he still had of turning the wafer into the flesh and blood of God. He was a sacrilege. Wherever he went, whatever he did, he defiled God.[10]

[10] Graham Greene, *The Power and the Glory* (N. Y.: The Viking Press, Compass Books Edition, 1958), pp. 263; 39.

At first, he had been proud to be the one priest who had not escaped. Then, he had fallen into drinking; one time, he had even given way to temptation and slept with a woman who later bore him a child. He had given way to despair—"the unforgivable sin"— but he had got over despair too. Now "he carried on, with spells of fear, weariness, with a shamefaced lightness of heart."

> Now that he no longer despaired it didn't mean, of course, that he wasn't damned—it was simply that after a time the mystery became too great, a damned man putting God into the mouths of men: an odd sort of servant, that, for the devil.[11]

> There was a time when he had approached the Canon of the Mass with actual physical dread—the first time he had consumed the body and blood of God in a state of mortal sin: but . . . it hadn't after a while seemed to matter very much, whether he was damned or not, so long as these others. . . .[12]

The whisky priest brings the same humility to the half-caste who seeks to betray him to the police and eventually does. "Christ had died for this man too: how could he pretend with his pride and lust and cowardice to be any more worthy of that death than this half-caste?" The half-caste becomes, in fact, the image of man for the priest—an image of sinful man but of man, nonetheless, created in the image of God rather than, as for Don Ardito, overpowered by Satan:

> At the center of his own faith there always stood the convincing mystery—that we were made in God's image—God was the parent, but He was also the policeman, the criminal, the priest, the maniac, and the judge. Something resembling God dangled from the gibbet or went into odd attitudes before the bullets in a prison yard or contorted itself like a camel in the attitude of sex. He would sit in the confessional and hear the complicated dirty ingenuities which God's image had thought out: and God's image shook now . . . with the yellow teeth sticking out over the lower lip; and God's image did its despairing act of rebellion with Maria in the hut among the rats.[13]

The whisky priest cannot look at a man without beginning to feel pity for him. So far from stressing the original sin that has separated man from God, he sees beauty even in what Satan carried down with him when he fell. "When you visualized a man or woman carefully, . . . it was impossible to hate. Hate was just a failure of imagination." He does not have to go from loving man in God to

[11] *Ibid.*, p. 83.
[12] *Ibid.*, p. 96.
[13] *Ibid.*, p. 136.

loving God in man. To him, "loving God isn't any different from loving a man—or a child. It's wanting to be with Him, to be near Him. . . . It's wanting to protect Him from yourself." Even when he has escaped across the border and knows that the half-caste is certainly taking him back into a trap, he cheerfully returns to Mexico in order to give a last confession to a dying gringo murderer. "There was no question at all that he was needed. A man with all that on his soul."

One of the singular aspects of this Modern "Saint" is the contrast, of which he himself is aware, between the time before the persecution of the priests, when he was innocent of any but the most venial sins and yet felt no love for any one, and now, when in his corruption he has learned to love. This is the central paradox of the book. Saintliness is not identified with moral perfection here. Man is sinful as such. It is identified rather with humility and with that genuine love and concern for others that enables one to forget even one's own salvation and damnation. Grace consorts more easily with evil than with good.

> Men like the half-caste could be saved: salvation could strike like lightning at the evil heart, but the habit of piety excluded everything but the evening prayer and the Guild meeting and the feel of humble lips on your gloved hand.[14]

In contrast to Eliot's Thomas à Becket, the whisky priest is very certain that he is not a saint or martyr. He interprets his staying when the other priests have left as pride and not the love of God. "Martyrs are not like me," he tells the lieutenant who has finally succeeded in catching him and will soon execute him. "They don't think all the time." He sees God as love but "a man like me would run a mile to get away if he felt that love around." The lieutenant suggests that he does not trust his God much. "If a man served me as well as you've served Him, well, I'd recommend him for promotion." But the whisky priest is interested neither in God's reward nor in God's mercy, only in God's justice, and that assures him that he is damned.

> "I don't know a thing about the mercy of God: I don't know how awful the human heart looks to Him. But I do know this—that if there's ever been a single man in this state damned, then I'll be damned too." He said slowly: "I wouldn't want it to be any different. I just want justice, that's all."[15]

[14] *Ibid.*, p. 228.
[15] *Ibid.*, p. 269.

Just before his execution his thoughts are on sainthood, to be sure, but on the impassable gulf between him and the saint. He might have become a saint—that was the only thing worth becoming—but as it was he was not even worthy of Hell:

> What an impossible fellow I am, he thought, and how useless. I have done nothing for anybody. I might just as well have never lived. . . . Tears poured down his face: he was not at that moment afraid of damnation—even the fear of pain was in the background. He felt only an immense disappointment because he had to go to God empty-handed, with nothing done at all. It seemed to him at that moment that it would have been quite easy to have been a saint. It would only have needed a little self-restraint and a little courage. He felt like someone who has missed happiness by seconds at an appointed place. He knew now that at the end there was only one thing that counted—to be a saint.[16]

If he pities himself at the end, it is, nonetheless, with a humility so authentic and touching that one feels impelled to see him as a Modern "Saint," even though he is not a traditional one. His sorrow for what he feels to be an empty and inauthentic existence does not mean he has turned from love and concern for others to concern for his own salvation. He has helped others all he can; he is not afraid of damnation; but he is sorry to disappoint God.

Graham Greene himself sees his "hero" as a modern and new type of saint. At the beginning of the novel, a devout mother is reading to her children a book about Juan, an exemplary martyr who died shouting, *"Viva el Cristo Rey!"* When her little boy asks whether the "whisky priest" who had taken refuge in their house overnight is like Juan, his mother says, "No, he is not—exactly—like Juan." Later, she tells her husband that she wishes they had never had him in the house. If they had caught him, he would have been one of your martyrs, replies the skeptical husband.

> "They would write a book about him and you would read it to the children."
> "That man—never."
> "Well, after all," her husband said, "he carries on. I don't believe all that they write in these books. We are all human."[17]

In the center of the book, Maria, the mother of his child, scornfully tries to persuade him to escape over the border:

> I know you're a bad priest. That time we were together—I bet that wasn't all you've done. I've heard things, I can tell you. Do you think

[16] *Ibid.*, p. 283f.
[17] *Ibid.*, p. 37.

God wants you to stay and die—a whisky priest like you? . . . What
kind of a martyr do you think you'll make? It's enough to make people
mock.[18]

This clear elimination of the whisky priest from the traditional category of martyr and saint is followed by an equally clear indication
that he is a type of Modern "Saint" by virtue of his humility and
selfless concern for the Church he serves: "That had never occurred
to him—that anybody would consider him a martyr. He said: 'It's
difficult. Very difficult. I'll think about it. I wouldn't want the Church
to be mocked. . . .'"

At the end, the ironic contrast between the traditional and the
modern saint is reversed. Now that he has been shot, the same mother
who before denied that he could ever be a martyr wants to buy a
relic and enroll him in the ranks of saints and martyrs of the Church.
It would do no harm to pray to him, she tells her children.

> "Of course, before we *know* he is a saint, there will have to be
> miracles. . . ."
> "Did he call *Viva el Cristo Rey?*" the boy asked.
> "Yes. He was one of the heroes of the faith."[19]

But to the skeptical boy he is not a traditional idealized saint. He
is an image of man. When the boy sees the lieutenant with the gun
in his holster that he had admired so much before, he spits on it.
It is not the obvious power of the State that now attracts him, but
the power of the man who suffers and dies for others.

The fact that we have had to leave the word "saint" in quotation
marks throughout means that we have not been able to come up
with an unqualifiedly positive affirmation that it is possible at once
to be a traditional saint and a man who embodies within himself
the contradictions of contemporary existence. The Modern "Saint"
takes these contradictions on himself rather than transcends them
through his personal holiness.

[18] *Ibid.*, p. 107.
[19] *Ibid.*, p. 298.

VI

THE
MODERN GNOSTIC

8

SIMONE WEIL

Aʟᴛʜᴏᴜɢʜ the saint is one of the most familiar categories and the Gnostic one of the least, the Modern Gnostic is a no less important type of contemporary image of man than the Modern "Saint."

The Gnostic was a member of an ancient sect that believed in salvation through an esoteric knowledge or revelatory vision open only to the few who knew they did not feel at home in an evil creation. Hans Jonas singles out radical dualism as the cardinal feature of Gnostic thought. This dualism expresses itself in every sphere— God and the world, spirit and matter, soul and body, light and darkness, good and evil, life and death. Its root is the belief that God is so transcendent that he has nothing to do with the world, and that it is an evil-creator god, or demiurgos, who has created and rules over the cosmos. Correspondingly, the divine aspect of man— the pneuma, or spirit—has nothing to do with the body and the soul or with the world. But man does not know that this essential aspect of himself is alien to the world, and therefore he must have knowledge of God (gnosis) before he can be transformed and thereby saved.

> To the divine realm of light, self-contained and remote, the cosmos is opposed as the realm of darkness. The world is the work of lowly powers which . . . do not know the true God and obstruct the knowledge of Him in the cosmos over which they rule. . . . The universe . . . is like a vast prison whose innermost dungeon is the earth, the scene of man's life. . . . As alien as the transcendent God is to "this world" is the pneumatic self in the midst of it. The goal of Gnostic

striving is the release of the "inner man" from the bonds of the world and his return to his native realm of light. The necessary conditions for this is that he *knows* about the transmundane God and about himself, that is, about his divine origin as well as his present situation.[1]

Gnosticism recurs in the history of the world's religions as a recognizable type with infinite variations. It has an equally deep and perennial hold on mythology and has again and again entered into the mainstream of intellectual history and even philosophy. In contemporary culture, too, it has often recurred, even if frequently in a mixed form.

Within the category of the Modern Gnostic, we must distinguish between those who directly follow the central principle of the ancient Gnostics, that is, the emphasis on the transcendent God unconnected with the world and hidden from man, and those who replace this transcendent God with an emphasis on the divinity found within the self. To the former class belong Simone Weil and, to a lesser extent, the Russian Orthodox theologian and personalist philosopher, Nicolas Berdyaev.

Simone Weil is the French Jewess who embraced a life of poverty and manual labor, yet one filled with intellectual creativity. She wore out her health in this way, and in the end literally starved to death by refusing, while in England, to eat more than the French under the Nazi occupation. She is, in a sense of the term special to her, a Modern "Saint," as Leslie Fiedler points out in his introduction to her *Waiting for God:* "Since her death, Simone Weil has come to seem more and more a special exemplar of sanctity for our time—the Outsider as Saint in an age of alienation, our kind of saint." Simone Weil saw herself in this same way:

> I do not want to be adopted into a circle, to live among people who say "we" and to be part of an "us," to find I am "at home" in any human *milieu* whatever it may be. . . . I feel that it is not permissible for me. I feel that it is necessary and ordained that I should be alone, a stranger and an exile in relation to every human circle without exception.[2]

Although devoted to Catholicism, she refused to join the Church, so long as the Church was exclusive. "The love of those things that are outside visible Christianity keeps me outside the Church."

[1] Hans Jonas, *The Gnostic Religion, The Message of the Alien God and the Beginnings of Early Christianity* (Boston: The Beacon Press, 2nd ed. rev., 1963), pp. 42; 44.
[2] Simone Weil, *Waiting for God*, translated by Emma Craufurd, with an introduction by Leslie A. Fiedler (N. Y.: G. P. Putnam Sons, a Capricorn book, 1959), p. 54.

So many things are outside it, so many things that I love and do not want to give up, so many things that God loves, otherwise they would not be in existence. All the immense stretches of past centuries, except the last twenty are among them; all the countries inhabited by colored races; all secular life in the white peoples' countries. . . .[3]

She expected to occupy this position for her whole lifetime, as indeed she did. "I should betray . . . the aspect of truth that I see, if I left the point, where I have been since my birth, at the intersection of Christianity and everything that is not Christianity." The native city to which the children of God owe their love is "the universe itself, with the totality of all the reasoning creatures it ever has contained, contains, or ever will contain." This is the hallmark of the Modern "Saint," the man who fulfills the unprecedented demand of the present:

> We are living in times that have no precedent, and in our situation universality, which could formerly be implicit, has to be fully explicit. It has to permeate our language and the whole of our way of life.
>
> Today it is not nearly enough merely to be a saint, but we must have the saintliness demanded by the present moment, a new saintliness, itself also without precedent.
>
> Maritain said this, but he only enumerated the aspects of saintliness of former days, which, for the time being at least, have become out of date. He did not feel all the miraculous newness the saintliness of today must contain in compensation. . . . The world needs saints who have genius, just as a plague-stricken town needs doctors.[4]

In contrast to the whisky priest, Simone Weil did not identify Christianity with the Church. She was not interested in being at the right hand of Christ's glory, but only in being crucified at his side. In fact, in distinct contrast to the Christian who thinks of his salvation as coming through Christ, she confessed that "every time I think of the crucifixion of Christ I commit the sin of envy." She was not only ready to accept suffering, she actively desired it. Yet her prescription to the Modern "Saint" is to seek nothing himself, but practice attention and listening in order that he may become subject to the divine compulsion.

We experience the compulsion of God's presence in strict and mathematical proportion to our attention and love. Prayer, to Simone Weil, is attention—"the orientation of all the attention of which the soul is capable toward God." Attention is the way of removing the center from oneself to the objective reality of what one en-

[3] *Ibid.*, p. 75.
[4] *Ibid.*, p. 98f.

counters. "Attention consists of suspending our thought, leaving it detached, empty, and ready to be penetrated by the object." Man is, at best, the slave ready to open the door as soon as the master knocks. "Above all our thought should be empty, waiting, not seeking anything, but ready to receive in its naked truth the object that is to penetrate it." Warmth of heart, impulsiveness, pity will not make up for a lack of this kind of attention through which alone one can receive into oneself the being that one is looking at, "just as he is, in all his truth." Weil goes so far as to demand that it "be publicly and officially recognized that religion is nothing else but a looking" —a curiously strident insistence for one who holds religion to be waiting, openness, and receptivity!

There is something paradoxical indeed in the humility that leads Weil to a complete denial of self in favor of objectivity and at the same time makes possible the most dogmatic and intolerant pronouncements on every subject. She was herself, like the saint she calls for, a genius, and she was anything but humble concerning her own intellectual accomplishments. She wished to destroy her "I" and attain the plane of truth and pure objectivity. But there is another "I" which she identified with this plane, and so far from denying it, she set it no practical limits. She found her "I" by denying it, found it, in fact, in a much more absolute way than would be possible to one who admitted that his own subjectivity entered into his relation to the truth that he possessed.

Perfection, to Weil, is the stage we have reached when the pressure of God's presence has taken possession of the whole soul. But at whatever stage, we must not, she holds, do anything more than we are irresistibly impelled to do, not even in the way of goodness. Receptivity has so completely replaced will that she declares that she would not reach out to take her own eternal salvation placed in front of her unless she had received the order to do so. Nor would she even mind. Even for the eternal salvation of all human beings, past, present, and to come, she would not act without an order; but in this case she would mind. "I am always ready to obey any order, whatever it may be. I should joyfully obey the order to go to the very center of hell and to remain there eternally."

This life of obedience ultimately means setting aside the human condition of freedom and responsibility in favor of a complete dependence on necessity and chance. "The most beautiful life possible has always seemed to me to be one where everything is determined, either by the pressure of circumstances or by [divine] impulses . . . and where there is never any room for choice." This same denial of the seriousness and responsibility of human freedom leads Simone

Weil to regard even her own probable death, which she anticipates going abroad, as concerning God and not herself. "I am really nothing in it all." "The only thing left to hope for is the grace not to be disobedient here below," she writes in her "Last Thoughts." "The rest is the affair of God alone and does not concern us."

There is such a thing as openness and receptivity which enables us to understand the truth of what meets us in ways that we otherwise could not. But an absolute obedience which removes the self from the self so that it apprehends not only from the other side but also *without its own side* is pure illusion. It simply ignores the self that stands in relation to this objective truth and that apprehends it from the ground of its existence as a self. Like Archimedes looking for a leverage point outside the earth with which to move it, Simone Weil preaches an impersonal and indiscriminate love of the universe in which the "soul loves the universe, not from within but from without; from the dwelling place of the Wisdom of God, our first-born brother. Such a love does not love beings and things in God, but from the abode of God." Weil claims, as some of the medieval mystics, to have gone back behind creation, to have abolished her own existence as a created being, and to see reality instead from above. Such identification with the standpoint of God seems at first sight the greatest humility and self-denial, but at second glance it seems the greatest self-affirmation and pride. Obedience to her "is the power of renouncing our own personality" which takes the impersonal God as the divine model. The love of our neighbor, by the same token, becomes completely anonymous and impersonal; even faith "is a secret between God and us in which we ourselves have scarcely any part." It would be impossible to carry pseudo-objectivism any further!

When Weil identifies Christian obedience with Marcus Aurelius' *amor fati* and writes, "I know from experience that the virtue of the Stoics and that of the Christians are one and the same virtue," she has left the immediacy and uncertainty of Biblical trust for the security and certainty of a universal, cosmic vision. The soul, to her, is created only to give its consent to the free passage through it of the divine, uncreated love of God. "The soul does not love like a creature with created love. . . . God alone is capable of loving God." She is ready to find the sweetness of the contact with the love of God in the very heart of affliction: "God's love for us is the very substance of this bitterness and this mutilation." Sometimes, affliction takes the form of Saint John of the Cross' "dark night." When this is so, only ceaseless waiting, with little hope of light, is possible. At a time like the present, however, the equivalent to the dark night may be the incredulity of the man who does not believe, but still loves God and cries out like a child who is hungry.

Simone Weil lived with the poor, but she did not seek actively to help them, as the Catholic Workers and the *prêtes ouvriers* have done. Nor was she really one of them. Her emphasis, even in friendship, is on the preservation of distance—to her the necessary consequence of creation itself. To be sure, she suggests that the direct contact with God could not lead to the disappearance of friendship and love of neighbor. But this is only because to her they *only become real through that contact*. "Previously they were half dreams. Previously they had no reality." In the language of *Heaven and Earth*, she loves men in God rather than God in men. This is partly a consequence of the Gnostic separation between heaven and earth which she assumes.

It is surely the Gnostic concern for saving knowledge that leads her to identify Christ with truth and even, in diametrical contrast to Dostoyevsky, to prefer truth to Christ. It is this strain, too, that leads her to see vitality as blind necessity and thus to reject Bergson's identification of the saints with *élan vital* in favor of an identification of them with supernatural truth. There is, she says, a real transcendent energy whose source is in heaven; it flows into us and performs actions through us. But Bergson's religious faith is "a 'pink pill' of a superior kind, which imparts an astonishing amount of vitality" and measures the infinity of Christ's Passion by historical, temporal, and human results. This is pragmatism, she rightly says, and pragmatism, she adds, "has encroached upon and profaned the very conception of faith."

Although herself a Jewess, Simone Weil had the typical Gnostic attitude toward the God and the religion of the Old Testament, which she identified with the Great Beast of the Apocalypse, the social structure of every collective. Her main reason for not joining the Church was that the Church is a "social structure," and "the social is irremediably the domain of the devil." The flesh only impels us to say *me*, but the devil impels us to say *us*; "or else to say like the dictators *I* with a collective signification." In the New Testament, the devil is often referred to as "the Prince of this World"—a reflection of the early Christian hostility to the world and the proto-Gnostic dualism which prompted it. Insofar as the Church "is a social structure," writes Simone Weil in *Waiting for God*, "it belongs to the Prince of this World." Weil distinguishes between a "collective language" and an "individual one," between the two of which there can be no agreement. The love of Christ is something essentially different from social enthusiasms, she explains.

The social is not only evil, it is irremediably so. If almost all of her friends have amused themselves by hurting her, this is not a human failing but only that "animal nature" in man that leads hens to rush in to peck the one that is wounded. It is a strictly mechanical necessity that leads men to hurt the person who is already made vulnerable by his suffering. "The animal nature in a man senses the mutilation of the animal nature in another and reacts accordingly." One is impelled to the remarkable conclusion that this Modern Mystic and "Saint" saw life in almost the same terms as William Golding in *Lord of the Flies*, where the animal nature of a group of stranded children becomes "the sow's head," or the devil, through those Nazi-like social enthusiasms that enable even the nicest boys on the island to join in murdering Simon, the lonely mystic who has come upon their pseudoprimitive dance. Weil cannot recognize affliction without the social factor. "There is not really affliction unless there is social degradation or the fear of it in some form or another." She seeks out such degradation, experiences it, and forms from it her world view. But her world, like that of the ancient Gnostic, is set in the sharpest possible contrast to the transcendent God. On the human, i.e., animal, level "compassion for the afflicted is an impossibility."

Still more terrible is the fact that during affliction the soul is not only submerged in a horror in which God is absent and there is nothing to love, but if in this darkness it ceases to love, "God's absence becomes final" and the soul "falls, even in this life, into something almost equivalent to hell." Thus, both the afflicters and the afflicted are at an infinite remove from God. Only the man in whom the human has been replaced by the divine can escape this dreadful necessity:

> Men have the same carnal nature as animals. . . . This phenomenon is as automatic as gravitation. Our senses attach all the scorn, all the revulsion, all the hatred that our reason attaches to crime, to affliction. Except for those whose whole soul is inhabited by Christ, everybody despises the afflicted to some extent.[5]

What is worse, the afflicted man despises himself. He turns his scorn, revulsion, and hatred inward. Affliction establishes itself in him like a parasite so that he is in complicity with it. "It is sometimes easy to deliver an unhappy man from his present distress, but it is difficult to set him free from his past affliction."

Weil's view of affliction is not merely psychology, not even animal psychology. It is part of a terrifying Modern Gnostic view of the

[5] Simone Weil, *Waiting for God, op. cit.*, p. 122.

"infinite distance separating God from the creature." In affliction this infinite distance "is entirely concentrated into one point to pierce the soul in its center" and introduce "into the soul of a finite creature the immensity of force, blind, brutal, and cold." The nail of affliction pierces "cleanly through all creation, through the thickness of the screen separating the soul from God." For, as in the ancient Gnostic worlds, God himself is separated from the divine element in the world by the harsh, cold, mechanical necessity of the cosmos. This is Weil's understanding of the crucifixion: "The infinite distance between God and God, this supreme tearing apart, this agony beyond all others, this marvel of love is the crucifixion." The crucified one, whom Weil envies, is identified by her with the accursed, and "nothing can be further from God than that which has been made accursed." In this accursedness, in this "blind mechanism," Weil sees God's Providence. "Heedless of degrees of spiritual perfection," it "continually tosses men about and throws some of them at the very foot of the Cross." The blindness and impersonality of the mechanism are the very heart of the affliction:

> Affliction is anonymous before all things; it deprives its victims of their personality and makes them into things. It is indifferent; and it is the coldness of this indifference—a metallic coldness—that freezes all those it touches right to the depths of their souls. They will never find warmth again. They will never believe any more that they are anyone.[6]

"Everything that we call evil is only this mechanism." Weil does not see any real freedom as the alternative to this necessity, as does another Modern Gnostic, Nicolas Berdyaev. If a man does not freely obey God, he nevertheless obeys as "a thing subject to mechanical necessity." If he does desire to obey God, "he is still subject to mechanical necessity, but a new necessity is added to it, a necessity constituted by laws belonging to supernatural things." That this last sentence implies some special knowledge of these supernatural laws that ordinary men do not have is a typically Gnostic touch. Weil's knowledge comprehends the realm of God as well as man, of the supernatural as well as the natural, and she clearly identifies herself with the subject who *knows* these matters. Yet as far as will goes, she sees herself and all men as utterly incapable of love. We *consent* to God's love for himself to pass through us, but as creatures of a cold, evil, mechanical creation, we ourselves cannot love.

One of the most remarkable manifestations of Simone Weil's Mod-

[6] *Ibid.*, p. 125.

ern Gnosticism is the curious combination of her concern for the criminal and her readiness to abandon him to the cold mechanism of creation, or at best offer him the cold comfort of a Christ unconnected with social justice. The inferior person treated unjustly should avoid both submission and revolt, she counsels. For him, "the supernatural virtue of justice consists in understanding that the treatment he is undergoing, though on the one hand differing from justice, on the other is in conformity with necessity and the mechanism of human nature." The victims of affliction are not human, they are things; only God present in us can lead us to think a human quality into them. Only through God can we "bring to them in their inert, anonymous condition a personal love." There is nothing human in man per se, and when God enters into him and makes him human we have to realize that "it is not we who love the afflicted in God; it is God in us who loves them." Like the ancient Gnostics, Weil's image of man is a negative one. For her, like them, man is created in the image of the harsh creator god, and the divine that enters into the soul is essentially alien both to the world and to man.

Taking this view to its extreme logical consequences, Weil arrives at an extraordinary attitude toward punishment. The justice of punishment no longer has to do with the crime, but only with the presence of God, or Christ, whom she thinks of not as the Incarnation of God, but as God himself. Although Christ spared the woman taken in adultery, says Weil, he did not abolish penal justice and allowed the stoning to continue. But in the New Testament story, Jesus says, "Let him who is without sin cast the first stone," and all the accusers of the woman caught in adultery leave one by one. "Woman, where are thy accusers?" Jesus says after the men have departed, and adds, "Neither do I accuse you. Go and sin no more." In an amazing *volte face*, Weil concludes from this story that wherever stoning is done with justice, it is Christ who throws the first stone! In place of Jesus' mercy and his humanity, Weil substitutes the Modern Gnostic's indifferentiation of this world and of human existence in favor of the alien transcendent within the soul. So long as the punishment is looked on as a sacrament, not even capital punishment can raise a moral or human question in Weil's mind:

> The stone which slays and the piece of bread which provides nourishment have exactly the same virtue if Christ is present at the start and the finish.

> The legal character of a punishment has no true significance if it does not give it some kind of religious meaning, if it does not make

of it the analogy of a sacrament; and therefore all penal offices, from that of the judge to that of the executioner and the prison guard, should in some sort share in the priestly office.

However the code may be reformed, punishment cannot be humane unless it passes through Christ. The severity of the sentence is not the most important thing. . . . It is important that the law should be recognized as having a divine character, not because of its content but because it is law. It is important that the whole organization of penal justice should be directed toward obtaining from the magistrates and their assistants the attention and respect for the accused that is due from every man to any person who may be in his power and from the accused his consent to the punishment inflicted, a consent of which the innocent Christ has given us the perfect model.

A death sentence for a slight offense, pronounced in such a way, would be less horrible than a sentence of six months in prison given as it is at the present day.[7]

It is not merely cold logic and the love of truth that can lead to such an inhuman sacramentalism as this. It is the radical, Gnostic dualism which sees the world as essentially incapable of being hallowed and demands that religion "limit itself strictly to the plane of supernatural love which alone is suitable for it." If begging and penal action without Christ are the two most frightful things on earth and "have the very color of hell," earth as a whole and human existence in its created state have this color, too, for Weil. As a result, man is completely depersonalized, his created freedom is totally denied, and between animality and the spirit no room is left for the uniquely human:

There is only one way of never receiving anything but good. It is to know, with our whole soul and not just abstractly, that men who are not animated by pure charity are merely wheels in the mechanism of the order of the world, like inert matter. After that we see that everything comes directly from God, either through the love of a man, or through the lifelessness of matter, whether it be tangible or psychic.[8]

There is no room in Weil for Abraham's and Job's contending with God. We must desire that everything that has happened should have happened "because God has permitted it, and because the obedience of the course of events to God is in itself an absolute good." Man must not "eat beauty," she says, and she herself starves to death; yet she pictures the soul as in the labyrinth of the Minotaur in which, if he does not lose courage and goes on walking, "it is

---

[7] *Ibid.*, pp. 152; 153; 155f.; italics added.
[8] *Ibid.*, p. 157.

absolutely certain that he will finally arrive at the center of the labyrinth. And there God is waiting to eat him." This is not simply
Eliot's Christ the tiger who springs in the new year and devours
us through the inversion of our ordinary values and the sacrifice of
self. It is an inverse cannibalism—the complete denial of the self
in favor of the unlimited affirmation of the Other with whom the
knowing self identifies itself!

Although Weil proclaims the necessity of everything here below,
she finds the search for good that ends in necessity "horrible." Thus,
she accepts, indeed overaccepts, the necessity of the world, but only
as the step toward fleeing the world. She may have seen her starving
to death as God's eating her, i.e., absolute obedience. It is hard for us
not to see it as suicide. What clearer denial of the created freedom
that she received can there be than her insistence on eating according
to a formula of how much others were fed rather than in terms of her
own actual needs—frail and tubercular as she was! In his introduction
to *Waiting for God,* Leslie Fiedler describes her death in exactly these
terms—not as obedience but as willfulness.

The Bible does not picture God as wanting to eat man but wanting him to live and live more abundantly. The Bible sees God as
good and creation as good, whereas Simone Weil asserts repeatedly
that "there is no true good here below." To affirm the moment of
history in which Simone Weil lived—that of the Nazi occupation
of France—was, to be sure, impossible. To take upon herself without flinching the full burden of that hour was unquestionably heroic.
But Simone Weil's genius was too corrosive, her humility too arrogant,
her life-denial too definitive, her rejection of creation too one-sided,
her "objectivity" too self-preoccupied. She did not humbly take upon
herself the contradictions of modern existence, as did Bernanos'
"country priest." Neither did she point a way forward through absurdity to where "life's hidden splendor lies forever in wait," as did
that other modern Jew and modern exile, Franz Kafka. Yet Simone
Weil *is* important for us—for her courage, her "waiting," her ruthless
honesty, her intellectual power, her suffering. In the midst of her
affliction she witnesses that whoever learns to feel the obedience of
the universe to God "recognizes things and events, everywhere and
always, as vibrations of the same divine and infinitely sweet words."

9

CARL JUNG

THE SECOND TYPE of Modern Gnostic replaces Weil's transcendent God by an emphasis on the divinity of the self. This type is not found as such in ancient Gnosticism, but two of its most important elements are. One of these is the focus on the knowledge of the divinity of the inner self. Robert Grant goes so far as to suggest that this concern for self-knowledge is the primary characteristic of Gnosticism.

> The Gnostic approach to life is thus a "passionate subjectivity" which counts the world well lost for the sake of self-discovery, . . . recognition of the divine element which constitutes the true self.[1]

Another element already present in ancient Gnosticism is the antinomianism of this latter type of Modern Gnostic. The Gnostic hostility toward the world led to two seemingly opposed forms of Gnostic morality: the ascetic and the libertine. Actually, both are consistent in that both hold the world to be either a negative obstacle to salvation or something which must be used as a mere means to the end of salvation. In practice, it was often the majority of the adherents who were ascetics (Simone Weil is typical of them), while an elite of *pneumatics*, or of "the perfect," took part in evil and deliberately inverted the old morality. The basis for this antinomianism was the belief that they were essentially holy regardless of their actions and that whatever contact they had with the world and with sin was necessarily a redeeming one. Jonas speaks of this as "the

[1] R. M. Grant, *Gnosticism and Early Christianity* (N. Y.: Columbia University Press, 1959), pp. 8–10.

nihilistic element contained in Gnostic acosmism," but it would be equally valid to say that much modern nihilism had important Gnostic roots or precedents. When Ivan Karamazov tries to draw the consequences of "the death of God," he not only decides that "all is lawful," as Sartre reechoes, but also, in typically antinomian, Gnostic fashion, that "for every individual . . . who does not believe in God or immortality, the moral law of nature must immediately be changed into the exact contrary of the former religious law and that egoism, even to crime, must become, not only lawful but even recognized as the inevitable, the most rational, even honourable outcome of his position."

"Only an immature or enslaved mind," writes Nicolas Berdyaev, would deduce from the doctrine of the importance of evil that one should choose to follow the path of wickedness "in order to enrich our consciousness and profit from a new experience." But this is exactly what the second, and perhaps the more widespread, type of Modern Gnostic does—the one who contrasts the evil of the social world with the good within. In so doing, of course, he no longer thinks of "evil" as really evil. The old moral conceptions of good and evil are relativized in favor of a new conception of good as the integration, or individuation, of the person and real evil as anything that stands in its way.

The chief representative of this type of Modern Gnostic is the Swiss psychiatrist, Carl Jung. Jung is, of course, the founder of one of the most important schools of psychoanalysis, and he cannot be properly understood outside of the context of the development of psychoanalysis in our century. Yet he was also explicitly concerned with Gnosticism from his early youth, and he consciously endeavored in his psychology to create a Modern Gnostic mythology that would recapture the psychic wisdom of the ancient Gnostics. This mythology includes a terminology essentially original to Jung: the "anima" and the "animus" as feminine and masculine parts of the soul, the "shadow" as the suppressed, irrational, and therefore negative part of the soul, the distinction between the personal unconscious and the collective unconscious, which latter contains the great psychological archetypes that Jung sees as universals, and the process of individuation as the shaping of an autonomous center in the unconscious through which the numinous contents of the collective unconscious can be integrated into a personal, if still largely unconscious, wholeness. Even this terminology, especially the anima, Jung freely admits to be Gnostic, though he claims that it is empirically supported by his experiences. But above and beyond this, in volume after volume, he richly documents his view of the individuation of the Self from Gnostic sources and from medieval alchemy, which he sees as a link between the Gnostics and modern psychology. It would be a mistake to look on Jung as metaphysician or theologian, as he himself never tires of telling us. He does not "believe" in these Gnostic myths, as did the Gnostics themselves, but accepts them as symbols of unconscious psychic processes. On the other hand, it would be equally erroneous to accept Jung's view that he is simply being empirical since, *Modern* Gnostic that he is, he turns to the unconscious with the same expectation of saving knowledge as the ancient Gnostic turned to the demiurge and the hidden God.

The naïveté of Jung's distinction between the "metaphysical" and the "empirical" is made possible by a simplicistic theory of knowledge which elevates the psyche from an indispensable corollary of knowledge to being both the creator of what is known and itself the highest reality. Man "himself is the second creator of the world, who alone has given to the world its objective existence." The understanding of "the empirical nature of the psyche" is "a matter of the highest importance and the very foundation of . . . reality" to the man of the twentieth century, writes Jung, "because he has recognized once and for all that without an observer there is no world and consequently no truth, for there would be nobody to register it." Jung complains that people criticize him as a Gnostic and ignore the facts from which he proceeds—facts which are of prime importance to him and which others are at liberty to verify. What he does not recognize is that the "facts" that he cites illustrate abundance (of square or circular mandalas, for example) but not universality, resemblance but not necessarily affinity, coincidence but not necessarily meaning. Moreover, the overwhelming mass of "facts" that he brings from ancient scripts, so far from leading to a cautious, empirical temper, avalanche into highly speculative conclusions which, if they are not precisely "metaphysical" postulates, are also anything but the "auxiliary concepts, hypotheses, and models" which he claims they are. They are, rather, the Modern Gnostic mythology which he himself explicitly aims at creating, but which he also forgets at the time when he wishes to fall back on the security of being "a doctor and scientist."[2] This syncretism of science and mythology is itself a

2 "Looked at theologically, my concept of the anima . . . is pure Gnosticism; hence I am often classed among the Gnostics. On top of that, the individuation process develops a symbolism whose nearest affinities are to be found in folklore, in Gnostic, alchemical, and suchlike "mystical" conceptions, not to mention shamanism. When material of this kind is adduced for comparison, the exposition fairly swarms with "exotic" and "far-fetched" proofs, and anyone who merely skims through a book instead of reading it can easily succumb to the illusion that he is confronted with a Gnostic system. In reality, however, individuation

typically modern response to the problem of a contemporary image of man. Jung follows the myth-mongers, of whom he is himself one of the foremost, in trying to deduce secondary meaning from the quasi-universality of enormous numbers of myths and symbols taken in and out of context.

Our concern, happily, is neither with Jung's implications for metaphysics and theology nor with the empirical verifiability of his system, but with the contemporary image of man which he, more fully than any modern psychologist, has drawn for us. It is this image of man which we characterize as Modern Gnostic—*Gnostic* in its concern for saving knowledge, in its attitude toward the unification of good and evil, in its pointing toward an elite of those who have attained individuation and got beyond the relativity of good and evil; *Modern* in the fact that none of the Gnostic symbols Jung uses have the transcendent value that they originally had, but all stand for transformations and processes within the psyche, shading as that does, for Jung, into a vast, collective, and essentially autonomous area that is reached through, but is not dependent on, the individual conscious ego. These two senses of Modern and Gnostic are put together for us by Jung himself in "The Spiritual Problem of Modern Man." He characterizes the widespread interest in all sorts of psychic phenomena in the modern world as comparable to and having a deep affinity with Gnosticism. He recognizes, quite rightly, that even Theosophy and Anthroposophy "are pure Gnosticism in a Hindu dress." But the significance of this spiritual interest Jung sees as lying exclusively within the psyche and in psychic energy. If the Christian symbol is Gnosis and the compensation of the unconscious still more so, Gnosis itself is rooted in the psyche, and it is psychic experience that is expressed in Jung's Gnostic myth. This concern with *having* psychic experience Jung labels "Gnostic."

> Modern man, in contrast to his nineteenth-century brother, turns his attention to the psyche with very great expectations; and . . . he does so without reference to any traditional creed, but rather in the Gnostic sense of religious experience. . . . The modern man abhors dogmatic postulates taken on faith and the religions based upon them. He holds

---

is an expression of that biological process . . . by which every living thing becomes what it was destined to become from the beginning. This process naturally expresses itself in man as much psychically as somatically. On the psychic side it produces those well-known quaternity symbols, for instance, whose parallels are found in mental asylums as well as in Gnosticism. . . . Hence it is by no means a case of mystical speculations, but of clinical observations and their interpretation through comparison with analogous phenomena in other fields."
C. G. Jung, *Psychology and Religion: East and West* (*Collected Works*, Vol. XI, translated by R. F. C. Hull; N. Y.: Pantheon Books, Bollingen Series XX, 1958), p. 306f.

them valid only insofar as their knowledge-content seems to accord with his own experience of the deeps of psychic life.[3]

Jung's equation of gnosis with psychic experience is typical of modern man. But in contrast to other modern advocates of "experience," Jung does not value all experiences, but only those found within, and particularly within the unconscious. Like the ancient Gnostic, he sees the outer world as evil, and even the inner world that is accessible to man becomes good only when it comes into touch with 'that hidden divinity within the soul—the unconscious. The spiritual change that has come over modern man has put such an ugly face on the world "that no one can love it any longer—we cannot even love ourselves—and in the end there is nothing in the outer world to draw us away from the reality of the life within." But this "life within" is not simply *experienced*, as Jung suggests: it is *known*, and that precisely in the Gnostic sense. Jung's equation of ancient Gnosticism with modern psychic experience makes sense, for what he is really talking about is the gnosis that he brings to this experience. This gnosis, so far from leading Jung to abandon himself to the uniqueness and concrete immediacy of any given experience, leads him to seek for the "universal meaning" in it, that is, the meaning which fits his own theories.

Our greatest help in reconverting this Modern Gnostic systematizing into Jung's image of man is his autobiography, *Memories, Dreams, Reflections*. This book, if any, gives us the proper human perspective into which to set his enormously rich and varied lifework. In it, we find Jung, from the first, an isolated, divided person with a powerful inner world of fantasies, visions, and dreams which he identifies with "Personality Number Two." If this inner division led him to bring "inner" and "outer" into some contact, it also led him to accept a lifelong conflict between them. Even more resolutely than Bergson, he tended to regard the inner as the good and the outer as either secondary and instrumental or bad. Many of Jung's statements in this book exemplify the Gnostic tendency to regard other people as merely a means to the fulfillment of one's own inner destiny:

> Other people are established inalienably in my memories only if their names were entered in the scrolls of my destiny from the beginning, so that encountering them was at the same time a kind of recollection.

[3] C. G. Jung, *Modern Man in Search of a Soul*, translated by W. S. Dell and Carl F. Baynes (N. Y.: Harcourt Brace & Co., 1934), p. 239.

From the beginning I had a sense of destiny, as though my life was assigned to me by fate and had to be fulfilled. This gave me an inner security. . . . Often I had the feeling that in all decisive matters I was no longer among men, but was alone with God.

I have offended many people, for as soon as I saw they did not understand me, that was the end of the matter so far as I was concerned. I had to move on. I had no patience with people—aside from my patients. I had to obey an inner law which was imposed on me and left me no freedom of choice. . . . For some people I was continually present and close to them *so long as they were related to my inner world.* . . . I had to learn painfully that people continued to exist even when they had nothing more to say to me. Many excited in me a feeling of living humanity, but *only when they appeared within the magic circle of psychology;* next moment, when the spotlight cast its beam elsewhere there was nothing to be seen. I was able to become intensely interested in many people; but *as soon as I had seen through them, the magic was gone.* In this way I made many enemies. A creative person has little power over his own life. He is captive and driven by his daimon.[4]

Even Jean Jacques Rousseau could not rival this confession of monological existence! Yet Jung did desire some relation to people other than that of the Modern Gnostic Psychologist looking at interesting specimens. He wanted to overcome his intolerable sense of isolation by convincing others that his Personality Number Two was not just his private aberration, but was a universal, if almost totally neglected, substratum of all men.

The consequence of my . . . involvement with things which neither I nor anyone else could understand, was an extreme loneliness. I was going about laden with thoughts of which I could speak to no one. . . . I felt the gulf between the external world and the interior world of images in its most painful form. I could not yet see that interaction of both worlds which I now understand. I saw only an irreconcilable contradiction between "inner" and "outer."

However, it was clear to me from the start that I could find contact with the outer world and with people only if I succeeded in showing . . . that the contents of psychic experience are real, and real not only as my own personal experiences, but as collective experiences which others also have. . . . I knew that if I did not succeed, I would be condemned to absolute isolation.[5]

---

[4] C. G. Jung, *Memories, Dreams, Reflections,* recorded and edited by Aniela Jaffé, translated by Richard & Clara Winston (N. Y.: Pantheon Books, 1961), pp. 5; 48; 357; italics added.
[5] *Ibid.,* p. 194f.

Jung looks upon his psychology as satisfying "the need for mythic statements" by a world view "which fits man meaningfully into the scheme of creation, and at the same time confers meaning upon it." Like other contemporary myth-mongers, he fails to recognize the difference between the dramatic immediacy of myth and the reflective mediacy of *Weltanschauung*. On the contrary, he clearly sees his own "myth" as a saving gnosis for contemporary man that would take the place of the no longer efficacious myth of Christianity. It is "the myth of the necessary incarnation of God"—"man's creative confrontation with the opposites and their synthesis in the self, the wholeness of his personality." "That is the goal," the "explanatory myth which has slowly taken shape within me in the course of the decades."

Memories, Dreams, Reflections abounds with Modern Gnostic motifs: Jung's early certainty that his first task was not to establish a relationship *with* God, but to know more *about* him; the view of God as wishing "to evoke not only man's bright and positive side but also his darkness and ungodliness"; the "cure" of a neurosis in one week through Jung's dream that his patient was meant to be a saint; sexuality as the expression of the chthonic, or earth, spirit, which Jung equates with "the 'other face of God,' the dark side of the God-image"; the confession that between 1918 and 1926 he "had seriously studied the Gnostic writers, for they too had been confronted with the primal world of the unconscious and had dealt with its contents, with images that were obviously contaminated with the world of instinct"; the testimony that it was the "comparison with alchemy, and the uninterrupted intellectual chain back to Gnosticism," which gave substance to his psychology; the emphasis on liberation not through imagelessness and emptiness, like the Hindus, but through active participation in every part of the psyche; the relativization of good and evil which converts both into "halves of a paradoxical whole"; the equation of "the wholeness of the self" brought about in the depths of the unconscious with "the divinity incarnate in man"; the equation of God with "a *complexio oppositorum*" for which "truth and delusion, good and evil, are equally possible." These motifs are capped by two, quintessentially Gnostic statements. The first deals with the radical dualism between good and evil, dark and light: "The sole purpose of human existence is to kindle a light in the darkness of mere being"—through making the unconscious conscious. In the second, Jung puts forward gnosis as the saving goal of his personal existence:

> My life has been permeated and held together by one idea and one
> goal: namely, *to penetrate into the secret of the personality*. Every-

thing can be explained from this central point, and all my works relate to this one theme.[6]

If this last statement makes Jung a Modern Gnostic, would not Freud and his offshoots in psychoanalysis be Modern Gnostics, too? The answer is emphatically yes. Here, too, we find the emphasis on a secret, saving knowledge. Here, too, we find a cult which gives the initiates power that the uninitiated cannot have.[7] Here too we have the tendency to see the world in dark terms and the emphasis on the need for liberation. But Freud, Jung suggests, saw only half of Gnosticism—the dark world given over to the wrathful creator god, or demiurge, of sexuality and not the "transcendent" spirit of the anima and the collective unconscious that Jung sees:

> Alchemy formed the bridge on the one hand into the past, to Gnosticism, and on the other into the future, to the modern psychology of the unconscious. This had been inaugurated by Freud, who had introduced along with it the classical Gnostic myths of sexuality and the wicked paternal authority. The motif of the Gnostic Yahweh and Creator-God reappeared in the Freudian myth of the primal father and the gloomy superego deriving from that father. In Freud's myth he became a daemon who created a world of disappointments, illusions and suffering. But the materialistic trend . . . had the effect of obscuring for Freud that other essential aspect of Gnosticism: the primordial image of the spirit as another, higher god who gave to mankind the . . . vessel of spiritual transformation, . . . a feminine principle which could find no place in Freud's patriarchal world.[8]

Jung's Gnostic myth is given significant, further extension in such works as *Psychology and Alchemy* and *Aion: Researches into the Phenomenology of the Self.* The concern of the psychotherapist, he tells us in the former work, is not what the patient does but how he does it, and this makes good and evil "ultimately nothing but ideal extensions and abstractions of doing," which "both belong to the chiaroscuro of life." In contrast to Weil, Jung sees Christ as not only not *condemning* the sinner, but *espousing* him. The medieval alchemists preferred "to seek through knowledge rather than to find through faith," and in this "they were in much the same position as modern man, who prefers immediate personal experience to belief in traditional ideas." If Jung here again equates knowledge with personal experience, he is still more modern in asserting that "the central ideas of Christianity are rooted in Gnostic philosophy, which, in accordance with psychological laws, simply *had* to grow up at a

---

[6] *Ibid.,* p. 206; italics added.
[7] *Cf.* Erich Fromm, *Sigmund Freud's Mission* (N. Y.: Harper & Bros., 1959).
[8] *Memories, Dreams, Reflections, op. cit.,* p. 201.

time when the classical religions had become obsolete." Jesus becomes the great prototype of the Modern Gnostic—the hero of a new "perennial philosophy":

> There have always been people who, not satisfied with the dominants of conscious life, set forth . . . to seek direct experience of the eternal roots, and, following the lure of the restless unconscious psyche, find themselves in the wilderness where, like Jesus, they come up against the son of darkness, an *antimimon pneuma*.[9]

In *Aion*, Jung asserts that the totality of the self is indistinguishable from the God image, while identifying the devil that the modern Jesus encounters with "the post-Christian spirit" of today. The end result of Christian consciousness through the centuries, writes Jung, "is a true *antimimon pneuma*, a false spirit of arrogance, hysteria, woolly-mindedness, criminal amorality, and doctrinaire fanaticism, a purveyor of shoddy spiritual goods, spurious art, philosophical stutterings and Utopian humbug, fit only to be fed wholesale to the mass man of today." What splits the world into irreconcilable halves today is modern man's lack of personal wholeness, and this Jung sees as remediable only through taking Christ as a symbol of the self. At the same time, Jung substitutes for Christ's teaching of *perfection* the archetypal teaching of *completeness*, which he identifies with Paul's confession, "I find then a law, that, when I would do good, evil is present with me." What Paul lamented, Jung affirms—namely, the experiencing of evil within oneself:

> Only the "complete" person knows how unbearable man is to himself. So far as I can see, no relevant objection could be raised from the Christian point of view against anyone accepting the task of individuation imposed on us by nature, and the recognition of our wholeness or completeness, as a binding personal commitment.[10]

Gnostic salvation of the soul in relation to the transcendent God is now equated with bringing the warring opposites of the conscious and unconscious into "a healthier and quieter state (salvation)." Though the history of the Gnostic symbol of the *anima mundi* or Original Man "shows that it was always used as a God image," we may assume, says Jung, "that some kind of psychic wholeness is meant (for instance, conscious + unconscious)." "I have not done violence to anything," Jung finds it necessary to explain. Psychology

---

[9] C. G. Jung, *Psychology and Alchemy* (*Collected Works*, Vol. XII, translated by R. F. C. Hull; N. Y.: Pantheon Books, Bollingen Series XX, 1953), p. 36.
[10] C. G. Jung, *Aion: Researches into the Phenomenology of the Self* (*Collected Works*, Vol. IX, Part II, translated by R. F. C. Hull; N. Y.: Pantheon Books, Bollingen Series XX, 1959), p. 70.

establishes "that the symbolism of psychic wholeness coincides with the God image." The Gnostics possessed the idea of an unconscious—the same knowledge as Jung's, "formulated differently to suit the age they lived in." To say that "each new image is simply another aspect of the divine mystery immanent in all creatures" is, to Jung, absolutely synonymous with saying that "all these images are found, empirically, to be expressions for the unified wholeness of man." What clinches this equation for Jung is his experience that the mandala structures which he finds in Gnosticism as elsewhere have in the dreams of his patients "the meaning and function of a centre of the unconscious personality." No ancient Gnostic could have had such a one-dimensional psychological view of religious symbols! But Jung, in all innocence, converts gnosis into his psychology, even as he converts his psychology into gnosis:

> Gnosis is undoubtedly a psychological knowledge whose contents derive from the unconscious. It reached its insights by concentrating on the "subjective factor," which consists empirically in the demonstrable influence that the collective unconscious exerts on the conscious mind. This would explain the astonishing parallelism between Gnostic symbolism and the findings of the psychology of the unconscious.[11]

Instead of seeing the Gnostics as they for the most part were—enormously abstruse system-builders and mythicizers—Jung turns them into modern thinkers, "theologians who, unlike the more orthodox ones, allowed themselves to be influenced in large measure by natural inner experience." The Gnostic dissolution of Christ's personality into symbols for the Kingdom of God is praised by Jung as representing "an assimilation and integration of Christ into the human psyche," through which human personality grows and consciousness develops. These achievements Jung sees as "gravely threatened in our anti-Christian age" (no longer, it seems, merely post-Christian!) "not only by the sociopolitical delusional systems" ("the murderous upsurge of bolshevistic ideas," as Jung puts it in another place) "but above all by the rationalistic hybris which is tearing our consciousness from its transcendent roots and holding before it immanent goals." Thus, Jung sees Gnosticism as both the antidote for and the natural expression of modern man.

Jung is not entirely unaware, however, that even as far as the content of the symbols is concerned he is a *Modern* Gnostic and not just a Gnostic. He consciously modifies the Gnostic systems, even as he modifies the Christian Trinity, to include a "Shadow Quaternio," an image of the hidden, dark, unconscious, irrational, evil side of

[11] *Ibid.*, p. 223.

man. This transition from the Anthropos, the divine image of man, to the Shadow was already prefigured, Jung claims, in the "historical development which led, in the eleventh century, to a widespread recognition of the evil principle as the world creator"—a typical expression of radical Gnostic dualism. But the need to balance the upward orientation of the psyche "by an equally strong consciousness of the lower man" is seen by Jung as "a specifically modern state of affairs and, in the context of Gnostic thinking, an obnoxious anachronism that puts man in the centre of the field of consciousness where he had never consciously stood before." Even this awareness of the difference between the ancient and the Modern Gnostic Jung quickly loses when he claims that "by making the person of Christ the object of his devotions he [man] gradually came to acquire Christ's position as mediator."

In his discussion of "The Development of Personality," Jung sets the true person, who has attained individuation, in contrast to convention, conformity, and the collective. Although he sees convention as a necessary stopgap, he leaves no question in our minds that the great person, the image of man for all men, is the one who defies convention for the sake of his own inner vocation and his own inner destiny. Of these great persons, Jung cannot speak highly enough. They are the heroes, leaders, saviors who discover "a new way to greater certainty"; they are the ones who achieve the "perfect realization of the meaning of existence innate in all things."

> These personalities are as a rule the legendary heroes of mankind, the very ones who are looked up to, loved, and worshipped, the true sons of God whose names perish not. They are the flower and the fruit, the ever fertile seeds of the tree of humanity. . . . They towered up like mountain peaks above the mass that still clung to its collective fears, its beliefs, laws, and systems, and boldly chose their own way.[12]

Here we have reached the very heart of Jung's image of man. To assess it as a direction for contemporary man we must ask what specific indications he offers as to what this "wholeness of the self" concretely means and implies. To be a person is to have a vocation, he writes, and "the original meaning of 'to have a vocation' is 'to be addressed by a voice.'" "The clearest examples of this," he adds, "are to be found in the avowals of the Old Testament prophets." But the "still small voice" or roaring lion that the prophets heard was always taken by them as an Other, as the address of God that

---

[12] C. G. Jung, *The Development of Personality* (*Collected Works*, Vol. XVII, translated by R. F. C. Hull; N. Y.: Pantheon Books, Bollingen Series, 1954), p. 174f.

came to them in the events and situations of their lives. Jung's conception of voice and vocation is quite different. He sees the true personality as trusting in his voice "as in God," but the voice comes not from God but from himself, his own inner destiny: "He *must* obey his own law, as if it were a daimon whispering to him of new and wonderful paths. Anyone with a vocation hears the voice of the inner man: he is *called.*" This does not mean, of course, that he consciously addresses himself. Rather just as Jung saw himself as split into two personalities, so he sees man in general as split into a conscious ego and an unconscious ground which is the potential arena of the true Self. He leaves us in no doubt as to which of these two is the dominant reality: "Only the tiniest fraction of the psyche is identical with the conscious mind and its box of magic tricks, while for much the greater part it is sheer unconscious *fact*, hard and immitigable as granite, immovable, inaccessible, yet ready at any time to come crashing down upon us at the behest of unseen powers." He also leaves us in no doubt as to which of these is the source of value: it is the unconscious which calls and guides, the conscious which listens and obeys, or, if it fails to obey, pays the price of neuroticism:

> The neurosis is thus a defence against the objective, inner activity of the psyche, or an attempt, somewhat dearly paid for, to escape from the inner voice and hence from the vocation. For this "growth" is the objective activity of the psyche, which, *independently of conscious volition,* is trying to speak to the conscious mind through the inner voice and lead him towards wholeness. Behind the neurotic perversion is concealed his vocation, his destiny: the growth of personality, the full realization of the life-will that is born with the individual.[13]

In this statement, we have the curious doctrine of a "life-will" which is realized "independently of conscious volition," which means independently of the will. For this to make any sense at all, Jung must be positing another "will" in the depths of the unconscious psyche, and in effect this is just what he does. In *Memories, Dreams, Reflections,* as we have seen, he attributes the fact that he could not be really interested in other people to his *daimon,* his guiding genius, while speaking of himself as the helpless victim. However much Jung may set the impersonal, collective unconscious in contrast to the modern collective as that which is realized only by the liberated, individuated person, it is curiously like totalitarianism in its reference of reality and value to a universal which allows room for individuality but not for true uniqueness:

[13] *Ibid.,* p. 183; italics added.

The psychic substratum upon which the individual consciousness is based is universally the same, otherwise people could never reach a common understanding. So in this sense, personality and its peculiar psychic makeup are not something absolutely unique. The uniqueness holds only for the individual nature of the personality.[14]

"The inner voice is the voice of a fuller life, of a wider, more comprehensive consciousness," writes Jung. Only through responding to this law of one's being and rising to personality does one attain to his life's meaning. But if one only becomes a personality through consciously assenting to the power of the inner voice, this assent still means the sacrifice of oneself to one's vocation. "That," says Jung, "is the great and liberating thing about any genuine personality." This means again that one must choose between one's conscious will and one's unconscious will, and the latter, the voice of the unconscious, Jung freely identifies with "the will of God." Like Weil, he sees this obedience as a necessity, rather than as the free response or failure to respond of the Bible. Like Weil, too, he sees the group as bound to another type of iron necessity, the laws of nature. "The group, because of its unconsciousness, has no freedom of choice, and so psychic activity runs on in it like an uncontrolled law of nature." In contrast to this group, but as the potential leader of it, Jung sets "the redeemer personality" for whom "our age calls." He is "the one who can emancipate himself from the inescapable grip of the collective and save at least his own soul, who lights a beacon of hope for others, proclaiming that here is at least *one* man who has succeeded in extricating himself from that fatal identity with the group psyche." By his very decision to put his own way above all other possible ways, "he has already fulfilled the greater part of his vocation as a redeemer." Exalting his own law above convention, he recognizes, in Nietzschean fashion, that "creative life always stands outside convention." When mere routine predominates, "there is bound to be a destructive outbreak of creative energy," but this destructive-creative energy is never a catastrophe "in the individual who consciously submits to these higher powers and serves them with all his strength." On the contrary, he "is able to cope with the changing times, and has unknowingly and involuntarily become a *leader*." If this notion of a "redeemer personality" who becomes a leader through following his unconscious "destiny" is disturbing, Jung's association of this leader with the dictator of the totalitarian states—the greatest apparatus of collective conformity known to man —is more disturbing still:

[14] *Ibid.*, p. 179.

The great liberating deeds of world history have sprung from leading personalities and never from the inert mass, which is at all times secondary and can only be prodded into activity by the demagogue. The huzzahs of the Italian nation go forth to the personality of the Duce, and the dirges of other nations lament the absence of strong leaders.[15]

There is a footnote to this last sentence which reads: "After this was written, Germany also turned to a Führer." In the original English translation, this footnote read: "Since then Germany, too, has found its leader."[16] Both translations, and especially the latter, raise the question, often raised before, of whether Jung saw in Hitler an embodiment of his "redeemer personality." We may wish to modify this question by reference to the fact that in his latest works Jung adds an attack on Naziism to the attacks on Bolshevism present throughout. But even so, we cannot fail to ask whether there is anything to prevent Jung's "redeemer personality" and "leader" from being a Hitler, whether or not Jung so intended.

It is hard to answer otherwise than no. Jung sees his leader personality as precisely the Modern Gnostic who unites good and evil within himself through taking part in both. Good and evil are both relativized here to mere functions of wholeness. Human values are transcended by "the voice of Nature, the all-sustainer and all-destroyer." "If she appears inveterately evil to us," says Jung, "this is mainly due to the old truth that the good is always the enemy of the better." But what is this "better" of which he speaks? It is that "individuation," or wholeness in the unconscious, which has no reference, check, or court other than itself, no direction, guide, or criterion by which to distinguish one voice of the archetypal unconscious from another. If we still recognize apparent evil in the unconscious, then it is our task, for the sake of this "better," to succumb to it in part so that we may realize our destiny as Modern Gnostic supermen:

> The inner voice brings the evil before us in a very tempting and convincing way in order to make us succumb. If we do not partially succumb, nothing of this apparent evil enters into us, and no regeneration or healing can take place. (I say "apparent," though this may sound too optimistic.) If we succumb completely, then the contents expressed by the inner voice act as so many devils, and a catastrophe ensues. But if we can succumb only in part, and if by self-assertion the ego can save itself from being completely swallowed, then it can assimilate the

15 *Ibid.*, pp. 167–8.
16 C. G. Jung, *The Integration of the Personality*, translated by Stanley Dell (N. Y.: Farrar & Rinehart, 1939), p. 305.

voice, and we realize that the evil was, after all, only a semblance of evil, but in reality a bringer of healing and illumination.[17]

What sort of "healing and illumination" does this "semblance of evil" bring? Jung's immediate answer is that "the inner voice is a 'Lucifer' in the strictest and most unequivocal sense of the word, and it faces people with ultimate moral decisions without which they can never achieve full consciousness and become personalities." But Jung's conception of a "moral decision" is very different from the old distinctions between right and wrong, just as the court of conscience for him is replaced by the criterion of wholeness and the address of the inner voice. If the healing that such "moral decision" leads to is not obvious, still less is the "illumination" it provides: "The highest and the lowest, the best and the vilest, the truest and the most deceptive things," reads the very next sentence, "are often blended together in the inner voice in the most baffling way, thus opening up in us an abyss of confusion, falsehood, and despair." What is the way out of this "confusion, falsehood, and despair"? It is succumbing in part to evil, or, as Jung puts it in a later writing, not succumbing to either good or evil, but rising above them, which means, once again, to relativize them. The Carpocratian Gnostic teaching of going along with one's own body in its instinctive demands is cited favorably by Jung in *Psychology and Religion* and is freely read by him into Taoism as what *must*, according to his own insights, be the secret of the Taoist's detachment:

> Have we, perhaps, an inkling that a mental attitude which can direct the glance inward to that extent owes its detachment from the world to the fact that *those men have so completely fulfilled the instinctive demands of their natures* that little or nothing prevents them from perceiving the invisible essence of the world? Can it be, perhaps, that the condition of such knowledge is freedom from those desires, ambitions, and passions, which bind us to the visible world, and *must not this freedom result from the intelligent fulfillment of instinctive demands*, rather than from a premature repression, or one growing out of fear?[18]

How can individuation be a goal in itself, independent of the way in which the individuated person moves to meet his world? What guidance does obeying the inner voice offer in distinguishing between the authentic and the inauthentic in the concrete context of

---

[17] *The Development of the Personality, op. cit.*, p. 185.
[18] C. G. Jung, "European Commentary" in *T'ai-i, The Secret of the Golden Flower*, translated and explained by Richard Wilhelm, translated into English by Cary F. Baynes (London: Kegan Paul, Trench, Trubner & Co., Ltd., 1931), pp. 80–1; italics added.

one's life relationships? What direction of movement as a person in the world is implied as the result of the unification of conscious and unconscious, good and evil? Is Jung's individuation in the last analysis an image of authentic existence for contemporary man or a substitute for one that makes one's concrete existence of secondary importance? How can psychic experience take the place of the traditional God as a voice, an address, a guidance when God is consistently identified by Jung with individuated man, and the new mystery that he proclaims is the mystery of God become man?

> A modern mandala is an involuntary confession of a peculiar mental condition. There is no deity in the mandala, nor is there any submission or reconciliation to a deity. *The place of the deity seems to be taken by the wholeness of man.*
>
> If we want to know what happens when the idea of God is no longer projected as an autonomous entity, this is the answer of the unconscious psyche. *The unconscious produces the idea of a deified or divine man.*
>
> The goal of psychological, as of biological, development is self-realization, or individuation. But since man knows himself only as an ego, and the self, as a totality, is indescribable and indistinguishable from a God-image, self-realization—to put it in religious or metaphysical terms—*amounts to God's incarnation.*[19]

The remarkable thing about these statements is that Jung sees no essential difference between modern man's relation to the inner self and ancient man's relation to the divine Other. Jung ascribes certain qualities of otherness to the archetypal unconscious, to be sure, in particular that sense of numinous awe of which Rudolph Otto has spoken. But he has robbed his commanding voice of its essential otherness by identifying it with one's own destiny, one's law, one's daimon, one's creativity, one's true self, one's life will. "Self-realization," as we have seen, is not the terminus for the contemporary image of man; it is at best the starting point. The word in itself carries no meaning, for we do not know what our true self is; we do not know the direction in which we must authenticate our existence in order to "realize" our selves. This is all the more the case when "self" is identified not with the whole body-soul person in his active relations with the world and other men, but with the "inner man," the self within, the unconscious center of "personal wholeness." The indications that Jung gives all seem to imply that the task of

19 C. G. Jung, *Psychology and Religion: West and East* (*Collected Works*, Vol. XI, translated by R. F. C. Hull; N. Y.: Pantheon Books, Bollingen Series, 1958), pp. 82; 96; 157; italics added.

authenticating one's concrete existence in the world is merely secondary and instrumental to realizing an inner wholeness in which both good and evil, authentic and inauthentic are relativized. "The vast majority needs authority, guidance, law," says Jung. But the pneumatic, or perfect man, the Gnostic elite, is able to put aside the law in favor of his own inner wholeness, his "soul":

> Mankind is, in essentials, psychologically still in a state of childhood—a stage that cannot be skipped. . . . The Pauline overcoming of the law falls only to the man who knows how to put his soul in the place of conscience. Very few are capable of this ("Many are called, but few are chosen"). And these few tread this path only from inner necessity, not to say suffering, for it is sharp as the edge of a razor.[20]

Whatever else "conscience" is, it has always been held to be the voice that prompted one to distinguish intrinsic right from wrong in concrete situations. Now this voice is put aside, along with the elemental seriousness of those situations and of one's desire to respond to them in the right way. In their place is the "inner necessity" which need not take either conscience or the situation seriously since both belong to the relatively less real and less valuable world of one's relations to others. Yet man's existence is, in important part, made up of these very relations. To make them extrinsic and instrumental inevitably means to destroy man's personal wholeness by dividing him into an essential inner self and an inessential social self. Submission *to* and deliverance *from* convention are an either/or for Jung that admits of no third alternative. The man who at the same time tries to follow his own way and adjust to the group inevitably becomes neurotic. The "wholeness of self" which the individuated man attains is the integration of the inner self, a wholeness that reduces the person in his relation to other persons to a mere *persona*, a mask, or social role, with at best only secondary significance. Thus, in his teaching as in his life, Jung is not really able to unite "inner" and "outer" and overcome the conflict between them. Instead, he demands a fundamental choice between them which makes the "outer" the instrument and material for the "inner."

Much of Jung's Modern Gnosticism is presented in scholarly guise. His *Answer to Job*, in contrast, is an explicitly personal statement. Like many ancient Gnostics, he begins by distorting the imageless God of the Old Testament into the evil creator god. Only a Modern Gnostic, however, could hold this god to be a projection of the

[20] C. G. Jung, *Two Essays on Analytical Psychology* (*Collected Works*, Vol. VII, translated by R. F. C. Hull; N. Y.: Pantheon Books, Bollingen Series, 1953), p. 237.

collective unconscious of mankind, as Jung does, and yet rant at it in a highly personal manner. Indeed, the resentment which Jung gives vent to in his diatribe against God might lead one to think that he projects his own father into the empty skies, à la Freud.

God, to Jung, is not conscious, and is therefore not man. Yet he is seen by Jung as conscious enough to be aware that he is inferior to man and at the same time human enough to be personally jealous! Like the evil, Gnostic creator god, the God of the Book of Job is only to be feared, and not to be loved or trusted. The two central motifs of the Bible and of the Book of Job—the wholehearted love of God and the unconditional trust in the relationship with God— are entirely absent in Jung's treatment of Job. In their place is a caricature of a wrathful, malicious deity that seems almost willfully projected into the text:

> One can submit to such a God only with fear and trembling, and can try indirectly to propitiate the despot with unctuous praises and ostentatious obedience. But a relationship of trust seems completely out of the question to our modern way of thinking. Nor can moral satis- faction be expected from *an unconscious nature* god of this kind. . . . Yahweh's allocutions have the unthinking yet nonetheless transparent purpose of showing Job *the brutal power of the demiurge*.[21]

Jung's Job, in short, "is set up as a judge over God himself." The central meaning of the whole book, which upholds Job's trust *and* his contending, but censures his gnosis—the desire of the creature to comprehend within his limited reason the creation that transcends him—is lost.[22] Jung's contending knows no trust and his gnosis no limits.

The very meaning of religion is changed by Jung from the direct dialogue between Job and God, which refuses to leave the ground of the immediate and the concrete, to a universal myth which has no concern for the unique and none for Job himself.

> Religion means, if anything at all, precisely that function which links us back to the eternal myth. . . . I would even go so far as to say that the mythical character of a life is just what expresses its universal hu- man validity.[23]

This turning away from the existential immediacy of lived life to "universal human validity" has the inevitable effect of depersonal-

21 C. G. Jung, *Answer to Job*, translated by R. F. C. Hull (Cleveland and N. Y.: The World Publishing Co., a Meridian Book, 1960), p. 53; italics added. *Answer to Job* is included in Jung, *Psychology and Religion, op. cit.*
22 For my interpretation of the Book of Job, see Maurice Friedman, *Problematic Rebel, op. cit.*, pp. 12–22.
23 Jung, *Answer to Job, op. cit.*, p. 95f.

izing man, of removing that freedom and that stamp of personal wholeness which make him a person. The very next sentence after the passage quoted above affirms: "It is perfectly possible psychologically, for the unconscious or an archetype to take complete possession of a man and to determine his fate down to the smallest detail." Not only does Jung see God as acting out of the unconscious of man, but as *forcing* him "to harmonize and unite the opposite influences to which his mind is exposed from the unconscious."

> Whatever man's wholeness, or the self, may mean *per se*, empirically it is an image of the goal of life spontaneously produced by the unconscious, *irrespective of the wishes and fears of the conscious mind*. It stands for the goal of the total man, for the realization of his wholeness and individuality *with or without the consent of his will*.[24]

How there can be any personal wholeness, individuality, or spontaneity in the face of a conscious self taken over and compelled by the unconscious is incomprehensible to me. Only an attitude such as this could lead Jung to ignore Job's deeply personal plea, "Thou shalt seek me and I will not be," in favor of the "answer to Job" that he finds in the historical development of the collective unconscious. "Job," I have said in *Problematic Rebel*, "is the true existentialist." Jung is anything but!

God for Jung is the "loving Father" who is unmasked as dangerous, unpredictable, unreliable, unjust, and cruel, in short "an insufferable incongruity which modern man can no longer swallow." Here, as in the modern mandalas, the place of God is gradually taken by deified man. Consciousness separates man from his instincts and makes him prone to error, but man's instincts themselves "give him an inkling of the hidden wisdom of God." Jung exalts the instincts themselves; this exaltation means "the inclusion of evil." The more consciousness lays claim to moral authority, says Jung, "the more the self will appear as something dark and menacing." One would think from this that the "evil" of the shadow lay only in the fact that it was suppressed, that the unconscious was not given its full due in the *complexio oppositorum* of the self. But, in fact, Jung again and again refers *all* moral valuation to the unconscious and leaves the conscious only the task of obeying.

The essential content of the unconscious, writes Jung, is *"the idea of the higher man* by whom Yahweh was morally defeated and who he was later to become." Man not only judges God, in Jung's reading; he ultimately replaces him. The apocalyptic writers such as Ezekiel foresee "what is going to happen, through the transformation

24 *Ibid.*, p. 183; italics added.

and humanization of God, not only to God's son as foreseen from all eternity, but to man as such." The incarnation of God in Christ is not enough; for Christ is perfect man, but not complete, i.e., sinful man. The new incarnation will be that of God in sinful man. *"God will be begotten in creaturely man."* This, Jung quite rightly remarks, "implies a tremendous change in man's status, for he is now raised to sonship and almost to the position of a man-god." The deification of man as "man-god" that Dostoyevsky foresaw as the abysmal consequence of "the death of God" is now openly hailed by Jung. *"God wanted to become man and still wants to."*

> From the promise of the Paraclete we may conclude that God wants to become *wholly* man; in other words, to reproduce himself in his own dark creature (man not redeemed from original sin).

> God . . . wants to become man, and for that purpose he has chosen, through the Holy Ghost, the creaturely man filled with darkness—the natural man who is tainted with original sin and who learnt the divine arts and sciences from the fallen angels. The guilty man is eminently suitable and is therefore chosen to become the vessel for the continuing incarnation, not the guiltless one who holds aloof from the world and refuses to pay his tribute to life, for in him the dark God would find no room.[25]

The uniting of God's antinomy must take place in man, says Jung, and "this involves man in a new responsibility." Man "has been granted an almost godlike power": he must know God's nature "if he is to understand himself and thereby achieve gnosis of the Divine."

Never has Jung's radical antinomian Gnosticism received clearer expression. Never has he stated so openly his goal of substituting for the Christian God-man the Modern Gnostic man-god who will achieve gnosis of the Divine through understanding himself. This does not mean a deification of the conscious ego. Jung warns again and again against the danger of the "inflation" to which the ordinary mortal, not freed from original sin, would instantly succumb if he saw himself as Christ, or as a complete God-man.

> Even the enlightened person remains what he is, and is never more than his own limited ego before the One who dwells within him, whose form has no knowable boundaries, who encompasses him on all sides, fathomless as the abysms of the earth and vast as the sky.[26]

In other words, there is for Jung a transcendence within in relation to which the conscious "I" knows its limits and its limitedness. This is of

25 *Ibid.*, pp. 179; 186.
26 *Ibid.*, p. 203.

great significance for avoiding that inflation of the conscious by the archetypal materials of the unconscious which leads the Simon Magi of every age to suicidal self-absolutization. But there is another, even greater danger, which Jung does not warn us of, and that is the danger of a divinization of the unconscious which leaves man at the mercy of the dark, irrational forces Jung worships as the dark side of God. Jung sees no middle ground between sinless man and sinful man, no possibility of sinful man's transforming and hallowing his instincts rather than simply celebrating them. By identifying the real "self" with the autonomous center in the unconscious, Jung is in danger of taking his own inner knowledge for the will of God and imposing it on others.[27]

In Jung's psychology, individuation is attained through the integration in the unconscious of the four faculties—thought, feeling, sensation, and intuition. Particularly central in this process of individuation is the "shadow," the suppressed part of the self. The shadow challenges the whole ego-personality and therefore usually meets with resistance. "To become conscious of it involves recognizing the dark aspects of the personality as present and real." If one does not make the shadow conscious, one invariably projects it onto one's environment, seeing all evil as outside of oneself. For that very reason, one is all the more threatened by the danger of its being unmasked within. Projections isolate the person from his environment by changing a real relation to it into an illusory one. The world is transformed "into the replica of one's own unknown face," and the subject "dreams a world whose reality remains forever unattainable."

"Real and fundamental change in individuals," writes Jung in *The Undiscovered Self*,[28] "can come only from the personal encounter between man and man, but not from communistic or Christian baptisms en masse, which do not touch the inner man." Jung recognizes that the mass state, for all its emphasis on the group, is an enemy of "mutual understanding and relationship of man to man," yet such human relationship is urgently needed for the real cohesion of our society, "in view of the atomization of the pent-up mass man, whose personal relationships are undermined by general mistrust." Love can only exist where mutual projections of the shadow are withdrawn, and in

[27] That Jung may not have entirely escaped from this danger is suggested by his celebration in *Answer to Job* of the new Roman Catholic dogma of the Assumption of Mary. He considers this dogma "to be the most important religious event since the Reformation"—not because of any of the reasons that the Catholic Church would hold to be important, but because it gives the feminine principle the place in the deity that Jung's psychology calls for!
[28] C. G. Jung, *The Undiscovered Self*, translated by R. F. C. Hull (Boston: Little, Brown & Co., 1958), p. 12; see pp. 10–13.

love—mutual, trusting human relationship—the real cohesion and strength of society belongs. "Nothing promotes understanding and *rapprochement* more than the mutual withdrawal of projections." A conscious recognition and consideration of our imperfections, of the shadow, is necessary if human relationship is to be established. Thus, Jung integrates his basic, more individualistic image of man with a new emphasis on mutual relationship by picturing the process of self-knowledge and individuation as a mutual one. This mutuality, however, is an essentially instrumental one in which each individual "psychic process" tends to regard the other with which it interacts as a function of its own personal development.[29]

[29] For my treatment of the quite different subject of Jung's approach to *psychotherapy*, see Maurice Friedman, "The Image of Man in Jung's Psychotherapy," *Psychoanalytic Review*, Winter 1966/1967, Vol. LIII, No. 4.

10

HERMANN HESSE

UNDER the influence of his own Jungian analysis, the great, German-Swiss novelist, Hermann Hesse, wrote a series of novels which not only give dramatic embodiment to Jung's Modern Gnostic, but carry this figure forward and plumb the depths of its problematic. *Demian, Siddhartha, Steppenwolf, The Journey to the East*, and *Magister Ludi* together form the most significant and profound presentation of the Modern Gnostic in contemporary literature. The central figures of these novels have an immediate personal appeal that no amount of discursive thought concerning dreams, myths, alchemy, or archetypal patterns in literature could have.

Demian, a novel published anonymously at the end of World War I, is at once explicitly Gnostic and thoroughly Jungian. The story of the novel is Emil Sinclair's search for self-realization. The book presupposes, as does Jung, that there is a "true self" to which one is called and destined. The dramatic interest lies in the ways in which that destiny manifests itself and the trials that Emil Sinclair goes through in struggling to listen to and follow his destiny. "I wanted only to try to live in obedience to the promptings which came from my true self. Why was that so very difficult?" reads the motto at the beginning. This struggle to obey one's true self is identified with the absence of an image of man in the contemporary world: "What that is, a real living man, one certainly knows less today than ever." The uniqueness of this "real living man" is seen not in the person himself, however, but in the convergence of all the world's phenomena in that person. Like Jung, the narrator sees man of value only to the extent that he "carries out the will of nature." "In everyone has the spirit taken

shape, in everyone creation suffers, in everyone is a redeemer crucified." Although the path of each man is toward "self-realization," in
realizing himself the individual helps nature project itself into "manhood."

Emil Sinclair begins, like Jung, with two personalities or two
worlds: one bright, orderly, respectable, good, sunny—the world of
his family; the other full of dark, "monstrous, tempting, terrible,
enigmatic goings-on," "beautiful and dreadful, wild and cruel." The
hierophant who initiates Emil into this second, dark world bears the
transparent name of Demian. He is the daimon, or guiding genius,
who issues from and leads Sinclair to his own self. Like the ancient
Gnostic Cainites, he holds that the sign of Cain is a distinction of the
bold men, the men of character, whom the weak fear and ostracize.
For Demian, as for Nietzsche, the whole of biblical morality is a product of the *ressentiment* of the weak against the strong. A young town
boy, Frank Kromer, obviously the Jungian "shadow," prepares Sinclair
for Demian's teaching by blackmailing him. "In my dreams he lived
as my shadow," says Sinclair, "and thus my fantasy credited him with
actions which he did not, in reality, do," such as encouraging Emil to
stab his father with a knife. What Sinclair suffered resistingly from
Kromer he suffers willingly from Demian, when the latter gains a far
subtler and surer ascendancy over him than Kromer's threats could
ever attain. "Was not a voice talking there, which could only come
from myself? . . . Which knew all in a better, clearer way than I myself?" Although in a different way from Kromer, Demian, too, is a
seducer who binds him "to the second, evil, bad world."

Yet Demian's goal is not dominance, but helping Sinclair to his
self-realization, and his aim is not the evil world per se, but the unification of the good and evil worlds in a higher synthesis. Like Jung,
he juxtaposes the unrepentant thief on the cross with the image of
Christ in order to point away from the *perfect* man to the *complete*
man. He is that himself—not an actual person, but a gynandromorphic
combination of man and woman, age and youth, an archetypal being
out of the collective unconscious, "somehow or other a thousand years
old, not to be measured by time, bearing the stamp of other epochs."
He bears the secret Gnostic wisdom of the ages—the desire to create
a God who will embody the devil as well—and through him Sinclair
realizes that his own problem is "a problem of humanity as a whole,
of life and thought in general." It is not he who introduces Sinclair
to the two worlds, but he shows him the need of unifying these words
—not in thought alone but in experience. "Only the thought that we
live through in experience has any value."

When Emil Sinclair feels sexual stirrings, he sublimates them in love for a Dantean "Beatrice" whom he is content to paint and dream about, but never address. With Beatrice, as with every other person in the story, he is interested only in the reflected image in his soul and not in the person herself. "I felt no emotion on seeing her, but I was often sensible of a harmony of sentiment, which seemed to say: we are connected, or rather, not you and I, but your picture and I; you are a part of my destiny." How startlingly similar this is to Jung's confession of his own relation to other people! Thoroughly Jungian, too, is Demian's statement that it is not the conscious ego which lives our life but the daimon within: "There is that in you, which orders your life for you, and which knows why you are doing it. . . . There is someone in us who knows everything, wills everything, does everything better than we do ourselves."

The teaching of *Demian* becomes still more explicitly Gnostic when Demian sends Sinclair an interpretation of a dream-bird that he has painted: "The bird fights its way out of the egg. The egg is the world. Whoever will be born must destroy a world. The bird flies to God. The name of the god is Abraxas." Here is the Gnostic theme of having to wake up from the evil world in order to find the saving knowledge. Here, too, is the Gnostic god, Abraxas, whom Jung himself celebrated in his youth as the deity that unites good and evil in itself,[1] or as *Demian* puts it, the "divinity on whom the symbolical task was imposed of uniting the divine and the diabolical," "the god, who was at the same time god and devil." In the teaching of the Cainites and of the Carpocratians, there is no suggestion of the transformation of evil into good. Rather the evil as such is propitiated, worshipped, and united with good in a higher "synthesis" that transcends and relativizes them both. This goal is imaged by Sinclair in his dreams as the embrace of a Great Mother figure. This figure, which Sinclair paints and which he later discovers to be Demian's mother, "Mother Eve," means for him a mixture of rapture and horror, divine worship and crime, "man and woman, the most sacred things and the most abominable interwoven, the darkest guilt with the most tender innocence." Now love for him is neither a dark, animal impulse, nor a pious spiritualized form of worship, but both. "It was the image of an angel and of Satan, man and woman in one, human being and animal, the highest good and lowest evil."

The aspect of the Modern Gnostic that *Demian* brings out most clearly is the absence of any genuine otherness. None of the main characters except Demian is real or important in himself. Many are shadow figures that are there only to guide Demian on his path. Nor

[1] See Martin Buber, *Eclipse of God* (N. Y.: Harper Torchbooks, 1957), pp. 85, 137; and Jung's reply in *Merkur* (Berlin, May, 1952) and *Spring* (1958).

is Demian ever concerned about anyone other than himself and his own destiny. Though he longs for contact with real life, it is his own self which always occupies his attention. Whatever comes to him he sees neither as chance nor as the independent will of another person, but as the effect of his own desires which leads him "compellingly to the object of which he stands in need." Each person is utterly alone in this sense, and at the same time part of the universal, but never in essential, direct relation with another person about whom he is concerned. Even when Sinclair has at last found Mother Eve, whom he has sought so long, he sees her only as a part of himself and a function of his self-realization: "I felt decidedly that it was not her person for which my whole being was striving, but that she was a symbol of my inward self, and that she wished only to lead me to see more deeply into myself." This attitude leads to total concern with one's "self-realization"—"one's only true vocation"—and complete unconcern with the persons with whom one deals. Even World War I, with which the novel ends, is seen in romantic, Modern Gnostic fashion as the expression of individual destinies, and the killing of others as merely a reflection of ones own inner soul on its way to gnosis:

> Even their wildest instincts were not actually directed against the enemy, their murderous and bloody work was an expression of their own inner being, of their cleft soul, which wished to rave and kill, to destroy and die, in order to be able to be born anew. A giant bird was fighting its way out of the egg, and the egg was the world, and the world had to go to ruin.[2]

If there is no real uniqueness in other persons, neither is there real uniqueness in history. In its place is Jung's collective unconscious, a universal, spiritual substratum which would make it possible for "a single, moderately gifted child, who had not enjoyed the slightest instruction," to "rediscover the whole process of things" and "produce gods, demons, paradises, the commandments and prohibitions, old and new testaments—everything."

The gnosis of *Demian* carries with it the sense of the initiated, or elite, who alone know the meaning of being a man. All men have the possibility of becoming human, but only those who become conscious of these potentialities possess them. Only those who can walk alone, fulfilling their destiny without examples or ideals, can join this special brotherhood. Despite his dependence on Demian and Mother Eve, it is intimated again and again that Sinclair is one of these. The complete loneliness of these people brings them together, a league of

[2] Hermann Hesse, *Demian: The Story of a Youth* (N. Y.: Henry Holt & Co., 1948), p. 204.

"Eastern Wayfarers," who have nothing in common but that each is seeking in his own way and that this seeking is seen, in true Jungian fashion, as originating "in dreams of the subconscious soul, dreams in which humanity is . . . feeling its way forward." These are the elite, or the awake, who carry out the will of nature "as men of the future." In the apocalyptic breakup of European civilization in World War I, the task of this Modern Gnostic elite is "to be, as it were, an island in the world, perhaps an example, in any case to proclaim that it was possible to live a different sort of life." They do not see themselves as living shut off from the world but "in its midst, only on another plane," separated from others "by a different sort of vision." It is in this spirit that Sinclair goes into the war, receives the kiss of the dying Demian, and learns that Demian is in him and is divine.

> When I find the key and step right down into myself, to where the pictures painted by my destiny seem reflected on the dark mirror of my soul, then I need only stoop towards the black mirror and see my own picture, which now completely resembles Him, my guide and friend.[3]

In the end, Demian and Mother Eve are not characters in a novel, but the messengers of the Gnostic redeemer god, whose dwelling is no longer in or above the cosmos, as with the ancient Gnostics, but in the soul. With little essential change in the personae, the Gnostic cosmology has been transformed by the Modern Gnostic into a psychology!

Hesse's next novel, *Siddhartha*, is an excellent example of that "pure Gnosticism in Hindu dress" of which Jung speaks in *Modern Man in Search of a Soul*. What characterizes this particular form of Modern Gnosticism, as we also find it in the thought of Joseph Campbell, Alan Watts, and others, is that it turns to the East for essentially Western purposes. Specifically, it takes the Hindu and Buddhist doctrines of an Absolute that is beyond good and evil and uses them for a typically Gnostic relativization of good and evil. For the Hindu, as long as man is himself in the relative world, good and evil are as real as he is. But the Westerner, weighed down by the guilt of a too strong "super-ego," wishes to relativize good and evil without leaving the ground of the self. So far from denying the individual self for the supreme reality of Atman, the Modern Gnostic looks toward the completion and even deification of self. The Hindu doctrine of the absolute, impersonal, transpsychic Self, and the Buddhist doctrine of nonself become transformed here into their opposite: a superman who in his

[3] *Ibid.*, p. 207.

own person is beyond good and evil since both are mere functions of his own becoming!

It is indeed a European, a Modern Gnostic conception that is subtly portrayed here through the constant juxtaposition of the spiritual pilgrimage of the young Brahmin Siddhartha with the figure of Sakyamuni, or the Buddha. Siddhartha evolves within himself a new teaching—not to escape from and destroy himself but to understand and learn from himself. Now the true Self is no longer identified with Atman, the absolute Self, but with Siddhartha, a particular being, who lives separated and different from everybody else. "I will learn from myself the secret of Siddhartha," he says to himself, and instead of scorning diversity for unity find unity in diversity. "Meaning and reality were not hidden somewhere behind things, they were in them, in all of them." Instead of seeing the visible world as *maya,* or the veil of illusion, Siddhartha now looks at the world in a simple, child-like way, without seeking to penetrate to any reality behind it. Instead of trying to put aside the senses and trap his Self in a net of thoughts, as he had done before, he now recognizes that both senses and thought are fine things behind which "lay hidden the last meaning."

> It was worth while listening to them both, to play with both, neither to despise nor overrate either of them, but to listen intently to both voices. He would only strive after whatever the inward voice commanded him, nor tarry anywhere but where the voice advised him.[4]

The celebration of the divine in the particular is characteristic of a certain type of mystic—the Zen Buddhist, the Taoist, the Hasid, Thomas Traherne, and William Blake. But to regard the senses and thought as worthy of being listened to only because through and in them one hears the command of the "inward voice" is unmistakably Modern Gnostic. It is this attitude which we have already seen in Jung.

Also, Modern Gnostic is the path that Siddhartha then takes—one of becoming a worldly man, who learns from a prostitute, a merchant, and a dice-thrower how to live the life of self-indulgence and debauchery so that through experiencing sin he may finally transcend the self that becomes enmeshed in it. After twenty years, Siddhartha experiences a profound revulsion, leaves his riches, and almost drowns himself in his disgust, only then to rediscover the true Siddhartha:

> I have had to experience so much stupidity, so many vices, so much error, so much nausea, disillusionment and sorrow, just in order to be-

---

[4] Hermann Hesse, *Siddhartha,* translated by Hilda Rosner (N. Y.: New Directions Paperback, 1951), p. 50.

come a child again and begin anew. But it was right that it should be so; my eyes and heart acclaim it. I had to experience despair, I had to sink to the greatest mental depths, to thoughts of suicide, in order to experience grace, to hear Om again, to sleep deeply again and to awaken refreshed again. I had to become a fool again in order to find Atman in myself. *I had to sin in order to live again.*[5]

Like Jung and like Demian, Siddhartha realizes that it is not enough to *think* the unification of good and evil, one must actually *experience* it. Only through this experience has he overcome the arrogance of knowledge that stood in the way of his losing his self.

In the last stage of his life, Siddhartha becomes a ferryman and learns from the old ferryman, Vasudeva, and still more from the river itself, how to listen, "to listen with a still heart, with a waiting, open soul, without passion, without desire, without judgment, without opinions." Many of the countless people whom they ferry across are drawn to talk and even to confess to these holy ferrymen. This quality of listening to the other, rather than to one's own inner voice, is something that has not characterized the Modern Gnostic up till now. Through his rebellious son, whom the dying courtesan Kamala leaves with him, Siddhartha learns what he had not been able to learn in his twenty years of worldliness: to love another, to lose himself in another person to such an extent as to forget himself.

> He felt indeed that this love, this blind love for his son, was a very human passion, that it was Sansara, a troubled spring of deep water. At the same time he felt that it was not worthless, that it was necessary, that it came from his own nature. This emotion, this pain, these follies also had to be experienced.[6]

There is no suggestion, for all this, that he can ever communicate with his son, who has to leave him and make his own way through pain and folly, just as *he* had to leave *his* father.

Siddhartha is healed of the wound that his love for his son has caused him, when he learns to listen to all the thousand voices of the river at once without binding his soul to any one particular voice. Then he hears the unity of them all, the word Om—perfection—and his Self merges into unity.

> From that hour Siddhartha ceased to fight against his destiny. There shone in his face the serenity of knowledge, of one who is no longer confronted with conflict of desires, who has found salvation, who is in harmony with the stream of events, with the stream of life, full of

[5] *Ibid.*, pp. 98–9; italics added.
[6] *Ibid.*, p. 125.

sympathy and compassion, surrendering himself to the stream, belonging to the unity of all things.[7]

Time is an illusion and with it the dividing line between world and eternity, suffering and bliss, good and evil. "Never is a man wholly a saint or a sinner," nor does he merely evolve from the one to the other. The potential Buddha *already* exists in the sinner. Like the ancient and the Modern Gnostic, Siddhartha sees the world not as in need of redemption, but already holy, already perfect.

> Every sin already carries grace within it, all small children are potential old men. . . . The Buddha exists in the robber and dice player; the robber exists in the Brahmin. . . . Everything that exists is good— death as well as life, sin as well as holiness, wisdom as well as folly. Everything is necessary, everything needs only my agreement, my assent, my loving understanding; then all is well with me and nothing can harm me. I learned through my body and soul that it was necessary for me to sin, that I needed lust, that I had to strive for property and experience nausea and the depths of despair in order to learn not to resist them, in order to learn to love the world, and no longer compare it with some kind of desired imaginary world, some imaginary vision of perfection.[8]

This recognition that everything is necessary and that it needs only one's loving assent is reminiscent of Nietzsche's *amor fati* and of Jung's obedience to the all-controlling will of the unconscious. It presents a picture of timeless unity, of serene and even humorous wisdom. But does it offer us an image of man, an image of a direction of authenticating existence for the man who does have to live in time, who is free, and who has to make real decisions?

This question becomes sharper and more agonized in *Steppenwolf*, Hesse's next great novel. Though the laughter of the immortals may still be heard at a distance, the hero of the novel is anything but serene and affirmative. In *Steppenwolf*, it becomes abundantly clear that the Modern Gnostic wisdom of *Siddhartha* was a vision of the unification of opposites that Hesse could not sustain except through a pain and perplexity quite foreign to *Siddhartha*. *Steppenwolf* is of great significance as an exploration of the extent to which the Modern Gnostic can and should be a "live option" for contemporary man. It is of equally great significance in its presentation of what I have called "the problematic of modern man"—the inner division of contemporary man, the crisis of motives and problematic of guilt, the paradox of the person in the modern world.[9] As much as any book with which we

[7] *Ibid.*, p. 139.
[8] *Ibid.*, p. 145f.
[9] See *Problematic Rebel, op. cit.*, Part V.

shall deal, *Steppenwolf* addresses itself squarely to the question we have asked in setting forth our theme: What contemporary images of man possess the right tension between the raw material of the absurd and the shaping force of a new direction toward authentic existence?

The real name of "the Steppenwolf" is Harry Haller, the initials of which are the same as Hermann Hesse's. The name Steppenwolf he has given himself in token of his inner division—a cultured, humane man and a wild, uncouth wolf of the steppes. But actually, as the "Treatise on the Steppenwolf" explains, Harry is not two different selves but many, and his task is not simply the reconciliation of nature and spirit, but the discovery of unity in baffling multiplicity. This struggle for the recognition of the multiplicity and the movement forward to the All-unity, Haller describes in the manuscript that he leaves behind. The young man who presents this manuscript to us opines that the adventures related in it are for the most part fictitious, but not in the sense of arbitrary invention. "They are rather the deeply lived spiritual events which he has attempted to express by giving them the form of tangible experiences." They are almost what one might expect if a gifted poet like Hesse were to set out to dramatize his Jungian analysis.

Hesse does not see them as simply the product of his own sickness or that of the Steppenwolf. They are rather "a document of the times," a document of the absence of a meaningful image of man. Caught between two ages, two modes of life, a whole generation "loses the feeling for itself, for the self-evident, for all morals, for being safe and innocent." As one of the strong and gifted men of this displaced generation, Haller must live outside all security and innocence. "He belongs to those whose fate it is to live the whole riddle of human destiny heightened to the pitch of a personal torture, a personal hell." If he is not an image of man in the full sense of the term, he is an image of modern man, of that man who both shares and is aware of the contradictions of our time. "It is hard to find [the] track of the divine," he exclaims, "in . . . this besotted humdrum age of spiritual blindness!" But he is not simply a representative of the negative of the age, as Kafka said of himself. Rather, he pursues the fleeting, fluttering significance of his life over its ruins; even while he suffers its seeming meaninglessness and madness, he hopes "secretly at the last turn of Chaos for revelation and God's nearness."

Like K. in Kafka's *Castle*, the Steppenwolf has sought a freedom which turns out to be isolation and death. The independence that he formerly wished for becomes his lot and his sentence. He belongs to "the suicides," those men who, whether they try to commit suicide or not, feel their ego "dangerous, dubious, and doomed," exposed to extraordinary risk, liable at any instant to plunge into the void. The aim of the suicide, according to the "Treatise on the Steppenwolf" which Haller finds, is not to perfect and mold the self but to liberate it "by going back to the Mother, back to God, back to the All." But for someone incapable of the extremes of the saint, and imprisoned, despite all rebellion, within the bourgeois world, it is only through humor that this liberation can be achieved:

> Humour alone, that magnificent discovery of those who are cut short in their calling to highest endeavour, those who falling short of tragedy are yet as rich in gifts as in affliction, humour alone (perhaps the most inborn and brilliant achievement of the human spirit) attains to the impossible and brings every aspect of human existence within the rays of its prism. To live in the world as though it were not the world, to respect the law and yet to stand above it, to have possessions as though "one possessed nothing," to renounce as though it were no renunciation, all these favourite and often formulated propositions of an exalted worldly wisdom, it is in the power of humour alone to make efficacious.[10]

Harry Haller is anything but a humorous person, however. He is weighted down by a heavy seriousness which even the "Magic Theater" into which he wanders is not able to cure. He is one of those who "must suffer the loneliness of the garden of Gethsemane" in order to become a man in the highest sense of the word—not one of the expendable millions, but "kingly men," "the immortals." "The long road to true manhood" which he must walk is not back to an illusory innocence and wholeness, which man never had, but forward via the Modern Gnostic way of experience and of sin, "ever further into sin, ever deeper into human life." Not narrowing the world and simplifying the soul, but taking the whole world into his soul must be his way. Although the "Treatise" contrasts the Western desire to preserve the ego with the Hindu desire to overcome it, the path that is pointed out for the Steppenwolf is that of "the expansion of the soul until it is able once more to embrace the All." The personality is not abolished, but lifted and enlarged; yet it is lifted through suffering. Man is not a fixed and enduring form, but an experiment and a transition:

> He is nothing else than the narrow and perilous bridge between nature and spirit. His innermost destiny drives him on to the spirit and to God. His innermost longing draws him back to nature, the mother.

[10] Hermann Hesse, *Steppenwolf*, translated by Basil Creighton, revised by Walter Sorell (N. Y.: The Modern Library, 1963), p. 60.

Between the two forces his life hangs tremulous and irresolute. What is commonly meant by the word "man" is never anything more than a transient agreement, a bourgeois compromise.[11]

Harry Haller understands this treatise as a sentence of death. Either he must kill himself or go through a painful transition which he has experienced many times. The mask of his present self must be torn off, and its ideal broken, and he must descend into a "deathly constriction and loneliness and unrelatedness," an "empty hell of lovelessness and despair." With every such growth in liberty and spiritual depth, he has experienced "an increasing chill of severance and estrangement." He has become the very embodiment of the Modern Exile.[12]

The passing years had stripped me of my calling, my family, my home. I stood outside all social circles, alone, beloved by none, mistrusted by many, in unceasing and bitter conflict with public opinion and morality. . . . Religion, country, family, state . . . meant nothing to me any more. The pomposity of the sciences, societies, and arts disgusted me.[13]

Harry is about to commit suicide when he meets Hermine, the feminine counterpart of his boyhood friend Herman. Hermine is at once his anima, and his hierophant, the Gnostic messenger who initiates him into the divine-diabolic mysteries. Like Mother Eve for Sinclair, Hermine is only a function of Haller's self-realization and in no sense an independent other. She is, as he says himself, his "magic mirror." "The reason why I please you and mean so much to you," she says, "is because I am a kind of looking-glass for you, because there's something in me that answers you and understands you." They are both exiles, Hermine the courtesan and Haller the Steppenwolf, and they are both, in good Gnostic terminology, "children of the devil." "The devil is the spirit, and we are his unhappy children. We have fallen out of nature and hang suspended in space."

Hermine presents Harry with a mistress, Maria; through her, he recovers the images of his past and with it the knowledge that the kernel of his life is noble. His outer life confronts him unceasingly with the absurd, but within he finds a series of pictures "indestructible and abiding as the stars," which make up the story of his life and the value of his being. Although he is not at home in the world, he is at home in the transcendent, the transcendent which he refers to the stars, but which he finds within. "It had been for all its wretchedness a princely life. . . . It had purpose and character and turned not on

[11] *Ibid.*, pp. 67–8.
[12] See Maurice Friedman, *Problematic Rebel*, Part III, "The Modern Exile."
[13] Hesse, *Steppenwolf, op. cit.*, p. 75f.

trifles, but on the stars." Like Jung, he now holds "the goal set for the progress of every human life" to be the unification of the inner opposites: "I had only to snatch up my scattered images and raise my life as Harry Haller and as the Steppenwolf to the unity of one picture, in order to enter myself into the world of imagination and be immortal." But this prospect in no wise portends any reconciliation with the world, which both Harry and Hermine see as irredeemably meaningless. People with a dimension too many, like them, people who want "music instead of noise, joy instead of pleasure, soul instead of gold, creative work instead of business, passion instead of foolery" find "no home in this trivial world of ours." At first, this seems like a critique of contemporary life, but Hermine suggests that it has actually always been the same. "Time and the world, money and power belong to the small people and the shallow people," asserts Hermine in true Gnostic fashion. "To the rest, to the real men belongs nothing . . . but death" *and* eternity. These "real men" she holds to be "the saints, . . . the true men, the younger brothers of the Saviour." But they are Gnostic saints whose only guide is their homesickness—their knowledge of not being at home here and their longing to return to the lost transcendent. These are the pneumatics who can reach holiness through sin. "There are many saints who at first were sinners. Even sin can be a way to saintliness, sin and vice."

After Hermine has led Harry Haller into "The Magic Theater," entrance to which is "for madmen only" and "the price of admission your mind," the jazz musician Pablo takes over from her the task of hierophant and guide. Pablo makes explicit for Harry the *Modern* Gnostic doctrine that the transcendent reality which he seeks outside the world in the sphere of "the immortals" can be found only within his own soul. And although this reality is still identified with "eternity," it is a curious Gnostic eternity in which time is redeemed into innocence by being transformed into space and in which all the experiences that Harry has had in his lifetime are relived in the present as Jungian images within the psyche:

> You have a longing to forsake this world and its reality to penetrate to a reality more native to you, to a world beyond time. Now I invite you to do so. You know, of course, where this other world lies hidden. It is the world of your own soul that you seek. Only within yourself exists that other reality for which you long. I can give you nothing that has not already its being within yourself. I can throw open to you no picture-gallery but your own soul. . . . I help you to make your own world visible. That is all.[14]

14 *Ibid.*, p. 197f.

Harry walks down a corridor with innumerable doors, each one of which opens on to exactly what he seeks—the images of experience that will enable him to escape from the prison of his so-called personality. Not unlike the well-known psychologist who took hallucinogenic drugs so often that he came to regard the everyday world to which he returned as "play," Pablo assures Harry that he will be able to leave "the farce of reality" behind him directly. Behind one door inscribed "All Girls Are Yours," Harry relives and completes all the partial experiences with girls from his earliest boyhood. In another, labeled "Jolly Hunting, Great Automobile Hunt," he throws his pacifism aside and takes part with nihilistic gusto in a war shooting down all the automobiles that come along the highway. In a burst of Jungian irrationalism, Harry glorifies his war as a defense of the image of man against that rationalism which reduces man to a mechanism:

> What we are doing is probably mad, and probably it is good and necessary all the same. It is not a good thing when man overstrains his reason and tries to reduce to rational order matters that are not susceptible of rational treatment. Then there arise ideals such as those of the Americans or of the Bolsheviks. Both are extraordinarily rational, and both lead to a frightful oppression and impoverishment of life, because they simplify it so crudely. The likeness of man, once a high ideal, is in process of becoming a machine-made article. It is for madmen like us, perhaps, to ennoble it again.[15]

What the Steppenwolf is reacting to is the mechanization and standardization of life against which we, too, must rebel for the sake of the image of man. But the form of the Steppenwolf's rebellion—the glorification of nihilism and killing—is hardly such as to ennoble man once again! Nor is it any particular comfort that these experiences are seen as taking place within the soul of the Steppenwolf. To the Modern Gnostic, as we have seen in *Demian,* these impulses may also be acted out since other people are seen as functions of one's own individuation as one is of theirs.

In place of the seriousness with which Harry has formerly taken his life—a seriousness which almost led him to take his life!—comes the realization that life is "child's play," as Hermine puts it. When he comes to the door inscribed, "How One Kills for Love," he finds the naked figures of Hermine and Pablo asleep on a rug after having made love. He plunges his knife into her breast and reflects ruefully that he has fulfilled Hermine's wish that he kill her even before she has ever been his. Harry's "sentence," pronounced by Mozart, is that he apprehend the "gallows-humour" of life. "You are to live and to learn

[15] *Ibid.,* pp. 212-3.

to laugh. You are to listen to life's radio music and to reverence the spirit behind it and to laugh at the bim-bim in it." The easy division between the trivial outer world and the transcendent world of the immortals is no longer allowed Harry. Instead, he has to encounter life, reverence the spirit that manifests itself through it but cannot be identified with it, and laugh at the absurdities with which its music is cluttered and obscured. The Steppenwolf goes forward on his endless way, knowing "that all the hundred thousand pieces of life's game are in his pocket," ready to begin the game afresh, and aware that he will sample life's tortures once more and shudder again at its senselessness. One day, he may learn how to laugh, but there is no suggestion that he will ever learn to live with others or to live in the world.

The Journey to the East is a slight, transitional work written between *Steppenwolf* and *Magister Ludi,* Hesse's last great novel. In it, H. H. joins the League of the Eastern Wayfarers, in which the fellowship of seekers already hinted at in *Demian* is expanded to include the seekers of all ages who now live in a contemporaneity with each other that has nothing to do with time. The journey itself is a spiritual rather than a geographical one. It is an incessant movement of believers toward the Home of Light, a wave in "the eternal strivings of the human spirit." Though this particular expedition has arisen in the troubled and confused time since the World War, the journey to the East has been going on for centuries and includes most of the salient venturings of the human spirit.

Two different images of man are offered in this book. One is of the servant, Leo, whose unaffected, cheerful, winning qualities lead everyone to love him and cause a crisis of confidence that H. H.'s group cannot overcome when he disappears. The other is that of the disciple who joins the League in its search for "the home and youth of the soul," but then loses his way through the reason and mockery of the world. Such disciples may spend the rest of their lives looking for the League but, being blind to it, come to believe it never existed. The servant as the image of man presages Joseph Knecht, the hero of *Magister Ludi,* whose name means "servant" and who rises to the top of the hierarchy through perfect obedience. The image of the believer who falls away presages what happens to H. H., to Hermann Hesse himself.

After the dissolution of his particular group, H. H. leads for years what Leo later describes as a "dreadful, stupid, narrow, suicidal life," in short, the life of the Steppenwolf before his meeting with Hermine. He cherishes only one goal that might give his life meaning—preserving, as one of the last survivors, some record of the League's journey. After pouring out all his bitterness, his complaints, and his indictments of himself in a long letter which he sends to Leo, H. H. is summoned before the High Throne of the League, and receives judgment from the President, Leo himself, who bears his radiant office as a true servant—"conscientiously, humbly, dutifully." He realizes now—and in this lies the essential movement beyond the subjectivity of the Modern Gnostic—that he has fallen into the error of taking his own experiences and feelings as a measure of the reality of the League. He had seen the League as a failure and regarded himself "as the survivor and chronicler of a concluded and forgotten tale, while I was nothing more than a run-away, a traitor, a deserter." Like Harry Haller, he is asked to learn more about himself. But the goal of this learning is not the individuation or unification of the self, nor the perspective that would enable him to laugh at the "bim-bim" of life's music. It is ceasing to set himself as his goal and taking on himself Leo's "law of service": "He who wishes to live long must serve, but he who wishes to rule does not live long."[16]

It is this new image of man which is continued, developed, and modified in *Magister Ludi*. The chronicle of the Magister Ludi, or Master of the Bead Game, looks back from a future some centuries hence to the present, condescendingly dubbed "the Age of Digest." The game itself is a musical, mathematical interrelationship of the great cultural and spiritual achievements of mankind. As such, it represents "a select, symbolical form of the quest for perfection, a sublime alchemy, a self-approach to the inherent spirit beyond all images and pluralities—and thus to God." It is a sort of latter-day Platonic "striving towards perfection, pure being and reality." This movement from becoming to being, from the possible to the real, is called "realization." Its goal is a "superiority to coincidence" based on a knowledge of the human tragedy and acceptance of man's destiny. It is "always a courage in the face of death, a courtliness, possessing within it a sound of superhuman laughter, of immortal serenity."

In sharpest contrast to Jung's definition of vocation and to Pablo's "Magic Theater," the "call" that comes to Joseph Knecht, as to others called to join the elite scholars, is an awakening of the soul, "so that inner dreams and premonitions are suddenly replaced by a summons from without." No longer is one's destiny seen as something that has already taken place within one, reflected only by outer events. Instead, these events themselves are a reality that calls the chosen ones to their vocation. Moreover, for Joseph Knecht, this event takes the form of an image of man through *response* to which he becomes him-

[16] Hermann Hesse, *The Journey to the East,* translated by Hilda Rosner (N. Y.: The Noonday Press, 1957).

self. This image of man is embodied in the Magister Musicae, who shows Joseph, almost without words, what music really means and brings him to presentness by his own concentrated presence. The Music Master is with Joseph at almost every important stage of his career. Other significant figures also act as images of man that play a part in his becoming, some of them, like the Benedictine historian Father Jacobus, outside the Order itself.

Creativity to Hesse has always meant spirit in fruitful tension with nature, but Castalia forgoes creativity. Joseph Knecht himself later describes the theory of the Game thus: "The whole of life, physical as well as spiritual, is a dynamic phenomenon, of which the Bead Game embraces basically only the aesthetic side, and that predominantly within the image of rhythmic events." Thus, the Bead Game has the gnosis and the concern with self-perfection of the Modern Gnostic without the vitalism and the emphasis on creativity. It also has Jung's dualism between the inner destiny and the outer person, which is seen as nothing other than a persona, or mask. Through writing up in detail imaginary past "incarnations," the scholars of the Bead Game "learned to consider one's person as a mask, as the transitory raiment of an entelechy." The Bead Game turns the particular into a mere symbol of the universal, the concrete historical event into a timeless artifact of meaning.

> In the spirit of the Bead Game everything was in actual fact all-significant. . . . Each symbol and each combination of symbols led, not hither and thither, not to single examples, experiments and proofs but towards the centre, into the mystery and vitals of the world, into primaeval conscience.[17]

The whole apparatus of the game is an elaborate gnosis that has nothing to do either with the immediacy of the mystic or the dynamism of the vitalist. It may reach the "mystery" of the world, but it does not reach its vitals, or, for that matter, its "primaeval conscience," for there is nothing primeval about it.

You bead-players deal with world history, complains Father Jacobus, "as a mathematician deals with mathematics, where nothing exists except laws and formulas—where there is no reality, good or evil, no time, no yesterday or tomorrow but only an eternal flat mathematical present." To Joseph's objection that one cannot deal with history without bringing some order into it, Father Jacobus points out the difference between an ordering which removes the concrete and unique events of history and one that leaves room for them:

---

[17] Hermann Hesse, *Magister Ludi,* translated by Mervyn Savill (N. Y.: Frederick Ungar, 1949), p. 109.

Whoever elects to study history . . . should have respect for the incomprehensible truth, reality and singularity of events. . . . History presumes in advance that one is striving with something impossible and yet necessary and of the greatest importance. To deal with history means to abandon oneself to chaos and yet to retain a belief in the ordination and the meaning. It is a very serious task, young man, and perhaps also a tragic one.[18]

In this statement, Father Jacobus has struck at the very heart of the Bead Game and of the Modern Gnostic in general. "The idea of the inner unity of all intellectual human effort, the thought of universality, has its perfect expression in our illustrious Game," says Joseph Knecht when he has become Magister Ludi. Like the Journey to the East, the Bead Game means a voyage of discovery into past cultures, ages, and countries, but like it, too, it means a contemporaneity of all ages, cultures, and events, a spatialization of time, which is the very opposite of true history. History means lived time—irreversible, uncollapsible, one-directional, unique, and irreducible.

In the course of his activities as Magister Ludi, Joseph Knecht discovers something that is in no way indicated by Leo's "law of service," and that is the meaning that is to be found in direct relationship between person and person. He discovers the joy of teaching and of educating. This means the struggle "for an exact identification between person and office," and it means simultaneously "the joy that ensues from the transplanting of knowledge already gained into other minds and of seeing it take on completely new appearances and radiations." To do this, he has to struggle with the personalities of the students, to gain and practice authority and leadership, but he does it for the sake of educating and not for the sake of his own self-realization.

Joseph Knecht believes in the possibility of communication with others, and, in delicate, effective ways, he helps them. He recognizes that no complete, unbroken communion is possible, but he never ceases to strive for communication—with the Castalia-disdaining world and with his own colleagues who have turned too much away from the world. Therefore, the radical Gnostic dualism which could look on the world as unqualifiedly evil and on the Castalian Order as unqualifiedly good, is not available to him. His conflict rather is to hold the right tension between these two worlds. The image of man which Joseph Knecht has found in the Music Master and which he believes to be the heart of the Order is the search for a true serenity that can accept life's abysses instead of fleeing from them:

[18] *Ibid.*, p. 153.

To achieve this serenity is my highest and noblest aim, and also that of many others: you will find it very often among the Fathers of our Order. This serenity is neither a pose nor self-complacency but the highest knowledge and love, the acceptance of all truth, the awareness at the edge of all depths and abysses, the virtue of the Saint and the Knight. It is imperturbable and increases with age and the approach of death; it is the secret of all beauty, and the quintessence of all art.[19]

Not even in the final wisdom of Siddhartha and the serene laughter of the immortals in *Steppenwolf* has Hesse pointed so convincingly to serenity as the image of man. Yet Joseph Knecht does not grow old and die in the Order like his beloved Music Master. Instead, he leaves his high office and breaks with the Order to go out into the world in order to find "a simple natural task—a human being who has need of me." In his letter to his fellow Magisters, he points out the dangers that lie in store for Castalia from its ignoring of history and the world, but it becomes clear to him during the time in which he is preparing his departure that "the actual cause of his alienation and desire to depart . . . lay simply in the fact that an empty and idle residue of himself, of his heart and his soul, now desired its rights and wished to fulfil them." We might be led by this to think that Knecht has fallen back from the "law of service" to the Modern Gnostic's goal of "individuation," were it not for the fact that what calls him to the world is not himself but the demand and need of other persons. He desires to trade hierarchy and power for simple, direct contact, a life of immediacy which is denied to the officials of the Order. "The same stern, clear, single and direct path which had led him . . . into the Order and to the office of Magister Ludi, was now leading him out of it again. That which had been a sequence of acts of awakening had at the same time been a series of leave-takings." An "awakening," he now realizes, is "not so much a question of realizing truth"—gnosis— "but of experiencing reality and of sustaining it." And reality is not simply found within his soul or within the Order. Joseph Knecht's personal way is ultimately more important to him than the hierarchy. Yet his personal way is not the voice of the "inner man." It is the call of a reality that cannot be swallowed into his soul yet places a demand on it. "I desire that there should be hazards, difficulties and dangers to face," he says to the Head of the Order; "I am hungry for reality, for tasks and deeds, and also for privation and suffering." In the same spirit, he defends his "awakenings" not as divine manifestations or absolute truth, but as existential reality. "They are monstrously real

[19] *Ibid.*, p. 286.

in their presence and inescapability, like some violent bodily pain or surprising natural phenomenon." "A naive sentiment for the simple, the whole and the healthy," has warned him against the spirit of the Bead Game "as being a specialist and virtuoso spirit, highly cultivated and richly elaborated admittedly, but one which was severed from the whole of life and humanity and which had become an arrogant solipsism." He is not fazed, therefore, by the accusation that he is concerned about his "private, subjective experiences, personal desires, personal developments and decisions."

When Joseph Knecht leaves Castalia and goes to the home of his old school friend, Designòri, it is with the understanding that he will tutor Designòri's rebellious young son. This task is to begin in the mountains, where the son flees ahead of him and he follows, considerably wearied from a sudden change of pressure that he cannot endure— a perfect metaphor for his too sudden plunge from rigid discipline into complete freedom. In the morning, the boy and he go out to the mountain lake together, and the boy, inspired by the lake, the sun, and his new teacher, does a spontaneous dance of devotion. When he comes to himself, the embarrassed boy flings himself into the lake and challenges his teacher to race him across it. Knecht knows that he has already overtaxed his strength with the too rapid mountain journey; yet he is afraid that if he renounces this test of strength "with the cool reasoning power of the adult" he will lose forever "the promise this morning hour had set in motion." He dives into the water and drowns of a heart attack. The too sudden plunge into the world, the imitation of an ecstasy and impulse that he could not share, lead Joseph Knecht to disaster. He is denied the acting upon the world that he desired. Yet his death is not without meaning, for it follows clearly from his decision to trade the office of Magister Ludi for that of tutoring. The Modern Gnostic has turned away from the world to the higher gnosis, and then he has turned back to the world. He has gone from Samsara to Nirvana and from Nirvana to Samsara. He must go through both of these stages, it seems. But when he finishes, he is a Modern Gnostic no longer. What he once secretly thirsted for he now makes his own—"love's embrace, birth, suffering and death."

If we look now at both types of Modern Gnostic—those like Weil who emphasize a transcendent God utterly removed from creation and those like Jung and the early Hesse who transform the reality that transcends the evil world to the Self within—we arrive at the remarkable conclusion that by opposite routes they reach essentially the same image of man. Weil hardly fits Grant's definition of Gnosticism as self-knowledge in any obvious sense, yet there is an inescapable corollary between the absolute denial of self and the absolute affirmation of it. Those who cannot follow Pascal's dictum that man is neither all nor nothing are alike whether they choose self-deification or self-denial! One is tempted to characterize this Modern Gnostic image of man as a union of animal and God; subhuman and superhuman, it seems to miss the human! What stands out above all else in the Modern Gnostic is the absence of any genuine otherness. Other people always prove to be hierophants who guide the self to its path or shadow figures on which he works out his inner destiny. Impulses for "evil" may be acted out, since other people are seen as functions of one's own individuation as one is of theirs. Even the absolute self-denial of Simone Weil affirms absolutely the knowing self that does the denying.

In the Modern Gnostic, even more than in the Modern Vitalist, man is split into one part that participates in life and one that looks on. Ultimately, the integration and individuation which the Magic Theater offers Harry Haller is nothing other than a free experimentation with the self. If it removes the illusion of the persona, or mask of outer personality, it also destroys the unity of the self by dividing it into the observer and the observed, the experimenter and that which is experimented upon! Even apart from the fact that this process fails to take seriously the independent otherness of the persons with whom one lives, it cannot lead to inner wholeness. At best, it can lead to a Modern Gnostic superman who does not take seriously the social roles that he plays in the world. The seeming spontaneity and freedom of this "game of life" is deceptive. The spontaneity that comes when the whole person responds freely, without concern for the by-products —the effects on the self—is entirely wanting here. Instead, there is an arbitrariness that puts the self forward even where it claims to show up the illusion of the self.

VII

PSYCHOLOGICAL MAN

11

SIGMUND FREUD

I<small>N HIS</small> brilliant study of Freud, the French philosopher Paul Ricoeur suggests that Freud is to be understood as a combination of two elements, force and meaning. Freud's interpretation of dreams and the other symbols of the unconscious is a deciphering of what has already entered into the realm of meaning through the meeting of libidinal energy and symbolic signification. By this same token, Freud represents a synthesis of two antithetical traditions, mechanism and rationalism, on the one hand, and romanticism and mysticism, on the other.[1]

Freud does indeed represent a golden mean between the behaviorists, who try to deal with psychology in purely mechanistic terms, and a psychologist like Jung, who converts everything into meaning. The behaviorists and operationalists, even when they correct their isolated psychological monads in favor of dyadic relations, are barred from an image of man in the full sense of the term by their resolutely external position in relation to their subject. Jung's opposite emphasis on meaning seen from within tends to lead him toward an all-encompassing gnosis.

Freud is the founder of psychoanalysis and the man who more than any other has made the image of Psychological Man into a "live option" for contemporary man. According to Philip Rieff, Freud has given us a new image of man. According to Erich Fromm, he has simply taken over the nineteenth-century economic image of man and recast it in psychological terms. Both statements are true. Freud has

[1] Paul Ricoeur's Terry Lectures on Freud will be published by Yale University Press in 1966.

taken seventeenth-century mechanism, eighteenth-century rationalism, nineteenth-century economics and biology, ancient Greek myths, an emergent philosophy of the unconscious,[2] and a touch of mysticism and forged them into a new and powerful image of man that has cast its shadow on our age as no other. Freud's "discovery of unconscious processes and of the dynamic nature of character traits," writes Erich Fromm, "is a unique contribution to the science of man which has altered the picture of man for all time to come."

It is only the reforging that Freud claims to be new, not the basic *Weltanschauung*, or world view, which he explicitly identifies as that of Science. He sees his own contribution as applying Science to the study of the human mind. By Science, Freud means, of course, an earlier, mechanistic philosophy of science which today's physicist and biologist would find unrecognizable. In the "Philosophy of Life" chapter of his *New Introductory Lectures,* Freud declares that there can be no way of regarding man other than the scientific:

> For the spirit and the mind of man is a subject of investigation in exactly the same way as any nonhuman entity. The contribution of the science of psychoanalysis consists precisely in having extended research to the region of the mind. Any other . . . view of the mind has a purely emotional basis.[3]

Freud thereby excludes from his image of man the concrete and unique human person who does not fit into scientific categories. He even excludes the central question of philosophical anthropology, the problem of what man is, of wherein lies man's uniqueness in comparison with all other animals. Freud does not deny that other views of the mind and of its relation to man might exist as an emotional need on the part of mankind, but he insists that we cannot admit them to real knowledge in any sense of the term.

> Science does well to distinguish carefully between illusion, the result of emotional demands of that kind, and knowledge. It is inadmissible to declare that science is one field of intellectual activity, and religion

2 Freud himself describes his relation to the numerous philosophies of the unconscious in the following, somewhat oversimplified, fashion: "It is true that philosophy has repeatedly dealt with the problem of the unconscious, but, with few exceptions, philosophers have taken up one or the other of the two following positions. Either their unconscious has been something mystical, something intangible and undemonstrable, whose relation to the mind has remained obscure, or they have identified the mental with the conscious and have proceeded to infer from this definition that that which is unconscious cannot be mental or a subject for psychology." *Totem and Taboo & Other Works* (*The Complete Psychological Works of Sigmund Freud,* Vol. XIII, translated under the editorship of James Strachey, Anna Freud, *et al.;* London: The Hogarth Press & The Institute of Psycho-Analysis, 1955), p. 178.
3 Sigmund Freud, *New Introductory Lectures on Psycho-Analysis,* translated by W. J. H. Sprott (N. Y.: W. W. Norton & Co., 1933), pp. 217-9.

and philosophy another and . . . that they all have an equal claim to truth. . . . Scientific research looks on the whole field of human activity as its own and must adopt an uncompromisingly critical attitude toward any other power that seeks to usurp any part of its province.[4]

That man has a soul, or psyche, belongs to the age-old wisdom of mankind. What is new about Psychological Man is that the psyche is now converted into the more impersonal "mind," that its main determinants are seen as residing in an impersonal and largely repressed "unconscious" mind, and that man, thus relatively depersonalized, is seen as existing, in the real sense of the term, not in his relation to the environment or to other people or to the world, but in his mind. Thus, Psychological Man usually means, to a greater or lesser extent, psychologism—the referring of both reality and value to the psyche. Knowing, of course, remains with the conscious mind, and for Freud, in greater measure than for Jung, value too lies in the conscious, or rather in the bringing of the unconscious into the conscious. "Where id was ego shall be," reads Freud's famous motto, and it is in Freud's book, The Ego and the Id, that we get perhaps his most concentrated presentation of his image of man, the image of man that he presupposes and that which he proclaims.

Freud distinguishes between two kinds of unconscious, one of which is capable of becoming conscious, such as something we are not thinking of but can think of if we wish to, and another which cannot become conscious, because it is repressed by the censor as too dangerous for the ego. The former Freud calls the "preconscious," the latter the "unconscious" proper. Although repressed, the unconscious is still the basic, determining force. Following Georg Groddeck's Book of the It, Freud holds that the ego is essentially passive, that we are "lived" by unknown and uncontrollable forces. Freud also follows Groddeck in naming these forces "the It," Latinized in the English translation into "the id." "The ego constantly carries into action the wishes of the id as if they were its own." This is as much as to say that the ego rationalizes the desires of the id. "The ego represents what we call reason and sanity, in contrast to the id which contains the passions." So far from seeing man as an essentially rational animal, as the ancient Greeks did, Freud holds that the ego only comes into existence as a splitting off from the id, resulting from identifications with the parents in the first years of life. The character of the ego, to Freud, is nothing other than a precipitate of abandoned object-choices. The word "object" here is particularly appropriate, for Freud does not see the cathexis as an essential relation with another person, but as an instinctual relation with oneself through the other person. It is like a closed circuit in which the other person is the intermediate transmitter, but never really the initiator or receiver.

By a similar process, the ego-ideal, or "super-ego," is developed. The ego-ideal originates to begin with in a direct and immediate identification with the father. The father becomes the image of man, both in the sense of what it means to be a man, a male, and also in the super-ego that governs the character ideals. The super-ego not only says, "You *ought to be* like your father in these and these ways," but also "You *must not be* like him in these other ways which are his prerogative." In his "Letter to His Father," Franz Kafka expressed this exactly by picturing his father as covering most of the map and leaving him only unimportant territories, not including, above all, marriage and the family, which would make him—unthinkable!—his father's equal.

Freud's concept of the super-ego has an especial significance for the image of man insofar as this includes a sense of authentic direction. Freud sets out to show, on the one hand, that the origin of all ego-ideals is in a repression of the Oedipus complex that is at the same time its heir. On the other hand, Freud rejects as unjust the accusation that psychoanalysis ignores "the higher, moral, spiritual side of human nature." Freud asserts, on the contrary, "that the ego-ideal answers in every way to what is expected of the higher nature of man." As "a substitute for the longing for the father, it contains the germ from which all religions have evolved" and the sense of worthlessness with which the believer judges himself. Similarly, social feelings rest on the basis of a common ego-ideal with the result that "the tension between the demands of conscience and the actual attainments of the ego is experienced as a sense of guilt." The difficulty here is that in explaining the origin of the super-ego, Freud also claims to depict its true nature. In so doing, he reduces all sense of "ought" to the "is," all sense of the normative to something purely descriptive, all sense of authentic direction freely chosen to value-free psychological necessity.

The Freudian super-ego cannot have room for all the highest of mankind, since it is precisely the highest—the intrinsic value of the ideal—that Freud has removed from it. Thus, the super-ego can not be equated with our image of man—first, because it is pure ideal, rather than the tension between what man is and what he ought to be, and, second, because it eliminates the possibility of real value decision, of the distinction between what is more and less authentic for oneself. Man, to Nietzsche, is the valuing animal, and without valuing the nut of existence is hollow. To Freud, he is the animal who *thinks* that he values, but whose valuations are really the product of psychological forces of which he is unaware. Freud even goes so far as to see the experiences of successive individuals of many generations as transformed into "experiences of the id, the impress of which is preserved by inheritance." Like Jung's collective unconscious, Freud's hereditary id stores up "vestiges of existences led by countless former egos," and he even speculates that "when the ego forms its super-ego out of the id, it may perhaps only be reviving images of egos that have passed away and be securing them a resurrection." Thus, Freud's super-ego is not only subject to the impersonal id and, as such, "to a great extent unconscious and inaccessible to the ego"; it is also not even truly individual. For Freud, as for Jung, the base of value and valuation is removed from the whole, conscious person, to impersonal, collective forces contained within the unconscious.[5]

Conscience, to Freud, is the tension between the ego and the ego-ideal. Although the super-ego condemns and criticizes the ego, a great part of the sense of guilt remains unconscious, "because the origin of conscience is closely connected with the Oedipus complex which belongs to the unconscious." This may have the effect of leading a person to commit a crime in order to find relief from a powerful but unconscious sense of guilt by fastening it on to something real and immediate. A Freudian interpretation of Dostoyevsky's *Crime and Punishment* would certainly see Raskolnikov in this light. This means that not only may there be neurotic and irrational guilt—and Freud's illumination of this area is certainly one of his greatest contributions to our contemporary image of man—but also that the super-ego as such is allied with the passions of the id rather than with the reason of the ego. It was the custom in earlier ages, especially the eighteenth and nineteenth centuries of enlightenment and progress, to identify the moral and the rational. In stark contrast, Freud unmasks the moral as containing within itself a large component of destructiveness and irrational sadism. In melancholia, for example, it is "a pure culture of the death-instinct" that holds sway. The ego struggles against the tendencies of the id, but the super-ego behaves as if the ego were responsible for these impulses and chastises it.

[5] At the end of *Totem and Taboo*, Freud posits a collective unconscious in an even more explicit fashion to explain the hereditary guilt that could enable the Oedipus complex (in this case acted out by the clan of sons who murder the father and establish their fraternal clan rules and ceremonies in simultaneous remorse and triumph) to become the foundation of all civilization and culture: "I have taken as the basis of my whole position the existence of a collective mind, in which mental processes occur just as they do in the mind of an individual. In particular, I have supposed that the sense of guilt for an action has persisted for many thousands of years and has remained operative in generations which can have had no knowledge of that action." *Op. cit.*, pp. 157–8.

"From the point of view of morality, the control and restriction of instinct, it may be said of the id that it is totally nonmoral, of the ego that it strives to be moral, and of the super-ego that it can be hyper-moral and then becomes as ruthless as only the id can be." This means that the id is displaced to the super-ego so that "the more a man controls his aggressiveness, the more intense become the aggressive tendencies of his ego-ideal against his ego." From this Freud concludes that when people seem to check their aggressiveness because of the standard set up by the ego-ideal, it is really the check on aggressiveness which produces the high standards. Not only does he unmask the id lurking behind seeming humaneness, but he fixes the *real* meaning of religion at this point too: "Even ordinary normal morality has a harshly restraining, cruelly prohibiting quality. It is from this, indeed, that the conception arises of an inexorable higher being who metes out punishment." The upshot of all this is that the super-ego stands in no moral relation to the ego, no matter how much it pretends to. "What lies hidden behind the ego's dread of the super-ego, its fear of conscience is the original threat of castration, the kernel round which the subsequent fear of conscience has gathered." Freud seems to speak metaphorically here, rather than literally, but in either case the old notion of conscience as a voice that calls one to what is intrinsically right in one's situation is replaced by conscience as the brute force exercised by the powerful over the powerless, now introverted within the psyche itself.

If the super-ego, or ego-ideal, is not the image of man, can we perhaps turn to the ego and find the image of man in its task of integrating id and super-ego? At first, it would seem so, and later Neo-Freudians, such as Anna Freud and Eric Erickson, have developed an ego psychology which makes the strengthening of the ego its goal and identifies this goal with the search for identity. For Freud, too, the task of psychoanalysis is helping the ego in its task of mastering the id. He sees the ego as the reality-tester which "arranges the processes of the mind in a temporal order and interposes the processes of thinking in such a way as to secure a postponement of motor discharges and control the avenues to motility." But this last office, to Freud, is more a question of form than of fact. For the ego is actually "a poor creature owing service to three masters and consequently menaced by three several dangers: from the external world, from the libido of the id, and from the severity of the super-ego." The ego is not only the ally of the id, which it pretends to control; "it is also a submissive slave who courts the love of his master."

Whenever possible, it tries to remain on good terms with the id; it draws the veil of its preconscious rationalizations over the id's unconscious demands; it pretends that the id is showing obedience to the mandates of reality, even when in fact it is remaining obdurate and immovable; it throws a disguise over the id's conflicts with reality and, if possible, over its conflicts with the super-ego too. Its position midway between the id and reality tempts it only too often to become sycophantic, opportunist and false, like a politician who sees the truth but wants to keep his place in popular favour.[6]

What are we to say, then, about Freud's tripartite structure of id, ego, and super-ego as an image of man? First, that it is of enormous importance for our contemporary image of man, because it is the way in which many of us have come to look on man. Second, that it serves as a very necessary protection against turning the image of man into an ideal or neglecting the real tensions, anxieties, and inner conflicts which must be taken into account by any image of man that is to be meaningful and helpful. But, third, that by excluding any intrinsic values, it has shorn off an indispensable dimension of the image of man, namely, that which seeks to find a true personal, a truly human direction. In fact, Freud sees no possibility of free response to an image of man and none of real choice *as a person* of the way forward. His very definition of morality as "the control and restriction of instinct" shows that he rules out the possibility of any personal wholeness into which the passions might enter as a full partner, accepting form and direction, but not needing to be curtailed, repressed, limited, and constrained.

Freud goes from the divided, sick man that he sees before him—a type of man that is very typical of our age—to a definition of human nature as such. In his description of what he sees, Freud is indeed realistic and "scientific," if one may use the latter term for a form of knowledge which does not admit of laboratory conditions. In extrapolating from what his patient is to what man is, he is neither. One may question, in fact, the very conception of "human nature" which is so important for Freud that, like the social theoreticians of the seventeenth and eighteenth centuries, he has to project it backward to primitive man. Man is not given to us in the universal, outside-of-history, social context, and the particularity of given situations and persons. Freud's picture of man as id, ego, and super-ego is a *construct* of man rather than an *image* of man. It is a synthetic combination of analytical subcategories which systematically excludes from its view the wholeness and uniqueness of the person. What I mean by "person"

[6] Sigmund Freud, *The Ego and the Id*, authorized translation by Joan Riviere (*The International Psycho-Analytical Library*, edited by Ernest Jones, No. 12, 4th ed.; London: The Hogarth Press and The Institute of Psychoanalysis, 1947), p. 83.

here is not the individual seen from the outside, as Freud sees him, but the actually existing person, seen from within, who knows himself, to some extent, as an "I" and not as an "it." Freud has an "ego," but he has no true "I," no actual subject, for as soon as one tries to make the "I" into an object, it ceases to be "I." This Freud never seems to notice, perhaps because he believes that the ego is "lived" by impersonal, instinctual passion. Id, ego, and super-ego are alike objects to Freud. Yet objects do not exist without a knowing subject—and that subject is Freud himself! Freud's construct of man displaces the center of human existence from the person into separate factors which enter into but cannot in themselves constitute man's wholeness.

Freud was not so poor a scientist as to fasten on any one theory and leave it at that. On the contrary, he constantly changed and grew as new evidence confronted him. One of the most important of these developments for his image of man is his view of "instincts." Freud's tendency toward a biological and even mechanistic image of man made him take over somewhat uncritically the concept of "instinct." Instinct, like human nature, is not a scientifically knowable reality. It is at best a hypothesis and at worst an unexamined postulate. As a result, in giving man over to the realm of "instinct," Freud deepened the split between man the knower and man the object of knowledge without in fact remaining on the scientific ground he so much coveted. He took over the view of the "pleasure principle" as dominating mental processes, and, like a latter-day Bentham, worked out the libidinal economy on strictly quantitative lines.

Yet there are two ways in which Freud used the notion of instinct that prevent his image of man from being as limiting as it may at first appear. The first of these is the mythical, which he adopted quite consciously and, as it were, hand in hand with the biological. However unfaithful he may have been to the original Oedipus myth, that he chose to express his central concept in mythical rather than in scientific terms shows a desire to grasp what man is in broader and less rigidly definable images than was customary in the science of his day. The same is true of his taking over the classical name, "eros," for the libidinal instinct, which he saw in his earlier writings as the primary psychological determinant.

The second way in which Freud went beyond the narrowly scientific was his development of the notion of a second instinct alongside that of eros, namely "thanatos," or the death instinct. Originally Freud held that hostility was a secondary principle, derived from the frustration of libidinal passion. His studies in the biological and psychological field of "repetition," and his examination of cases of sadism and of "shell shock," or hysterical paralysis, led him to postulate a destructive, death-desiring impulse as equally basic to that of love. This concept develops from a somewhat more limited biological and psychological notion in *Beyond the Pleasure Principle* to a general theory of human nature in *Civilization and Its Discontents*. On the basis of this principle, Freud could argue against Einstein that war is inevitable, the hope for lasting peace illusory.

Although Freud's theory of the death instinct has not decisively entered into Freudian psychoanalysis, and still less into popular Freudianism, it represents, as set forth in *Civilization and Its Discontents*, Freud's most far-reaching and significant image of man. Here, he sees man not in himself but in his relation to "culture"—"the sum of the achievements and institutions which differentiate our lives from those of our animal forebears." Culture serves the double purpose "of protecting humanity against nature and of regulating the relations of human beings among themselves." The decisive step toward civilization comes when the power of a united number is substituted for the power of a single man. Like the social-contract theory of Plato's Adeimantus and of Hobbes, this means that members of the community restrict their possibilities of gratification. The community now takes on a moral sanction, and its united strength is opposed as "Right" against the strength of any individual, which is condemned as "brute force."

This united strength is never more than a social contract, however. It cannot convert man into a cell in an organic whole, like the ant or the bee. Man will always defend his claim to individual freedom against the will of the multitude, says Freud, and this makes central the task of finding a satisfying solution between individual claims and those of the civilized community. "It is one of the problems of man's fate whether this solution can be arrived at in some particular form of culture or whether the conflict will prove irreconcilable." Freud seems to take the latter view—not only because of the frustrations of the id attendant upon civilization, but also, as we shall see, because of the death instinct. Instinct need not be gratified, it may be sublimated, and it is this sublimation "that makes it possible for . . . scientific, artistic, ideological activities, to play such an important part in civilized life." But sublimation, though it is not so harmful to the individual as repression, is paid for at a price: "It is impossible to ignore the extent to which civilization is built up on renunciation of instinctual gratifications, the degree to which the existence of civilization presupposes the non-gratification . . . of powerful instinctual urgencies."

An example of the price paid by sublimation is what happens to genital love when it is sublimated. Genital love is man's greatest gratification, says Freud, but through it "he becomes to a very dangerous degree dependent on a part of the outer world, namely, on his chosen love-object, and this exposes him to most painful sufferings if he is rejected by it or loses it through death or defection." Freud wryly observes that while the wise men of all ages warn against sex for just this reason, for most people it retains its attraction. Yet, some people protect themselves by turning away from the sexual aim, and with it the uncertainties and disappointments of genital love, to a general love of all mankind. The "unchangeable, undeviating, tender attitude" which results "has little superficial likeness to the stormy vicissitudes of genital love," but it is nevertheless derived from it. With a bold stroke, Freud takes Saint Francis of Assisi—perhaps the most famous image of humble love in Western civilization—as his prime example of "using love to produce an inner feeling of happiness." Freud scolds Saint Francis because his love was indiscriminate, for "not all men are worthy of love." Thus, Saint Francis is not an image of man, after all, because the love of others he seems to represent is neither possible nor desirable!

Freud extends this attack to "love thy neighbor as thyself." I cannot love my neighbor as myself, he says, for he is not worthy of my love. Who then is? Only the man who "is so like me in important respects that I can love myself in him" or he who "is so much more perfect than I that I can love my ideal of myself in him" or "the son of my friend, since the pain my friend would feel if anything untoward happened to him would be my pain." In other words, to be worthy of love, the other must be a function of myself. Freud *deduces* the true motive of Saint Francis' love from his general theory of sex and sublimation. He is unconcerned with the actual life of the man whose love of Brother Sun, Sister Water, Brother Fire, and Brother Wolf has been for men through the centuries an image of the possibility of loving others without referring them in the first instance to oneself. In the place of Saint Francis, Freud offers us a love which centers entirely around the self and yet is held up for us as mature "object love" as opposed to Francis' immature narcissism!

So far, Freud's discussion of love brings in only the one instinct, eros. But now he moves decisively to the death instinct, which he sees as operating not only to bring the individual organism to its own death, but also to destroy others. On the basis of this second instinct, and of his own view of man, he presents a devastating image of man which no man who lives in the world today can afford to ignore:

> Not merely is this stranger on the whole not worthy of love, but, to be honest, I must confess he has more claim to my hostility, even to my hatred. He does not seem to have the least trace of love for me,

does not show me the slightest consideration. If it will do him any good, he has no hesitation in injuring me, never even asking himself whether the amount of advantage he gains by it bears any proportion to the amount of wrong done to me. What is more, he does not even need to get an advantage from it; if he can merely get a little pleasure out of it, he thinks nothing of jeering at me, insulting me, slandering me, showing his power over me; and the more secure he feels himself, or the more helpless I am, with so much more certainty can I expect this behaviour from him towards me. . . .

The bit of truth behind all this—one so eagerly denied—is that men are not gentle, friendly creatures wishing for love, who simply defend themselves if they are attacked, but that *a powerful measure of desire for aggression has to be reckoned as a part of their instinctual endowment.* The result is that their neighbour is to them not only a possible helper or sexual object, but also a temptation to them to gratify their aggressiveness on him, to exploit his capacity for work without recompense, to use him sexually without his consent, to seize his possessions, to humiliate him, to cause him pain, to torture and to kill him.[7]

Homo homini lupus, Freud concludes: Man is a wolf to man. "Who has the courage to dispute it in the face of all the evidence in his own life and in history?"

Who indeed? In the years since Freud's death in 1939 there has been as much new evidence of "man's inhumanity to man" as in the whole of recorded history up till that time: the Nazi extermination of six million Jews and a million gypsies, the bombing of German cities, the atomic destruction of Hiroshima and Nagasaki, the slave-labor camps of the Soviet Union, the wars and uprisings and systematic exterminations. The view of man as an essentially good, rational creature who will gladly co-operate with others in his own self-interest is no longer a live option. Freud had the prescience and the courage to state this long before Golding's *Lord of the Flies* became the favorite mirror of sophisticated teen-agers and of their shocked but unprotesting parents. Such evidence cannot be excluded from any serious contemporary image of man.

It is evidence, nonetheless, of how man *acts* and not of what man *is.* Like the myths that Freud uses, it is a plausible, perhaps even a convincing hypothesis, but one that can never be scientifically verified. Since we cannot know either instinct or human nature outside a historical context, we cannot categorically assert, as Freud has, that the desire for aggression is a part of man's instinctual nature. It would

[7] Sigmund Freud, *Civilization and Its Discontents,* translated by Joan Riviere (N. Y.: Doubleday Anchor Books, 1958), pp. 59–61; italics added.

be equally possible to say with Erich Fromm that the destructiveness which man vents on other men is the product of an authoritarian character structure which is, in turn, the product of one or another type of authoritarian society. What is *not* possible is to ignore the enormous amount of hostility and destructiveness that men have displayed toward one another in history and in our own day. Rousseau held that man is by nature good and that it is only civilization that makes him bad. Freud, with much greater realism, recognizes that civilization is inseparable from man. In this sense, it is meaningless to ask what man is "by nature," since we only know him as a social and civilized being. For the same reason, it is not necessary or even possible to accept Freud's view of "human nature" at face value. But it *is* necessary to confront his view of man with utter seriousness, to recognize the presumption in its favor, unprovable though it is, and to take it into our own, hopefully larger, image of man.

Freud's view of "civilization and its discontents" leads him to the curious position of making moral judgments against the super-ego, which he has defined as the sole source of moral judgments. "In commanding and prohibiting with such severity," he complains, "it troubles too little about the happiness of the ego, and it fails to take into account sufficiently the difficulties in the way of obeying it—the strength of instinctual cravings in the id and the hardships of external environment." As a result, Freud sees the therapist as "obliged to do battle with the super-ego and work to moderate its demands." From his moral judgment of the individual super-ego, Freud turns to a moral judgment of the ethical standards of the cultural super-ego, the norms of society. It, too, enjoins a moral "ought" which cannot possibly be fulfilled. It presumes unlimited power of the ego over the id such as does not exist even in normal people. This exorbitant demand produces revolt or neurosis or makes individuals unhappy.

Freud has reduced both conscience and morality to their origins in the fear of castration and the need of the individual to repress instinctual gratification for the sake of protection against nature and other men. On what ground, then, does he make a moral judgment against the conscience and the ethical demands of the culture? He must presuppose another set of values, which are not merely extrinsic products of psychological and cultural determinants, but are intrinsic values, good in themselves. The word "happiness," which Freud frequently uses, is the only clue to what this other set of values is. "It is very far from my intention to express any opinion concerning the value of human civilization," Freud writes. He ascribes to himself a complete impartiality as to the question of whether civilization is worth the effort, an impartiality which he holds to be all the easier to him "since I know very little about these things." I "am sure only of one thing," he adds—with a definiteness which gives the lie to his humility—"that the judgements of value made by mankind are immediately determined by their desires for happiness." In making values a product of the desire for happiness, Freud has reduced all that seems to be of value in itself to a mere instrument for reaching ends of self-gratification. This is all the more the case since Freud tends to regard happiness not as the well-being of the whole person, like Aristotle's *eudaimonia*, but as the maximizing of pleasure and the minimizing of pain. Nonetheless, Freud's touching plea for the individual against the claims of his own super-ego and that of the culture shows that he does not, in the end, look on man merely from without, as a psychological mechanism, but also from within as a being with some value of his own, and therefore with some claim to happiness.

The reality of unconscious compulsion makes it impossible to assert the existence of full, conscious freedom. But it is equally impossible to reduce man to a purely deterministic system. The human reality—of the well man as well as of the ill—is a complex intermixture of personal freedom and psychological compulsion, a paradoxical phenomenon that can be understood only from within.[8] In Freud's image of man, there is no place for freedom and spontaneity—with one curious, yet all-important exception. However Freud may explain it theoretically, the goal of psychoanalysis is the liberation of the indi-

[8] For this reason, as I have stated in *Problematic Rebel*, Dostoyevsky throws more light on this phenomenon than Freud: "The problem of the relation of personal freedom to psychological compulsion cannot be solved by the attempt to reduce man to a bundle of instinctual drives, unconscious complexes, the need for security or any other single factor. . . . Motivation is inextricably bound up with the wholeness of the person, with his direction of movement, with his struggles to authenticate himself. This wholeness of the person in his dynamic interrelation with other persons Dostoievsky guards as no psychoanalytic theory ever has. In Dostoievsky we never see a metaphysical freedom or free will separate from conditioning factors; rather, we see the free will shining through and refracted by the sickness which shapes and exasperates so many of Dostoievsky's characters. . . . No general theory of psychogenesis and no general knowledge of a person will tell us in advance what will be his actual mixture of spontaneity and compulsion in any particular situation. Hence Dostoievsky's contribution to the problematic of modern man is in this respect superior to Freud's psychogenic determinism." (See Maurice Friedman, *Problematic Rebel*, op. cit., pp. 255–7.)

Dostoyevsky is interested in mental illness, but not in psychogenesis. Freud, in contrast, especially in his early thought, is absorbed with the question of origins and tends to make this all-important. "Now for the first time," writes Freud, "psycho-analysis enables us to construct a 'psychography' of a personality." It is not the business of psychoanalysis to undertake such criticism itself, Freud cautions, since "the fact that a theory is psychologically determined does not in the least invalidate its scientific truth." But it does, it seems, invalidate every other type of truth if we are to go by *The Future of an Illusion* and Freud's other writings on religion and morality.

vidual from past fixations and traumas so that he may be free to respond to and live with the reality of the present.

There is an important theoretical grounding for this exception
worked out in the course of Freud's later thought. It rests, first of all,
on the fact that, despite his reduction of conscience to the fear of
castration, the constructs of id, super-ego, and ego are not regarded
by Freud as psychogenic explanations, but as structures of the mind
that is already developed. It rests, secondly, on the fact that the ego
is the reality-tester. In its function of helping the individual to adjust
to reality and to modify or compromise between the demands of
super-ego and id, it already implies the existence of real freedom. A
corollary of this fact is Freud's tendency to regard consciousness itself as freedom, especially when it succeeds in recognizing repressed
material and integrating it into the ego. The goal of Freudian psychoanalysis—"Where id was ego shall be"—itself describes a movement
from psychological determinism to personal freedom. Finally, the
movement from psychogenic determinism to freedom may be seen in
the development of the "reality principle" from a utilitarian extension
of the "pleasure principle" in Freud's early thought to an independent
arbiter of reality in *The Ego and the Id* and to an acceptance of one's
own death and of the tragic limitations of human existence in *Civilization and Its Discontents*.[9]

Freud's recognition of the debt that each of us owes to nature—
the inescapable reality of one's personal death—leads him to a realistic
limitation of the tendency of the infantile and narcissistic ego to regard itself as if it were omnipotent and immortal. Similarly, his understanding of the "death instinct" leads him to a realistic limitation of
the tendency of civilizations to regard their progress and achievement
as capable of indefinite extension. Freud's death instinct recognizes
the tragic limitations of human existence as few psychoanalytic theories have done. The Greek tragic hero, I have written, "finds his
place again and again through discovering his potentialities *and*
his fateful limitations. These two together—man's potentialities and his
limits—constitute the Greek tragic vision."[10] In contrast to Erich
Fromm's typically modern, one-sided emphasis on self-realization,
Freud captures something of the Greek tragic vision. Yet he does so
without any possibility of the belief in an order such as the Greek
moira with which man can reconcile himself and through which he
can find meaning. In this respect, he is not the Modern Promethean

9 I am indebted for this last insight to the penetrating seminar of Paul Ricoeur
on "The Reality and the Pleasure Principle in Freud" given for The Council on
Existential Psychology & Psychiatry, October 31–November 1, 1964.
10 Maurice Friedman, *Problematic Rebel, op. cit.*, p. 28; italics added.

who defies order or the ancient Oedipus who accepts it, but the Modern Exile who understands man's alienation as man and views it as his inescapable condition.

To Freud, more than to any other single man, go the credit and the blame for ushering in the age of the Psychological Man. On the credit side are the deeper insights into human passions and conflicts, into the complex inner divisions and internecine strife of man in general and of modern, civilized man in particular. Also on the credit side is that moral concern which makes Freud desire to limit the harsh reign of the super-ego in favor of the more moderate combination of repressions and instinctual satisfactions which a liberated and mature ego can afford. Freud's juxtaposition of the reality and pleasure principles and later of the love instinct and the death instinct afford him a delicately balanced realism which accepts the tragic limitations of life yet believes in the melioristic possibilities afforded by reason when it operates in psychoanalysis as a neutral scientific instrument of inquiry.

On the debit side of the ledger must be entered that overwhelming and overweening individualism which makes Freud reduce the social relationships between men to secondary products of individual, instinctual gratifications. Even more serious for the image of man is that psychologism which translates the meaning of human existence into internal, psychic categories and dimensions. Along with this goes that unmasking which reduces all conscious motivations to unconscious determinants. Freud thereby removes the intrinsic meaning of any "ought" that might guide an individual toward authentic personal existence.

VIII

THE
MODERN PRAGMATIST

12

WILLIAM JAMES, JOHN DEWEY, GEORGE HERBERT MEAD, AND HARRY STACK SULLIVAN

THOUGH pragmatism is an outgrowth of British empiricism, in its emphasis on judging both truth and value by what is effective in a given situation it is indigenous to America. The true philosophical originator of pragmatism is Charles Peirce, but it is William James who popularized it and who made it into a "live option" as a contemporary image of man. James points out in "The Sentiment of Rationality" that while some matters, such as the future movements of the stars and the facts of past history, are completely determined, others are influenced by our personal contribution, including a subjective energy which depends on faith in the result. From this, he derives the notion that the verification of the view that the world has a moral character depends on the fruit of those actions resulting from that theory, on whether these harmonize with and amplify it so that one does not have to alter the essential formulation. This verification does not depend on a single philosopher, but on the experience of the entire human race. "All the evidence will not be 'in' till the final integration of things, when the last man has had his say." One must act, and one must act "as if" the world is moral; that action is itself part of a verification which will never be completed. This leaves us with the problem of whether our moral faith becomes true through our action, i.e., proves itself workable in harmony with the practical effects, or whether we must act "as if" it is true, disregarding practical effects—which we will never be in a position to judge—so long as we have the subjective conviction that our moral faith is true.

In "The Moral Philosopher and the Moral Life," James attacks the notion of an a priori *ought* that exists in some Platonic world of ideas in favor of the position that claim and obligation are coextensive. *"Without a claim actually made by some concrete person there can be no obligation, . . . there is some obligation wherever there is a claim."* Desires are valid because they exist, imperative to the extent of their amount. The only force of appeal is our own heart's responsiveness to the claim, says James, which is tantamount to saying that there is a claim, but that claim has no claim unless we acknowledge it in our subjectivity. James says that *"the essence of good is simply to satisfy demand"*; yet, he also says that "the feeling of the inward dignity of certain spiritual attitudes, as peace, serenity, simplicity, veracity; and of the essential vulgarity of others, as querulousness, anxiety, egoistic fussiness, etc.—are quite inexplicable except by an innate preference of the more ideal attitude for its own pure sake." If the "demand" should arise, then, because we *feel* something good, as the latter sentence suggests, then we have a logical circle from which it is difficult to escape. It is this circle and the dependence on verification through consequences that one can know only *after* one has acted which raise the most serious questions concerning the concrete meaning of pragmatism.

If "every real dilemma is in literal strictness a unique situation . . . a universe without a precedent, and for which no adequate previous rule exists," then it will not help us much in responding to the present situation to know the consequences of past ones. James recognizes this himself, but he seems content to settle for knowledge after the fact—"the cries of the wounded"—without much concern for the problem of the man who must make a moral decision in the present:

> He knows that he must vote always for the richer universe, for the good which seems most organizable, most fit to enter into complex combinations, most apt to be a member of a more inclusive whole. But which particular universe this is he cannot know for certain in advance; he only knows that if he makes a bad mistake the cries of the wounded will soon inform him of the fact.[1]

Will he be able to heal or comfort the wounded by explaining that he now realizes that he has made a "bad mistake"? A liberal rabbi once preached a sermon in which he raised the question of how the Israelites could know who was right—the prophet Jeremiah, who predicted that they would be taken to exile in Babylon, or the competing prophet who assured them of safety and security? The answer that he gave was that one could judge by history, by results. That is all well

[1] William James, *Essays in Pragmatism*, edited with an introduction by Alburey Castell (N. Y.: Hafner Publishing Co., 1949), p. 83.

and good for us who look back on the event. But how could it help those who had to make a fateful choice in the present!

William James' answer to this question would be that they had to decide and act whether they could know the consequences or not. His classic formulation of this principle in "The Will To Believe" is that there are certain options which are *live, forced, momentous,* which we cannot sit out. These must be decided by our passional natures, and even a decision not to decide and to leave the question "open," "is itself a *passional decision . . . attended with the same risk of losing the truth.*" Even if we should agree that moral choices are live, forced, momentous options that we cannot postpone or expect science to decide for us, it does not follow that we shall be *able* to decide that one thing or another is moral. The problem of the bases of ethical decisions is no less acute for James' having removed them, like Pascal, to the heart.

In his conclusion to *Varieties of Religious Experience,* James writes, "God is real since He produces real effects." We must distinguish between two quite different kinds of effects, however, one which is real and one which is not. The saints, mystics, converts, and fundamentalists whom James studied, all wholeheartedly believed in a God Who was something more than their own unconscious, and this belief transformed and energized their lives. James and his readers, on the other hand, wish to partake of the good results by acting *as if* they, too, believed. Such a "belief" can never be wholehearted, since one part of one knows that one is acting *as if.* One does not act spontaneously, for the sake of what one believes, but with calculation in hopes of attaining *élan vital,* peace of mind, or "successful living." Precisely through this double-mindedness, the by-products of the truly religious life (not all of which are happy ones) are absent. As Jesus remarked, "if thy eye be single, thy whole body is full of light." If it be double, the effect is darkness! One may respect the witness of the religious man, but "a will to believe" is a contradiction in itself. It is autosuggestion, hypocrisy, or magic, but it is not religious reality.

The true is the expedient in our way of thinking, says James, as the right is the expedient in our way of behaving. He sees this expediency as corrected by further experience, but he does not thereby solve the problem of having reduced the true and the good to the purely instrumental. We must still ask the question, "Instrumental to what?" To this question, James seems to have no answer except a vague vitalism of the "richer" and "the fuller" which we cannot even know we will attain. Ideas are true insofar as they help us get into satisfactory relation with other parts of our experience, says James, following Dewey's instrumentalism. But he has no suggestion as to what makes a relation "satisfactory." New truth is a go-between which smooths over transitions, he says. "It marries old opinion to new fact so as ever to show a minimum of jolt, a maximum of continuity." This may seem self-evident in the smooth functioning of a machine, but it is anything but clear why the "minimum of jolt" and the "maximum of continuity" should be a prime value for human life and the criterion of truth.

"If theological ideas prove to have a value for concrete life," says James in "What Pragmatism Means," *"they will be true, for pragmatism, in the sense of being good for so much."* But what is the criterion of "value for concrete life?" Orthodox theological opinions instead of heretical ones?—mildly liberal ones instead of radical ones? —ones that do not trouble the social order or ones that produce social reform? Here again we are caught in a hopeless circle. Pragmatism's "only test of probable truth is what works best in the way of leading us, what fits every part of life best and combines with the collectivity of experience's demands, nothing being omitted." If we knew what was meant by "leading us" and by fitting "every part of life best," and if we knew what ways of combining with experience are better and what worse, then this sentence might have some meaning. But if we knew all this, we should already have a sense of values, a direction of authentic personal and social existence, and we should not need the aid of pragmatism!

One trait that James can justly claim for the Modern Pragmatist, because he emobdies it so strikingly himself, is openness. He sees pragmatism as anti-intellectual, anti-metaphysical, concerned with the particular, devoted, to facts, but not weighted down with the materialistic bias under which ordinary empiricism labors. It has no objections to using abstractions, just so they enable one to get about among particulars.

> She has in fact no prejudices whatever, no obstructive dogmas, no rigid canons of what shall count as proof. She is completely genial. She will entertain any hypothesis, she will consider any evidence. . . . Pragmatism is willing . . . to follow either logic or the senses and to count the humblest and most personal experiences. She will count mystical experiences if they have practical consequences. She will take a God who lives in the very dirt of private fact—if that should seem a likely place to find Him.[2]

Unfortunately, John Dewey's instrumentalism does not carry forward the openness of James' Pragmatic Man. It is an empiricism which

[2] *Ibid.*, p. 157.

excludes not only mysticism and God, but also James' willingness to "count the humblest and most personal experiences"—"the very dirt of private fact."

Dewey denies the classical mind-body dualism in favor of an experimental naturalism. He emphasizes man's organic continuity with nature and the environment and the development of man's reasoning powers as a natural product of organic evolution. Dewey conceives of mind as the conscious adaptation of the organism to the social and natural environment. He insists on the integration of thought and emotion, of learning and experience, but he tends to look on the "person" as a collection of potentialities and the education of the person as the development of these potentialities. Dewey has had an enormous influence on education in the United States through precisely this image of man.

The starting point of Dewey's "reconstruction in philosophy," as of his image of man, is his attack on the separation of some things as ends-in-themselves and others as means-in-themselves. He holds this separation to be a heritage of ancient Greek civilization, "in which only those activities were called 'useful' which served living physiologically rather than morally, and which were carried on by slaves or serfs to serve men who were *free* in the degree to which they were relieved from the need of labor that was base and material." In opposition to Plato and Aristotle, Dewey regards intelligence "not as the original shaper and final cause of things, but as the purposeful energetic reshaper of those phases of nature and life that obstruct social well-being." Man's ego does not create the world. It is "the agent who is responsible through initiative, inventiveness and intelligently directed labor for re-creating the world, transforming it into an instrument and possession of intelligence." Dewey identifies this view with modern science.

Like James, Dewey holds that the criterion of truth is, "By their fruits shall ye *know* them": "That which guides us truly is true—demonstrated capacity for such guidance is precisely what is meant by truth." Like James, too, he assumes that we know what it means to be guided "truly"; yet this presupposes some sense of truth other than the pragmatic. He speaks in Jamesian language when he emphasizes "the belief in a plurality of changing, moving. individualized goods" and when he holds that "principles, criteria, laws are intellectual instruments for analyzing individual or unique situations." He is not concerned with true, noncomparable uniqueness, however, but only with that comparable individuality which may be used as materials for his scientific generalizations. "The primary significance of the unique and morally ultimate character of the concrete situation is to transfer the weight and burden of morality to intelligence." He defines the part played by intelligence not as entering into the response to the unique, or pointing back to it, but as abstracting from its concreteness, destroying its wholeness, blurring its vividness:

> A moral situation is one in which judgment and choice are required antecedently to overt action. . . . What is needed is to find the right course of action, the right good. Hence, inquiry is exacted: observation of the detailed makeup of the situation; analysis into its diverse factors; clarification of what is obscure; discounting of the more insistent and vivid traits; tracing the consequences of the various modes of action that suggest themselves; regarding the decision reached as hypothetical and tentative until the anticipated or supposed consequences which led to its adoption have been squared with actual consequences. This inquiry is intelligence.[3]

In some respects, Dewey comes quite close to our understanding of the way in which the image of man enters into personal becoming, namely, not as a fixed, final end but as a part of the stream of becoming itself, in such wise that the present can never be taken to be merely a crude instrument for ideal ends purely extrinsic to it. "No one can possibly estimate," Dewey writes, "how much of the obnoxious materialism and brutality of our economic life is due to the fact that economic ends have been regarded as merely instrumental." Again, in entire accord with our understanding of the image of man, Dewey writes, "No individual or group will be judged by whether they come up to or fall short of some fixed result, but by the direction in which they are moving." The image of man is not an ideal at all; it is a *direction of becoming*, starting not with the future and the abstract, but with the present situation, with where one is. What makes that image authentic for any given person is precisely its *direction*. But this Dewey immediately seems to lose sight of when he declares that "the process of growth . . . becomes the significant thing" and that "growth itself is the only moral 'end.'" Growth may be in a meaningful direction or it may be a malignancy. The mere fact of process of growth does not guarantee the "improvement and progress" with which Dewey equates it.

At one point, Dewey almost seems to be ready to state what the meaningful direction is:

> Government, business, art, religion, all social institutions have a meaning, a purpose. That purpose is to set free and to develop the capacities of human individuals without respect to race, sex, class or

---

[3] John Dewey, *Reconstruction in Philosophy*, enlarged edition, with a new introduction by the author (Boston: The Beacon Press, 1948), p. 163f.

economic status. And this is all one with saying that the test of their value is the extent to which they educate every individual into the full stature of his possibility.[4]

This is a statement of values that most of us would accept as the very heart of democracy, as an expression of our goals and of our image of man. But there is *nothing*, either in James' pragmatism or in Dewey's instrumentalism, that necessarily leads to or implies these values. Rather, they are value assumptions which Dewey holds quite apart from that pragmatism which he claims to be the source of all values. We know that he associates these values with pragmatism, just as John Stuart Mill associates the democratic social concept that each is equal to one with his utilitarianism. But this association is not necessary, and in responding positively to it, we are not responding to pragmatism per se.

Dewey's "ethics of potentiality," moreover, makes all things serve the purpose of releasing and fulfilling potentiality, but leaves "potentiality" itself a vague, neutral term without any value direction of its own. We have the potentiality to murder as well as to create. Were fulfilling all potentialities our goal, the one activity would have as high moral value as the other. If, on the other hand, Dewey means by "potentialities" only "good" potentialities, then we have once again the question of which is the best direction in which to develop potentialities.

In *Theory of Valuation*, Dewey makes clear that what he is concerned with is the dynamic process of valuing and valuation and not abstract values taken in themselves. Particularly helpful here is his concept of a "means-ends continuum." Instead of beginning with an abstract aim and assuming that one will reach it by a quite separate means, one recognizes that the end grows quite naturally out of the means, that there may be five or six or a hundred more end products than one has in mind. To say that one is fighting "to make the world safe for democracy" does not ensure that democracy will result. The immediate end, once attained, becomes the means to some further end. Dewey distinguishes between that "prizing" which is a feeling and that "appraising" which is the use of intelligence to bring about the prized aim, but he also recognizes that the two intermingle at every stage. An end comes in view only "when there is some trouble to be done away with, some need, lack, or privation to be made good, some conflict of tendencies to be resolved by means of changing existing conditions." The removal of this negative state of affairs will make possible the fulfillment of highly positive values. When all this is said,

[4] *Ibid.*, p. 186.

however, one is compelled to reiterate, on the subtler plane to which Dewey's *Theory of Valuation* has brought us, that his whole notion of valuation is a purely instrumental one. Even the testing of interests and desires by their postponement brings us no nearer to understanding why the fulfillment of a desire should in itself be desirable.

In *A Common Faith*, Dewey points out that the harmonizing of the self is made possible only through imagination, that the very idea of personal wholeness "is an imaginative, not a literal, idea." More significant, still, he recognizes the contradiction involved in the idea of integration of the self with reference only to itself. Integration must be coupled with a certain direction of movement beyond the self:

> The unification of the self throughout the ceaseless flux of what it does, suffers, and achieves, cannot be attained in terms of itself. The self is always directed toward something beyond itself and so its own unification depends upon the idea of the integration of the shifting scenes of the world into that imaginative totality we call the Universe.[5]

The self is, indeed, always directed toward something beyond itself. Dewey sees this direction as toward the "Universe." It would, indeed, be unthinkable for man to live without some imaginative apperception of a "world"—a unified totality over against him of which he also sees himself as a part. But we may question whether this is enough, whether anyone ever attains unification of the self in reference to the universe. Does it not come into being rather in responding again and again to one or another concrete image of man? "Mankind" and the "universe," "man" and "the world" are proper corollaries, but I, the self, need another I, other I's, even if at times in imaginative and fictitious form, if I am to become a real person and achieve personal unification.

Dewey is concerned with replacing the image of man as standing in relation to a particular, supernatural Being by the image of man as becoming himself through an open, even reverent co-operation with nature. He sees the origin of ideals as an entirely natural one:

> It emerges when the imagination idealizes existence by laying hold of the possibilities offered to thought and action. There are values, goods, actually realized upon a natural basis—the goods of human association, of art and knowledge. The idealizing imagination seizes upon the most precious things found in the climacteric moments of experience and projects them. We need no external criterion and guarantee for their goodness.[6]

[5] John Dewey, *A Common Faith* (New Haven: Yale University Press, 1934), p. 19.
[6] *Ibid.*, p. 48.

If we take this statement out of the context of "natural" versus "supernatural" and bring it back to the human, we must ask how we distinguish among the welter of our experiences as to which are more precious and which are less. Nazism also represented an ideal produced by the imaginative projection of idealized experience. Are all ideals of equal value then?

Dewey answers this question to his own satisfaction, if not to ours, by his concept of "the community of causes and consequences in which we, together with those not born, are enmeshed."

> The continuing life of this comprehensive community of beings includes all the significant achievement of men in science and art and all the kindly offices of intercourse and communication. It holds within its content all the material that gives verifiable intellectual support to our ideal faiths. A "creed" founded on this material will change and grow, but it cannot be shaken.

> The things in civilization we most prize are not of ourselves. They exist by grace of the doings and sufferings of the continuous human community in which we are a link. Ours is the responsibility of conserving, transmitting, rectifying, and expanding the heritage of values we have received that those who come after us may receive it more solid and secure, more widely accessible and more generously shared than we have received it. Here are all the elements for a religious faith, that shall not be confined to sect, class, or race. Such a faith has always been implicitly the common faith of mankind. It remains to make it explicit and militant.[7]

What distinguishes this image of man is its exalted tone, its inspiring vision of the whole surge forward of mankind, *and* its lofty disregard for the problems of actual men trying to find their way forward through repeated decisions between one direction and another! To celebrate all ideals is to celebrate none. To imagine all movement as progress is to depreciate all those who strive to discriminate day by day as to which is a better way and which is a worse. Dewey would say, of course, that these are matters that can be decided by intelligence, by science. But intelligence and science per se cannot select or create an image of man, however useful they are in illuminating and leading toward it. Dewey is opposed to the separation of ideal from existent, yet he talks of ideals in as vague and general a manner as the most abstract idealist. It does indeed remain to make this "common faith" explicit and militant: as Dewey has stated it, it is incapable of becoming either.

Through his concern with the active interrelation between man and his social environment, Dewey attains a preliminary glimpse of the understanding of the self as a social product that was later developed by George Herbert Mead and Harry Stack Sullivan. Bodies are only individual in the physical sense, says Dewey. "Individuality in a social and moral sense is something to be wrought out. It means initiative, inventiveness, varied resourcefulness, assumption of responsibility in choice of belief and conduct." Dewey clearly does not regard the self as *merely* a product of the social environment. On the contrary, its active response plays a very important part in the attainment of real individuality. At the same time, he recognizes the enormous importance of the social environment in the molding of character, particularly in relation to education. "When self-hood is perceived to be an active process it is also seen that social modifications are the only means of the creation of changed personalities." Institutions, from this point of view, are to be judged by their educative effect, by the types of individuals they foster.[8]

Dewey's concern with the interaction of man and nature prevents him from making any sharp distinctions between the natural and social environment. In contrast, his disciple and colleague, George Herbert Mead, makes the social environment all-important and tends to reduce the natural, including the animals, to functions of human existence. The fundamental emphasis of Mead in his central book, *Mind, Self and Society,* is that the self is a product of the social process, rather than something which exists independently of and prior to that process. "Selves can only exist in definite relationship to other selves."

> The self is not something that exists first and then enters into relationship with others, but it is, so to speak, an eddy in the social current and so still a part of the current. It is a process in which the individual is continually adjusting himself in advance to the situation to which he belongs, and reacting back on it.[9]

The self is constituted, for Mead, by mutual interaction, and self-consciousness is nothing other than consciousness of social relations—of how others see one. The basic social act, according to Mead, is becoming an object to oneself, and mind and thinking are both products of this act. The mind is the expression in one's own conduct of the social situation, and thinking is carrying on a conversation with the socialized self which results from becoming an object to oneself.

For Mead, the earliest stage of the development of the self is "the

[8] *Reconstruction in Philosophy, op. cit.,* pp. 194; 196.
[9] George H. Mead, *Mind, Self, and Society, From the Standpoint of a Social Behaviorist,* edited by Charles W. Morris (Chicago: The University of Chicago Press, 1934), p. 182.

internalization and inner dramatization, by the individual, of the external conversation of significant gestures which constitutes the chief mode of interaction with other individuals belonging to the same society." Mead shows the self arising in a child through play and the game in which the child takes the attitude of the other and carries on a conversation with the other. This taking on the role of the other—perhaps the most basic point in Mead's social behaviorism—has significant implications for our understanding how a person develops through his relation to his image of man.

Mead indicates two stages in the development of the self. The first is the internalization of the attitude of particular people and responding to those particular people. The second is the internalization of a "generalized other" which expresses the attitude of society as a whole. Despite this distinction, Mead sees them as operating on the individual in the same way. "These social or group attitudes are brought within the individual's field of direct experience, and are included as elements in the structure or constitution of his self, in the same way that the attitudes of particular other individuals are." The objectivity of the "generalized other" is the basis for communication. Society arises through the institutionalizing of the responses which the community stimulates in the individual. This institutionalizing of responses does not prevent a dialogue between the individual and the community. It is through this very dialogue, in fact, that the community changes and develops new institutions. The human social process, unlike that of the insects, works through the individual and finds its expression in him. The implication of democracy is "that the individual can be as highly developed as lies within the possibilities of his own inheritance, and still can enter into the attitudes of the others whom he affects."

One of Mead's most fruitful ideas for our understanding of the image of man is his distinction between two different selves which appear together and constitute the personality—the "I" and the "Me." The "Me" is the organized response of the other that we have taken into ourselves, and the "I" is our reaction to this organized response. Only through both of these—the internalization and the response—do we acquire conscious selves. There remains, nonetheless, an element of the unexpected and unpremeditated in the response of the "I" which is not present in the "Me." "The 'Me' represents a definite organization of the community there in our own attitudes, and calling for a response, but the response that takes place is something that just happens." This means that for all Mead's characterization of the self as "an eddy in the social current," he leaves room for an element of freedom and spontaneity through which the becoming of the individual can be understood as a *dialogue* between the person and his image of man rather than as an entirely conditioned response.

> The "I" gives the sense of freedom, of initiative. The situation is there for us to act in a self-conscious fashion. We are aware of ourselves, and of what the situation is, but exactly how we will act never gets into experience until after the action takes place.[10]

The corollary of this recognition of the freedom and spontaneity of the "I" is Mead's insistence that for all its individuality the "I" is a social self which can be realized only in relation with others.

On the basis of his contrast between the "Me" and the "I," Mead makes a distinction between the "conventional individual," who acts entirely according to habitual social response, and the "definite personality," who reacts in an individual way to the social situation and really brings about a change in this situation through his reaction. The realization of the "I" self is the most important value and goal for Mead, but he also recognizes the value and necessity of the "Me." If it were not for the organized "Me," society could not exist. Moreover, the "I" finds its expression through the "Me." It is possible to isolate oneself from others through manners, but it is also possible to get outside oneself and open up to others. In this latter case, the "I" may fuse with the "Me" in such a way that the individual takes on the larger values of the community. This fusion of the "I" and the "Me" is the source of sympathy for others. This fusion can take place only if social institutions have not become inflexible and stereotyped. The institutionalized "Me" must be of such a nature as to allow the "I" to find expression through it.

> Oppressive, stereotyped, and ultra-conservative social institutions . . . which by their more or less rigid and inflexible unprogressiveness crush or blot out individuality, or discourage any distinctive or original expressions of thought and behavior in the individual selves or personalities implicated in and subjected to them are undesirable but not necessary outcomes of the general social process of experience and behavior.[11]

One realizes oneself as a self, according to Mead, only as one takes the attitude of the other. One takes this attitude over against one's self, in fact, for the self only has meaning in its existence over against the other self. Through language, for example, one "gets a new soul." "He puts himself into the attitude of those that make use of that language. He cannot read its literature, cannot converse with those that belong to that community without taking on its peculiar atti-

[10] *Ibid.*, p. 197.
[11] *Ibid.*, p. 299.

tudes." Communication, for Mead, is the organizing process in the community which makes possible "putting one's self in the place of the other person's attitude, communicating through significant symbols." This taking of the attitude of the other is the basis of human sympathy, for it means a sympathetic identification with the other and a tendency to respond to his social situation in the way that he does. "What is essential is the development of the whole mechanism of social relationship which brings us together, so that we can take the attitude of the other in our various life-processes." This relation of man to the "world" is built up more concretely, and more convincingly than Dewey's imaginative unity of the self and of the universe.

In his statement about man's relation to animals, Mead equates absence of socialized personality with a total absence of rights. This suggests an undue emphasis on society as in itself the supreme value and reality. The "social self" of Mead tends to swing uneasily back and forth between the ideal society as one which works through the individual and gives him the maximum possible expression for his "I," and the self as merely "an eddy in the social current."

The American psychiatrist, Harry Stack Sullivan, developed his image of man far more under the influence of George Herbert Mead and American pragmatism than of Freud and Jung. Sullivan takes interpersonal relations as the true nexus of the self and, by the same token, of mental health and mental illness. Sullivan distinguishes between the pursuit of satisfactions, which pertains to man's bodily needs, and the pursuit of security, which pertains to his cultural needs. It is the latter, not the former, which he holds to be crucial in mental illness. The child is formed and educated through the anxiety he experiences from the disapproval of significant others or the relief and pleasure he feels from their approval. The personality is a larger whole than the self. Many of the impulses and performances of the personality are not noted because they are outside the awareness of the self. A curious reversal thus takes place. Instead of anxiety's serving to prevent one's feeling, thinking, or doing what significant others disapprove, it serves to protect the self from the awareness that it is engaging in such disapproved things.

Relationships with other people are an indispensable part of one's development as a person and a self. "The human being requires the world of culture, cannot live *and be human* except in communal existence with it." This is absolutely true in the earlier phases of personality development, but it is true in a different sense when the child moves from the juvenile to the preadolescent stage. Only then does there arise a capacity to love in which "the satisfactions and the security which are being experienced by someone else, some particular other person, begin to be as significant to the person as are his own satisfactions and security."

> If another person matters as much to you as do you yourself, it is quite possible to talk to this person as you have never talked to anyone before. The freedom which comes from this expanding of one's world of satisfaction and security to include two people, linked together by love, permits exchanges of nuances of meaning, permits investigations without fear of rebuff or humiliation, which greatly augments the consensual validation of all sorts of things.[12]

"Consensual validation" means a truth, a world, that is discovered with others, not through being objectively established, but through being interpersonally shared and tested out. This is the period in which a real world community is illuminated. Instead of being imprisoned within his self in autistic, self-referring isolation, one is open to some comparing of notes, some checking and counterchecking. This consensual validation leads one to feel human in a new sense—through the appreciation of the common humanity of people, through sympathy for the other fellow whether one knows him directly or only by report.

When a person does not experience this consensual validation, he not only fails to develop his feeling of humanity, but he also fails to develop as a person. He becomes less and less aware of his interpersonal performances, and as a result more and more dissociated. Only by skilful use of responsive speech, "our most specialized tool of communication," can we overcome the privacy of our personal worlds. Those who do not succeed in bridging this gap lead existences which are unstable and less than human, inauthentic not in terms of some moral judgment, but in terms of their existence itself:

> There are people among us whose integration of interpersonal situations is chiefly characterized by lack of duration. These people live through a great number of fugitive, fleeting, involvements with other people—and even with the more tangible of the institutions of the particular society in which they have their being. They are disappointing to everyone who is interested in them. They are themselves always disappointed in other people—but this does not make them bitter, nor does it excite them to inquiry as to what may be the matter. Without troubling to think it out, they exemplify the saying that all the world is queer, except. . . . They move through life giving many of the appearances of human beings; they just miss being human—and they

[12] Harry Stack Sullivan, *Conceptions of Modern Society* (N. Y.: W. W. Norton Co., 1940), p. 20.

do not lack fluency in verbal behavior. They almost always say the right thing. They often say it well. But it signifies very little.[13]

Sullivan tends to see the ideal norm in terms of "a fully rational way of life" and normative rules as the expedients that must be adopted in the long period before this norm will be realized. Unfortunately, these normative rules become embodied in religion and law in such a way that they become relatively static and highly resistant to change, hence "least apt to keep closely in step with the developing culture-complex." Sullivan seems to make adjustment to the culture the norm, which is almost equivalent to having no norm at all. Not that the norm should be abstract or static and unchanging. But it cannot merely keep up with cultural change: it must respond to it and, if necessary, contend with and set a limit to it. This absence of a norm, of a direction of movement toward authenticity, is evident in Sullivan's statement, "One achieves mental health to the extent that one becomes aware of one's interpersonal relations." If the patient sees himself as others see him, he will be both well and good in the only senses that Sullivan holds significant.

Sullivan explicitly rejects Freud's notion of the formation of conscience as an introjection of the values of father and/or mother. What Sullivan is concerned with is the actual anxiety-diminishing and anxiety-increasing experiences of the child in its interpersonal relations with significant others. In other words, Sullivan is substituting dynamic relationship—verbs—for the more static, noun-based thinking of Freud: "This dynamism is an explanatory conception; it is not a thing, a region, or what not, such as superegos, egos, ids, and so on." By the same token, Sullivan cannot exclude from his understanding of mental illness the consideration of the actual culture in which the patient lives. In an ideal culture, the parental group would reflect the essence of the social organization for which the young are being trained in living. What actually happens is that one discrete excerpt of a culture comes in conflict with another, as a result of which "the self-system in its actual functioning in life in civilized societies as they now exist, is often very unfortunate." Sullivan is also aware of the part that the image of man plays in human becoming: "A great deal of the learning which the child achieves is on the basis of human examples." These examples lead to a healthy dramatization in which the child acts *as if* he were this person. The dramatization only becomes harmful when it is used to conceal violations of co-operation and to deceive authority-invested figures.

Instead of holding with Freud that man "has an actual need for being cruel and hurtful to his fellows," Sullivan sees malevolence and hatred developing from the child's experience of being denied tenderness. When a child expresses a need for tenderness, its parents sometimes reject and even hurt the child, with the result that as a juvenile the child "makes it practically impossible for anyone to feel tenderly toward him or to treat him kindly," beating them to it by his own display of attitude. Malevolence, as Sullivan sees it, is "just an elaboration of this earlier warp," the vicious circle which comes when parents fail "to discharge their social responsibility to produce a well-behaved, well-socialized person." If Jung errs on the side of valuing the inner man as against the social, and Freud straddles the fence on this issue, Sullivan goes to the other extreme in making the sole criterion of authentic personal existence being "well-behaved" and "well-socialized." The impossible only became possible in Nazi Germany because so many Germans were so well-behaved and well-socialized in relation to that particular society that they did not dare to stand against it! Sullivan seems to have no room in his thinking for Socrates' drinking a cup of hemlock because the Athenians considered him a threat to good behavior and good socialization.

If one assumes a democratic society, what Sullivan says may seem quite practical, though even then it gives no guidance as to what sort of behavior is a truly social response and what is not. Would Sullivan rule out the conscientious objector, the strike, the nonviolent sit-downs and sit-ins because they arouse social antagonisms, or would he broaden his definition of the social so far as to include whatever anyone did? If the former, he has no value but adjustment to society, therefore nothing which is a value in itself. If the latter, he offers the stamp of approval after the decision, but no guidance at all before. Sullivan's conception of "orientation in living" falls into the same dilemma of pragmatism. It is clearly his image of the sort of man he wishes to produce through therapy, yet it is entirely functional:

> One is oriented in living to the extent to which one has formulated, or can easily be led to formulate (or has insight into), data of the following types: the integrating tendencies (needs) which customarily characterize one's interpersonal relations; the circumstances appropriate to their satisfaction and relatively anxiety-free discharge; and the more or less remote goals for the approximation of which one will forego intercurrent opportunities for satisfaction or the enhancement of one's prestige. The degree to which one is adequately oriented in living is, I believe, a very much better way of indicating what we often have in mind when we speak about how "well integrated" a person is, or what his "character" is in the sense of good, bad, or indifferent.[14]

14 Harry Stack Sullivan, *The Interpersonal Theory of Psychiatry,* edited by Helen Swick Perry and Mary Ladd Gawel (N. Y.: W. W. Norton & Co., 1953), p. 243f.

Happily, Sullivan's image of man does not end here. On the contrary, he develops further implications of his interpersonal approach that lead him to a much broader conception of human maturity and health. Although he seems to have founded his whole system on anxiety, he now attests that loneliness can brush aside the activity of the self-system. "Under loneliness, people seek companionship even though intensely anxious in the performance. . . . The fact that loneliness will lead to integrations in the face of severe anxiety automatically means that loneliness in itself is more terrible than anxiety." This means that our relations to others are not just a system of being approved or disapproved, that we need them for themselves and not just for their bolstering of our own selves. Sullivan distinguishes three "needs": "the need for personal security—that is, for freedom from anxiety; the need for intimacy—that is, for collaboration with at least one other person; and the need for lustful satisfaction, which is connected with genital activity in pursuit of the orgasm." The fact that he speaks of "the need for intimacy" shows the psychologism that still dominates his thinking. He has already defined intimacy as caring about the other person's needs as much as one's own. If this is so, he cannot be a "need" of mine without making my concern for his needs a function of my own and therefore by definition less of a concern for him than for myself. But this is as much of a language vestige as it is a reduction of the relationship to a function of the self. Sullivan not only recognizes that the need for intimacy and that for lust cannot be identified, but also points out that they are often quite at variance with each other as well as with the need for security.

Sullivan includes in his thought an open relationship to another person which would have been quite impossible for Freud, for whom love at its best could never be anything but a mutual exploitation for the fulfillment of individual, instinctual needs. This open relationship is not easily attained in our culture. "The cultural influences which are borne in upon each person include very little which prepares members of different sexes for a fully human, simple, personal relationship together." The result is often a split between lust and intimacy in which the former is directed to "the prostitute" and the latter to "the good girl." The satisfaction of lust then takes place at the cost of one's self-esteem, while the relationship which allays loneliness and anxiety is not a full relationship. Nor is this split only present in adolescence. Some of Sullivan's most biting comments are on the false part that sex plays in our culture—not as satisfaction of a genuine need but as a means of enhancing prestige: "In this culture the ultimate test of whether you can get on or not is whether you can do something satisfactory with your genitals or somebody else's genitals without undue anxiety and loss of self-esteem."

In his discussion of "late adolescence," Sullivan presents his most complete image of man, his image of what it means to be fully human. Late adolescence begins with discovering what one likes in the way of genital behavior and how to fit it into the rest of one's life, and it proceeds *"through unnumbered educative and eductive steps to the establishment of a fully human or mature repertory of interpersonal relations, as permitted by available opportunity, personal and cultural."* The goal of being fully human means, to Sullivan, freedom of living. But since living takes place in interpersonal relations, these relations must be real ones. Sullivan sees a restriction to freedom of living not in the fact that the individual is prevented by others from full "self-expression," but in the fact that many people settle for "pseudosocial ritual": "Each person is busily engaged with people, but nothing particularly personal transpires. . . . There are a remarkable number of people who have ways of being social as the devil without having anything to do with the other people concerned." Thus, Sullivan's use of the term "interpersonal" is not merely descriptive but normative as well. Not every type of relationship between people leads to the "fully human," but only that into which people really enter as persons and in which they really have to do with others.

For Sullivan, human maturity, self-respect, and genuine interpersonal relations are necessary corollaries. It is only the immature person who must derogate others for the sake of his own security, and just in so doing demonstrate his own lack of self-respect. The mature person will be recognized by his sympathetic understanding of the limitations, interests, possibilities, and anxieties of those with whom he lives. Thus, the *need* for intimacy that leads to collaboration with others also leads to a transcending of the language of individual needs in favor of "a very lively sensitivity to the needs of the other and to the interpersonal security or absence of anxiety in the other." Thus, much in Sullivan's latest thought points the way beyond the pragmatic functionalism of his earlier image of man.

13

ERICH FROMM
AND "SELF-REALIZATION"

IN THE writings of the American psychotherapist, Erich Fromm many of the types of contemporary images of man that we have discussed intermingle—the Modern Socialist, the Modern Vitalist, the Modern Mystic, and also, of course, Psychological Man. Despite the variegated nature of Fromm's thought and the influences on it, he is recognizable in many important respects as the Modern Pragmatist—more exactly, as that higher level of the Modern Pragmatist presented to us by John Dewey in his ethics of potentiality. Fromm's emphasis on "self-realization" makes him perhaps more representative of the current image of man, especially in America, than any other man.

In contrast to Freud's psychology, with its biological individualism and its innate competitiveness and aggression, Fromm sees the key problem of psychology as "that of the specific kind of relatedness of the individual towards the world and not that of the satisfaction or frustration of this or that instinctual need *per se*." Following Karl Marx and Harry Stack Sullivan, Fromm sees man as *primarily* a social being, i.e., social in his very self and not just in his needs. Psychology, as a result, is "psychology of interpersonal relationships." Fromm disagrees emphatically with Freud's view that history is "the result of psychological forces that in themselves are not socially conditioned." But he also disagrees with those theories, "more or less tinged with behaviorist psychology," that assume "that human nature has no dynamism of its own and that psychological changes are to be understood in terms of the development of new 'habits' as an adaptation to new cultural patterns." (*Escape from Freedom*) Human nature is not infinitely malleable, and the human factor is one of the dynamic elements in the social process.

In *Escape from Freedom,* Fromm goes beyond Freud and Sullivan in his emphasis on freedom which he sees as characterizing human existence as such.

> Human existence begins when the lack of fixation of action by instincts exceeds a certain point; when the adaptation to nature loses its coercive character; when the way to act is no longer fixed by hereditarily given mechanisms. In other words, *human existence and freedom are from the beginning inseparable.*[1]

Human freedom, however, depends on the successful emergence of the individual from his primary ties to an individualized state. He finds fulfillment not through organic or symbiotic union with others, but through "his active solidarity with all men and his spontaneous activity, love and work, which unites him again with the world . . . as a free and independent individual." But the loss of ties that gave people security, plus coercive economic, social, and poltical conditions often make freedom an unbearable burden. The result is "sado-masochism"— an unhealthy, nonproductive, dominance-submission relation to others —and with it the loss of the true self. Sado-masochism, as Fromm uses the term, is not a sexual phenomenon, or even an expression of hostility, as Freud later saw sadism, but an attempt to overcome the anxiety produced by being a separate person through a symbiotic union with another in which that separateness is forgotten. For this reason, a sadist is as dependent on the person he dominates as a masochist is on the person who dominates him. In fact, says Fromm, the two always go together. Even Hitler and Napoleon saw themselves as subject to destiny, while even the most masochistic of persons usually finds at least one person to lord it over. Both sadism and masochism are equally an "escape from freedom."

Dostoyevsky's "Underground Man," in *Notes from the Underground,* is a perfect illustration of Fromm's sado-masochistic character. He invites humiliation from his friends and in turn humiliates Lisa, a prostitute whom he visits, while pretending to take on the role of her guardian. "To avenge my wounded pride on someone," he says to Lisa later, "to get my own back, I vented my spite on you and I laughed at you. I had been humiliated, so I too wanted to humiliate someone; they wiped the floor with me, so I too wanted to show my power." "I cannot love without feeling that I have someone completely in my power, that I am free to tyrannise over some human being," says this inveterate masochist who is always placing himself in a position where other people will trample on him and treat him without respect. Another striking illustration from literature is Captain

---

[1] New York: Rinehart & Co., 1941, p. 32.

Ahab in Herman Melville's *Moby Dick*. In his relations with the members of his crew, we know Captain Ahab only as the overpowering sadist, yet he too sees himself as subject to some power above him: "I am the Fates' lieutenant; I act under orders," cries Ahab to his first mate. "Look thou, underling! that thou obeyest mine."

Fromm sees freedom as a corollary of the wholeness of the personality. "Positive freedom consists in the spontaneous activity of the total, integrated personality." Such spontaneity comes through "the acceptance of the total personality and the elimination of the split between 'reason' and 'nature.'" The foremost component of spontaneity is love—not the dissolution of the self in another person or the possession of another but the spontaneous affirmation of others while preserving the individual self. Love for Fromm means the overcoming of separation without the elimination of otherness. Work, too, is a part of spontaneity—not compulsion or domination of nature, but an act of creation that unites one with nature without dissolving one in it. "The basic dichotomy that is inherent in freedom—the birth of individuality and the pain of aloneness—is dissolved on a higher plane by man's spontaneous action."

Freedom and the organic growth of the self are possible, says Fromm, only if one respects the uniqueness of the self of other persons as well as one's own self. This most valuable achievement of human culture is in danger today, declares Fromm. One may question, however, whether respect for another is as much the achievement of culture as it is of a relation of directness, mutuality, and presentness that enables one to see the other in his concrete uniqueness as of value in himself. One may also question Fromm's definition of "a genuine ideal as any aim which furthers the growth, freedom, and happiness of the self." The very meaning of these terms depends on one's image of man and one's sense of one's own personal direction. "Life has an inherent tendency to grow, to expand, to express potentialities," writes Fromm, recapitulating Bergson's emphasis on creativity and dynamism. But the question of the image of man—that of the meaningful direction of this growth and of these potentialities—remains unanswered.

In *Man for Himself* Fromm recognizes that what man *is* cannot be understood without including what man *ought* to be. "It is impossible to understand man and his emotional and mental disturbances without understanding the nature of value and moral conflicts." Yet he joins himself to the Modern Pragmatist in defining the source of values in purely pragmatic terms, the good being that which contributes to the mature and integrated personality, vice being that which destroys it.

The character structure of the mature and integrated personality, the productive character, constitutes the source and the basis of "virtue." . . . "Vice," in the last analysis, is indifference to one's own self and self-mutilation. Not self-renunciation nor selfishness but self-love, not the negation of the individual but the affirmation of his truly human self, are the supreme values of humanistic ethics. If man is to have confidence in values, he must know himself and the capacity of his nature for goodness and productiveness.[2]

Fromm presents us here with a succession of terms to each of which we have a positive emotional response—"mature," "integrated," "productive," affirmation of the truly human self"—but to none has he given concrete content. He defines values in terms of "the mature and integrated personality" and "the truly human self," yet these terms themselves imply values and would have to be defined in terms of values. Thus, Fromm offers us one set of explicit, conscious values which are merely instrumental and another of implicit, assumed values the source of which he does not explore. Fromm bifurcates "conscience" into an authoritarian conscience that demands submission out of fear—not too different from Freud's conception of the conscience as the introjection of the censure of the father—and a humanistic conscience which is "the guardian of our integrity." The humanistic conscience "is the voice of our true selves which summons us back to ourselves, to live productively, to develop fully and harmoniously— that is, *to become what we potentially are.*" But what is meant by the "true self" and by becoming "what we potentially are?" Fromm knows the beneficial results of authentic existence, but he cannot point to such existence itself.

An important contribution that Fromm does make to the problem of discovering what is authentic is his recognition that pleasure, the subjective experience of satisfaction, is in itself deceptive and not a valid criterion of value. The masochist is only the most striking example of those who take pleasure in what harms them. A man, as his dreams often reveal, may think himself happy and in fact be deeply anxious and wretched underneath. Happiness is more than a state of mind. It is an expression of the total personality. "Happiness is conjunctive with an increase in vitality, intensity of feeling and thinking, and productiveness." It is "the indication that man has found the answer to the problem of human existence; the productive realization of his potentialities." Although Fromm speaks in this book of "existential dichotomies," he seems to ignore the possibility of a tragic conflict between realizing one's potentialities to the full and playing one's part in a historical situation which may call on one to sacrifice this realization, and perhaps life itself. The man who realizes his poten-

[2] Erich Fromm, *Man for Himself: An Inquiry into the Psychology of Ethics* (N. Y.: Rinehart & Co., 1947), p. 7.

tialities productively is one with the world and at the same time preserves the integrity of his self, writes Fromm. Fromm would recognize that such harmony of self and world is not possible in our society, but he seems to assume that all that is needed is a change of social conditions for it to be brought about. The only thing he speaks of as inherently tragic is that one dies without ever having realized all one's potentialities.

Fromm's definition of "a genuine ideal as any aim which furthers the growth, freedom, and happiness of the self" vitiates his emphasis on spontaneous relations to others by making self-realization the goal and relations to others the means to that goal. In contrast to this emphasis on self-realization, Fromm defines love, in *Man for Himself* and in *The Art of Loving*, as "care, responsibility, respect, and knowledge." These terms all imply a mutual relation with others that see the other as of value in himself. Fromm recognizes this explicitly in taking responsibility back to its root meaning of "respond" and in further defining love as "the wish for the other person to grow and develop" and as "the expression of intimacy between two human beings under the condition of the preservation of each other's integrity." The great popularity of psychology, Fromm points out in *The Art of Loving*, indicates an interest in the knowledge of man, but "it also betrays the fundamental lack of love in human relations today. Psychological knowledge thus becomes a substitute for full knowledge in the act of love, instead of being a step toward it." Love, to Fromm, is "a paradoxical two-in-oneness" in which both separateness and togetherness prevail. It means the response to another in his uniqueness, accepting him *as he is:*

> Responsibility could easily deteriorate into domination and possessiveness, were it not for a third component of love, *respect*. Respect is . . . the ability to see a person as he is, to be aware of his unique individuality. Respect means the concern that the other person should grow and unfold as he is. Respect, thus, implies the absence of exploitation. I want the loved person to grow and unfold for his own sake, and in his own ways, and not for the purpose of serving me.[3]

The knowledge of another in love, similarly, is not that sadism which seeks to know his last secret in order to dominate him, but "the active penetration of the other person," a union in which "I know you, I know myself, I know everybody—and I 'know' nothing." This distinction between knowing an object and knowing in relation takes Fromm beyond *Man for Himself*, where he defines the science of man as

[3] Erich Fromm, *The Art of Loving* (*World Perspectives*, Vol. IX; N. Y.: Harper & Brothers, 1956), p. 28.

observing the reactions of man to various individual and social conditions and from these observations making inferences about man's nature. Now Fromm recognizes that the image of man is not derived from empirical observation and scientific inference, but from the dialogue between man and man: "In the act of loving, of giving myself, in the act of penetrating the other person, I find myself, I discover myself, I discover us both, I discover man." Fromm does not mean by this knowing in relation a knowledge that can ever be fully objectified. "The only way of full knowledge lies in the *act* of love: this act transcends thought, it transcends words. It is the daring plunge into the experience of union."

In Fromm's discussion of "the objects of love," however, love loses its character as responsibility, respect, care, and knowledge. "Love is not primarily a relationship to a specific person," Fromm writes; "it is an *attitude*, an *orientation* of *character* which determines the relatedness of a person to the world as a whole." While it may be true that "if I truly love one person, I love all persons, I love the world, I love life," it is not true that one begins with love for all human beings before one is able to love any specific human being. This retreat into the universal destroys the very character of love as a relation to an actual other person. I must love him in his concrete uniqueness, and not as part of a general attitude, if I am to care for him, respect him, respond to him, and truly know him. One may go from particular love to ever-more inclusive love of others. But one cannot go from love of humanity to love of the individual, for the simple reason that love of humanity is an abstract idea or a general emotion that remains essentially within oneself and does not itself imply a relation to any actual other person.

In the end, Fromm sacrifices even the separateness, the paradoxical two-in-oneness on which he had insisted before, in favor of a view of love as an identity of one person with another.

> In essence, all human beings are identical. We are all part of One; we are One. This being so, it should not make any difference whom we love. Love should be essentially an act of will, of decision to commit my life, completely, to that of one other person. . . . All men are part of Adam, and all women part of Eve.[4]

This view is a useful corrective to the romantic notion that love simply *happens* to one—a passive act of falling in love rather than a decision, commitment, an act of will. What is more, Fromm qualifies his statement of identity by the recognition that "We are all One—yet every one of us is a unique, unduplicable entity." He recognizes, as a result,

[4] *Ibid.*, p. 55f.

that erotic love is not only an act of love but also an individual attraction between two specific persons. Nonetheless, in his affirmation of identity, which plays an important part in the rest of the book, Fromm leaves his earlier understanding of love for one closer to the Upanishads' "Husband is not dear because of husband but because of the Self within the husband." This means losing sight of the actual person, for the person exists only in uniqueness and not in an identity with all others that is simply complemented by individuality.

The nature of an individual's love for God corresponds to the nature of his love for man, states Fromm. But this is hardly true for Fromm himself, whose usual recognition of the otherness of the other in the healthy, mature relation between man and man entirely disappears in his various discussions of religion. In *Man for Himself*, Fromm postulates a split between man and a cold, meaningless universe. Not only is man *for* himself, as the title of the book suggests, he is also *by* himself. There is only one solution to man's problem, says Fromm:

> to acknowledge his fundamental aloneness and solitude in a universe indifferent to his fate, to recognize that there is no power transcending him which can solve his problem for him. Man must accept the responsibility for himself and the fact that only by using his own powers can he give meaning to his life. . . . If he faces the truth without panic he will recognize that *there is no meaning to life except the meaning man gives his life by the unfolding of his powers, by living productively;* and that only constant vigilance, activity, and effort can keep us from failing in the one task that matters—the full development of our powers within the limitations set by the laws of our existence.[5]

To know what is meant by living productively and by the full development of one's powers, one must *already* have meaning in life, meaning that can be actualized through man's meeting with life, but that cannot be produced from man's side alone. Meaning is a relationship between man and the world. By positing that the world is indifferent to man and that no meaningful relation to it is possible, Fromm has undercut all the ground on which creativity, productivity, and all his other favorite terms rest.

In human relations, Fromm affirms the self *and* the other and denies that one must choose between self-love and love of others. In religion, Fromm posits the self *or* the other, denying a priori the possibility that man may "fulfill himself" in relation to what transcends him. In both spheres, however, he allows the pragmatic motif to dominate. He defines ethics in terms of what produces a mature, integrated personality, and he defines religion in the same extrinsic way. "Good" or

[5] *Ibid.*, p. 45.

"bad" in religion, as in ethics, is a function of the psychological effect of a type of relationship, rather than of any intrinsic value or disvalue in the relationship itself. What matters to the psychologist, writes Fromm in *Psychoanalysis and Religion*,[6] is what human attitude a religion expresses and what kind of effect it has on man, whether it is good or bad for the development of man's powers. Again, we have the curious pragmatic inversion which makes the development of man's powers the end, that for which these powers are developed the means.

Fromm's categories of transcendent and immanent are themselves based on and presuppose the values by which he judges some religions as authoritarian, and therefore bad, and others as humanistic, and therefore good. Yet Fromm nowhere adequately deals with the sources of these values that he presupposes. If he refers them back to the nature of man, he also defines man's nature in terms of these values. This confusion in Fromm's thinking about religion and values is shown most clearly in the ending of *Psychoanalysis and Religion*. Having defined the God of humanistic religion as "the symbol of man's own powers," he now describes the attitude of this religion as the devotion of life to "the aim of becoming what one potentially is, a being made in the likeness of God." If man is a being made in the likeness of God and God is a symbol of the powers of man, we have a perfect circle! What this contradiction suggests is a still deeper unclarity as to the relation between such essentially instrumental terms as "power," "potentiality," and "creativity" and the values of love, fairness, kindness, and relatedness that Fromm espouses. In *The Art of Loving* God is again created in man's image while values are taken for granted. Thus, the image of man, which Fromm assumes will emerge into full light through the recovery of man's alienated creativity, retreats into still greater darkness.

As a social psychologist and therapist seeking to understand man, Fromm has unquestionably contributed to a climate of concern and to a feeling of humanity that has advanced the search for a contemporary image of man. One of the finest statements of the problem of attaining such an image is that which Fromm himself makes at the end of *The Art of Loving*:

> While we teach knowledge, we are losing that teaching which is the most important one for human development: the teaching which can only be given by the simple presence of a mature, loving person. In previous epochs of our own culture, or in China and India, the man most highly valued was the person with outstanding spiritual quali-

[6] Erich Fromm, *Psychoanalysis and Religion* (New Haven: Yale University Press, 1950).

ties. Even the teacher was not only, or even primarily, a source of information, but his function was to convey certain human attitudes. In contemporary capitalistic society—and the same holds true for Russian Communism—the men suggested for admiration and emulation are everything but bearers of significant spiritual qualities. . . . Movie stars, radio entertainers, columnists, important business or government figures—these are the models for emulation. . . . Yet . . . if one considers the fact that a man like Albert Schweitzer could become famous in the United States, if one visualizes the many possibilities to make our youth familiar with living and historical personalities who show what human beings can achieve as human beings, . . . if one thinks of the great works of literature and art of all ages, there seems to be a chance of creating a vision of good human functioning, and hence of sensitivity to malfunctioning. If we should not succeed in keeping alive a vision of mature life, then indeed we are confronted with the probability that our whole cultural tradition will break down.[7]

In *Beyond the Chains of Illusion,* Fromm presents his own image of man in terms of his dialogue with other images of man. In opposition to Freud, Fromm holds that the most powerful motive for repression is not fear of castration, but of isolation and ostracism. "Man has to be related, he has to find union with others, in order to be sane." Like Sullivan, therefore, Fromm sees man's strongest fear as the loneliness which threatens his sanity. This often leads the individual to blind himself to the reality behind the illusions his group puts forward, rather than risk ostracism. Yet man is also afraid of isolation from the humanity inside him, from his conscience and reason. When a society is not human, the individual is forced into a conflict between social and human aims. He can only resolve this conflict in favor of the human if he "has transcended the limits of one's society and has become a citizen of the world." One source of such transcending, Fromm suggests, is his unconscious, which to Fromm is neither good nor evil, rational nor irrational, but both—all that is human. The unconscious is the whole man, the universal man, minus the social part, whereas consciousness is the social man, "the accidental limitations set by the historical situation into which an individual is thrown." "To become aware of one's unconscious," therefore, "means to get in touch with one's full humanity and to do away with barriers which society erects within each man and, consequently, between each man and his fellowman." Fromm goes even beyond Jung here in his valuing of the unconscious; for Jung never suggests that it is itself the ultimate, but only the material which can be shaped into the autonomous center of the self.

[7] *The Art of Loving, op. cit.,* p. 117f.

There is a necessary connection, Fromm points out, between knowledge through relation, openness and uniqueness:

> I understand man only in the situation of being related to him, when he ceases to be a split-off object and becomes part of me or, to be still more correct, when he becomes "me," yet remains also "not-me." . . . Only if I am open to him and respond to him, and that is, precisely, if I am related to him, do I see my fellowman; and to see him is to know him. . . . To be open is the condition to enable me to become filled with him, to become soaked with him, as it were; but *I* need to be *I*, otherwise how could *I* be open? I need to be myself, that is, my own authentic, unique self.[8]

One aspect of this openness for Fromm is intelligence, but intelligence is itself a type of openness:

> Intelligence, aside from the native faculty, is largely a function of independence, courage, and aliveness; stupidity is equally a result of submission, fear, and inner deadness. . . . In order to reduce the general level of stupidity, we need not more "intellect" but a different kind of character: men who are independent, adventurous, and who are in love with life.[9]

To recognize oneself as part of humanity, to live according to love, justice, truth, to develop one's powers of love and reason, "to see one's identity with all beings, and to give up the illusion of a separate, indestructible ego," to recognize the equality of all men in the spiritual realm—these are the ideals that Fromm sets forth as the true religion. By the very fact of being human, man is asked the question of how to overcome the split between himself and the world—through regression to a prehuman form of existence or through full development of his human powers of love and reason "until he reaches a new harmony with his fellowman and with nature." The first answer Fromm sees as inauthentic and destructive, the second as difficult but productive, intensifying man's vital energies in the very effort to reach it. To choose life instead of death, man must enlarge the margin of freedom that is given to him, giving up the quest for ultimate answers in favor of "a degree of intensity, depth and clarity of experience which gives him the strength to live without illusion, and to be free." This path, says Fromm, leads to a "sense of heightened aliveness in which I confirm my powers and my identity." But to reach it, one needs an image of

[8] Erich Fromm, *Beyond the Chains of Illusion: My Encounter with Marx and Freud* ("The Credo Series"; N. Y.: Simon and Schuster, A Trident Press Book, 1962), p. 149f.
[9] *Ibid.*, p. 154f.

man, an education which is effective because "the best heritage of the human race" becomes "reality in the person of the teacher and in the practice and structure of society." It is not learning abstract concepts, but responding to an image of man that produces real change: "Only the idea which has materialized in the flesh can influence man."

What makes the norms that Fromm affirms the universal, productive, primary ones and the ones that he denies the tribal, destructive, secondary ones? Many of us would go along with much that Fromm says and yet be troubled by the vagueness of his image of man, which he threatens to leave either functional or pragmatic or abstractly idealistic. How does one become a "citizen of the world?" How does one get beyond the illusion of one's ego? What makes the universal a value in itself? We may agree that "to risk doing what is right and human, and have faith in the power of the voice of humanity and truth, is more realistic than the so-called realism of opportunism," and not be much clearer as to what direction of movement in any concrete situation is implied by the words "right," "human," and "truth." Fromm recognizes that freedom is more than freedom *from*, it is also freedom *to*, that the capacity to say "no" meaningfully implies the capacity to to say "yes" meaningfully. "The 'yes' to man is the 'no' to all those who want to enslave, exploit, and stultify him." Insofar as social injustice is in question, this is evident, and Fromm has stood courageously as a socialist and as a worker for One World who wants to create the new type of man who can make such a world possible. Insofar as the image of man is concerned—the direction to authentic personal existence—he has left us with an affirmation of man and of "self-realization" without the direction that would make these terms meaningful.

In probably conscious response to those who have accused him of ignoring the repressed negative aspects discovered by depth psychology, Fromm discusses in *The Heart of Man* "the most vicious and dangerous form of human orientation." This is the love of death, malignant narcissism, and symbiotic-incestuous fixation, three orientations which combine in their extreme form into a "syndrome of decay" that prompts destruction and hate for their own sake. In opposition to the necrophilous person, Fromm posits a *"biophilic ethics"* which is clearly his own image of man:

> Good is all that serves life; evil is all that serves death. Good is reverence for life, all that enhances life, growth, unfolding. Evil is all that stifles life, narrows it down, cuts it into pieces. Joy is virtuous and sadness is sinful. . . . The conscience of the biophilous person is not one of forcing oneself to refrain from evil and do good. It is not the super-ego described by Freud, which is a strict taskmaster, em-

ploying sadism against oneself for the sake of virtue. The biophilous conscience is motivated by its attraction to life and joy; the moral effort consists in strengthening the life-loving side in oneself.[10]

Attractive as this emphasis is, it does not bring us appreciably closer to an image of man than the "productive orientation" of Fromm's *Man for Himself*, to which Fromm himself refers. Not even the status which Fromm gives this image by his claim that "the pure biophile is saintly" can rescue it from the fatal ambiguity of what is mean by "life." Fromm cannot capture *man* in the sheer love of life since man's relation to life is different from that of the rest of life. Life is not worth loving and enjoying unless implicit in the concept of life is living well. Growth is not necessarily a good unless implicit in the concept of growth is growth in a direction that realizes positive values. Fromm's syndrome of growth does indeed imply such values—love, independence, openness—but for that very reason his scheme is circular. His ethics of growth rests on another set of ethics which in turn he seeks to ground in the ethics of growth.

In narcissistic love, the partner exists only as a shadow of the other person's narcissistically inflated ego, in contrast to genuine love in which there is real separateness and each exists for the other in his own right. The love of the stranger and of the enemy to which the Old and New Testaments point is based on the realization that the stranger is fully human because *you* are fully human. But in manifest contradiction to the separateness of the partners which he recognizes as essential to love, Fromm declares: "To love the stranger and the enemy is possible only . . . if 'I am thou.'" Only through overcoming narcissism, says Fromm, can we "progress toward the most important 'new frontier' that exists today—man's development into a completely human being."

Throughout a good deal of this book, Fromm talks in terms of the tradition of the Hebrew Bible, according to which man can never overcome the "evil urge" once for all, although he can direct this urge into the service of God. At other times, however, he falls into a doctrine of perfectionism entirely foreign to the Hebrew Bible. From this latter point of view, he speaks of the "completely free person" not only as loving, productive, and independent but as someone whose character structure is such that he "is not free to choose evil."

Fromm is at his best when he turns away from his notions of saintliness and total freedom to the recognition of the subtle interplay of freedom and determinism that make up the life of the average man.

[10] Erich Fromm, *The Heart of Man, Its Genius for Good and Evil*, Vol. XII of *Religious Perspectives*, edited by Ruth Nanda Anshen (N. Y.: Harper & Row, 1964), p. 47.

Fromm's concrete approach to the problem of freedom of choice shows *awareness* to be the decisive factor in choosing the better rather than the worse. One of the most common misunderstandings of any philosophy that points to personal wholeness—one that Fromm himself has contributed to by his penchant for perfectionism—is the notion that wholeness is a finished state of being which the saint or perfected man attains and which no one else can approach. Fromm also points to another freedom, however, the freedom to choose. This freedom is only an abstraction, Fromm says, unless one recognizes that it is a concrete part of a life process. "The degree of our capacity to make choices varies with each act, with our practice of life." Every choice that is made with relatively greater personal wholeness, I would say, leads to greater freedom and greater wholeness. Every choice that is made with relatively less personal wholeness leads to more restricted freedom and more partial wholeness.

> Each step in life which increases my self-confidence, my integrity, my courage, my conviction also increases my capacity to choose the desirable alternative, until eventually it becomes more difficult for me to choose the undesirable rather than the desirable action. On the other hand, each act of surrender and cowardice weakens me, opens the path for more acts of surrender, and eventually freedom is lost.[11]

Not only decision but also the awarness that one is deciding is essential. Many people fail in the art of living, Fromm declares, because they are not aware they stand at a fork in the road, because they do not decide while they still have alternative answers.

Fromm sums up his image of man in terms of the understanding of evil as "man's loss of himself in the tragic attempt to escape the burden of his humanity." One cannot cease being human even at the most archaic levels of regression, and therefore all evilness is tragic. The degrees of evilness are the same as the degrees of regression—the strivings against life, the love of death, the incestuous-symbiotic striving to return to the womb, the soil, the inorganic, the narcissistic self-immolation which imprisons man in the "hell" of his own ego and makes him an enemy of life. Man is free to choose as long as his inclinations to regress *and* to move forward are still in some balance. If his heart hardens to such a degree that there is no longer a balance of inclinations, then he is no longer free to choose. But even this hardening of the heart is a specifically human and not a nonhuman phenomenon. To be human is to be faced with the never-ending task of making choices and of recognizing that wrong choices make us incapable of saving ourselves. If man becomes indifferent to life, then there is no longer any hope that he will choose the good.

[11] *Ibid.*, p. 136.

No awareness will help us if we have lost the capacity to be moved
by the distress of another human being, by the friendly gaze of another person, by the song of a bird, by the greenness of grass.[12]

The Modern Pragmatist has to some extent bequeathed us the same
problem as the Modern Vitalist—that of finding a direction which
would make meaningful the emphasis on what "works," on what has
"real effects," on social adaptation, and, in the case of Fromm, on "self-
realization." Self-realization cannot be made the goal without vitiating
its very meaning as the attainment of authentic existence. Such an
existence cannot be measured in terms of the self alone, but in terms
of the meaning that the self attains through giving itself in relation to
what is not itself, to other selves and other beings. If one means by
self-realization no more than realizing the empirical self that one is,
then one is already at one's goal. If one means, on the other hand, a self
one has not yet become but can become, then one must still discover
which of the many selves one can become is one's "real" self. "Potentiality" is essentially neutral. Only the direction of "potentiality" makes
it good or bad. Values cannot be based on self-realization or the
realization of man's powers. On the contrary, we cannot define ourselves or our potentialities apart from the direction we give them, apart
from what we become in relation to others. This direction, this becoming, implies a movement toward the authentic, toward values,
toward the image of man.

[12] *Ibid.*, p. 150.

IX

THE
EXISTENTIALIST

14

THE ATHEIST
EXISTENTIALIST:
NIETZSCHE AND SARTRE

THE existentialist is one of the most important types of contemporary images of man. Yet it is even more difficult to define and delimit than the other types we have portrayed. The popular mind tends to lump together under existentialism everything from Salvador Dali to Simone de Beauvoir, the Frenchman in the *cave* on *la rive gauche* to the beatnik in San Francisco. Jean-Paul Sartre defines existentialism as existence preceding essence, which means that man invents himself and has no meaning or value prior to his doing so. This definition does not even fit Sartre's own philosophy, much less the many other schools of existentialism. Sartre also distinguishes between the atheist and the religious existentialists and implies that the former somehow represent the mainstream. This division grossly oversimplifies and distorts the actual situation. In Part V of *The Worlds of Existentialism*, I present sixteen thinkers in a subtle shading from atheist to humanist to religious to theological existentialism, and the large majority are in one sense or another religious!

Another reason that Sartre's division is misleading is that it obscures real differences and similarities of attitude which are often more important than the question of whether or not a particular thinker professes a belief in God. Camus never ceased to speak of himself as an atheist, yet the later Camus is closer in attitude to the theist Buber than he is to the atheist Sartre.[1] That there is a significant difference in the image of man of explicitly atheistic and explicitly theological existentialists we can see by dealing with Nietzsche and Sartre in one

[1] As I have demonstrated through my contrast between "the Modern Promethean" and "the Modern Job" in *Problematic Rebel.*

chapter and Kierkegaard, Berdyaev and Tillich in the next. But that nonreligious and religious existentialists may converge even more significantly than they diverge we shall also see in the following chapter on "The Existentialist of Dialogue."

As I have pointed out, there is no single philosophy that can claim to set the standard for what existentialism is, despite the claims of Sartre on the one hand and of the followers of Martin Heidegger on the other:

> "Existentialism" is not a philosophy but a mood embracing a number of disparate philosophies; the differences among them are more basic than the temper which unites them. This temper can best be described as a reaction against the static, the abstract, the purely rational, the merely irrational, in favor of the dynamic and the concrete, personal involvement and "engagement," action, choice, and commitment, the distinction between "authentic" and "inauthentic" existence, and the actual situation of the existential subject as the starting point of thought.[2]

Beyond this common temper, however, the issues that divide the existentialists are frequently even more important than the temper which unites them.

Although there is too much of the vitalist in Nietzsche to justify classifying him entirely as an existentialist philosopher, his teaching of the "will to power," of "the death of God," of the importance of the self, of man as a valuing animal, of the uniqueness of each man's way—all bring him clearly within our focus. Like all existentialists, Nietzsche is strongly critical of inauthentic existence—of those who live simply to live:

> Alas! There cometh the time when man will no longer give birth to any star. Alas! There cometh the time of the most despicable man, who can no longer despise himself.
>
> "We have discovered happiness"—say the last men, and blink thereby. . . .
>
> They have left the regions where it is hard to live; for they need warmth. One still loveth one's neighbour and rubbeth against him; for one needeth warmth. . . .
>
> A little poison now and then: that maketh pleasant dreams. And much poison at last for a pleasant death. . . .
>
> No shepherd, and one herd! Everyone wanteth the same; everyone is equal: he who hath other sentiments goeth voluntarily into the madhouse.[3]

---

[2] *The Worlds of Existentialism: A Critical Reader,* edited with introductions and a conclusion by Maurice Friedman (N. Y.: Random House, 1964), pp. 3-4.
[3] Friedrich Nietzsche, *Thus Spake Zarathustra, op. cit.,* p. 11f.

As opposed to these "last men," Nietzsche celebrates those who will have the strength to destroy old values and create new ones. Before the new can be created, the old must be destroyed, but this holy Nay unto duty is for the sake of a new beginning, "a holy Yea unto life: *its own* will, willeth now the spirit; *his own* word winneth the world's outcast." It is not just a matter of replacing old values by new, but of throwing off the tyranny of values imposed from the outside in favor of values which are created by one's own will to power.

Through his creation of new values, man recovers his alienated freedom. Those who sought to reach "all gods and backworlds" with a "death-leap," "a poor ignorant weariness unable to will any longer," are unmasked by Zarathustra as life-deniers. The true source of reality and of value is human existence, man, the self within. Nietzsche's ego, unlike Freud's, cannot be looked at as an object because it is the *subject* of all sensing and feeling:

> But that "other world" is well concealed from man, that dehumanised, inhuman world, which is a celestial naught; and the bowels of existence do not speak unto man, except as man. . . .
>
> Yea, this ego, with its contradiction and perplexity, speaketh most uprightly of its being—this creating, willing, evaluing ego, which is the measure and value of things.
>
> And this most upright existence, the ego—it speaketh of the body, and still implieth the body, even when it museth and raveth and fluttereth with broken wings. . . .
>
> A new pride taught me mine ego, and that teach I unto men: no longer to thrust one's head into the sand of celestial things, but to carry it freely, a terrestrial head, which giveth meaning to the earth!
>
> Instruments and playthings are sense and spirit: behind them there is still the Self. The Self seeketh with the eyes of the senses, it hearkeneth also with the ears of the spirit. . . .
>
> Behind thy thoughts and feelings, my brother, there is a mighty lord, an unknown sage—it is called Self; it dwelleth in thy body, it is thy body.[4]

Nietzsche, like Dewey, rejects the "eternal values" in favor of valuing and valuation. But valuing to Nietzsche is neither pragmatic nor instrumental: it is the very center of human existence, what makes man man:

> Values did man only assign to things in order to maintain himself—he created only the significance of things, a human significance! Therefore, calleth he himself "man," that is, the valuator.

---

[4] *Ibid.*, pp. 28–30; 33.

Valuing is creating: hear it, ye creating ones! Valuation itself is the
treasure and jewel of the valued things.

Through valuation only is there value; and without valuation the
nut of existence would be hollow. Hear it, ye creating ones!

Change of values—that is, change of the creating ones. Always does
he destroy who hath to be a creator.[5]

The recognition of valuation as both the product and center of
human existence leads Zarathustra to attack "the eternal reason spider
and the eternal reason cobweb," that hypostasization of reason that
attempts to substitute universals and abstractions for the concrete,
particular realities of human existence. He attacks in particular the
idealist who "proves" his assertion that reality and thought coincide
by turning away from the irreducible particularity that he confronts
to a smooth, rationalized thought world:

"Will to Truth" do ye call it, ye wisest ones, that which impelleth
you and maketh you ardent?

Will for the thinkableness of all being: thus do *I* call your will!

All being would ye make thinkable: for ye doubt with good reason
whether it be already thinkable.

But it shall accommodate and bend itself to you! So willeth your will.
Smooth shall it become and subject to the spirit, as its mirror and reflection.[6]

One of the most important aspects of idealist philosophies that existentialism rebels against is the postulate that only the universal is
meaningful. Even Hegel sees the process of history as the movement
of universal spirit, and his concrete universal is a part of a dialectic
in which the particular becomes subject to the universal. From the
standpoint of the universal, the way of man is a rational, universal
way. From the standpoint of the existentialist, the way of man is
unique for each particular man because each man is unique and each
is in a unique situation. "This—is now *my* way,—where is yours?" says
Zarathustra. "Thus did I answer those who asked me 'the way.' For
the way—it doth not exist!" The unique way must also be the way
that is entered with one's whole person and not with merely rational
decision:

Ah, that ye would renounce all half-willing, and would decide for
idleness as ye decide for action!

Ah, that ye understood my word: "Do ever what ye will—but first
be such as *can will*.[7]

[5] *Ibid.*, p. 6of.
[6] *Ibid.*, pp. 122–3.
[7] *Ibid.*, p. 190.

The specifically atheistic quality of Nietzsche's existentialism, as of Sartre's, lies in his belief that man not only *ought* to recover his alienated freedom and create new values for himself, but that he has no option but to do so. When Zarathustra meets the old saint in the forest, the saint asks for a gift. But Zarathustra hurries away lest he take something from him and exclaims to himself: "This old saint in the forest hath not yet heard of it, that *God is dead!*" The death of God is not a theological statement. It is a historical one. It designates a change in the human relationship to the transcendent. The important part of it is not that man no longer believes in the existence of God, but that the transcendent is now without effective power in guiding his life, in giving him a base for value decisions. The contemporary German existentialist Martin Heidegger interprets this saying of Nietzsche's in explicitly existentialist terms of the contrast between a world of ideal essences and values and the world of the "here and now." To Nietzsche, says Heidegger,

> God is the designation for the realm of ideas and ideals. This realm of the transcendent has been considered since Plato, or more precisely, following the late Greek and Christian interpretation of Platonic philosophy, as the true and truly real world. Compared to it the world of the senses is but the here and now, a transitory world and therefore but appearance and unreality. . . . Nietzsche's statement "God is dead" means that the transcendent is without effective power. . . . If God as ground of the transcendent and end of all that is real is dead; if the transcendent world of ideas has lost its binding and, above all, its evocative and constructive force, then there remains nothing to which man can turn for support and guidance. . . . The true is that which truly is. The good is that on which everything depends. The beautiful is the order and unity of that-which-is in its entirety. These ultimate values, however, begin to devaluate as soon as the conviction spreads that the ideal world cannot and will never be effected within the real world.[8]

This proclamation of "the death of God" implies the very recognition that underlies this book—the absence of an image of man in response to which one can grope one's way toward authentic personal existence. The "death of God," as I have pointed out, "does not mean that modern man does not 'believe' in God, any more than it means that God Himself has actually died."

> Whether or not one holds with Sartre that God never existed or with Buber that God is in "eclipse" and that it is we, the "slayers of God," who dwell in the darkness, the "death of God" means the awareness of a basic crisis in modern history—the crisis that comes when

man no longer knows what it means to be human and becomes aware that he does not know this. This is not just a question of the relativization of "values" and the absence of universally accepted mores. It is the absence of an image of meaningful human existence, the absence of the ground that enabled Greek, Biblical, and Renaissance man to move with some sureness even in the midst of tragedy.[9]

It is the *ways* in which God died in *Thus Spake Zarathustra* that reveal the fundamentally atheist or, more precisely, nihilist quality of Nietzsche's statement. The first way, we are told, is that God choked to death out of compassion for man. Here, the Jewish and Christian insight into a God who dwells in the high and holy places *and* with those who are humble and contrite of heart is converted into a loss of belief in all transcendence. God now is only immanent. Not equal to the sufferings of his miserable creatures, he is not even an immanent *divine* force, but merely absurd. "The transcendence is without effective power." The second way in which God dies is through the problem of evil. Like Omar Khayyám, and unlike Jeremiah, from whom the Sufi poet got the figure of the potter and the pots, Zarathustra sees God as cause and man as purely determined effect, so that the indictment of God for man's evil rests on the prior assumption that there is no reality to human freedom, to our existence as persons:

> He was also indistinct. How he raged at us, this wrath-snorter, because we understood him badly! But why did he not speak more clearly?
> And if the fault lay in our ears, why did he give us ears that heard him badly? If there was dirt in our ears, well! who put it in them?
> Too much miscarried with him, this potter who had not learned thoroughly! That he took revenge on his pots and creations, however, because they turned out badly—that was a sin against *good taste*.
> There is also good taste in piety: *this* at last said: "Away with *such* a God! Better to have no God, better to set up destiny on one's own account, better to be a fool, better to be God oneself!"[10]

This last exclamation—"better to be God oneself!"—resumes the specifically modern motif that we have already seen in Jung, the combination of the abhorrence of the transcendent with a tendency to the deification of man—in Jung's case the "self" which comes into being in the unconscious, in Nietzsche's the ascent of the higher man toward the superman. As in Jung's *Answer to Job*, too, there is the curiously personal note of resentment against a transcendent God who is held at the same time not to be there at all!

9 *Problematic Rebel, op. cit.*, p. 52.
10 *Thus Spake Zarathustra, op. cit.*, pp. 291–2.

The motif of the deification of man carries with it not only the grandeur of man's ascent to the superman, but also the fear of modern man before an infinite that threatens to crush him—"the heartless voids and immensities of the universe that stab us from behind with the thought of annihilation," to quote Melville's Ishmael in *Moby Dick*. This combination of the glorification of man and the confession of his impotence is shown in the other two ways in which God dies in *Thus Spake Zarathustra*. With the sublime logic of the man who begins with his own existence as the reference point for all other reality, Zarathustra states: "But that I may reveal my heart entirely unto you, my friends: *if* there were gods, how could I endure it to be no God! *Therefore* there are no gods." How could he bear to exist if he knew that over against him was an eternity that dwarfed his time, a reality that limited his consciousness, an Other which he could see only as hostile, so deeply has existential mistrust become the very principle of his world view?

When Zarathustra meets the "ugliest man," however, there is no suggestion of any heroic Promethean self-assertion of man against the infinite. The ugliest man is the murderer of God, but he murdered him out of sheer self-defense:

> "Thou couldst not *endure* him who beheld *thee*,—whoever beheld thee through and through, thou ugliest man. Thou tookest revenge on this witness!"

> "But he—*had* to die: he looked with eyes which beheld *everything* —he beheld men's depths and dregs, all his hidden ignominy and ugliness.
> His pity knew no modesty: he crept into my dirtiest corners. This most prying, over-intrusive, over-pitiful one had to die.
> He ever beheld *me*: on such a witness I would have revenge—or not live myself."[11]

The existential mistrust of the ugliest man is even deeper than that of Zarathustra. He cannot affirm his own existence. Therefore, any witness must be not only hostile, but, what is still worse, a mirror forcing him to look at his own shame. "To understand all is to forgive all," said Voltaire. But the ugliest man knows that it is precisely if his real motives, his innermost soul were understood that it would be impossible to forgive. This, too, is a specifically modern motif. To many people today, even psychoanalysis, and still more "self-analysis," is a means of escaping from the *shame* of the self by seeing oneself as an object, in categories, or as rationally comprehensible and explicable. This means that one is not responsible as the unique person that one is, but only in terms of a social role.

[11] *Ibid.*, pp. 294; 297.

Does this mean that Zarathustra ends in nihilism, that he leaves us with no positive image of man? There is certainly an attempt to portray such an image—through the three motifs of the will to power, the Superman, and the eternal return. The direct sequence to the statement that "God is dead" is the proclamation of the Superman—not the glorification of man as he is but of man as something to be surpassed, as the bridge between the animal and the Superman. The Superman is no fixed goal: it is the direction of movement that comes into being when our will to power creates new values. "Let your will say: The Superman *shall be* the meaning of the earth!" In this statement, Nietzsche agrees with Sartre's formula that existence precedes essence. There is no meaning of the earth simply waiting to be discovered. It must be created by you yourself, by the striving upward of your will to power. One reaches the hour of great contempt when even one's happiness becomes loathsome to one as "poverty and pollution and wretched self-complacency." But at that very hour one says: "My happiness should justify existence itself!" Man is a bridge and not a goal. He is an "overgoing," but he is also a "downgoing." The evolution upward to the Superman takes place through our strivings, through our will to power, but also through our defeats since the will to power expresses itself dialectically in the competition between the will to power of one man and another, of one nation and another. Since it is valuation that makes man man, one cannot get beyond the relative values of competing groups to man except through letting this process of will and struggle continue until it has created man out of the welter of men.

Nietzsche's rejection of the old morality takes place on the basis of implicit moral values (the higher selfishness, the right kind of friendship and marriage, joy in life, world affirmation). Values, to him, are the product of a "will to power" which justifies itself by the creation of new values and the progress toward the "Superman." Yet the Superman is an undefined direction which we can only assume to be upward if we take for granted the very values that are to be created. In other words, Nietzsche is a great moralist in his critique of existing morals, but if we try to extrapolate an image of man from this critique or from his teaching of the Superman, we will find that Nietzsche has given us no real direction as to which expression of the will to power is more authentic and which less.

To Jean-Paul Sartre, man is his own project and remains responsible for himself no matter what he does. Sartre rejects every traditional notion of human nature in favor of the image of man as one who invents himself. Thus he holds, like Bergson, that actuality precedes potentiality. Man "is only what he wills himself to be after this thrust toward existence," says Sartre in his famous essay *Existentialism*. By this, he does not mean a conscious decision, but the project that man becomes through that earlier, more spontaneous choice whereby he comes into relation to existence and takes responsibility for it. This leads Sartre to the position that our responsibility is not only for ourselves but for everyone else. "I am creating a certain image of man of my own choosing. In choosing myself, I choose man." The truth behind this statement is that I must be ready to accept responsibility for the way in which what I choose to become affects others. The distortion is the injunction to act as if I were the only variable, the only locus of freedom and responsibility. If I am, as Sartre says, "alone with no excuses, condemned to be free," then this aloneness includes the impossibility of taking full responsibility for the image of man that any other person chooses. I may only say that this is what I have chosen man to be in myself and witness to the image of man I wish to become. I may not also choose it for others.

In utmost contrast to Freud, Sartre sees man as completely free. There is no fixed and given human nature, no determinism, no God to give us values or commands and legitimize our conduct, no passion whose power could remove our responsibility for ourselves. "Man is free, man is freedom." While he recognizes society as one's situation, he admits of no conditioning by society that could excuse one's conforming to that situation. Also in contrast to Freud, Sartre begins with the prereflective *cogito* or consciousness. Only this gives man dignity, he claims. He would never consent, like Freud, to see the ego as an object; or, like Jung, to see it as determined by deep forces of the unconscious; or, like Mead, to see it as "an eddy in the social current"; or, like Sullivan, to see it as thoroughly interpersonal. To live means to be *involved* in a *situation* in which *one must make a choice, without reference to preestablished values,* but also *without arbitrariness.* "In choosing his ethics, he makes himself." To Sartre, the only possibility of creating a human community is to accept the human condition—that we exist, that we must work, that we are mortal, that we are involved, that we must choose, and that in choosing we invent ourselves and take full responsibility for our lives:

> To say that we invent values means nothing else but this: life has no meaning *a priori.* Before you come alive, life is nothing: it's up to you to give it a meaning, and value is nothing else but the meaning that you choose.[12]

[12] Jean-Paul Sartre, *Existentialism,* translated by Bernard Frechtman (N. Y.: The Philosophical Library, 1947), p. 58.

Sartre's atheism is not concerned with proving that God does not exist. Rather it says—and this is a much more drastic statement—that nothing would be changed if God did exist. He refuses to join either with those who say we can keep God and make Him into a function or reflection of human values, or those who say we can do away with God "as a useless and costly hypothesis" and keep all the old norms of civilization and progress:

> The existentialist . . . thinks it very distressing that God does not exist, because all possibility of finding values in a heaven of ideas disappears along with Him: there can no longer be an *a priori* Good, since there is no infinite and perfect consciousness to think it. Nowhere is it written that the Good exists, that we must be honest, that we must not lie; because the fact is we are on a plane where there are only men. Dostoevsky said, "If God didn't exist, everything would be possible." That is the very starting point of existentialism.[13]

Dostoyevsky thought that by taking the "death of God" to its logical conclusions, he could show the absurdity of Ivan Karamazov's "All is permitted," and by this dialectical process bring men back to God. Sartre accepts the most extreme consequences without batting an eye. "I'm quite vexed that that's the way it is," he says; "but if I've discarded God the Father, there has to be someone to invent values."

In his play, *The Flies,* Sartre takes over the ancient Greek myth of Orestes and Electra in order to bring out by contrast his view of man's complete freedom and total responsibility. Orestes steps forth as the modern existentialist hero, resolutely defying Zeus for the sake of liberating the people of Argos from the superstitious fears and blind guilt that keep them prisoners. Having been made free, Orestes cannot be one with Nature, for he *is* his freedom, no matter how much anguish this brings him. "Outside nature, against nature, without excuse beyond remedy, except what remedy I find within myself," he proclaims. Every man must find his own way burdened with a freedom that he cannot escape, a forlornness that brings him up short every time he tries to flow unthinkingly with the stream of life. "Human life begins on the far side of despair."

A somewhat more modern and more convincing dramatization of Sartre's atheistic existentialism is his play *The Devil and the Good Lord.* Goetz, the hero, discovers that God does not exist, that God is the loneliness of man, and that it is man alone who decides on Evil and invents Good. "If God exists, man is nothing," he says in an echo of Dostoyevsky's "man-god," and by implication draws the conclusion that if He does not exist, man is everything. God is an absence, a

---

[13] *Ibid.,* p. 26f.

silence, and now the absence of God, the absence of the witness, makes life real for man. At the same time, it makes man aware of his dependence on others for his own existence. *"How real* you have become since He no longer exists," Goetz says to his beloved, and adds: "Look at me, don't stop looking at me for one moment: the world has been struck blind; if you turned away your head, I should be afraid of annihilation."

The note of the Modern Promethean rings through these two plays, the man who feels he recovers his alienated freedom and creativity by destroying the Transcendent over against him.[14] It is a note of noble rebellion which seems to carry with it its own meaning. But what happens when man has accepted the "death of God" and no longer romanticizes the rebellion against a God who does not exist? Sartre's powerful early novel *Nausea* answers this question. Man discovers himself to be *de trop*. His existence is superfluous; it is without justification. It cannot take on meaning through immersing oneself in historical research or through identifying oneself with the burghers whose pictures line the walls of the chief room in the city hall. At all of these respectable, solid citizens the hero—Antoine Roquentin—thumbs his nose. But he also thumbs his nose at himself—at everything he has ever been, at everything he is and might become. Perhaps if I could write a novel, he lamely concludes, I might give meaning to my existence.

Mathieu Delarue, the hero of Sartre's trilogy of novels *The Roads of Freedom,* has less nausea than Roquentin, but even in his gratuitous sacrifice of himself at the end of the third novel, he is anything but a positive image of man. The first novel of the trilogy, *The Age of Reason,* is the most conscious and significant treatment of the problem of the man who recognizes that he is "condemned to be free." Mathieu is a thirty-five-year-old professor of philosophy who wishes to keep himself free from any bourgeois ties. However, he has in effect settled down to a thoroughly bourgeois existence as an employee of the government and as the lover of a mistress with whom he has spent four nights a week for the past seven years. Marcelle becomes pregnant through Mathieu's carelessness, and it is this situation and his attempts to cope with it which are the focal point of the whole novel. Mathieu assumes, without asking, that Marcelle wants an abortion, whereas she is more and more drawn to keep the child, but does not tell him. This misunderstanding provides the central irony of the book.

[14] See Maurice Friedman, *Problematic Rebel, op. cit.*, Part IV, "The Modern Promethean."

What makes this central irony so biting is that it turns on Mathieu's ideal of remaining free and forces him to confront the futility of a life which is free without being committed. To Marcelle, Mathieu's freedom is his personal vice, that which makes him different from other people. To Mathieu, it is the only thing a man can do: "If I didn't try to assume responsibility for my own existence, it would seem utterly absurd to go on existing." Mathieu's old friend, Sarah, tells him of her abortion—throwing the fetus down the drain like a dead rat—and says that he does not realize what he is going to do. But he rejects her assumption that life is its own justification:

> "And when you bring a child into the world, do you realize what you're going to do?" asked Mathieu wrathfully.
> A child: another consciousness, a little center-point of light that would flutter round and round, dashing against the walls, and never be able to escape.[15]

This figure of consciousness fluttering against walls from which it cannot escape is an apt metaphor for Sartre's image of man. He is a sort of latter-day Cartesian dualist who, if he does not make a strict division between mind and body, nonetheless holds consciousness to be free only when it transcends itself through its own becoming, its inner emptiness—*pour soi*—but bound when it must see itself as an object seen by others, as attached to the body, as conditioned and imprisoned within its own incarnation—*en soi*. The dialectic between these two modes of consciousness never issues either into a Bergsonian possibility of flowing with existence or into Maurice Merleau-Ponty's existence for others—*pour autrui*. Inner division and conflict with others are the two built-in postulates of Sartre's image of man.

When Mathieu was seven, his uncle had left him alone in a room with a three-thousand-year-old vase, telling him to be sure not to touch it. But to Mathieu this vase represented everything that deprived him of freedom and made his existence *de trop*, and he proceeded with childish directness to regain his freedom:

> How frightening it was to be a little ball of bread crumb in this ancient fire-browned world, confronted by an impassive vase three thousand years old! He had turned his back on it, and stood grimacing and snuffling at the mirror without managing to divert his thoughts; then he had suddenly gone back to the table, picked up the vase, which was a heavy one, and dashed it on the floor—it had just happened like that, after which he had felt as light as gossamer. . . . He had thought: "I did it," and felt quite proud, freed from the world,

15 Jean-Paul Sartre, *The Age of Reason*, translated by Eric Sutton (N. Y.: Bantam Books, 1959), p. 48.

without ties or kin or origins, a stubborn little excresence that had burst the terrestrial crust.[16]

When he was sixteen, he repeated this process intellectually, determining that he would be free and betting with himself "that his whole life should be cast in the semblance of that unique moment." It is this bet which shapes Mathieu's image of himself and his image of man:

> Mathieu was not, in his own eyes, a tall, rather ungainly fellow who taught philosophy in a public school, nor the brother of Jacques Delarue, the lawyer, nor Marcelle's lover, nor Daniel's and Brunet's friend: he was just that bet personified.[17]

This is the *for-itself* of Mathieu's subjectivity that cannot be fixed in any category. But he would be in "bad faith" were he not to recognize that he also exists as an object to others and to himself—the *in-itself*. He thinks of his own words about freedom as empty, pompous commonplaces of the intellectual and sees himself as an official worried about money, an empty person waiting for nothing. When Mathieu goes to visit his lawyer-brother Jacques to ask for money for the abortion, Jacques points out that the coming child is the logical result of a situation which he entered of his own free will, yet he wants to suppress it and not accept the consequences of his acts. "Your whole life is built upon a lie," he taunts. He wants a comfortable life and the appearance of liberty, the advantages of marriage without its inconveniences. He has fallen into a habit of life with Marcelle which entails respect and obligations without adventure or even vivid pleasure. To all this, Mathieu retorts, through clenched teeth and with a sort of shame, that he cares little whether he is a bourgeois. "All I want is to retain my freedom." Jacques' response is a telling confrontation that sums up Mathieu as nothing else in the book:

> "I should myself have thought," said Jacques, "that freedom consisted in frankly confronting situations into which one has deliberately entered, and accepting all one's responsibilities. But that, no doubt, is not your view: you condemn capitalist society, and yet you are an official in that society; you display an abstract sympathy with Communists, but you take care not to commit yourself, you have never voted. You despise the bourgeois class, and yet you are a bourgeois, son and brother of a bourgeois, and you live like a bourgeois."[18]

Mathieu's confrontation with his communist friend Brunet is even more unpleasant for him, for Mathieu envies Brunet and would like

[16] *Ibid.*, p. 52f.
[17] *Ibid.*, p. 53.
[18] *Ibid.*, p. 118.

to be able to join him in his cause, "You need to commit yourself," Brunet says to him. "You live in a void, . . . you're an abstraction, a man who is not there." *Da-sein*—to be there, in situation, in the world, is the essence of the existentialism that Sartre took over from Heidegger. Brunet's comment thus goes straight to the heart of Sartre's philosophy: how can one use one's freedom so as to have a responsible, committed existence through which one is really "there?" Brunet tells Mathieu that the only answer is, having freed himself from the bourgeoisie, to renounce his freedom and join the proletariat. Otherwise he will live his life in parentheses, a slave of his own freedom, and die without ever having waked up. Mathieu himself agrees. Brunet to him is a man—he has *chosen* to be a man:

> A man with powerful, rather knotted muscles, who deals in brief, stern truths, a man erect and self-enclosed, sure of himself, a man of this earth, impervious to the angelical allurements of art, psychology, and politics, a whole man, nothing but a man. And Mathieu was there, confronting him, irresolute, half his life gone, and still half-raw, assailed by all the vertigoes of non-humanity; and he thought; "I don't even look like a man."[19]

Mathieu responds that if he chooses, he must choose Brunet's side, "there is no other choice." Why he feels this way is as incomprehensible, given his philosophy of freedom, as his inability to commit himself given the fact that he feels this way! Brunet says of himself that nothing can deprive his life of meaning or prevent its being a destiny, like the life of every comrade, while Mathieu admits that his freedom is a burden to him, which he longs to exchange "for a good sound certainty."

Applying Sartre's idea of self-deception to Brunet and Mathieu, we would be tempted to say that Mathieu is in bad faith because he wishes to be pure *for-itself* without any *in-itself*, with the result that he lives an uninvolved, uncommitted life. But we would also say that Brunet is in bad faith because he has made himself an incarnation of the *in-itself*, a solid being, a masculine man, a courageous comrade, at the expense of renouncing his freedom to transcend what he *is* by what he may *become*. Mathieu would never thumb his nose at Brunet as Antoine Roquentin did at the pictures of the burghers in the city hall. He envies Brunet's ability to *choose* to be a communist. But he cannot choose this himself, and he cannot renounce that philosophy of freedom which seems to be his sole *raison d'être*—the justification of an existence which, by his own definition, cannot be justified.

It is his responsibility to the child that he was, the child who took

[19] *Ibid.*, pp. 131-2.

freedom as its destiny, that makes him defy all those who wish to fix him in his place, his activity, and his social role:

> "A life," thought Mathieu, "is formed from the future just as bodies are compounded from the void." . . . The far-off days of childhood, the day when he had said: "I will be free," the day when he had said: "I will be famous," appeared to him even now with their individual future, like a small, circled individual sky above them all, and that future was himself, *himself* just as he was at present, weary and a little overripe, they had claims upon him across the passage of time past, they maintained their insistencies, and he was often visited by attacks of devastating remorse, because his casual, cynical present was the original future of those past days. It was he whom they had awaited for twenty years, it was he, this tired man, who was pestered by a remorseless child to realize his hopes; on him it depended whether these childish pledges should remain forever childish or whether they should become the first announcement of a destiny.[20]

Later on, Mathieu thinks of his freedom in less romantic terms than that of destiny:

> "It is *by my agency* that everything must happen." Even if he let himself be carried off, in helplessness and in despair, even if he let himself be carried off like an old sack of coal, he would have chosen his own damnation; he was free, free in every way, free to behave like a fool or a machine, free to accept, free to refuse, free to equivocate; to marry, to give up the game, to drag this dead weight about with him for years to come. He could do what he liked, no one had the right to advise him, there would be for him no Good nor Evil unless he brought them into being. All around him things were gathered in a circle, expectant, impassive, and indicative of nothing. He was alone, enveloped in this monstrous silence, free and alone without assistance and without excuse, condemned to decide without support from any quarter, condemned forever to be free.[21]

Mathieu's pitiful attempts to raise money for the abortion fall afoul of Marcelle's desire to have the baby, a desire encouraged by Mathieu's friend, Daniel, who has been seeing Marcelle secretly in the role of benevolent protector. Daniel tells Mathieu that he will marry Marcelle himself *and* that he is a homosexual. Mathieu realizes that in his own relation to Marcelle he has been "a sort of embodied refusal, a negation," and wonders intrigued whether freedom is not doing just what Daniel has done—*acting* and in such a way that one cannot go back on it. He, in contrast, has not acted. He remains alone, no freer than before, but stripped of the illusion that if Marcelle did

20 *Ibid.*, p. 234.
21 *Ibid.*, pp. 275–6.

not exist, his life would have been freer. His life, he concludes, has been "much ado about nothing."

> Various tried and proved rules of conduct had already discreetly offered him their services: disillusioned epicureanism, smiling tolerance, resignation, flat seriousness, stoicism—all the aids whereby a man may savor, minute by minute, like a connoisseur, the failure of a life. . . . It's true, it's really true: I have attained the age of reason."[22]

The assertion of freedom is empty if it is not bound up with taking responsibility for choices that one makes. But neither Mathieu nor his author seems any farther along at the end of the book as to how to combine this total freedom and this total responsibility, how to put together Mathieu and Brunet and make of them one believable image of man. Sartre's Orestes has the double heroism of the ancient tragic hero who acts for the sake of the order and of the Modern Promethean who rebels against that order in the name of man. Mathieu has neither. He cannot glean any heroism from his freedom since he does not believe in the order to start with. Nor can he make his freedom a destiny, since he is nothing but a projection into the future which no one and nothing can justify but himself.

It is not in the portrayal of the authentic, but in the merciless keenness with which he sees through the inauthentic, that Sartre is at his best. One example of *mauvaise foi,* or self-deception, that Sartre cites is the pathologically frigid woman who tries to detach herself in advance from the pleasure she dreads by making up household accounts during the sexual act. Another is the girl who does not want to break the magic charm when the boy takes her hand, yet at the same time does not want to admit to herself what he is after—since "the desire cruel and naked would humiliate and horrify her." She escapes from her dilemma by contemplating her body as if from above as a passive object to which events can *happen* while thinking of the relationship itself as an intellectual one.

Sartre's finest portrayal of bad faith, and with it of inauthentic existence, is his "Portrait of the Anti-Semite." He explains the anti-Semite as an unconscious Manichean who believes that if only evil is destroyed, good will automatically reign supreme. He is also a sadist who finds it amusing and sexually exciting to attack unarmed men. But above all, he is a man in bad faith who wishes to escape man's fate of being a subject and become purely an object—a being of a fixed nature who need not be responsible and who need not bear the anguish of freedom:

[22] *Ibid.,* p. 342.

He is a man who is afraid. Not of the Jews of course, but of himself, of his conscience, his freedom, of his instincts, of his responsibilities, of solitude, of change, of society and the world; of everything except the Jews. . . . *By adhering to antisemitism, he is not only adopting an opinion, he is choosing himself as a person. He is choosing the permanence and the impenetrability of rock,* the total irresponsibility of the warrior who obeys his leaders—and he has no leader. . . . *Antisemitism, in a word, is fear of man's fate. The antisemite is the man who wants to be pitiless stone, furious torrent, devastating lightning:* in short, *everything but a man.*[23]

An important aspect of bad faith, or self-deception, is its intersubjective dimension. We exist because others see us, as Daniel writes to Mathieu in *The Reprieve,* and yet their look robs us of ourselves by turning us into an object. A man looking through a keyhole into a room hears footsteps which come up the hall and stop behind him. He who was the moment before a subject turning other persons into objects is now deprived of his own subjectivity by this person looking at him. Thus, our concrete relations with others are wholly governed by our attitudes with respect to the object which we are for the Other. "The Other *looks* at me," writes Sartre in *Being and Nothingness,* "and as such he holds the secret of my being, he knows what I am. Thus the profound meaning of my being is outside me, imprisoned in an absence." The original meaning of the relationship with others is conflict. The Other steals my being from me, and I recover myself only through absorbing him. Nonetheless, I exist by means of the Other's freedom: for I need his freedom as a reflection through which I am aware of myself. Therefore, I have no security in making him into an object, but must try instead to get hold of his freedom and reduce it to being a freedom subject to my freedom. This to Sartre, as to Proust before him, is the essence of love. "The lover does not desire to possess the beloved as one possesses a thing; he . . . wants to possess a freedom as freedom."

It is love that frees us from that state of being *de trop* which Sartre has described so vividly in *Nausea.* "We now feel that our existence is taken up and willed even in its tiniest details by an absolute freedom." Unfortunately, our desire to be loved in this way must provoke a conflict since in fact the beloved sees the lover as an object among others and uses him as such. The beloved cannot will to love; as a result, he must be seduced. Love is, in fact, nothing but an enterprise

[23] Jean-Paul Sartre, "Portrait of the Anti-Semite" in Walter Kaufmann, ed., *Existentialism from Dostoyevsky to Sartre* (N. Y.: Meridian Books, 1956), pp. 286–7; italics added.

of seduction. In sex, this seduction takes the form of the incarnation of the Other's freedom in his flesh.

Both desire and love are doomed to failure. At any moment, the Other can awaken, through a third person or by himself, and make me appear as an object—hence the lover's perpetual insecurity. If one wishes, through masochism, to immerse oneself in pure objectivity before the abyss of the Other's subjectivity, one ends by finding the Other's objectivity which, in spite of oneself, frees one's own subjectivity. If one tries instead to look at the Other's look, attempting to confront the Other's freedom on the ground of one's own freedom, one ends by converting the other into an object. If, thirdly, one tries through sadism to possess the other as an object, nevertheless "the Other as freedom and my objectivity as my alienated-self are there, unperceived, . . . given in my very comprehension of the world and of my being in the world."

For Sartre, I never really know the other subject directly but only as a part of my own consciousness and by indirect inference. Even that I am aware of "the look" of the Other does not in the least mean that I am aware of how the Other really sees me. I see his eyes seeing me, but I do not see *through* his eyes. Dostoyevsky's *Notes from the Underground* and T. S. Eliot's "The Love Song of J. Alfred Prufrock" both portray men incapable of action and involvement because of their awareness of how others see them. Yet in each case this awareness is an obviously distorted projection which bears little correspondence to reality. The Underground Man speaks of the painful sensation of being looked at by others and ends by declaring himself "just a fly, an odious obscene fly, more intelligent, more highly developed, more noble than anyone else (I had no doubts about that), but a fly that was always making way for everyone, a fly insulted and humiliated by everyone." Prufrock speaks of "the eyes that fix you in a formulated phrase" and concludes by saying that he has "heard the mermaids singing, each to each. I do not think that they will sing to me." In Sartre, too, there is no "each to each." The possibility of a direct knowledge of the other, the possibility of a full and direct mutuality, is ruled out by him in advance and on principle. His intersubjectivity does not, in fact, transcend the world of isolated consciousness that divides each man from the other.

At the same time, Sartre makes it impossible to fall back into the illusion of individualism where one acts as if one could exist as a pure subject unconcerned with others and how they see one. He also makes impossible the romantic illusion of Tristan and Iseult in which each person loses his personal identity in a closed world of two. At the end of *The Age of Reason*, Mathieu's finally coming to experience

Marcelle's side of the relationship signals its end rather than its ful-fillment. In Sartre's play, *No Exit,* two women and a man find them-selves, after death, shut together in a room. One of the women is a Lesbian, and the man is a socialist leader who, through cowardice, did not fight in the war. No two of them can relate to, or make love to, each other without interference by the third. Their intercourse pro-ceeds in a hopeless, frustrating circle of futility. Each acts as the torturer of the others, and they cannot, even when they try, forget about the others.

> INEZ: To forget about the others? How utterly absurd! I *feel* you there, in every pore. Your silence clamors in my ears. . . . You're every-where, and every sound comes to me soiled because you've intercepted it on its way. Why, you've even stolen my face; you know it and I don't! . . . You're a coward, Garcin, because I wish it. I wish it—do you hear?—I wish it. And yet, just look at me, see how weak I am, a mere breath on the air, a gaze observing you, a formless thought that thinks you. . . .
>
> GARCIN: So this is hell. I'd never have believed it. You remember all we were told about the torture-chambers, the fire and brimstone. . . . There's no need for red-hot pokers. Hell is—other people![24]

There are three conclusions which we are compelled to draw from *No Exit.* One is that we are inextricably linked together. The second is that you are not your potentialities but your life—what you have actually done with it. The third is that since human existence means other people, human existence is hell! Each of these conclusions challenges traditional images of man, but none of them—nor all taken together—offers us an image of man. Man for Sartre, as he him-self concludes, "is a useless passion."[25]

[24] Jean-Paul Sartre, *No Exit and Three Other Plays,* translated by Stuart Gilbert (N. Y.: Vintage Books, 1955), pp. 23; 44–7.

[25] There is a sense in which both Nietzsche and Sartre might be considered a special variant of the Modern Gnostic. According to Hans Jonas, one of the great authorities on Gnosticism, modern nihilism, particularly as it is expressed in the existentialism of Nietzsche, Sartre and Heidegger, has many similarities to an-cient Gnosticism. There is the same emphasis upon man's alienation, forlornness, and "thrownness" in a universe in which he cannot feel at home, a world where he can only know himself as in exile. There is the same proclamation as in antinomian Gnosticism that the absence of God from this world carries with it the legitimization of what is ordinarily held to be immoral. Ordinary man must abide by the law, but the *pneumaticos,* the spiritual, or higher man, "does not belong to any objective scheme." He "is above the law, beyond good and evil, and a law unto himself in the power of his 'knowledge.' " (Hans Jonas, *Gnostic Religion* [Boston: Beacon Press Paperbacks, 1963], Epilogue—"Gnosticism, Exis-tentialism, and Nihilism," pp. 332–40).

15

THE THEOLOGICAL
EXISTENTIALIST: KIERKEGAARD,
BERDYAEV, AND TILLICH

Is THE starting point of existentialism the "death of God," as Sartre claims? No, if this means, as it does for Sartre, that existentialism draws the logical consequences of an atheistic position. The large majority of existentialists are not atheists, and there is nothing in existentialism per se that necessitates atheism. Atheism, in its negative way, is as much of a metaphysical and essentialist position as that of any theologian. Nietzsche, Sartre, Heidegger, and Buber all speak of the "death of God," but to each it means something essentially different—to Nietzsche, the loss of a base for values that makes way for the will to power which creates new values and leads to the Superman; to Sartre, the necessity of inventing one's own values and choosing oneself as an image of man for all men; to Heidegger, a void that cannot be filled by any superman but the occasion, nonetheless, for a new succession of divine images arising out of man's clarifying thought about Being; to Buber, the "eclipse of God" which comes when God answers man's turning away by seeming to be absent Himself.

The German-American theologian, Paul Tillich, has said that existentialism provides the questions while the religious traditions, or essentialism, provides the answers. This is only partially true. An essential difference between the so-called religious existentialists, which makes them quite as varied as the nonreligious, is that some of them understand the "answers" in as thoroughly existentialist terms as the questions, while others follow an existentialist analysis of the human condition or the situation of modern man with an appeal to traditional theology as the only valid response to that situation. Although one cannot draw any clear lines here, we may distinguish between *religious existentialists,* such as Martin Buber, Franz Rosenzweig, and Gabriel Marcel, and *existentialist theologians,* such as Søren Kierkegaard, Paul Tillich, and Jacques Maritain. It is the latter whom we shall deal with in this chapter.

Although Søren Kierkegaard lived in the first half of the nineteenth century (1813–55), he is a thinker whom one cannot help considering contemporary by virtue of his thought, his style, and his enormous influence. Insofar as there is any one founder of the philosophy of existence, it is he. It is he who sounds the clarion call that is echoed and reechoed in all existentialism—the evocation of the existential subject. Kierkegaard opposes the "Single One," the true or authentic individual, to "the crowd," which he equates with untruth. But unlike Nietzsche and Sartre, he sees this Single One as set in a direct relation with a transcendent God. Before this relationship can come into being, a man must have discovered his true inwardness, and it is with all the passion of this inwardness that Kierkegaard clings to the "absurd" and attacks the "system." This is in the first instance an attack on the historical system of Hegel, but by implication on any system which helps one evade the task of ethical and religious living as a Single One.

Every man must render an account to God as an individual, says Kierkegaard in *Purity of Heart Is To Will One Thing.* "The most ruinous evasion of all is to be hidden in the crowd in an attempt to . . . get away from hearing God's voice as an individual." By "individual," he does not mean someone who is "different" from others, but someone who stands alone, in a unique relation with God, in which he takes responsibility as a person for every act and attitude of his life. Even when the crowd has silenced the voice of conscience, man continues to belong to his conscience. At one time, this voice may tell a man to select from among the thousands of possibilities the one that is his duty. This is the stage of the ethical. At another, it may pull him out of the security of the universal and force him to "suspend the ethical" in favor of an absolute relation to God. This is the religious stage. In either case, one is called on to be an authentic individual, to take responsibility for his whole personal existence. In *Concluding Unscientific Postscript,* Kierkegaard contrasts this man with the one who tries to subsume his existence under the system:

> Being an individual man is a thing that has been abolished, and every speculative philosopher confuses himself with humanity at large; whereby he becomes something infinitely great, and at the same time nothing at all. . . . To be a particular individual is world-historically absolutely nothing, infinitely nothing—and yet, this is the only true

and highest significance of a human being, so much higher as to make every other significance illusory.[1]

Initially, one's human nature is an abstract potentiality, but the task life sets one is to become subjective. To become subjective means to recognize that one exists as an exposed, limited individual, one whose knowledge arises from his own involvement in existence. The subjective individual knows that, so far from being identical with universal reason looking down on history from above, his very knowing is bound up with his finitude, his consciousness of existence, his awareness of death. This does not mean that he thinks about death all the time, but the knowledge that he will die conditions his relation to each moment of life. "In the same degree that I become subjective, the uncertainty of death comes more and more to interpenetrate my subjectivity dialectically." World-historical consciousness does not die. A particular person does.

In Kierkegaard, the relation between man and man tends to be secondary and inessential—an obstacle to becoming a Single One and to having an absolute relation to the Absolute. "Every man should be chary about having to do with 'the others,'" says Kierkegaard in his essay "That Individual," "and essentially should talk only with God and with himself—for only one attains the goal." He speaks, in this essay, of love for one's neighbor as that which can arise only when one has separated oneself from the crowd. But even this love he understands as a secondary by-product of becoming a Single One. If Sartre has an intersubjectivity that stops short of any direct meeting between subjects, Kierkegaard will not allow the relation between man and man any essential place at all:

> There is no immediate relationship, ethically, between subject and subject. When I understand another person, his reality is for me a possibility, and in its aspect of possibility this conceived reality is related to me precisely as the thought of something I have not done is related to the doing of it.

> Every human being is gloriously constituted, but what ruins so many is, among other things, also the wretched tittle-tattle between man and man about that which should be suffered and matured in silence, this confession before men instead of before God, this hearty communication between this man and that about what ought to be secret and exist only before God in secrecy, this impatient craving for intermediary consolation.[2]

[1] Søren Kierkegaard, *Concluding Unscientific Postscript*, translated by David F. Swenson (Princeton: Princeton University Press, 1941), pp. 112; 134.
[2] *Ibid.*, pp. 284–5; 437.

One might think from the above that Kierkegaard has an over-simplified, perhaps even a romanticized image of man, like the stern, solitary, and life-denying preacher in Ibsen's *Brand,* who is said to have been modeled on Kierkegaard. In the dimension of the intersubjective, this is true. Yet Kierkegaard has an insight into the complex, dialectical self-relationship of the existential subject that has never been surpassed. This is particularly true of his concepts of "the sickness unto death" and of "dread." The sickness unto death Kierkegaard defines in part as "despair at not willing to be oneself; or still lower, despair at not willing to be a self; or lowest of all, despair at willing to be another than himself, wishing for a new self." Kierkegaard's concept of dread, or *Angst,* has led to the insistence of Tillich and of many existential psychotherapists that anxiety is not simply repressed fear, as Freud held, but is a basic, irremovable ingredient of personal existence.

One of Kierkegaard's most important insights for the image of man is that the existential subject cannot be understood as the mere product of inner or outer conditioning. It cannot be turned into an object, as Freud wishes to do, or "explained" as a link in a chain of causes. Instead of a deterministic development of the self, Kierkegaard sees a radical confrontation with possibility that makes the most important points in the self's history those in which it falls from innocence into experience, or "leaps" from the stage of the aesthetic man, who makes the world his oyster, to the ethical man, who subordinates the wealth of possibility to the one thing which is his duty. "No science can state what the self is, without stating it in perfectly general terms," says Kierkegaard in *The Concept of Dread.* "The real 'self' is first posited by the qualitative leap." This leap takes place in dread. Dread leads every individual to reenact the "original sin" in which man plunges from innocence to sin. This plunge is not made in innocence, for one has left that stage; nor is it made in sinfulness, for one does not yet know good or evil. It is the paradoxical transition that leads one to prefer a concrete actuality, even a fallen one, to the unbearable tension of possibility:

> Dread is the dizziness of freedom which occurs when . . . freedom . . . gazes down into its own possibility, grasping at finiteness to sustain itself. In this dizziness freedom succumbs. . . . That very instant everything is changed, and when freedom rises again it sees that it is guilty. Between these two instants lies the leap, which no science has explained or can explain. He who becomes guilty in dread becomes as ambiguously guilty as it is possible to be. Dread is a womanish debility in which freedom swoons. . . . In dread there is the egoistic infinity

of possibility, which does not tempt like a definite choice, but alarms [aengster] and fascinates with its sweet anxiety [Beaengstelse].[3]

Kierkegaard's correlation of freedom, possibility, and dread results in his insight into "demonic shut-inness." This is the state in which the suffering of freedom and possibility is so great that the individual uses his freedom to deny himself. Like Captain Ahab, whom Melville compares to a grisly bear sucking its paws in a hollow tree all the winter, he shuts himself away from God, from his fellowmen, and from himself. "The demoniacal is unfreedom which would shut itself off," but is unfreely revealed. "The freedom lying prone in unfreedom revolts upon coming into communication with freedom outside and now betrays unfreedom in such a way that it is the individual who betrays himself against his will in dread." Authentic existence is not something one can decide for or against with impunity. The man who tries to deny his freedom and his responsibility becomes divided against himself. He is, literally, "sick unto death."

Dread is the great teacher about what it means to be a man. When a person graduates from the school of possibility, he "knows more thoroughly than a child knows the alphabet that he can demand of life absolutely nothing, and that terror, perdition, annihilation, dwell next door to every man, and has learned the profitable lesson that every dread which alarms (aengste) may the next instant become a fact." Even when reality rests heavily on such a man, he will extol it, remembering "that after all it is far, far lighter than the possibility was."

Kierkegaard's *Either/Or* is concerned with the qualitative leap from the aesthetic man to the ethical man. The aesthetic man enjoys the richness of possibility without ever having to make a real personal decision or commit himself to any one course. He exists as one who *experiences,* but not as a person who is really involved with life. He is the Don Juan who recognizes no claim that would bind him to the woman he enjoys and forsakes. The ethical man, in contrast, decides and commits himself, and in so doing sacrifices the many things that he might want to do for the one thing that he *ought* to do. This "ought" he discovers through the universal; for to Kierkegaard, as to Kant and Hegel, the realm of the moral is the universal, and the ethical man is one who subordinates his individual self to the universal. In *Fear and Trembling,* however, Kierkegaard is concerned with the qualitative leap from the ethical man to the religious man, and this latter, paradoxically, shows the most supreme obedience precisely in the fact that he will not subordinate himself to the universal, but

[3] Søren Kierkegaard, *The Concept of Dread,* translated with introduction by Walter Lowrie (Princeton: Princeton University Press, 1944), p. 55f.

discovers what he "ought" to do from moment to moment in direct, personal relation to God. This latter "ought," so far from being a moral one, means the "suspension of the ethical" in favor of a religious command that violates ordinary morality. From the outside, the religious man appears no different from the aesthetic man who puts himself before the universal. But the seeming selfishness of the religious man arises from the fact that he obeys a divine command made directly to him as a person, a command that excepts him from the impersonal obligations of the moral order. This means that he has left the realm of the universal for that of the unique.

In *Fear and Trembling*, Kierkegaard presents two images of man. One is Agamemnon—the tragic hero, or "knight of infinite resignation," who sacrifices his daughter Iphigenia for the sake of the safety of the Greek ships, thus subordinating his individuality to the universal order. The other is Abraham—the "knight of faith." Abraham has no reason that he can advance as does Agamemnon. He is commanded by "an absolute relationship to the Absolute" to "suspend" the ethical principles enjoined by the universal order and sacrifice his son, Isaac. Kierkegaard's "knight of faith" stands, like Biblical man, in a unique relationship to God, not mediated by any order or universal law. In every other respect, however, he differs decisively from the Biblical Abraham after whom he is modeled. In place of Abraham's direct trust, he has a faith of tension and of paradox. He must choose *between* God and creation, for there is no longer, for Kierkegaard, as there is for Biblical man, the possibility of finding God in creation. He rejects society and culture for the lonely relation of the "Single One" to God, thereby losing any contact with concrete otherness that might act as a check on the reality of the voice that addresses him. As a result, in its very affirmation of faith, Kierkegaard's concept of the "knight of faith" is a consequence and an expression of the "death of God": it entails the loss of faith in the universal order and in the society that purports to be founded on it, the "suspension of the ethical" and the relativization of ordinary ethical values that follows from it, the rejection of creation—the world and society—as an obstacle to the relationship with God, and the paradoxical "leap of faith" that is necessary to attain any sort of contact with God.[4] All this is not to imply that Kierkegaard is really an atheist existentialist in disguise. On the contrary, although he has exercised a decisive influence on atheist as well as religious existentialists, he is more important than any other figure in making the image of man of religious and theological existentialism a live option for modern man. Nonetheless, we must recognize

[4] Much of the material from this paragraph is taken from Maurice Friedman, *Problematic Rebel, op. cit.*, p. 52f.

that Kierkegaard's concept of the suspension of the ethical represents a serious curtailment of the realm in which the moral "ought" operates. Although Kierkegaard was very far from Dostoyevsky's "man-god" with his theory of the higher men for whom all things are allowable, he joins Raskolnikov and Ivan Karamazov in his denial of the divine sanction which society has customarily claimed for itself.

The "knight of infinite resignation" is the man who gives up the "finite" for the sake of the "infinite." As Kierkegaard sacrificed his fiancée, Regina Olsen, for God, he renounces forever the temptation to finitude, embodied in woman above all else. The "knight of infinite resignation" retains his love on a plane of perfect harmony without needing any actual contact with the beloved, who is lost to him the instant he has made the movement of resignation.

> He has no need of those erotic tinglings in the nerves at the sight of the beloved, etc., nor does he need to be constantly taking leave of her in a finite sense, because he recollects her in an eternal sense. . . . He has comprehended the deep secret that also in loving another person one must be sufficient unto oneself. He no longer takes a finite interest in what the princess is doing. . . . What the princess does, cannot disturb him, it is only the lower natures which find in other people the law for their actions, which find the premises for their actions outside themselves. If on the other hand the princess is like-minded, . . . she will introduce herself into that order of knighthood . . . which proves its immortality by the fact that it makes no distinction between man and woman. The two will preserve their love young and sound, she also will have triumphed over her pains, even though she does not, as it said in the ballad, "lie every night beside her lord."[5]

Kierkegaard's order of knighthood which makes no distinction between man and woman is anything but concrete and existential. Kierkegaard confesses, however, that he himself is not a true knight of infinite resignation: "There was one who also believed that he had made the movement; but lo, time passed, the princess did something else, she married—a prince, let us say—then his soul lost the elasticity of resignation. Thereby he knew that he had not made the movement rightly; for he who has made the act of resignation infinitely is sufficient unto himself." It is precisely this self-sufficiency which Freud mocked as the fear of genital love. Is Kierkegaard right in setting self-sufficiency as the goal and judging himself because he fell short of it? Or does authenticity lie in the exact opposite—having the courage *not* to be self-sufficient, not to trade in an actual relationship for an ideal

[5] Søren Kierkegaard, *Fear and Trembling* and *The Sickness Unto Death*, translated by Walter Lowrie (N. Y.: Doubleday Anchor Books, 1954), p. 55f.

harmony? It is almost as if he expected her, too, to settle down for life in the contemplation of their broken engagement and was quite unprepared for her moving on and marrying someone else!

Kierkegaard's most complete image of man is the knight of faith, in whose irreducible uniqueness the highest meaning attainable by man is embodied. Faith, to Kierkegaard, is reached "by virtue of the absurd," but existence itself, the totality of life lived with faith, is not absurd:

> If there were no eternal consciousness in a man, if at the foundation of all there lay only a wildly seething power which writhing with obscure passions produced everything that is great and everything that is insignificant, if a bottomless void never satiated lay hidden beneath all—what then would life be but despair?[6]

Kierkegaard is no stranger to the passions that Freud and Jung discovered in the unconscious, but he insists that the basic meaning of human existence remains inalienably personal. "Each becomes great in proportion to his *expectation*," says Kierkegaard, one by expecting the possible, another by expecting the eternal, but the greatest of all is Abraham, the knight of faith who expected the impossible—namely, that he would still somehow get Isaac back after being ready to sacrifice him. "Our age is not willing to stop with faith, with its miracle of turning water into wine, it goes further, it turns wine into water." But even those rare individuals who reach faith stop far short of Abraham. Kierkegaard knows of the sorrow that can derange a man's mind, and he knows through his own personal experience that there is "a strength of will which is able to haul up so exceedingly close to the wind that it saves a man's reason, even though he remains a little queer." But what appalls his soul, what is the only prodigy, is "to be able to lose one's reason, and therefore the whole of finiteness of which reason is the broker, and then by virtue of the absurd to gain precisely the same finiteness."

Kierkegaard's Abraham is ready in all good faith to sacrifice Isaac and yet believes by virtue of the absurd that he will get him back, whereas Kierkegaard himself uses up all his strength and will in resignation and has nothing left for faith. This faith by virtue of the absurd stands in part in the tradition of Tertullian's *credo quia absurdum est*. In *Concluding Unscientific Postscript*, true Christian faith consists in recognizing that the incarnation of God in Christ is historically absurd, yet affirming it with all the passion of inwardness: "If I wish to preserve myself in faith I must constantly be intent upon holding fast the objective uncertainty, so as to remain out upon the deep, over

[6] *Ibid.*, p. 30.

seventy thousand fathoms of water, still preserving my faith." The
existential inwardness gives the passion, but the content of that passion is a transcendent historical fact, higher than all possibility, the
rock on which Christianity is built. It is in this sense that we must call
Kierkegaard an existentialist *theologian*.

There is another, related meaning of Abraham's faith, however, and
that is the direct, unmediated relationship between Abraham and God.
This is in no way a proposition of knowledge or a universally meaningful state of being, but a concrete event, which must be renewed from
moment to moment, absolutely unique and without any justification
outside of itself. Resignation is an act of the will, which comes from
man's own side of the relationship, but his faith that nonetheless he
will get Isaac back means trusting the other side. If he were sure he
would get Isaac back, then the sacrifice would not be real and neither
would the trust. It would be a magic manipulation of the Other
which would allow it no possibility of a free response. The knight of
faith, in contrast, walks "in fear and trembling," open to what will
come to him and trusting in a grace which, since it is never within the
power of his will, is never assured. "The knights of infinite resignation
are easily recognized: their gait is gliding and assured." But the knight
of faith looks from the outside like a Philistine or a tax collector.

> One can discover nothing of that aloof and superior nature whereby
> one recognizes the knight of the infinite. He takes delight in everything,
> and whenever one sees him taking part in a particular pleasure, he
> does it with the persistence which is the mark of the earthly man
> whose soul is absorbed in such things. . . . With infinite resignation
> he has drained the cup of life's profound sadness, he knows the bliss
> of the infinite, he senses the pain of renouncing everything, the dearest
> things he possesses in the world, and yet finiteness tastes to him just
> as good as to one who never knew anything higher. . . . He con-
> stantly makes the movements of infinity, but he does this with such
> correctness and assurance that he constantly gets the finite out of it,
> and there is not a second when one has a notion of anything else.[7]

Although the knight of faith seems more humble and less assured
than the knight of infinite resignation, he has a boldness that the latter
lacks, the readiness to approach the Absolute directly and to enter
into an unmediated relationship with it. Kierkegaard demands that
even the man born in humble circumstances "should not be so inhuman toward himself as not to be able to think of the King's castle
except at a remote distance, dreaming vaguely of its greatness and
wanting at the same time to exalt it and also to abolish it by the fact

[7] *Ibid.*, p. 5of.

that he exalted it meanly." He should step forward confidently, not impudently rushing from the street into the King's hall, but daring, nonetheless, "to enter those palaces where not merely the memory of the elect abides but where the elect themselves abide." Like K. in Kafka's *Castle*, he does not merely want to relate to the Castle "through channels," but to reach the high officials directly and speak to them as person to person. "And what will help him is precisely the dread and distress by which the great are tried."

Kierkegaard's knight of faith has no more concern with the direct relation between man and man than his knight of infinite resignation. Here above all, in fact, the Single One stands in lonely relation to God. "The one knight of faith can render no aid to the other. . . . In these regions partnership is unthinkable . . . for only the individual becomes a knight of faith as the particular individual." Even the relationship of Abraham to Isaac never attains that immediacy, in Kierkegaard's eyes, which marks the relationship of Abraham to God. The only thing that stands in the way of Abraham's sacrificing Isaac, in Kierkegaard's account, is not his direct love for this son of his old age, but a universal injunction against murder. Even the command of God, for Kierkegaard, is not the direct command of a concrete situation, but a universal injunction to sacrifice in which the knight of faith decides, within his own subjectivity, what he must renounce. "Every more precise explication of what is to be understood by Isaac the individual can give only to himself." Hence, Kierkegaard sees no claim arising from the relationship itself that might lead him to question whether the voice that asks him to sacrifice is really the voice of God. The "command" is removed from the situation into the coils of subjectivity.

"The hero does the deed and finds repose in the universal, the knight of faith is kept in constant tension." To give oneself up to the universal, as does the knight of infinite resignation, requires enthusiasm and courage, but it also gives security because the renunciation is for the universal. The knight of faith has no such security.

> He who believes that it is easy enough to be the individual can always be sure that he is not a knight of faith, for vagabonds and roving geniuses are not men of faith. The knight of faith knows, on the other hand, that it is glorious to belong to the universal. He knows that it is beautiful and salutary to be the individual who translates himself into the universal, who edits as it were a pure and elegant edition of himself, as free from errors as possible and which everyone can read. . . . But he knows also that higher than this there winds a solitary path, narrow and steep; he knows that it is terrible to be born outside the universal, to walk without meeting a single traveller. . . .

Even the most tired of tragic heroes walks with a dancing step compared with the knight of faith, who comes slowly creeping forward.[8]

Kierkegaard's knight of faith, born outside the universal, anticipates Kafka's Modern Exile, the man who knows no security of being at home and cannot find any. But there is open to Kierkegaard's man a higher meaning of lonely relation to God that is never accessible to Kafka's. The knight of faith attains a "marvelous glory" that the Agamemnons—the knights of infinite resignation who do their deeds for the universal—can never attain. "He becomes God's intimate acquaintance, the Lord's friend, and (to speak quite humanly) . . . he says 'Thou' to God in heaven, whereas even the tragic hero only addresses Him in the third person." Thus, Kierkegaard anticipates by half a century William James' assertion in his essay "The Will to Believe" that to the religious man the universe is not an "It" but a "Thou" and every relationship possible between persons is possible with it. Kierkegaard broke through the philosophers' equation of the universal and the Absolute to the higher meaning found in the relationship between the Absolute and the particular.

This is a curtailed particularity, for all that; for Kierkegaard does not allow the full reality of his relationship to Regina or Abraham's love for Isaac to enter into the uniqueness of the particular moment. What makes him the first existentialist philosopher is that he places the unique above the universal. What makes him less than a full existentialist is that he divides the person into an essential, essentially individual part which enters into relationship with God, and an inessential, social part which must be depreciated and devalued if the individual is to authenticate himself. Thus, Kierkegaard finds it necessary to sacrifice his relationship with Regina Olsen for that with God.

It is Kierkegaard, nonetheless, who has taught the generations that follow the inescapable central significance of authenticity for meaningful personal existence. He has made the demand for the authentic into a central aspect of any contemporary image of man.

Is not the thing most needed an honest seriousness which dauntlessly and incorruptibly points to the tasks? . . . Whatever the one generation may learn from the other, that which is genuinely human no generation learns from the foregoing. . . . Thus no generation has learned from another to love, no generation begins at any other point than at the beginning.[9]

No contemporary thinker stands more clearly in the line of Kierkegaard than Nicolas Berdyaev. The very emphasis on freedom and sub-

[8] *Ibid.*, pp. 86–8.
[9] *Ibid.*, p. 130.

jectivity that forms the core of his Modern Gnostic dualism stands at the center of his personalism and his existentialism. "Personality," writes Berdyaev in *Slavery and Freedom*, "is recognized only as a subject, in infinite subjectivity, in which is hidden the secret of existence." This emphasis on subjectivity places Berdyaev in unalterable opposition to the general, the universal, the system.

> Personalist philosophy must recognize that spirit does not generalize but individualizes, that it creates, not a world of ideal values, suprahuman and common, but a world of personalities with their qualitative content, that it forms personalities. The triumph of the spiritual principle means, not the subordination of man to the universe, but the revelation of the universe in personality.[10]

Like Kierkegaard too, Berdyaev distinguishes between the alienation of the self in the objective and the transcendence of the self in the existential meeting with God. But Berdyaev extends this existential communion to include the meeting with other people.

Unlike Kierkegaard, Berdyaev is unwilling to surrender the field of ethics to the universal. Instead of contrasting ethics and religion, he contrasts two different types of ethics—the universalist and the personalist—and thereby avoids that dualism between God and the world which makes Kierkegaard's suspension of the ethical so problematic:

> Personalist ethics signify just that going out from the "common" which Kierkegaard and Shestov consider a break with ethics, which they identify with standards of universal obligation. The personalistic transvaluation of values regards as immoral everything which is defined exclusively by its relation to the "common"—to society, the nation, the state, an abstract idea, abstract goodness, moral and logical law—and not to concrete man and his existence.[11]

From this point of view, there cannot be one, ethical "ought" and another, religious "ought" which contradicts it. There is only the "ought" that arises again and again out of "concrete man and his existence." This "ought" is bound up in the strongest terms with the existential subject, with the person.

Berdyaev tends to equate the social with evil. He goes to surprisingly Kierkegaardian lengths, in fact, to divorce the social and the good altogether. "In its essence the moral is independent of the social," he writes in *The Destiny of Man*. Although man is both a social and a spiritual being, "it is only as a spiritual being that man can know the good as such." As a social being, man knows evil—"the feud between the

---

[10] Nicolas Berdyaev, *Slavery and Freedom*, translated by R. M. French (N. Y.: Charles Scribner's Sons, 1944), p. 28f.
[11] *Ibid.*, p. 43.

Creator and the creature which overshadows our whole existence."
Although Berdyaev recognizes that there can be an organic community
(*sobornost*) which is not evil, in general he sees the socialization of
man as that which destroys his freedom of spirit and conscience and
subjects him to the tyranny of society and of public opinion. Berdyaev
goes so far, indeed, as to deny that personality can be socialized. The
person, by this fact, becomes an inner spiritual essence that has nothing to do with man's social self. The latter is reduced to a mere social
role, the triumph of social routine, "the tyranny of the average and
common over the personally individual." Berdyaev sees *all* organization as a dominance which contracts the dignity of personality by
objectivizing it. As a result, "man falls under the sway of the will to
power, of money, of the thirst for pleasure, glory, etc., which are destructive of personality."

Berdyaev sees man as at one and the same time a free, spiritual and
creative being, who prefers the free creation of spiritual values to happiness, and a sick being, divided in himself and influenced by a dark
subconscious. Man is the point of intersection of two worlds: "in him
there takes place the conflict between spirit and nature, freedom and
necessity, independence and dependence." Personality, as a result,
presupposes asceticism, that concentration of inward strength that
refuses to acquiesce in a mingling with impersonal forces, both within
man and in the surrounding world.

One of the forms in which these evils of outer social and inner
psychological compulsion combine is sex. Berdyaev tends, on the
whole, to see sex as a negative force that binds man to the world of
matter and necessity. "The whole being of man is affected by the horror of sex and the force of sexual polarity," he writes in *The Destiny
of Man*. Sexual energy may be the source of the urge of creative life,
but sex per se is an enslaving principle, strongest of all in women, in
whose nature sex is deeper and more complete than in man's. There
is a possibility of sublimating and transfiguring the passions, however,
by purifying them from lust. This purification liberates man from the
slavery of sex and allows a free creative element to enter into his
passion, that love in which even sexual union is a part of the spiritual
union with the loved one. "At its highest love is always the vision of
the face of the loved one in God."

Paul Tillich is even more consciously an existentialist theologian
than Berdyaev. Tillich sees man as the question, not the answer. The
answer comes from divine revelation, a grace beyond man's power.
But this answer is meaningful only in terms of the question, and the
question is "man himself in the conflicts of his existential situation."

Man cannot help ask the question because "his very being is the question of his existence." "He asks 'out of the depth,' and this depth is he himself." Only the question of human finitude, of finite freedom, makes the answer of the eternal, or infinite freedom, meaningful. Only the question implied in human estrangement makes the answer of divine forgiveness meaningful.

Tillich's clearest statement of man's existential question is his book *The Courage to Be*. Instead of seeing the human being as something that is self-evident, he sees it as something that exists only through the courage which affirms itself in spite of the anxiety that ·arises through the existential awareness of nonbeing. Nonbeing may be taken to stand here for all forms of changing and perishing and passing away, everything that always makes the flux of becoming threatening to the I that knows that it exists, but also that it will cease to be. As such, it is most clearly represented in the fear of death—not the specific fear of death that looms up at a certain moment in a given situation, but that awareness of death with which our existence is shot through. Thus, in contrast to Freud, Tillich affirms an ontological, nonneurotic anxiety. "Anxiety, if not modified by the fear of an object, anxiety in its nakedness, is always the anxiety of ultimate nonbeing." It is anxiety about the human situation as such. This anxiety "cannot be eliminated. It belongs to existence itself." "It is the anxiety of not being able to preserve one's own being which underlies every fear and is the frightening element in it."

Tillich distinguishes between three basic types of ontological anxiety: the anxiety of fate and death, the anxiety of emptiness and meaninglessness, and the anxiety of guilt and condemnation. The first threatens man's ontic self-affirmation, the second his spiritual self-affirmation, and the third his moral self-affirmation. All three of these anxieties belong to existence itself and cannot be removed by any form of psychoanalysis that brings repressed fears into consciousness. The anxiety of fate arises out of the contingent character of our existence. There is much that happens that is not only unpredictable but seems to be a matter of irrational chance rather than of any ultimate necessity. Behind this anxiety of fate at every moment stands death— the ultimate contingency.

Already implied in this anxiety, as a corollary, is the anxiety of emptiness and meaninglessness, for man's very being includes his relation to meanings. Nietzsche sees vitality as itself creating new values, whereas Tillich recognizes that vitality must always be *accompanied by* intentionality. Man "is human only by understanding and shaping reality, both his world and himself, according to meanings and values." In this sense, Tillich marks a decisive step beyond the vitalist in understanding the problem of the image of man. Man's vital power cannot be seen separately from its relations to meanings. In fact, the two are interdependent. "Man's vitality is as great as his intentionality. . . . Vitality is the power of creating beyond oneself without losing oneself." To exist to Tillich means to be a centered self, but by the same token to exist means to transcend oneself in relation to what is not oneself. "The more power of creating beyond itself a being has the more vitality it has." But if the *meaning* of existence is lacking, man's very existence is threatened. "The anxiety of meaninglessness is anxiety about the loss of an ultimate concern, of a meaning which gives meaning to all meanings." In this insight, Tillich also goes beyond the pragmatists, who, content with the immediate meanings of practical functioning, never face the abyss which arises when all of these activities are attacked at their root by a corrosive doubt that empties them of all significance. This question is not a metaphysical one, or even a conscious intellectual one. It is a pervasive sense of futility that robs one of the motive force to carry on day after day.

Another related existential question is whether our actions stand up under scrutiny, whether we can affirm them as morally good. Tillich does not see this question as one imposed by an external social code. It is the question that the individual asks himself. But it is not, for all that, a subjective or arbitrary question. He is not free *not* to ask it, and when he does ask, he does so not as the self that acts, but as the self that judges.

> Man's being, ontic as well as spiritual, is not only given to him but also demanded of him. He is responsible for it; literally, he is required to answer, if he is asked, what he has made of himself. He who asks him is his judge, namely he himself, who, at the same time, stands against him. . . . Man is essentially "finite freedom"; freedom not in the sense of indeterminacy but in the sense of being able to determine himself through decisions in the center of his being. Man, as finite freedom, is free within the contingencies of his finitude. But within these limits he is asked to make of himself what he is supposed to become to fulfill his destiny.[12]

In the place of the traditional opposition between "free will" and "determinism," Tillich offers the subtler insight that man is limited, yet is free and responsible within these limitations. In place of Freud's opposition between the pleasure-seeking individual and the morality-imposing society, Tillich offers the more sophisticated insight that man both shapes his reality according to values and judges himself by

[12] Paul Tillich, *The Courage to Be* (New Haven: Yale University Press, 1952; Yale Paperbounds, 1959), p. 51f.

those values. The combination of these two insights results in the recognition that for every man without exception "a profound ambiguity between good and evil permeates everything that he does, because it permeates his personal being as such." If one tries to avoid this situation either through denying all validity to morality or through the opposite tack of a rigid adherence to a legalistic morality, "the anxiety of guilt lies in the background and breaks again and again into the open, producing the extreme situation of moral despair."

Despair in general arises when "a being is aware of itself as unable to affirm itself because of the power of nonbeing." This despair leads to a Kierkegaardian desire to get rid of the self and the corollary despair of being unable to do so. "Despair appears in the form of reduplication, as the desperate attempt to escape despair." Courage cannot remove anxiety since anxiety is existential, but it can take the anxiety of nonbeing into itself. He who does not succeed in doing this can avoid the extreme situation of despair by escaping into neurosis. He still affirms himself, but on a limited scale, thus avoiding nonbeing by diminishing being. No matter how strong the self-affirmation of the neurotic, the self that is affirmed is a reduced one, some of whose potentialities are not admitted to actualization. He who lives in the prison produced by pathological anxiety "is unable to leave the security given to him by his self-imposed limitations." Similarly, in the pathological forms of the anxiety of guilt and condemnation, the horror of feeling condemned is so strong that it makes responsible decisions and any kind of moral action almost impossible. There is exaggeration of guilt where little or none is present. "Yet the awareness of real guilt and the self-condemnation which is identical with man's existential self-estrangement are repressed, because the courage which could take them into itself is lacking." Pathological anxiety produces an unrealistic security as a defense against fate and death, an unrealistic perfection as a defense against guilt, and an unrealistic certitude as a defense against doubt and meaninglessness.

According to Tillich, "man essentially has a world because he has a fully centered self." By the same token, the healthy man can transcend every given environment in the direction of his world. Only when he loses his world does he become *subject* to his "environment," rather than creatively encountering it as a part of his world. "Only in estrangement can man be described as a mere object of environmental impact." Thus, when one's unity as a person disintegrates, one's world also "falls to pieces" and is no longer a meaningful whole. One's world feels completely unreal and one's self empty. Thus, one's personal unity does not exist for its own sake and in its own terms, as Jung seems to suggest, but is dependent on its content, its direction of transcending itself to meet the world. When the finite self attempts to be the center of everything, it gradually ceases to be the center of anything.

This alienation from the meaningful encounter with things that enables them to speak to us is not for Tillich the primary stage of man's existence. Primary is his essential bond with the world, his essential goodness. His existential estrangement from the world is the second stage, and there is a third—the progress of the self beyond essence and existence to a new being in which the cleavage is overcome and healed. On this basis, Tillich criticizes Freud as trying to define man's essential nature in terms of his existential estrangement. Freud's very notion of an infinite libido which can never be satisfied and which produces the death instinct is an illustration of this distortion in his image of man. At the same time, Tillich values highly Freud's insight into man's existential estrangement. He "saw more about human nature than all his followers who, when they lost the existentialist element in Freud, went more to an essentialist and optimistic view of man."[13]

The theological answer which Tillich gives to the existential question has to do with the source of that courage which enables one to affirm being despite the threat of nonbeing. In order to accept ourselves, Tillich explains in *The Courage to Be,* one needs to be accepted by the Power of Being itself. One needs, what is more, to accept being accepted, and this requires a self-transcending courage of confidence, "for being accepted does not mean that guilt is denied." One cannot escape the abyss of meaninglessness, but one can find a hidden meaning within it. To do this one must go beyond the reliance on anything limited—one's own or anyone else's finite power—to "that which is unconditional itself and which we experience as unconditional in a person-to-person encounter." Tillich wishes to go beyond the divine Thou which is encountered by Kierkegaard to the transpersonal "ground of being itself." "The theologians who speak so strongly and with such self-certainty about the divine-human encounter should be aware of a situation in which this encounter is prevented by radical doubt and nothing is left but absolute faith." True courage to be must combine the courage to participate in the whole of being that is found in mysticism and the courage to be a solitary self that is found in Kierkegaard. "The courage to be in its radical form is a key to an idea of God which transcends both mysticism and the person-to-person encounter." Courage takes radical doubt, the doubt about God, into itself, and makes God into a living God—the self-affirmation of Being itself which prevails against nonbeing. Tillich sees the "personal" God of theological theism as "a being beside others and as such a part of the whole of reality." At the same time, this limited God is the subject that makes us into objects and deprives us of our freedom as persons by His omnipotence and omniscience.

> I revolt and try to make *him* into an object, but the revolt fails and becomes desperate. God appears as the invincible tyrant, the being in contrast with whom all other beings are without freedom and subjectivity. . . . This is the God Nietzsche said had to be killed because nobody can tolerate being made into a mere object of absolute knowledge and absolute control. This is the deepest root of atheism. . . . It is also the deepest root of the Existentialist despair and the widespread anxiety of meaninglessness in our period.[14]

The only alternative that Tillich sees to this despair of atheistic existentialism is the transcendence of theism in "absolute faith"—the accepting of being accepted without somebody or something that accepts. Kierkegaard's I-Thou relation to the God of theism cannot enable one to take the anxiety of doubt and meaninglessness into the courage to be. But mysticism, too, must be transcended, for "mysticism does not take seriously the concrete and the doubt concerning the concrete"—the world of finite values and meanings. The divine-human encounter is paradoxical, however, for in it the God above the God of theism is present, although hidden. It is the Thou, but it is also nearer to the I than the I is to itself. Here, personalism and the transpersonal go hand in hand—so well indeed that one wonders why Tillich need posit the "God above God" as a separate logical or theological category. Knowing for Tillich is knowing in the relationship of faith, but at a still deeper level it is the knowledge which gives the ground for that relationship. To this extent, Tillich shores up the existential encounter with God with the essentialist *gnosis* that takes refuge in comprehensive concepts. The question that this raises concerning Tillich's existentialist theological image of man has never been posed more sharply than by Tillich's disciple and friend, the late David E. Roberts:

> I have always been mystified as to how he could be so flexible, concrete, vital, and "close to home" on the one hand, and so schematic, abstract, abstruse, and remote on the other. . . . The schematic aspect . . . is an asset wherever it is used analytically and organizationally, that is, where it is used to clarify concepts and to show their interrelatedness. But it becomes a liability at the point where existential problems, after being high-lighted, are swallowed into an abyss. Somehow Tillich, like God, manages to engulf distinctions without blurring

14 Tillich, *op. cit.*, p. 185.

them. He fully realizes (again, no doubt, like God) that such problems are met, in so far as they ever are, by living rather than by
constructing systems. But it is a weird experience, which I have under-
gone many times, to have problems answered with great sensitivity
and patience, by being brought into connection with some relevant
segment of the system, only to discover later that I do not happen to
be the man who carries this system around in his head.[15]

If we substitute "Hegel" for "God" in Roberts' comparison, the point
he is making becomes clearer still. Existentialism, which begins with a
reaction against Hegel's universal system, is always in danger—either
by way of philosophy or by way of theology—of ending by incorporating its insights into some new Hegelian dialectic. The reaction against
system ends in system. The reaction against *Weltanschauung* ends in
Weltanschauung!

The mixed metaphor of a personal acceptance and forgiveness by a
transpersonal *Ground* of Being is a troublesome one. It suggests an
earthquake which opens up and swallows one. Yet the Ground of
Being for Tillich is not merely a logical, theological, or metaphysical
concept. It is also a living presence that undergirds the relation between the I and the Thou, whether the latter be divine or human.

> Absolute faith, or the state of being grasped by the God beyond
> God, is not a state which appears beside other states of the mind. It
> never is something separated and definite, an event which could be
> isolated and described. It is always a movement in, with, and under
> other states of the mind. It is the situation on the boundary of man's
> possibilities. It *is* this boundary. Therefore it is both the courage of
> despair and the courage in and above every courage. It is not a place
> where one can live, it is without the safety of words and concepts, it
> is without a name, a church, a cult, a theology. But it is moving in the
> depth of all of them. It is the power of being, in which they partici-
> pate and of which they are fragmentary expressions.[16]

---

[15] David E. Roberts, "Tillich's Doctrine of Man" in Charles W. Kegley & Robert
W. Bretall, editors, *The Theology of Paul Tillich* (*The Library of Living Theologians,* Vol. I; N. Y.: The Macmillan Co., 1956), p. 130. *Cf.* Tillich's reply to
Roberts on p. 329f.
[16] *The Courage to Be, op. cit.,* p. 188f.

THE EXISTENTIALIST
OF DIALOGUE:
MARCEL, CAMUS, AND BUBER

ORE significant than the issue between atheistic and theological existentialists is the issue between those existentialists who see existence as grounded in the self and those who see it as grounded in the dialogue between man and man. Except for Paul Roubiczek's *Existentialism for and Against* and my own book *Worlds of Existentialism,* this issue has been seen as only a secondary one. That this has been the case is due to the confusion surrounding the term "intersubjectivity."

Almost every existentialist philosopher has undertaken a fundamental critique of Descartes' *cogito.* Descartes asserts in his *Meditations* that, although one can doubt everything else, one cannot doubt that one is doubting. Descartes takes this immediate awareness of doubt as the adequate foundation of his own existence and indirectly of his body, other people, the material world, and God. All this is implied in his formula, "I think, therefore I am." Practically every existentialist philosopher has objected to the impoverishment and objectification of subjectivity that has resulted from identifying the "I" with a "thinking thing." The Cartesian *cogito* does not know the existential subject in all his wholeness and concreteness—the willing, feeling, thinking person who decides and acts and does so from the limited perspective of his particular life-situation seen from within.

Another objection to Descartes' *cogito* is that it begins by assuming the reality of one's own "I" while doubting the reality of all other selves. With the partial exception of Kierkegaard, every modern existentialist has criticized this aspect of the *cogito* in favor of the recognition that we live in a world of intersubjectivity. "I challenge you to show me where one personality ends and another begins," wrote Dostoyevsky, who also said, "I love, therefore I exist." Even Sartre and Albert Camus, who explicitly accept the *cogito* as the starting point of philosophy, affirm intersubjectivity. "I rebel, therefore *we* exist," says Camus in *The Rebel*, and Sartre writes:

> The philosophies of Descartes and Kant to the contrary, through the *I think* we reach our own self in the presence of others, and the others are just as real to us as our own self. Thus, the man who becomes aware of himself through the *cogito* also perceives all others, and he perceives them as the condition of his own existence. He realizes that he cannot be anything (in the sense that we say that someone is witty or nasty or jealous) unless others recognize it as such. In order to get any truth about myself, I must have contact with another person. . . . In discovering my inner being I discover the other person at the same time, like a freedom placed in front of me which thinks and wills only for or against me. Hence, let us at once announce the discovery of a world which we shall call intersubjectivity; this is the world in which man decides what he is and what others are.[1]

There is at the same time an important difference between those existentialists who regard the relations between subjects as an additional dimension of self but see existence primarily in terms of the self, and those who see the relations *between* selves as central to human existence. Neither Heidegger nor Sartre could join Buber, Marcel, and Karl Jaspers in the recognition that I *become* a self with other selves and am confirmed in my uniqueness through being made present by others in dialogue.

Dialogue, or the "I-Thou" relationship of openness and mutuality between man and man, is not to be confused with interpersonal relations in general. Dialogue includes a reality of over-againstness and separateness quite foreign to Sullivan's definition of the self as entirely interpersonal. Moreover, neither Sullivan nor Mead makes any basic, clear distinction between indirect interpersonal relations in which men know and use each other as subject and object—the "I-It" relation in Buber's terms—and direct, really mutual interpersonal relations in which the relationship itself is of value and not just a means to some individual satisfaction or goal. This latter relationship Buber calls "the interhuman." In interhuman relationships, the partners are neither two nor one. Rather, they stand in an interaction in which each becomes more deeply himself as he moves more fully to respond to the other.[2]

[1] Jean-Paul Sartre, *Existentialism, op. cit.*, p. 44f.
[2] Some of the material in the above three paragraphs has been taken from Maurice Friedman, *The Worlds of Existentialism, op. cit.*, pp. 9; 11; 173; 542f.

In his *Metaphysical Journals*, Gabriel Marcel explains that the *I* only exists as it is confronted by a *Thou*, "for whom in turn I myself am a *Thou*." He who loves me discovers me to myself through his presence. The other "only exists for me in so far as I am open to him, in so far as he is a Thou." Marcel tells of how he ran into a schoolfellow whom he had not seen for a good forty years:

> I remembered him as a boy with red cheeks and bright eyes; I re-discovered him as an old gentleman with a flaccid face, whose eyes were quite expressionless. There was nothing in the quality of these two appearances, nor in my feelings about them, that could confirm that they were two appearances of the same person. . . . There was nothing within me that, when I saw my old comrade, cried out joy-ously: "So it is you, so it is really you again."[3]

Marcel develops this distinction between the Thou and the He in terms of his concept of *presence*. A man may be in the same room with us and yet not really be present, not make his presence felt. I may communicate with him without communion. He will understand what I say, but he will not understand *me*, and his reflection of what I have said makes my own words unrecognizable to me. He "interposes him-self between me and my own reality" and makes me a stranger to myself. In contrast, when someone really makes his presence felt, "it can refresh my inner being; it reveals me to myself, it makes me more fully myself than I should be if I were not exposed to its impact." Even in the living presence of another, however, one may shut oneself off and not recognize the Thou at all. "The intersubjective can only be acknowledged freely, and that implies further that it is always within our power to deny it." Since man does not exist through himself but through the Thou, his freedom is the trial in which he makes the decisive option whether to open himself to the Thou or to close him-self from it.

Unmistakably atheist though he is, the French writer Albert Camus must be counted, along with a number of the religious existentialists, as an existentialist of dialogue.[4] Camus sees man as existing through rebellion, whether it be rebellion against God, tyranny, or the absurd. This is the image of man that Camus presents in *The Rebel*. But in

---

[3] Gabriel Marcel, *Reflection and Mystery*, translated by G. S. Fraser (*The Mystery of Being*, Vol. II; Chicago: Henry Regnery, Gateway Books, 1960), p. 230f.
[4] A few years ago, Irving Howe wrote an article for *Dissent* on Camus' collection of essays, *Resistance, Rebellion, and Death*. The title of the article, "Albert Camus: The Life of Dialogue," surprised me because it took over the subtitle of my own book *Martin Buber: The Life of Dialogue*. But the article surprised me still more, for in it Howe recognized (as I thought no one other than myself had) that dialogue is central to the later Camus' attitude and thought. "Albert Camus," Howe concluded, "lived the only life worth living: the life of dialogue."

the course of this book he goes beyond the rebellion of the Modern Promethean, who finds it enough to overthrow the power that has alienated him from his own freedom to the rebellion of the Modern Job, who contends, but who also trusts in the midst of his contending and therefore respects what he is rebelling against.[5] The revolution which respects no limits leads immediately to new tyranny. True "rebellion must respect the limit it discovers in itself—a limit where minds meet and, in meeting, begin to exist." This meeting Camus understands as "dialogue," not just in the sense of two people talking, but of a real effort at mutual understanding, mutual acknowledgment, and mutual respect. It is dialogue which Camus sees as the highest value, not in the Platonic sense of an objective value that has always existed, but in the sense of the value which men have created in their life together, in their co-operation and in their struggles:

> The mutual recognition of a common destiny and the communication of men between themselves are always valid. Rebellion proclaimed them and undertook to serve them. . . . It opened the way to a morality which, far from obeying abstract principles, discovers them only in the heat of battle and in the incessant movement of contradiction. Nothing justifies the assertion that these principles have existed eternally; it is of no use to declare that they will one day exist. But they do exist, in the very period in which we exist. With us, and throughout all history, they deny servitude, falsehood, and terror.[6]

Here is an existentialism which does not *invent* values, as Sartre, nor create them through the will to power, as Nietzsche, yet discovers them in the concrete situations of life rather than in the "celestial nought." Camus sees these values as endangered by everything which *in fact*, rather than in mere profession, limits the dialogue between man and man. There is no true master-slave relationship, to Camus, for "it is impossible to speak with a person who has been reduced to servitude."

> Instead of the implicit and untrammeled dialogue through which we come to recognize our similarity and consecrate our destiny, servitude gives sway to the most terrible of silences. If injustice is bad for the rebel, it is not because it contradicts an eternal idea of justice, but because it perpetuates the silent hostility that separates the oppressor from the oppressed. *It kills the small part of existence that can be realized on this earth through the mutual understanding of men.* In the same way, since the man who lies shuts himself off from other men, falsehood is therefore proscribed and, on a slightly lower level, murder and violence, which impose definitive silence. *The mutual understand-*

[5] I have taken these categories from my *Problematic Rebel, op. cit.*
[6] Albert Camus, *The Rebel: An Essay on Man in Revolt,* translated by Anthony Bower (N. Y.: Vintage Books, 1956), p. 283f.

ing and communication discovered by rebellion can survive only in the free exchange of conversation.[7]

In rejecting the alternatives of the master and the slave, Camus also rejects the choice between being a "victim" or an "executioner." The true man refuses to be either. But the only way to avoid this alternative is through the dialogue in which one stands one's own ground and recognizes the ground of the other. This dialogue has produced mankind as it is, and it is this which is threatened today by "a vast conspiracy of silence" in which terror takes the place of persuasion, in which man is submerged in History and can no longer tap the equally real part of himself found in contemplating the beauty of nature and of human faces.

> We live in a world of abstractions, of bureaus and machines, of absolute ideas and of crude messianism. We suffocate among people who think they are absolutely right, whether in their machines or in their ideas. And for all who can live only in an atmosphere of human dialogue . . . this silence is the end of the world.[8]

Camus is not attacking industrialism here in favor of a pastoral society or intellectualism in favor of emotions. He is indicating the stance that must be taken in the midst of industrialism and intellectualism if these are not to become the weapons of a terrifying monologue that will suffocate the human even as it silences the reality of each person's standing his own ground and having his own point of view. This stance, to Camus, does not consist of opposing one ideology to another, but in passing beyond all ideology to that concreteness of day by day existence which meets the real problems as they come and responds to them as it can. This means defending dialogue against the slavery, injustice and lies which destroy it. It means taking "on the job of keeping alive, through the apocalyptic historical vista that stretches before us, a modest thoughtfulness which, without pretending to solve everything, will constantly be prepared to give some human meaning to everyday life."

Camus' "Letters to a German Friend" who has become a Nazi are a remarkable instance of dialogue which confirms one's enemy even while one opposes him, respecting in him the humanity which he does not respect in others. For Camus, this meant the overcoming of hatred without weakening in any way the determination to resist and oppose. The true opposition to dictatorship is that freedom which is based on intelligence *and* on mutual understanding.

[7] *Ibid.*, p. 283f. italics added.
[8] Albert Camus, "Neither Victims Nor Executioners," translated by Dwight MacDonald, in Paul Goodman, editor, *Seeds of Liberation* (N. Y.: George Braziller, 1964), p. 27.

Camus brings the same attitude to the dialogue between believer and unbeliever. He recognizes in his address at a Dominican monastery that dialogue is not based on a pseudo-reconciliation in which each side gives up what it really believes for the sake of apparent agreement:

> The world needs real dialogue, . . . falsehood is just as much the opposite of dialogue as is silence, . . . the only possible dialogue is the kind between people who remain what they are and speak their minds. . . . I shall not . . . try to pass myself off as a Christian in your presence. I share with you the same revulsion from evil. But I do not share your hope, and I continue to struggle against this universe in which children suffer and die.[9]

If the voice of Rome against the Nazis was muted and indirect at the time when the executioners multiplied and solitude spread like a plague, then Camus demands of the Christians that they speak out loud and clear and voice their condemnation in such a way that not the slightest doubt could rise in the heart of the simplest man. This means the readiness to leave abstractions and confront the bloodstained face of contemporary history. It means the readiness to speak up and to pay personally. It also means, as Camus points out in his quarrel with Marcel over Spain, the readiness to condemn tyranny whether it agrees with one's ideas or does not.

> Between the forces of terror and the forces of dialogue, a great unequal battle has begun. . . . I believe it must be fought, and I know that certain men have resolved to do so. . . . The program for the future is either a permanent dialogue or the solemn and significant putting to death of any who have experienced dialogue.[10]

> Tyrants indulge in monologues over millions of solitudes. If we reject oppression and falsehood, on the other hand, this is because we reject solitude. Every insubordinate person, when he rises up against oppression, reaffirms thereby the solidarity of all men.[11]

It is dialogue again for which Camus calls in the murderous conflict between French colonials and Arabs in his own native country, Algeria. Policies of retaliation and torture kill all possibility of free discussion and prevent the essential dialogue between the races from taking place. To live as free men, in contrast, means to live "as men who refuse either to practice or to suffer terror." Terror is the enemy of all dialogue. There is no hope that a totalitarian society will evolve

[9] Albert Camus, *Resistance, Rebellion, and Death,* translated by Justin O'Brien (N. Y.: The Modern Library, 1960), p. 5f.
[10] *Ibid.,* p. 55.
[11] *Ibid.,* p. 77.

in any way except toward a still worse terror. The scaffold does not become more liberal or the gallows more tolerant. What defines a totalitarian society is the single party, the party of monologue, which allows no other voice but its own. Only a plurality of parties, only a plurality of voices, "allows one to denounce, hence to correct, injustice and crime," such as the disgraceful torture "as contemptible in Algiers as in Budapest."

In his lengthy attack on the French guillotine and on capital punishment in general, Camus again focuses on that dialogue which demands compassion as well as justice, recognition of human solidarity with the criminal as well as sympathy for his victim. Here too, as in rebellion, a limit is set to the final condemnation that turns the voice of one man into an absolute monologue that suppresses the voice of the other: "Compassion does not exclude punishment, but it suspends the final condemnation. Compassion loathes the definitive, irreparable measure that does an injustice to mankind as a whole because of failing to take into account the wretchedness of the common condition."

Contrary to the common notion of the artist as the one who defies society in order to express his individual self, Camus sees the artist, too, as discovering his task only in the heart of the life of dialogue. "Art cannot be a monologue." Even when an artist appeals to posterity, he is turning from his deaf contemporaries "to a more far-reaching dialogue with the generations to come." In Camus' story "The Artist at Work," no one can tell whether the word the dying artist writes on the canvas is "solitary" or "solidary." To Camus it is both. If the artist bears solitude, it is not for the sake of self-expression, but for the sake of genuine dialogue. Even Camus' understanding of the creation of art is dialogical.

> Art is neither complete rejection nor complete acceptance of what is. It is simultaneously rejection and acceptance, and this is why it must be a perpetually renewed wrenching apart. . . . In order to paint a still life, there must be confrontation and mutual adjustment between a painter and an apple. . . . The artist can neither turn away from his time nor lose himself in it. . . . At the very moment when the artist chooses to share the fate of all, he asserts the individual he is.[12]

The thinker who more than any other has pointed to the "life of dialogue" as an image of man is Martin Buber. "The man who thinks existentially vouches for his word with his life and stakes his life in his thought," writes Buber. He "pledges himself to the truth and verifies it by being true himself." All of Buber's mature thought bears

[12] *Ibid.*, p. 202f.

the stamp of the existential: his insistence on the concrete, on the unique, on the everyday, on the situation rather than the "ism," on response with one's whole being and the personal wholeness that comes into being in that response.

At the center of Burber's existentialism stands existential trust. This is the "holy insecurity" which is willing to go out to meet the unique present, rather than taking refuge in orientation and knowing one's way about. The man of "know how" wants to master the situation. The man of existential trust is able to accept the unique which is present in each new situation, despite all resemblance to the past. Real presentness means for Buber, as for Marcel, presence—being open to what the present brings by bringing oneself to the present, allowing the future to come as it comes, rather than attempting to turn it into a predictable replica of the past. Existential trust refuses the security of the false Either/Ors in favor of the insecurity of the "narrow ridge." Buber has repeatedly expressed his image of man in this figure of a man who renounces the broad upland of a system, with its series of sure statements about the absolute, in favor of "a narrow rocky ridge between the gulfs where there is no sureness of expressible knowledge but the certainty of meeting what remains undisclosed."

> According to the logical conception of truth only one of two contraries can be true, but in the reality of life as one lives it they are inseparable. The person who makes a decision knows that his deciding is no self-delusion; the person who has acted knows that he was and is in the hand of God. The unity of the contraries is the mystery at the innermost core of the dialogue.[13]

The life of dialogue realizes the unity of the contraries in meeting others *and* in holding one's ground when one meets them. This is the existential trust that "all real living is meeting," that meaning is open and accessible in the lived concrete, that transcendence addresses us in the events of everyday life, that man's true concern is not *gnosis*—unraveling the divine mysteries—but *devotio*—the way of man in partnership with creation.

In *The Worlds of Existentialism*, I have pointed to an important divergence between those existentialists who are basically concerned with a phenomenological and existential analysis of the human situation and those who are concerned with pointing to the unique situation and the unique image of man. Buber's existentialism is essentially a pointing to the lived concrete. True humanism is not just an intellectual movement, writes Buber in "Hebrew Humanism." It encompasses all

[13] Martin Buber, *Israel and the World. Essays in a Time of Crisis* (N. Y.: Schocken Books, 1963), p. 17.

of life's reality. When the human element threatens to pale and disintegrate in an entire epoch of world history, it is still possible to turn to an age when it existed in its full strength and purity.

> Humanistic understanding sees literary tradition as the authority and the standard, for it shows us how to distinguish between what is human and what is inhuman; it bears witness to man and reveals him.[14]

A human pattern evolved under an utterly different set of historical conditions can help us realize humanity in our time if we discover the timeless elements in this image of man, those which plumb the history of that era so deeply and uniquely that they also speak to the special conditions and tasks of ours.

Unlike Tillich, who sees the existential—the contemporary situation—as providing the question while the essential—the tradition—provides the answer, Buber sees the existential aspect as lying both in the question *and* in the answer. One cannot know what is asked of one before the real question which addresses one in the present situation. Therefore, the answer must be something more than the adaptation of an already existing tradition. The situation provides the question, but you yourself must provide the answer. Even if it is an answer informed by tradition, it is still made in "fear and trembling," out of that depth of personal uniqueness where one hears the call to one's inmost being. It is this double activity of hearing the unique address of the situation and responding from one's personal wholeness and uniqueness that characterizes Buber's image of man.

> In spite of all similarities every living situation has, like a newborn child, a new face, that has never been before and will never come again. It demands of you a reaction which cannot be prepared beforehand. It demands nothing of what is past. It demands presence, responsibility; it demands you. I call a great character one who by his actions and attitudes satisfies the claim of situations out of deep readiness to respond with his whole life, and in such a way that the sum of his actions and attitudes expresses at the same time the unity of his being in its willingness to accept responsibility.[15]

Responsibility, to Buber, means response, the response of the whole person to what addresses him in the lived concrete. The "ought" must be brought back to lived life, says Buber, from where it swings in the empty air. Therefore, there can be no moral code which is valid in advance of particular situations. Rather, one moves from the concrete

14 *Ibid.*, p. 243.
15 Martin Buber, *Between Man and Man*, translated by Ronald Gregor Smith, with an introduction by Maurice Friedman (N. Y.: Macmillan Paperbacks, 1965), p. 114.

situation and the deep-seated attitudes which one brings to that situation to the decision and response which produces the moral action. This does not mean for Buber, as for Sartre, that one rejects all norms and "invents" one's own values. Rather, as Buber says in his criticism of Sartre,

> one can believe in and accept a meaning or value, one can set it as a guiding light over one's life if one has discovered it, not if one has invented it. It can be for me an illuminating meaning, a direction-giving value only if it has been revealed to me in my meeting with Being, not if I have freely chosen it for myself from among the existing possibilities.[16]

Like Camus, Buber sees values as the product of the way in which man meets what confronts him in history. As a child, Buber tells, he learned "the problematic relationship between maxim and situation" through being confronted by a situation in which two boys entertained the rest of the class with mimic games of an ever more pronouncedly sexual character. When the master asked the young Buber to tell him what he knew of these boys, Buber screamed, "I know nothing." The master replied, "You are a good boy. You will help us." At this point, Buber began to understand the difference between the "good" as automatic obedience to authority and the good as the new response that the present situation demands. "The true norm," Buber concludes, "demands not our obedience but ourselves." It does not want us to repress one part of ourselves in order to obey with the other, but to respond with all that we are, our passions and our reason, our sensing and our intuiting.

> No responsible person remains a stranger to norms. But the command inherent in a genuine norm never becomes a maxim and the fulfillment of it never a habit. Any command that a great character takes to himself in the course of his development does not act in him as part of his consciousness . . . , but remains latent in a basic layer of his substance until it reveals itself to him in a concrete way . . . whenever a situation arises which demands of him a solution of which till then he had perhaps no idea. . . . In moments like these the command addresses us really in the second person, and the Thou in it is no one else but one's own self. Maxims command only the third person, the each and the none.[17]

No one has ever understood the Ten Commandments, Buber has said, unless he has heard the Thou of the command as addressing himself in his particular situation.

[16] Martin Buber, *Eclipse of God. Studies in the Relation between Religion and Philosophy,* translated by Maurice S. Friedman, et al. (N. Y.: Harper Torchbooks, 1957), pp. 69–70.
[17] *Between Man and Man, op. cit.,* p. 114.

Buber's classic presentation of his pholosophy of dialogue is his poetic little book *I and Thou*. Here, he distinguishes between the I-Thou relationship which is direct, mutual, and present, and the I-It, or subject-object, relation in which one relates to the other only indirectly and nonmutually, knowing and using him. The I-Thou relationship is the only one in which I know the other in his uniqueness, for it is the only one in which I may perceive him in his wholeness and as of value in himself. The difference between these two relationships is not the object to which one relates: one can relate to a cat, a tree, or a painting as one's Thou, and one can and often does relate to a man as It. What is decisive is the relationship itself—whether it is sharing or possessing, imposing on the other or helping him to unfold, valuing the relationship in itself or valuing it only as a means to an end. Persevering in an unbroken I-Thou relationship is impossible: rather, the I-Thou and the I-It should alternate in such a way that ever more of the world of It is brought into the world of Thou. In this sense, the I-Thou is the basic relationship for Buber, for through it one becomes truly human. But its authentication would not be possible were it not for the civilized structure and ordering of the world of It. Without the world of It man cannot live, says Buber, but if he lives in this world alone, he is not a man. I-It is not evil in itself, but its predominance prevents the return to the Thou and leads to meaninglessness, evil, or even insanity.

The I-Thou philosophy is concerned with the difference between mere existence and authentic existence, between being human at all and being more fully human, between remaining fragmented and bringing the conflicting parts of oneself into an active unity, between partial and fuller relationships with others. No one ever becomes a "whole person." But one may move in the direction of greater wholeness through greater awareness and fuller response in each new situation. By the same token, no one can say that you "ought" to have an I-Thou relationship in every situation. The only "ought" for Buber is the *quantum satis*—the sufficient amount of your resources in this situation. This "ought" recognizes the practical limitation of your resources from moment to moment as opposed to any general doctrine of original sin or of the death instinct. It also recognizes the practical, and sometimes tragic, limitations of the situation. These, however, cannot be known in advance. "I cannot know how much justice is possible in a given situation," Buber once wrote me, "unless I go on until my head hits the wall and hurts."

The psychological is only the accompaniment of the dialogue between man and man. What is essential is not what goes on within the minds of the partners in a relationship but what happens *between* them. For this reason, Buber is unalterably opposed to that psychologism which wishes to remove the reality of relationship into the separate psyches of the participants. "The inmost growth of the self does not take place, as people like to suppose today," writes Buber, "through our relationship to ourselves, but through being made present by the other and knowing that we are made present by him." Being made present as a person is the heart of what Buber calls confirmation.

Confirmation is interhuman, but it is not simply social or interpersonal; for unless one is confirmed in one's uniqueness as the person one can become, one is only seemingly confirmed. The schoolmaster offered the child Buber confirmation at the price of his giving up his true wholeness and uniqueness which told him that something else was called for in this situation than merely obeying authority. The confirmation of the other must include an actual experiencing of the other side of the relationship so that one can imagine quite concretely what another is feeling, thinking, and knowing without falling into that identification which leads one to leave one's own ground and lose sight of one's own side of the relationship. This is no empathy for it does not abolish the basic distance between one self and the other. It is rather a bold swinging over into the life of the person one confronts, through which alone I can make him present in his wholeness, unity, and uniqueness.

This experiencing of the other side is essential to the distinction which Buber makes between "dialogue," in which I open myself to the otherness of the person I meet, and "monologue," in which, even when I converse with him at length, I allow him to exist only as a content of my experience. In *Between Man and Man,* Buber distinguishes among three types of "dialogue": *genuine dialogue,* whether spoken or silent, in which "each of the participants really has in mind the other or others in their present and particular being and turns to them with the intention of establishing a living mutual relation between himself and them"; *technical dialogue,* "which is prompted solely by the need of objective understanding"; and *monologue disguised as dialogue,* "in which two or more men, meeting in space, speak each with himself in strangely tortuous and circuitous ways and yet imagine they have escaped the torment of being thrown back on their own resources."

Real dialogue is hidden in odd corners. It need not be with someone one knows well or at all (as Harvey Cox mistakenly assumes in *The Secular City* when he suggests for urban life an anonymous "I-You" relationship to supplement Buber's "I-Thou"). It can break out "in the tone of a railway guard's voice, in the glance of an old newspaper vendor, in the smile of the chimney-sweeper." It does not mean having much to do with others—"I know people who are absorbed in 'social activity' and have never spoken from being to being with a fellowman." It means seeing the other as absolutely not oneself, and nevertheless communicating with him. It does not always mean love. It may even mean hatred, if it is straightforward and personal. But it means confirming the other even while opposing him.

Technical dialogue is communication which makes no pretense of relating to the other as a Thou. It is that which makes it possible for men today to think of a "communications industry," with relatively little concern for the truth that is communicated or the persons to whom it is to be communicated and enormous concern for the "techniques" of communication, i.e., of propaganda, advertising, and social manipulation.

The most confusing aspect is monologue disguised as dialogue. This is Dale Carnegie's formula for "winning friends and influencing people." Memorize people's names and flatter their egos so that they will think that you care about them personally, when in fact you are simply trying to make a good sale. The effect of such open education in manipulation is an ever-growing cynicism in which you *expect* the other to have a "line," to be trying to put something over on you, to pretend to care about you as a person in order to get your money or possess you sexually, but in fact to be interested only in what is in it for him.

This decline in genuine dialogue in favor of the empty forms of dialogue has been going on since World War I, in Buber's observation. Wherever a man lets the other exist only as part of himself, "dialogue becomes a fiction, the mysterious intercourse between two human worlds only a game, and in the rejection of the real life confronting him the essence of all reality begins to disintegrate." In the Eros of dialogue, the person really experiences the love relationship from the side of the other, who has become wholly present as a person to him. But in the Eros of monologue, everything becomes a game of mirrors.

Many years I have wandered through the land of men, and have not yet reached an end of studying the varieties of the "erotic man" (as the vassal of the broken-winged one at times describes himself). There a lover stamps around and is in love only with his passion. There one is wearing his differentiated feelings like medal-ribbons. There one is enjoying the adventures of his own fascinating effect. There one is gazing enraptured at the spectacle of his own supposed surrender. There one is collecting excitement. There one is displaying his "power." There one is preening himself with borrowed vitality. There one is delighting to exist simultaneously as himself and as an idol very unlike himself. There one is warming himself at the blaze of what has fallen to his lot. There one is experimenting. And so on and on—all the manifold monologists with their mirrors, in the apartment of the most intimate dialogue![18]

The very language of love today with its emphasis on the intensity of "feeling" that is awakened by the "love object" to which one has "transferred" one's affections betrays the thoroughly monological way in which love is regarded.

What is true of love is true of all monologue disguised as dialogue. In it, the Thou seems to be addressed, but if one responds personally one discovers, like Eliot's Prufrock, that "that is not what I meant at all." Buber reserves his special irony for this preservation of the form of I-Thou emptied of all content:

A *debate* in which the thoughts are not expressed in the way in which they existed in the mind but in the speaking are so pointed that they may strike home in the sharpest way, and moreover without the men that are spoken to being regarded in any way present as persons; a *conversation* characterized by the need neither to communicate something, nor to learn something, nor to influence someone, nor to come into connexion with someone, but solely by the desire to have one's own self-reliance confirmed by marking the impression that is made, or if it has become unsteady to have it strengthened; a *friendly chat* in which each regards himself as absolute and legitimate and the other as relativized and questionable; a *lovers' talk* in which both partners alike enjoy their own glorious soul and their precious experience— what an underworld of faceless spectres of dialogue![19]

Real love is not constituted by feelings, not even the most intense and sincere feelings, for real love takes place *between* I and Thou. It is the responsibility of an I for a Thou, of which feelings are only the accompaniment. "But love without dialogic, without real outgoing to the other, reaching to the other, and companying with the other, the love remaining with itself—this is called Lucifer." What is true of love is true of dialogue in general. One cannot enter genuine dialogue unless one is a real person. "Dialogue between mere individuals is only a sketch." But in contrast to Jung, Buber sees dialogue as the goal and individuation as the by-product. When one becomes integrated, it is so one may go forth to meeting. If one falls back instead on the enjoyment of one's wholeness, then even that wholeness disintegrates. What is more, the way to the personal wholeness that makes possible real dialogue is dialogue itself. "By what could a man from being an individual so really become a person as by the strict and sweet ex-

[18] *Between Man and Man, op. cit.,* pp. 29-30.
[19] *Ibid.,* pp. 19-20.

periences of dialogue which teach him the boundless contents of the boundary?"

Buber cannot follow George Herbert Mead in seeing the self as "an eddy in the social current." "What is said here is the real contrary of the cry, heard at times in twilight ages, for universal unreserve. He who can be unreserved with each passerby has no substance to lose." But he objects with equal vigor to Kierkegaard's advice to "be chary in having to do with the other." "He who cannot stand in a direct relation to each one who meets him has a fulness which is futile." Kierkegaard's notion that in order to come to God he had "to remove the object," namely his fiancée Regina Olsen, Buber considers a sublime misunderstanding of God.

> Creation is not a hurdle on the road to God, it is the road itself. We are created along with one another and directed to a life with one another. Creatures are placed in my way so that I, their fellow-creature, by means of them and with them find the way to God. . . . God wants us to come to him by means of the Reginas he has created and not by renunciation of them. . . . The real God lets no shorter line reach him than each man's longest, which is the line embracing the world that is accessible to this man.[20]

Kierkegaard wishes to reach God by joining hands with him *above* the world, writes Buber, whereas we wish to reach him by joining hands with him *around* the world.

Buber makes a similar critique of his own early mysticism. He tells that, when he was younger, he spent several hours a day in a mystic meditation that divided the world into "illumination and ecstasy and rapture held without time or sequence" and an everyday world that served either as obstacle to or preparation for this life beyond. The "illegitimacy" of this dualism was brought home to Buber by an event of "judgment," an experience of "conversion" from mystic ecstasy to the task of hallowing the everyday. After a morning of such religious enthusiasm, he was visited by a young man who came with a question that Buber later learned was one of life and death. He was friendly and attentive yet not really present in spirit. He answered the questions which the young man put, but failed to guess the one which he did not put. "What do we expect when we are in despair and yet go to a man? Surely a presence by means of which we are told that nevertheless there is meaning." When he learned that this young man had been killed in the trenches of World War I—not in suicide as some have thought but, as Buber has written me, "out of a despair which did not oppose its own death"—he accepted this as a judgment on a religious life that extracted him from the everyday and deprived him of that wholeness of presence with which he might have responded to the claim of the other. In place of the fullness of the mystic experience, Buber writes, he now has only "the everyday out of which I am never taken." "I know no fulness but each mortal hour's fulness of claim and responsibility."

This event of judgment is an excellent example of what Buber means by "existential guilt." Existential guilt, to Buber, is not "bad faith," or self-deception, as it is for Sartre, nor the failure to answer the call of one's ownmost conscience, as for Heidegger, nor the failure to realize one's potentialities, as for Fromm and Rollo May. It is the guilt that one has taken on oneself as a person in a personal situation. By the same token, it is the injury of that common order which one recognizes as the foundation of one's own existence as well as that of others. As such, it is neither objective nor subjective, cultural nor neurotic, but dialogical: the failure to become the person one is called to become through responding in each new concrete situation to that which addresses and claims one. Although the mystical experience seems self-validating to those who have it, Buber recognizes that human existence must be more broadly defined than this "flight of the alone to the Alone." That mystical philosophy which leads one to aim at unity with the All by sacrificing the full seriousness of the everyday is certainly an exalted form of being inauthentic, says Buber, but it is nonetheless inauthentic.

For this reason, Buber criticizes that modern individualism which looks toward the mystical doctrine of the East or toward the use of mescaline for "the great general indulgence in the security of being identical with the Self of being."

> The flight from the common cosmos into a special sphere that is understood as the true being is, in all its stages, from the elemental sayings of the ancient Eastern teachings to the arbitrariness of the modern counsel to intoxication, a flight from the existential claim on the person who must verify himself in We. It is flight from the authentic spokenness of speech in whose realm a response is demanded, and response is responsibility.[21]

Real, uncurtailed, personal existence begins not when one says to the other, "I am you," as the Hindu Upanishads do when they state, "Husband is not dear because of husband but because of the Self in the husband." It begins when one says, "I accept you as you are," in

[21] Martin Buber, *The Knowledge of Man*, edited and translated with an introductory essay by Maurice Friedman (London: George Allen & Unwin, 1965; N. Y.: Harper & Row, 1966), p. 107f.

your otherness and uniqueness. The typical mark of the inauthentic man of today, whether he be the one who has taken flight in the collective or in individualism, is that he does not really *hear*, he does not really *listen* to another. In so doing, he becomes guilty not just to the other but to the common world that men are building together, to the common We. "In our age in which the true meaning of every word is encompassed by delusion and falsehood and the original intention of the human glance is stifled by tenacious mistrust, it is of decisive importance to find again the genuineness of speech and existence as We."

Existence as We can never mean for Buber that the individual merely conforms to society or subordinates his own self to the collectivity. It means that each contributes to the common order from where he is and from what he is. From this standpoint, Kierkegaard's existential guilt, according to Buber, would be that he did not overcome his melancholy and make real his relationship with Regina and that, failing to make real that relationship, he then viewed all social relationships as secondary and inessential, incapable of being made authentic. In opposition to Kierkegaard, Buber says that one ought not to separate oneself on principle from the body politic, but that one should at the same time try to "de-crowd" the crowd so that it is bound, not bundled.

Buber sees marriage as the exemplary bond, for marriage means that I can only share in Present Being if I take seriously the fact that the other *is*, answering his address and answering for him as one entrusted to me. Through marriage, I enter into relation with otherness, "and the basic structure of otherness, in many ways uncanny but never quite unholy or incapable of being hallowed, in which I and the others who meet me in my life are inwoven, is the body politic." Real marriage leads to "vital acknowledgment of many-faced otherness—even in the contradiction and conflict with it."

> That the men with whom I am bound up in the body politic . . . are essentially other than myself, that this one or that one does not have merely a different mind, or way of thinking or feeling, or a different conviction or attitude, but has also a different perception of the world, a different recognition and order of meaning, a different touch from the regions of existence, a different faith, a different soil: to affirm all this, to affirm it in the way of a creature, in the midst of the hard situations of conflict, without relaxing their real seriousness, is the way by which we may officiate as helpers in this wide realm entrusted to us as well, and from which alone we are from time to time permitted to touch in our doubts, in humility and upright investigation, on the other's "truth" or "untruth," "justice" or "injustice." But to this we are led by marriage, if it is real, with a power for which

there is scarcely a substitute, by its crises and the overcoming of them which rises out of the organic depths.[22]

Buber carries this experiencing of the otherness in marriage into the sexual act itself. In love "imagining the real" takes place not as some Emersonian meeting of soul and soul, but with the whole body-soul person. It includes an experiencing of the other's response in sexual intercourse that is far more radical than Sartre's incarnation of the other's freedom:

> A man caresses a woman, who lets herself be caressed. Then let us assume that he feels the contact from two sides—with the palm of his hand still, and also with the woman's skin. The twofold nature of the gesture, as one that takes place between two persons, thrills through the depth of enjoyment in his heart and stirs it. If he does not deafen his heart he will have—not to renounce the enjoyment but—to love.
>
> I do not in the least mean that the man who has had such an experience would from then on have this two-sided sensation in every such meeting—that would perhaps destroy his instinct. But the one extreme experience makes the other person present to him for all time. A transfusion has taken place after which a mere elaboration of subjectivity is never again possible or tolerable to him.[23]

True lovers have a bipolar experience, a contemporaneity at rest. They receive the common event from both sides at once "and thus for the first time understand in a bodily way what an event is." The lover feels the inclination of the head on the neck of his beloved as an answer to the world of his own silence without leaving his own feeling of self-being. He does not assimilate the beloved into his own soul or attempt to possess her freedom. He vows her faithfully to himself and turns to her in her otherness, her self-reality, with all the power of intention of his own heart. This is not Sartre's otherness of the object nor even of the alien subject that makes me into an object. It is the otherness of the other who lives with me as Thou, who faces me as partner, who affirms and contends with me, but vows me faithfully to being as I vow him.

In the relations between parent and child and teacher and student, it is again the recognition of otherness, of the uniqueness that has its own right and must grow in its own way, which informs the mutual contact and the mutual trust.

> Trust, trust in the world, because this human being exists—that is the most inward achievement of the relation in education. Because this human being exists, meaninglessness, however hard pressed you are

[22] Between Man and Man, op. cit., p. 61f.
[23] Ibid., pp. 96–7.

by it, cannot be the real truth. Because this human being exists, in the darkness the light lies hidden, in fear salvation, and in the callousness of one's fellow-men the great Love.[24]

For this trust to exist, the teacher or parent must be really there, really facing the child, not merely there in spirit. To let himself be represented by a phantom would be a catastrophe for the child. To be there he need possess none of the perfections which the child imagines, but "he must have gathered the child's presence into his own store as one of the bearers of his communion with the world, one of the focuses of his responsibilities for the world." He does not have to be concerned with the child at every moment, but he must have gathered the child into his life in such a way "that steady potential presence of the one to the other is established and endures."

The catastrophe for the child comes not if the parent or teacher turns out to be less than perfect, but if he is trying to *seem* to be a certain type of person in order to win the approval or dependence of the child. To Buber, the essential problem of the sphere of the interhuman is this duality of being and seeming. The man who lives from his being may wish to influence others, but he does not concern himself with how he appears to others, or try to appear in a certain way in order to gain confirmation from the other. The seeming man, in contrast, "prepares a face to meet the faces that he meets," as Eliot's Prufrock puts it. He produces a look which is meant to appear to be a spontaneous utterance, but is actually only concerned with the effect it produces. In the interhuman realm, "truth" does not mean saying whatever comes to mind, but letting no *seeming* creep between oneself and the other. It does not mean letting go before another, but granting him a share in one's being. "This is a question of the authenticity of the interhuman, and where this is not to be found, neither is the human element itself authentic." The temptation to seeming arises out of the need to be confirmed. To yield to this temptation is man's essential cowardice; to resist it is his essential courage. Some men become so thoroughly seeming that one is tempted to think of this as their fixed nature. But Buber claims that he has never known a young person who struck him as irretrievably bad, nor an older one who was bad by his essential nature. "Man as man can be redeemed."

This does not mean any optimistic notions about present-day man. If the perception of the other's wholeness, unity, and uniqueness is only possible when I step into an elemental relation with him and make him present as a person, then by the same token the analytical, reductive, and deriving look that predominates between man and man today stands in the way of this perception.

> This look is a reductive one, because it tries to contract the manifold person, who is nourished by the microcosmic richness of the possible, to some schematically surveyable and recurrent structures. And this look is a deriving one, because it supposes it can grasp what a man has become, or even is becoming, in genetic formulae, and it thinks that even the dynamic central principle of the individual in this becoming can be represented by a general concept. An effort is being made today radically to destroy the mystery between man and man. The personal life, the ever-near mystery, once the source of the stillest enthusiasms, is leveled down.[25]

Needless to say, this critique of the modern "look" applies not only to the "look" of Sartre but to that of Freud. In opposition to the attempt to reduce man to one or another complex, Buber proposes envisaging man as a whole. The isolation of elements and partial process hinders the comprehension of the whole. "The search for the center of gravity shifts it." No one phenomenon should be made so much the center of attention that everything else is derived from it. "Rather, they should all be made starting points—not singly but in their vital connection." In isolating the conflicts of superego and id, Freud misses the real context in which this dualism of repression and sublimation takes place—namely, the sickness of modern man that is produced by the decay of organic community and results in a crisis of confidence, or trust.

> Where confidence reigns man must often, indeed, adapt his wishes to the commands of his community; but he must not repress them to such an extent that the repression acquires a dominating significance for his life. . . . Only if the organic community disintegrates from within and mistrust becomes life's basic note does the repression acquire its dominating importance. The unaffectedness of wishing is stifled by mistrust, everything around is hostile or can become hostile, agreement between one's own and the other's desire ceases, for there is no true coalescence or reconciliation with what is necessary to a sustaining community, and the dulled wishes creep hopelessly into the recesses of the soul. . . . Now there is no longer a human wholeness with the force and the courage to manifest itself. . . . The divorce between spirit and instincts is here, as often, the consequence of the divorce between man and man.[26]

Buber holds "that there resides in every man the possibility of attaining authentic human existence in the special way peculiar to

25 *The Knowledge of Man, op. cit.,* p. 8of.
26 *Between Man and Man, op. cit.,* p. 196f.

him." Individuation is "the indispensable personal stamp of all realization of human existence." But in contrast to Fromm, Buber holds that the goal is not self-realization, but the meaning that arises in the fulfillment of one's created task, one's response to that part of creation in which one is set:

> The self as such is not ultimately the essential, but the meaning of human existence given in creation again and again fulfills itself as self. The help that men give each other in becoming a self leads the life between men to its height. The dynamic glory of the being of man is first bodily present in the relation between two men each of whom in meaning the other also means the highest to which this person is called, and serves the self-realization of this human life as one true to creation without wishing to impose on the other anything of his own realization.[27]

Only he finds meaning who no longer aims at happiness, or at meaning for that matter, but forgets himself in the response to what calls him out in the deepest level of his being.

> That meaning is open and accessible in the actual lived concrete does not mean it is to be won and possessed through any type of analytical or synthetic investigation or through any type of reflection upon the lived concrete. Meaning is to be experienced in living action and suffering itself, in the unreduced immediacy of the moment. Of course, he who aims at the experiencing of experience will necessarily miss the meaning, for he destroys the spontaneity of the mystery. Only he reaches the meaning who stands firm, without holding back or reservation, before the whole might of reality and answers it in a living way. He is ready to confirm with his life the meaning which he has attained.[28]

Good to Buber is only that which is done with the whole being. Evil is passion without direction, or action without passion, both of which mean lack of true decision. True decision does not mean that one *is* whole; it means that one is moving toward wholeness through genuine response in dialogue.

> It is a cruelly hazardous enterprise, this becoming a whole, becoming a form, of crystallization of the soul. Everything in the nature of inclinations, of indolence, of habits, of fondness for possibilities which has been swashbuckling within us, must be overcome, and overcome, not by elimination, by suppression, for genuine wholeness can never be achieved like that, never a wholeness where downtrodden appetites lurk in the corners. Rather must all these mobile or static forces,

seized by the soul's rapture, plunge of their own accord, as it were, into the mightiness of decision and dissolve within it.[29]

Buber's most concentrated and comprehensive image of man is his classic little book, *The Way of Man according to the Teachings of the Hasidim*. On the basis of Hasidic tales, Buber expounds six stages that point the way to authentic personal existence and to the life of dialogue. In the first, "heart-searching"—God's "Where art thou, Adam?"—is seen as the question which breaks in on every man who has turned his life into a system of hideouts, the question which asks him where he is in his life. Only when he has begun to respond to this question with his existence will his life become a way. But this question is not introspection of any sort. It is, on the contrary, the voice of otherness that brings the self-encapsulated man back into dialogue. There is a demonic question which says, "From where you have got to, there is no way out." This is a sterile heart-searching "which leads to nothing but self-torture, despair and still deeper enmeshment." The true heart-searching, in contrast, means that response to the address of the other which helps one find one's particular way. "If a man does not judge himself," says the Hasidic Rabbi Nachman of Bratzlav, "all things judge him." This means that anything may stand in that relation of otherness which will call him to account by enabling him to see his own life from a perspective outside himself. And he adds: "All things are messengers of God to him." All things in "judging" him can call him back to genuine dialogical existence.

The second stage is "the particular way," that unique task which every person has and which no one else will ever have. "When I get to heaven, they will not ask me, 'Why were you not Moses?'" said the Hasidic rebbe Zusya, "but 'Why were you not Zusya?'" Why did you not become what only you were called to become? Without the image of man, Moses, he could not have become Zusya, but he could never become Zusya by merely imitating Moses. He had to respond to this image of man in his unique way. One's very existence as a person places on one the demand to authenticate one's life. If we recognize this, we are still left with the all-important question of how we discover "what we truly are." Buber answers that a man knows his particular way through that knowledge of his essential quality and inclination which is revealed to him by "his central wish, that in him which stirs his inmost being." This is no romanticism of emotion, rather the recognition that only the wholeness which includes the "central wish" can lead to the recognition of his unique task. Often, this recognition comes only in the form of the "evil" urge that seeks to lead him astray; for he

[29] Martin Buber, *Good and Evil: Two Interpretations* (N. Y.: Scribner's Paperbacks, 1961), p. 129.

has gotten so out of touch with his own strongest feelings that he knows them only in the guise of what seems to be tripping him up on his path to success.

The third stage is that resolution which seeks personal unity through doing whatever one does "all of a piece" and not "patchwork," until one attains a steadier unity than before and can maintain one's wholeness with a "relaxed vigilance." The fourth stage is "to begin with oneself," to recognize that in conflicts with others, it is our own inner contradictions which again and again foster misunderstanding and mistrust. The cause of conflict between me and my fellowman, says Buber, is that I do not say what I mean and that I do not do what I say. This is another way of saying that I do not respond as a whole person, that I am not really present, really responsible, really "there." As a result, I lead people to expect something which later I am quite unwilling to follow through on. This is not a matter of sticking to a rigid external code, but of a spontaneity which is not mere fragmented impulse, but the expression of my wholeness as a person. It is that which places the stamp of personal uniqueness on all my utterances, gestures, and actions. Though my actions cannot be predicted even by those who stand in the closest relationship to me, through these gestures and actions I may be recognized ever again and ever more strongly as the unique person that I am.

Though one begins with oneself, one does not end with oneself. One does not aim at oneself, but at the task that one has to fulfill. One comprehends oneself, including the resources as a person that enable one to transform relationships by bringing a new response to them, but one is not preoccupied with oneself—neither with one's salvation, one's guilt, nor one's neurosis, one's genius, one's frustration, nor one's grievances. "True, each is to know itself, purify itself, perfect itself, but not for its own sake—neither for the sake of its temporal happiness nor for that of its eternal bliss—but for the sake of the work which it is destined to perform upon the world."

Buber calls the final stage "Here Where One Stands." The culmination of all the other stages is the return to the lived concrete, the hallowing of the everyday. We all feel at times as if true existence had passed us by, says Buber, and so we search for it somewhere, anywhere but where we are. But the treasure is buried under our own hearth. The true name of all the paradises which people seek by chemical or other means, writes Buber in his criticism of Huxley's advocacy of mescaline, is situationlessness. One may stand in one's situation, one may resist it, one may change it if need be, "but situationlessness is no true business of man." Here where you stand is your situation, that which addresses you and claims you.

The environment which I feel to be the natural one, the situation which has been assigned to me as my fate, the things that happen to me day after day, the things that claim me day after day—these contain my essential task and such fulfillment of existence as is open to me.[30]

God places himself in man's hand's. He "dwells wherever man lets Him in." But we let God in only where we really stand, where we live a true life. "Man cannot approach the divine by reaching beyond the human; he can approach Him through becoming human. To become human is what he, this individual man, has been created for."

That psychotherapist who above all others made his lifework and his lifeway that of the life of dialogue is the late Swiss psychiatrist Hans Trüb. What had the greatest influence on Trüb was not Buber's doctrine, but the meeting with him as person to person, and it is from this meeting that the revolutionary change in Trüb's method of psychotherapy proceeded. Trüb tells how the closed circle of the self was again and again forced outward toward relationship through those times when, despite his will, he found himself confronting his patient not as an analyst but as human being to human being. From these experiences, he came to understand the full meaning of the analyst's responsibility. The analyst takes responsibility for lost and forgotten things, and with the aid of his psychology he helps to bring them to light. But he knows in the depths of his self that the secret meaning of these things which have been brought to consciousness first reveals itself *in the outgoing to the other*.

The psychotherapist in his work with the ill is *essentially a human being.* . . . Therefore he seeks and loves the human being in his patients and allows it . . . to come to him ever again.[31]

The personal experience which caused Trüb to move from the dialectical psychology of Jung to "healing through meeting" was, he tells us, an overwhelming sense of guilt. This guilt was no longer such as could be explained away or removed, for it was subjectively experienced as the guilt of a person who had stepped out of real relationship to the world and tried to live in a spiritual world above reality. It is just here, in the real guilt of the person who has not responded to the legitimate claim and address of the world, that the possibility of transformation and healing lies. Guilt does not reside in the person, says Buber. Rather, he stands, in the most realistic sense, in the guilt that envelops him. Similarly, the repression of guilt and the

[30] *Hasidism and Modern Man, op. cit.,* pp. 172–4.
[31] *The Worlds of Existentialism, op. cit.,* p. 497.

neuroses which result from this repression are not merely psychological phenomena, but real events between men. Therefore, the man who is sick from existential guilt must follow a path made up of three stages in order to be healed. First, he must illuminate his guilt by recognizing that, however different he may now be, he is the person who took this burden of guilt on him; second, he must persevere in this illumination; and third, he must repair the injured order of the world, either with the person he wronged or by establishing a new dialogical relation at some other point. In T. S. Eliot's *Cocktail Party*, Sir Henry Harcourt-Reilly tells Edward that he must learn to live with his guilt but there is nothing that he can do about it in relation to the person toward whom he is guilty. Buber, in contrast, holds that guilt means a rupture of the dialogical relationship, an injury of the existential order of "the common," and as such must be repaired by again entering into dialogue with that person or with the world.

A significant extension of the image of man as the life of dialogue is the theory of "will and willfulness" developed under Buber's influence by the psychiatrist, Leslie H. Farber. Farber sees genuine will as an expression of real dialogue, arbitrary willfulness as a product of the absence of dialogue. The proper setting of wholeness is dialogue. When this setting eludes us, "we turn wildly to will, ready to grasp at any illusion of wholeness (however mindless or grotesque) the will conjures up for our reassurance." This is a vicious circle, for the more dependent a person becomes on the illusion of wholeness, the less he is able to experience true wholeness in dialogue. "At the point where he is no longer capable of dialogue he can be said to be *addicted* to his will." Willfulness then is nothing other than the attempt of will to make up for the absence of dialogue by handling both sides of the no longer mutual situation. No longer in encounter with another self, he fills the emptiness with his own self, and even that self is only a partial one, its wholeness having disappeared with the disappearance of meeting. "This feverish figure, endlessly assaulting the company, seeking to wrench the moment to some pretense of dialogue, is . . . the figure of man's separated will posing as his total self."

We experience "a mounting hunger for a sovereign and irreducible will, so wedded to our reason, our emotions, our imagination, our intentions, our bodies, that only after a given enterprise has come to an end can we retrospectively infer that will was present at all." This is the will of the whole being rather than of isolated willfulness, of freedom rather than bondage, of dialogue rather than monologue. One way out of the impasse of the disordered will may be despair, Farber suggests. Despair may provide "the very conditions of serious-

ness and urgency which bring a man to ask those wholly authentic—
we might call them tragic—questions about his own life and the
meaning and measure of his particular human-ness." When despair is
repudiated, these questions will not be asked. The failure to confront
these questions may mark the turning to the inauthentic.[32]

The Atheist Existentialist sees the problem of finding authentic personal direction as clearly as anyone, but he gets no further than the
creation or invention of new values through one's own will to power
or conscious choice. The Theological Existentialist has an even more
profound existential analysis of the situation of modern man and of
man in general than the Atheist, and he has more of an answer to the
problem he sets. But the answer tends to derive from tradition without
being existentialist itself, and to this extent his image of man is often
something less than contemporary. The Existentialist of Dialogue is
less likely to fall into the subjectivism of the Atheist Existentialist,
which gives personal participation without direction, or the ob-
jectivism of the Existentialist Theologian, who points to essentialist
answers somewhat at the expense of the unique response to the unique
situation.

In contrast to Jung's emphasis on "individuation," the life of dialogue emphasizes the person. This means that the locus of value is not
within but *between*. To a great many people, existentialism means an
overwhelming preoccupation with the self—with the experiencing of "I
am," good faith with oneself, or the realization of one's "ownmost potentialities." For the Existentialist of Dialogue, the person is inseparable from his vocation, the "I" unthinkable without the dialogue
which calls it into personal existence.

> Each man has need of the personal confirmation that can come only
> when he knows his "calling"—his existence in the fullest sense of the
> term—as an answer to a call. No man is able simply to confirm him-
> self. He may be able to do without the admiration of crowds, but he
> cannot do without that silent dialogue, often internalized within him-
> self, through which he places his efforts within the context of a mutual
> contact with what is not himself. He needs to feel that his work is
> "true"—both as a genuine expression of the reality that he encounters
> in his life and as a genuine response to some situation or need that
> calls him.[33]

[32] *Ibid.*, pp. 455–62. The essays by Leslie H. Farber from which these selections
were taken—"Will and Willfulness in Hysteria," "Despair and the Life of Suicide," "The Therapeutic Despair," "Schizophrenia and the Mad Psychiatrist"—are
included, together with others, in Leslie H. Farber, *The Ways of the Will* (N. Y.:
Basic Books, 1966).
[33] Maurice Friedman, *Problematic Rebel, op. cit.*, p. 365.

X

THE
ABSURD MAN

17

SAMUEL BECKETT
AND THE EARLY CAMUS

OUR LAST, most decidedly modern and problematic type of contemporary image of man is the Absurd Man. The roots of the Absurd Man may be clearly found in the nineteenth century. His most explicit foreshadowing perhaps is Kierkegaard's "faith by virtue of the absurd." But he is even more startlingly prefigured in the complete severance of social relations and social expectations by Melville's Bartleby the Scrivener, with his calm "I prefer not to." [1] The Absurd Man is present, too, in Ivan Karamazov's cry of rebellion. "The absurd is only too necessary on earth," Ivan says to his brother Alyosha. "The world stands on absurdities, and perhaps nothing would have to come to pass in it without them." Ivan not only disclaims understanding but wanting to understand. In his insistence on the particular, he is perhaps a prototype of the existentialist. But in his insistence on the absurdity of the particular, he anticipates the Absurd Man. "If I try to understand anything I shall be false to the fact and I have determined to stick to the fact." By "the fact" Ivan means irreducible realities such as the torture and death of innocent children. No future harmony can justify such facts, and it is this which leads Ivan to turn in his ticket while there is still time, rejecting not God but His world.[2]

One of the clearest statements of the absurd occurs in a work of a

[1] See my discussion of "Bartleby the Scrivener" in *Problematic Rebel, op. cit.*, pp. 93–5, and my essay "Bartleby and the Modern Exile" in Howard P. Vincent, ed., *Bartleby the Scrivener* (Kent (Ohio) State Univ. Press, 1966), pp. 64–81.
[2] Fyodor Dostoyevsky, *The Brothers Karamazov*, translated by Constance Garnett (N. Y.: The Modern Library, 1943), pp. 298–300.

writer who sought most earnestly for meaning—Hermann Hesse. In *Steppenwolf*, the author of "The Treatise on the Steppenwolf" states that the life of men like Harry Haller consists "of a perpetual tide, unhappy and torn with pain, terrible and meaningless." Certain acts may shine out above the chaos of their lives, but until they see their destiny to immortality they are likely to live with "the desperate and horrible thought . . . that perhaps the whole of human life is but a bad joke, a violent and ill-fated abortion of the primal mother, a savage and dismal catastrophe of nature." In *Steppenwolf*, of course, the absurd is not the last word. Mozart is heard through the static, the voice of the immortals through the meaninglessness of everyday life.

The Absurd Man really emerges in full stature in the writings of Samuel Beckett. Intentionally or not, Beckett's play *Waiting for Godot* is a parody of Simone Weil's *Waiting for God*. The two main characters, Estragon and Vladimir, spend a lifetime "waiting for Godot." Their sense of time is characterized by that very blocking of the future and fragmentation of the present which the phenomenological psychiatrist, Eugene Minkowski, speaks of in "Findings in a Case of Schizophrenic Depression." In fact, there could be no better description of the tormented temporality of *Waiting for Godot* than Minkowski's statement: "Each day life began anew, like a solitary island in a gray sea of passing time." There is no reason to say that Mr. Godot is God, for there is no reason to suppose that in the world of the absurd God exists, even in Simone Weil's anguished sense. But there is an abundance of religious motifs which can be taken neither seriously nor ironically. In the total context, they appear as a parody of even such harsh religious consolation as Simone Weil offers. The parallels with Weil's *Waiting for God* are numerous and explicit: the discussion of the thief on the cross beside the Saviour; the repeated suggestion of the tree as the cross; the frequent mention of prayer, supplication, listening; the recognition that they have no rights any more; and the paradoxical waiting for someone whom they do not know, have not seen, and would not know if they saw him. There is the suggestion of man (Lucky) propitiating God (Pozzo) so that he will give up the idea of parting with him. There is a longing for death —"Will night never come?"—and the seeming acceptance of suffering from God for reasons that only God knows. There is the constant comparison with the crucified Christ, reminiscent of Weil's "I envy Christ his crucifixion" and even such explicit Weil-ian statements as "When you seek you hear. . . . That prevents you from finding." Above all, what is important is not that they know that Godot exists, but that Godot should know that they exist. It is *their* existence that is in doubt, not as a fact but through lack of confirmation, lack of being needed, wanted, called. Waiting for Godot means, for them, waiting to be called into existence. Pending this, they always find something to pass away the time, or as Gogo puts it more exactly, "to give us the impression that we exist." Didi responds to Gogo, "Yes, yes, we're magicians." "Christ have mercy on us!" says Didi near the end of the play, and both agree to hang themselves tomorrow, from the flowering tree-cross—unless Godot comes, in which case they will be saved.

"We are not saints, but we have kept our appointment," Estragon nobly asserts. "How many people can boast as much?" "Billions!" responds Estragon with devastating bathos. This is the final commentary on Vladimir's pathetic monologue which precedes it:

> Let us do something, while we have the chance! It is not every day that we are needed. *Not indeed that we personally are needed. Others would meet the case equally well, if not better.* To all mankind they were addressed, those cries for help still ringing in our ears! But at this place, at this moment of time, all mankind is us, whether we like it or not. Let us make the most of it, before it is too late! Let us represent worthily for once the foul brood to which a cruel fate consigned us! . . . In this immense confusion one thing alone is clear. We are waiting for Godot to come. . . . Or for night to fall.[3]

The mock high style of this passage carries at once bathos and poignance and points not to irony but the absurd. Simone Weil says in *Waiting for God* that one thing is sure: when one asks God for bread, one may trust that He will not give one a stone. But it is a stone—a burial stone—that the dog is given which, in the poem recited by Vladimir at the beginning of the second act of *Waiting for Godot*, comes to the kitchen to try to get some bread. And it is a stone that Vladimir and Estragon are given in *Waiting for Godot*.

In the first act, time is carefully measured by Pozzo, the man with the watch, the whip, and the slave-animal-man Lucky, whom he makes carry his possessions and whom he whips when he falls under the burden of them. Estragon complains: "Nothing happens, nobody comes, nobody goes, it's awful!" and Vladimir suggests that time has stopped. But Pozzo, cuddling his watch to his ear, says, "Don't you believe it, sir, don't you believe it. . . . Whatever you like, but not that." But in the second act, Pozzo has gone blind, his watch has disappeared, and time has stopped. When Vladimir tries to remind him of what took place yesterday, Pozzo says: "Don't question me. The blind have no notion of time. The things of time are hidden from them too," and later, suddenly furious, Pozzo exclaims:

---

[3] Samuel Beckett, *Waiting for Godot*. Tragicomedy in two acts (N. Y.: Grove Press, 1954), p. 51f.; italics added.

Have you not done tormenting me with your accursed time? It's abominable. When! When! One day, is that not enough for you, one day like any other day, one day he went dumb, one day I went blind, one day we'll go deaf, one day we were born, one day we'll die, the same day, the same second, is that not enough for you? [*Calmer*.] They give birth astride of a grave, the light gleams an instant, then it's night once more.[4]

Vladimir picks up this same theme while Estragon is sleeping, and it becomes almost a summation of the play and of the image of human existence that it presents:

Tomorrow, when I wake, or think I do, what shall I say of today? That with Estragon, my friend, at this place, until the fall of night, I waited for Godot? That Pozzo passed, with his carrier, and talked to us? Probably. But in all that what truth will there be? . . . Astride of a grave and a difficult birth. Down in the hole, lingeringly, the grave-digger puts on the forceps. We have time to grow old. The air is full of our cries. . . . At me too someone is looking, of me too someone is saying, He is sleeping, he knows nothing, let him sleep on. [*Pause*.] I can't go on.[5]

The slave Lucky presents a terrifying caricature of man when Pozzo whips him and commands him to "think" for the entertainment of Gogo and Didi. The content of the much-misnamed Lucky's thinking might seem at first glance to bear out the assertion of some that *Waiting for Godot* is a dramatization of Weil's *Waiting for God*. There are quasi-theological references to "the existence of a personal God . . . with white beard . . . outside time without extension Who from the heights of divine apathia divine athambia divine aphasia loves us dearly with some exceptions for reasons unknown but time will tell and suffers . . . with those who for reasons unknown but time will tell are plunged in torment." But these references are punctuated by "quaquaquaqua," the speech is rattled off in an unbearable, ever more hysterical cumulation, and it is finished when Pozzo, Vladimir, and Estragon all throw themselves on Lucky and silence him. The measuring of man yields an image of one who "in spite of the progress of alimentation and defecation wastes and pines wastes and pines" in the face of the death of God: "and then the earth in the great cold the great dark the air and the earth abode of stones in the great cold alas alas in the year of their Lord six hundred and something the air the earth the sea the earth abode of stones in the great deeps the great cold on sea on land."

4 *Ibid.*, p. 57b.
5 *Ibid.*, p. 58f.

All Beckett's works seem concerned with the long, slow process of dying. Beckett's characters endlessly and painfully drag themselves through a wasteland of nonpresence and nonexistence, the ultimate goal and relief of which is death. "Don't mind me. Don't take any notice of me. I do not exist. The fact is well known," says Mrs. Rooney in *All That Fall*, and Mrs. Fitt says: "I suppose the truth is I am not there, Mrs. Rooney, just not really there at all. I see, hear, smell, and so on, I go through the usual motions, but my heart is not in it." Such plot as there is in the play—the meeting of a train which is unexpectedly late because a child has fallen (or been thrown?) to its death from the train—is robbed of any possible dramatic tension by the general absurdity. "Did you ever wish to kill a child?" the blind Mr. Rooney asks his wife and adds, after a pause, "Nip some young doom in the bud." If human existence has neither meaning nor value, then the taking of a child's life does not mean a tragic foreshortening but sparing a doomed creature the misery of a lifelong dying. For the Buddha, too, existence was seen as suffering, but, however negatively stated, there was a positive deliverance from suffering in the cessation of existence in Nirvana. In Beckett's world there is no positive deliverance from suffering, only quick or slow death.

Beckett's *Endgame* is a secular apocalypse. It is the world of a Modern Gnostic who has neither the transcendent God of Simone Weil nor the belief in the Self within of Jung and Hesse, but only the forlornness, the endless sense of abandonment in a world where man never can be at home.

CLOV: I look at the wall.
HAMM: The wall! And what do you see on your wall? Mene, mene? Naked bodies?
CLOV: I see my light dying.[6]

The occupation of looking at the wall with which Melville depicted the absurdity of Bartleby's existence over a century ago is now taken up by Beckett into a world where the Absurd Man is no longer the exception but the rule. "*Mene, mene tekel upharsin*" are the Hebrew letters that appear in fire on the wall during Belshazzar's feast in the Book of Daniel. They represent a stern word of judgment—"You have been weighed in the balances and found wanting"—but they also imply by this very judgment that there is such a thing as authentic existence. The accountability is the corollary of the duty *and* the possibility of genuine existence. The judgment is in large part the judgment of the inauthentic existence itself. In the history of peoples as

6 Samuel Beckett, *Endgame. A Play in One Act*, translated from the French by the author (N. Y.: Grove Press, 1958), p. 12.

in the history of the individual, according to the Hebrew Bible, the sinner cannot stand under the judgment because his way vanishes, because the inauthentic way is not a way at all but a losing of one's way.

In Beckett's world, in contrast, there is no way to lose, no authentic existence which is possible, and hence no judgment or accountability. By the same token, there is no image of man in the sense of a direction of authentic existence. There is only realism, honesty, and despair. These three also exclude the possibility of a hedonistic life in which man can escape from the anguish and boredom of his existence through pleasure. There are no naked bodies to be seen on the wall either. All that the wall reflects to Clov, all that the wall reflects to Beckett is the undeniable fact that one's light is dying. To Clov's question, "Do you believe in the life to come?" Hamm replies, "Mine was always that." Some religions have portrayed this life as meaningful because it is a forecourt of a real existence to come. Other religions and philosophies have suggested that the highest reality is accessible in this life, that meaning is to be found in the "lived concrete," to use Buber's phrase. Beckett's world excludes both possibilities. There is no hope for the future, no meaning in the present. Our life is always a life to come because it never reaches real existence now. To Hamm's question, "Did you ever have an instant of happiness?" Clov replies, "Not to my knowledge." Needless to say, our life never reaches real existence in the future either. "You're on earth, there's no cure for that!" says Hamm to himself.

The corollary of the absurdity of individual existences is also the meaninglessness of the relations between man and man. With Buber's central assertion, "All real living is meeting," Beckett might have no theoretical disagreement. All he would say is that there is no real living and no meeting. The absurdity of imagining that one can help or save others is underscored by Hamm in a soliloquy: "Get out of here and love one another! Lick your neighbor as yourself!" This soliloquy ends by reverting to the absurdity of one's own existence and with it the *Waiting for Godot* view of time as an endless series of meaningless moments:

> Moment upon moment, pattering down, like the millet grains of . . . [*he hesitates*] . . . that old Greek, and all life long you wait for that to mount up to a life.[7]

Life is an "endgame" since it adds up to no more than dying, and dying offers such comfort as is to be found in this cheerless world. In his final soliloquy Hamm sums up:

7 *Ibid.*, p. 70.

Old endgame lost of old, play and lose and have done with los-
ing. . . .
You CRIED for night; it comes—
[*Pause. He corrects himself.*]
It FALLS: now cry in darkness. . . .
Moments for nothing, now as always, time was never and time is over,
reckoning closed and story ended.[8]

The absurdity of personal existence, of the dialogue between man
and man, and of the search for beauty and order in the world converge in the ironic comment of Clov before this final soliloquy:

CLOV [*fixed gaze, tonelessly, towards auditorium*]: They said to me,
That's love, yes, yes, not a doubt, now you see how—
HAMM: Articulate!
CLOV [*as before*]: How easy it is. They said to me, That's friendship,
yes, yes, no question, you've found it. They said to me, Here's the
place, stop, raise your head and look at all that beauty. That order!
They said to me, Come now, you're not a brute beast, think upon these
things and you'll see how all becomes clear. And simple! They said
to me, What skilled attention they get, all these dying of their wounds.[9]

No one could give more skilled attention than Beckett to those dying
of the wounds of living. He even allows the suggestion of the prospect
of happiness when the longed-for end comes. "When I fall I'll weep
for happiness," says Clov as he exits. But this is not that lullingly
nostalgic and dreamlike happiness with which the Victorian poet
Algernon Swinburne envisages death in "The Garden of Prosperine":

> From too much love of living,
> From hope and fear set free,
> We thank with brief thanksgiving
> Whatever gods may be
> That no life lives forever
> That dead men rise up never
> That even the weariest river
> Winds somewhere safe to sea.

Even romanticism lends a sort of meaning to the absurd, however
emotional. Beckett accepts no such meaning. The fact of life is its
ultimate meaninglessness.

Beckett's image of the Absurd Man is developed in breathtaking
fashion in his trilogy of novels *Molloy, Malone Dies,* and *The Unnamable.* The novel form allows Beckett an extra dimension of sub-

[8] *Ibid.,* p. 82f.
[9] *Ibid.,* p. 80.

jectivity through which he communicates a further intensity of the absurd—the absurdity of one's relation to oneself, of one's existence as a name, a person, an "I." It also allows him a greater play of wit, humor, patience, courage, and a kind of overall compassion and acceptance which, if it does not amount to an image of man in the sense of giving any positive direction, is something more than an image of inauthenticity.

Molloy and Moran—the man who sets out to find Molloy in the second half of *Molloy*—give a picture of hopeless, miserable, infinitely painful dragging oneself on. Molloy is sympathetic in a pitiable sort of way; Moran is unsympathetic. But it does not seem to matter in the end. Both belong to the "gallery of moribunds" of which Moran speaks, "the rabble in the head" of Beckett, but also of Moran, and of the unnamable I. Molloy's hopeless, absurd, interminable journey can be summed up in his own words:

> All my life, I think, I had been going to my mother, with the purpose of establishing our relations on a less precarious footing. And when I was with her, and I often succeeded, I left her without having done anything. And when I was no longer with her I was again on my way to her, hoping to do better the next time.[10]

Molloy's crutch-clutching progress is in the same measure a regress. His goal most of the time is that things shall be no worse than elsewhere. His usual feeling is "so terror-stricken that I was virtually bereft of feeling, not to say of consciousness, and drowned in a deep and merciful torpor shot with brief abominable gleams." His world is so far gone into the absurd that, so far from defining it as the nostalgia for the rational, as the lucid Camus does, he takes up a position exactly the opposite. He cannot follow that Cartesian rationalism which assumes that because an idea is clear it must, or at least should, be true. "All that is false may more readily be reduced, to notions clear and distinct, distinct from all other notions." Molloy's progress-regress is movement without meaning. All is muck, but "it's good to have a change of muck, to move from one heap to another a little further on, from time to time." According to his own statement, Molloy has progressed through all the sciences—astronomy, geology, anthropology, psychiatry, magic—but he dwells most frequently in "a place . . . deserted by magic, because devoid of mystery." In this "place" he attains something close to a mysticism of the absurd:

> I listen and the voice is of a world collapsing endlessly, a frozen world, under a faint untroubled sky, enough to see by, yes, and frozen

10 Samuel Beckett, *Molloy. A Novel,* translated by Patrick Bowles in collaboration with the author (N. Y.: Grove Press, 1955), p. 118.

too. And I hear it murmur that all wilts and yields, as if loaded down, but here there are no loads, and the ground too, unfit for loads, and the light too, down towards an end it seems can never come. For what possible end to these wastes where true light never was, nor any upright thing, nor any true foundation, but only these leaning things, forever lapsing and crumbling away, beneath a sky without memory of morning or hope of night. . . . Yes, a world at an end, in spite of appearances, its end brought it forth, ending it began, is it clear enough? And I too am at an end, when I am there, my eyes close, my sufferings cease and I end, I wither as the living can not.[11]

Moran, commissioned to find Molloy, ends up like him. "I don't like men and I don't like animals. As for God, he is beginning to disgust me." "I knew that all was about to end," he says, "or to begin again, it little mattered which, and it little mattered how, I had only to wait." Even the search for identity, so popular in our age, is seen by Moran not as a goal but as a misfortune.

To tell the truth, I not only knew who I was, but I had a sharper and clearer sense of my identity than ever before, in spite of its deep lesions and the wounds with which it was covered. And from this point of view I was less fortunate than my other acquaintances. I am sorry if this last phrase is not so happy as it might be. It deserved, who knows, to be without ambiguity.[12]

The second stage on the journey to the self—which is, at the same time, a journey to solipsism—is *Malone Dies*. Malone's "half-truths" are the same as those of Beckett's other Absurd Men: "I used not to know where I was going, but I knew I would arrive, I knew there would be an end to the long blind road." For him the noises of nature, of mankind, and even his own "were all jumbled together in one and the same unbridled gibberish." Not even the "facts" of life and death can withstand the absurdity of his so-called existence.

What matter whether I was born or not, have lived or not, am dead or merely dying, I shall go on doing as I have always done, not knowing what it is I do, nor who I am, nor where I am, nor if I am.[13]

Like one of the characters he describes, he is "flayed alive by memory, his mind crawling with cobras." The anguish of his existence expresses itself in the image of striking his bony but sensitive head with a hammer, for it is "the seat of all the shit and misery." As long as Malone can remember, he has had the sensation of a blind

11 *Ibid.*, p. 53.
12 *Ibid.*, p. 233.
13 Samuel Beckett, *Malone Dies*, translated by the author (N. Y.: Grove Press, 1956), p. 52.

and tired hand delving feebly in his particles and letting them
trickle between its fingers. It plunges into the sand of his existence
with its elbows, at first sleepily and then stirring, "wakes, fondles,
clutches, ransacks, ravages, avenging its failure to scatter me with
one sweep."

For all this, Malone's death is not merely passively experienced by
him:

> There is no good pretending, it is hard to leave everything. The
> horror-worn eyes linger abject on all they have beseeched so long, in a
> last prayer, the true prayer at last, the one that asks for nothing. And
> it is then a little breath of fulfillment revives the dead longings and a
> murmur is born in the silent world, reproaching you affectionately
> with having despaired too late.[14]

There is even an anticipation of the existence, behind or beneath
Malone, of that unobjectifiable, ungraspable subject which is the
core of *The Unnamable:*

> My concern is not with me, but with another, far beneath me and
> whom I try to envy. . . . To show myself now, on the point of
> vanishing, at the same time as the stranger, and by the same grace,
> that would be no ordinary last straw. Then live, long enough to feel,
> behind my closed eyes, other eyes close. What an end.[15]

In *The Unnamable* the journey to solipsism is completed. The Unnamable "I" strips away one layer after another of his social selves—
variously named Mahood, Worm, or simply "they"—in order to reach
by negation the silent, unspeaking, unspeakable within. This process
is so thorough that he wants to dispense with the use of "I" altogether since every thing that "I" says or does is really what "they"
have made it say or do. Of itself it is nothing and does nothing. "I
have been here, ever since I began to be, my appearances elsewhere
having been put in by other parties." Nor is there any suggestion
that this search for the unnamable within will lead to either identity,
meaning, or humanity. Quite to the contrary, these are the very
things which he is stripping off and with it the image of man as we
have discussed it, namely, the polar tension between one's uniqueness
and one's humanness. Since his "I" is unreachable, it is a mystery to
him how he can be indebted for information to persons with whom
he has never been in contact.

These persons are present, nonetheless, in his reflections throughout
the book. They wish him to believe that he is dependent on God,

14 *Ibid.,* p. 107.
15 *Ibid.,* p. 19.

that he must swallow the existence of his fellow creatures. Above all, "they" are trying to put over on him the notion that he is alive and exists. Though he does not see them, they are watching him, "like a face in the embers which they know is doomed to crumble," and he continues to make noise "in obedience to the unintelligible terms of an incomprehensible damnation." The chief dupery of all is that which tries to entice him into recognizing himself as a man, "tottering under the attributes peculiar to the lords of creation, dumb with howling to be put out of my misery." For an instant, or years, he fell into the temptation, stopping after each thrust of his crutches to devour a narcotic and measure the distance gone, the distance yet to go. But then he withdrew his adhesion, and whatever else his "I" is, it ceased to be man.

Even to speak of himself, he must use their language, but this is still a step toward the silence. "Nothing will remain of all the lies they have glutted me with. And I'll be myself at last, as a starveling belches his odourless wind, before the bliss of coma." They think that he can "never make a gesture but their cast must come to life." "But within, motionless, I can live, and utter me, for no ears but my own." Their humanity threatens to stifle "the little murmur of un-consenting man, . . . the little gasp of the condemned to life, rotting in his dungeon garrotted and racked." But even though he has no language but theirs, he will find a way of saying what he is, "so as not to have not lived in vain, and so as to go silent, if that is what confers the right to silence." He does not want meaning. He wants to strip away meaning to reveal the absurd at the heart of his being. "I'll say what I am, so as not to have not been born for nothing."

To do this, he must say what he is not. To begin with, "these maniacs let loose on me from on high for what they call my good," and after that the image of himself as winding his endless ways, or as walking on hands and knees, crawling on his belly or rolling on the ground, and finally, only the trunk remaining (in sorry trim), stuck into a deep jar with a cement collar round his neck, his skull bare and covered with pustules and bluebottle flies. He has been sufficiently assassinated, sufficiently suicided to stand on his own feet, he says to himself. But still, it's a lot to ask of one creature "that he should first behave as if he were not, then as if he were, before being admitted to that peace where he neither is, nor is not, and where the language dies that permits of such expressions." He wants to be "let loose in the unthinkable, unspeakable" and cannot under-stand why, "with their billions of quick, their trillions of dead, that's not enough for them, I too must contribute my little convulsion, mewl, howl, gasp and rattle, loving my neighbour and blessed with

reason." They will only take him seriously when he pukes his heart
out, spews it up whole along with the rest of the vomit. He is like
dust, out of which they want to make man; he is "matter, pawed
and pummelled endlessly in vain."

> One alone turned towards the all-impotent, all-nescient, that haunts
> him. . . . Come into the world unborn, abiding there unliving, with
> no hope of death, epicentre of joys, of griefs, of calm. . . . The one
> outside of life we always were in the end, all our long vain life long.
> Who is not spared by the mad need to speak, to think, to know where
> one is, where one was, during the wild dream, up above, under the
> skies, venturing forth at night. The one ignorant of himself and silent,
> ignorant of his silence and silent, who could not be and gave up try-
> ing. . . . He who seeks his true countenance, let him be of good
> cheer, he'll find it, convulsed with anguish, the eyes out on stalks.[16]

In a remarkable variation on his search for the self, the narrator
suggests that he is perhaps a tympanum dividing the inner and the
outer, two surfaces and no thickness—"on the one hand the mind,
on the other the world, I don't belong to either." This is the refusal
once for all to follow Descartes in identifying the I with the mind
which seems to speak it and speak for it, any more than one can
identify it with the world which speaks to it. The I will be grasped,
if at all, only in terms of its middle position between two realities
that it is not—the outside and the inside. The I is everything, and
it is also nothing:

> All words, the whole world is here with me, I'm the air, the walls,
> the walled-in one, everything yields, opens, ebbs, flows, like flakes,
> I'm all these flakes, meeting, mingling, falling asunder, wherever I go
> I find me, leave me, go towards me, come from me, nothing ever but
> me, a particle of me, retrieved, lost, gone astray, I'm all these words,
> all these strangers, this dust of words, with no ground for their settling,
> no sky for their dispersing, coming together to say, fleeing one another
> to say, that I am they, all of them, those that merge, those that part,
> those that never meet, and nothing else, yes, something else, that I'm
> something quite different, a quite different thing, a worldless thing in
> an empty place, a hard shut dry cold black place, where nothing stirs,
> nothing speaks, and that I listen, and that I seek, like a caged beast
> born of caged beasts born of caged beasts born of caged beasts born
> in a cage and dead in a cage, born and then dead, born in a cage and
> then dead in a cage.[17]

[16] Samuel Beckett, *The Unnamable*, translated by the author (N. Y.: Grove Press,
1958), p. 82f.
[17] *Ibid.*, p. 139.

Most of the time the I that the I seeks seems to be, in *The Un-namable*, "a wordless thing in an empty place, a hard shut dry cold black place, where nothing stirs, nothing speaks," and yet the listening and the speaking remain inescapably bound up with "the sinned-against silence" as long as the book lasts. He is not even sure in the end which I he is not—the one that left the silence and talks on, or the one that never left the silence, that is made of the silence. At the end of *The Unnamable*, one glimpses both the final release of the suffering talker into the silence of death and the birth of the confused fetus into life.

> Perhaps they have carried me to the threshold of my story, before the door that opens on my story, that would surprise me, if it opens, it will be I, it will be the silence, where I am, I don't know, I'll never know, in the silence you don't know, you must go on, I can't go on, I'll go on.[18]

If Beckett's Absurd Man is the image of man cut off from humanity and imprisoned in an absurd and unnamable self, this also, to a less extreme degree, is the Absurd Man of the early Camus. In his early play, *Caligula*, Camus portrays a young Roman emperor whose love for his sister Drusilla is metamorphosed on her death into an overwhelming conviction of the absurdity of life. Mourning, for him, takes the form of a determination to force this absurd to its logical conclusions until his indifference to the death of others finds its inevitable dénouement in his own death. In other words, *Caligula* is, in the most extreme form imaginable, a portrayal of what Leslie Farber calls the "life of suicide." Having arrived at the conclusion that "men die and they are not happy" and the emotional protest that "things as they are . . . are far from satisfactory," Caligula now wants the moon—the impossible. With his almost godlike power as Roman emperor, he is determined to make the impossible possible or bring down his empire and himself in the attempt. "I wish men to live by the light of truth, and I've the power to make them do so." Before this change, he is pictured as someone who tried to be just and to spare others suffering. Now he wants only injustice and suffering, and he gets them both in full measure. He seeks a freedom that he believes can be won only by the recognition that this world has no importance. But he knows that the road to this freedom is anguish—"How hard, how cruel it is, this process of becoming a man"—and he accentuates this anguish to the utmost by a mad, inhuman logic which tolerates no contradictions. He wants to be a

[18] *Ibid.*, p. 179

god, to tamper with the scheme of things, "to drown the sky in the sea, to infuse ugliness with beauty, to wring a laugh from pain." If he cannot reduce the sum of suffering and make an end of death, he will make suffering and death so universal as to make an end of life. "He is converting his philosophy into corpses," complains Cherea, the man who ultimately organizes his assassination, "and— unfortunately for us—it's a philosophy that's logical from start to finish." Cherea sees no way to meet this threat but to allow this logic to follow its bent until it founders in sheer lunacy. His fear of Caligula is not just the fear of death but the fear of the absurd meaning of life that Caligula forces on his subjects:

> All I wish is to regain some peace of mind in a world that has re-gained a meaning. What spurs me on is not ambition but fear, my very reasonable fear of that inhuman vision in which my life means no more than a speck of dust.[19]

Caligula describes himself as single-minded for evil. Deep within himself he is aware of "an abyss of silence, a pool of stagnant water and rotting weeds." Where Scipio, his young poet friend, finds soli-tude and the beauty of nature, he finds "gnashings of teeth, hideous with jarring sounds and voices." He teaches the hard lesson of in-difference, of the equivalence of all things in nothingness. He chooses to play the part of fate, to wear "the foolish, unintelligible face of a professional god." When he pictures his own assassination, which he has done "everything needed" to bring about, he rejoices to see "in all those faces surging up out of the angry darkness, convulsed with fear and hatred, . . . the only god I've worshipped on this earth; foul and craven as the human heart." If Caligula embodies Farber's life of suicide, he also embodies, again in the most extreme form, what Farber holds lies behind this life: willfulness. Contem-plating his own approaching death, he says to himself angrily:

> Logic, Caligula; follow where logic leads. Power to the uttermost; willfulness without end. Ah, I'm the only man on earth to know the secret—that power can never be complete without a total surrender to the dark impulse of one's destiny.[20]

He exults in the fact that security and logic cannot go together, that he has used his power to create for his subjects "a world where the most preposterous fancy may at any moment become a reality, and the absurd transfix their lives, like a dagger in the heart." But he

[19] Albert Camus, *Caligula and Three Other Plays*, translated by Stuart Gilbert (N. Y.: Vintage Books, 1958), p. 22. The three other plays are *The Misunder-standing, The State of Siege,* and *The Just Assassins.*
[20] *Ibid.,* pp. 49–50.

does not recognize that what he romantically characterizes as "total self-surrender to the dark impulse of one's destiny" is really the willfulness of the isolated will, separated from the living dialogue that gave it meaning. But meaning is now precisely what he does not want, except in the utterly negative form of the denial that there is any meaning. To Caligula all actions, like all lives, are on an equal footing—because none amounts to anything. Even this negative feeling is not enough to fill the emptiness within.

> How strange! When I don't kill, I feel alone. The living don't suffice to people my world and dispel my boredom. I have an impression of an enormous void when you and the others are here, and my eyes see nothing but empty air. . . . Only the dead are real.[21]

Erich Fromm, with good reason, takes Camus' Caligula as a prime example of the necrophilous man. But there is an awareness in Caligula's necrophilia that does not quite fit the picture. He knows that against him is not only stupidity, but also "the courage and the simple faith of men who ask to be happy." He proclaims himself as the man who has reached "beyond the frontier of pain . . . a splendid, sterile happiness." Even had Drusilla lived, he could not have borne to love her, for he was not willing to grow old beside her. His real suffering is not that death snatched her out of the blue, but the recognition that grief too cannot last, that even grief is vanity.

When Caligula confronts himself in the mirror just before he is assassinated, he weeps because there is nothing in this world, or in the next, made to his stature. But he also recognizes that his search for the impossible has never done anything but bring him face to face with himself. He has come to hate himself and with it the "freedom" in which he is imprisoned. "I have chosen a wrong path, a path that leads to nothing." He concludes that his freedom is not the right one, that he has not succeeded in becoming the image of man that liberates mankind. "We shall be forever guilty."

Writing in 1957 about this play written nineteen years before, Camus underlines this conclusion:

> If his truth is to rebel against fate, his error lies in negating what binds him to mankind. One cannot destroy everything without destroying oneself. . . . *Caligula* is the story of a superior suicide. . . . Caligula accepts death because he has understood that no one can save himself all alone and that one cannot be free at the expense of others.[22]

---

[21] *Ibid.*, p. 68.
[22] *Ibid.*, p. vi.

This statement "foreshadows" Camus' later image of man, but it is a foreshadowing that is implicit in *Caligula* only in seed. The passages in Camus' 1957 preface to *The Misunderstanding* (1943) seem even more of a retrospective reading-in of a positive meaning than those on *Caligula*. Camus explains the suffocating, claustrophobic atmosphere of the play by the historical and geographical situation in which he lived then: the mountains of central France during the Nazi occupation. He suggests in addition, however, that the play be looked at as an attempt to create a modern tragedy whose morality is not altogether negative:

> A son who expects to be recognized without having to declare his name and who is killed by his mother and his sister as a result of the misunderstanding—this is the subject of the play. Doubtless, it is a very dismal image of human fate. But it can be reconciled with a relative optimism as to man. For, after all, it amounts to saying that everything would have been different if the son had said: "It is I; here is my name." It amounts to saying that in an unjust or indifferent world man can save himself, and save others, by practicing the most basic sincerity and pronouncing the most appropriate word.[23]

Granted that the son would not have been killed if he had not stuck to his foolish notion of making his mother and sister love him before revealing to them that he is the son and brother who left them twenty years before. Yet there is much more of the absurd in this play than Camus' prefatory remarks indicate. The real drama is not so much that of the innocent and provokingly duty-bound husband as it is that between mother and daughter, habitual murderers bound together by this tie and by a common hopelessness. The mother is reluctant to kill this stranger not because she feels guilty, but because she is weary. "Life is crueler than we," she says, and the daughter, though insisting on going through with the murder, also wants it to be the final one: "Yes, my soul's a burden to me, I've had enough of it. I'm eager to be in that country, where the sun kills every question."

Jan, the son, is accompanied by his wife, Maria, but he will not let her spend the night with him, and he insists on going through with his plan of not making himself known. He justifies himself by saying that it is not so much an idea as the force of things that carries him along. "It takes time to change a stranger into a son." But Maria replies, with acute prescience, "By pretending to be what one is not, one simply muddles everything. . . . There's something . . . something morbid about the way you're doing this." She knows

23 *Ibid.*, p. vii.

that he is speaking to her with the voice of his loneliness and not his love, and that his desire to redeem himself from exile and es-trangement by forcing her to leave him is denying that immediacy of love which has no time for dreams and dreads every separation. On the other hand, her advice to him to speak from the heart could hardly be less appropriate to the heartless situation into which he comes. He wonders, and with good reason, whether he will be made welcome. Although he has a faithful heart which soon builds up memories and attachments if given a chance, his sister rebuffs even the most ordinary sociality, and his mother confesses that she had forgotten her husband before he died and that she only knows her daughter because she has kept beside her all these years. She de-clares she is too old to love a son. "Hearts wear out, sir." The daugh-ter adds, "If a son came here, he'd find exactly what an ordinary guest can count on: amiable indifference, no more and no less." She is not so explicit as to add, "plus murder," but she warns him that he is in a house where the heart isn't catered to. The bleak years in this little spot of Central Europe have drained all the warmth out of this house and its occupants. Martha is angered at Jan's confiding innocence, and this, her mother points out, is an unsound decline from the indifference that they brought to their task in the past.

When Jan is alone in his room that night, he experiences fear—"fear of the eternal loneliness, fear that there is no answer." He finds an answer, but not the one he is looking for. Martha, who has her-self become unsure, is reconfirmed in her determination by Jan's description of the land of sea and sunshine from which he comes and to which she hopes to go by means of his money. She brings him a cup of tea with a sleeping potion in it, and he drinks it be-fore the mother has a chance to come in and stop him. As mother and daughter look at the sleeping man, they rationalize the drown-ing they are about to carry out by the thought that he, like other men, can never know peace except through the mercy of death. Martha impatiently adds that had he realized sooner that no one would ever find warmth or comfort or contentment in this house, he would have spared them the trouble of killing him. But it is not just the house of which his innocence is unaware, it is also life. They have had to teach him that this world is for dying in.

When Jan's passport reveals his identity after he has been drowned, it is his turn to teach his mother and sister something about the world in which they live. The mother learns that her heart, which had seemed indifferent to everything, could not help grieving over her son's death, that "in a world where everything can be denied, there are forces undeniable; and on this earth where nothing's sure we have our certainties." A mother's love for her son is now her bitter certainty, and drowning herself is now her only recourse. Martha learns that, though her mother has loved her, she is bound more closely to the son who deserted her so many years before than to Martha, who has stuck by her. Martha says that, even if she had recognized Jan, it would have made no difference, for the only person to whom she lowers her head is her mother. Like Cain, she cries out that she is not her brother's keeper—"What concern of mine was it to look after my brother? None whatever!" But, unlike Cain, she sees herself as the innocent one to whom injustice has been done, for now she is an outcast in her home with no hope of attaining the sun and sea for which she longed. Her exile is beyond remedy. She has shed blood for her mother's love, and is left with nothing but her "very rightful anger" and her hatred of "this narrow world in which we are reduced to gazing up at God." She is an exile and a rebel, one who will go down to her death protesting and unreconciled.

If *The Misunderstanding* is a sublime and depressing example of what Martin Buber calls "mismeeting," there is hardly a hint in it that in an absurd world meeting is possible. Despite Camus' suggestion to the contrary, the real problem of communication in *The Misunderstanding* could not have been solved by the commonsense directness which would say, "It is I." It is the encounter of smug innocence and bitter, exiled guilt. Between these two there is an abyss which Martha recognizes clearly, which leaves her not remorseful but angry at the brother she has killed; for he has had the happiness that she has been denied. Like a Greek tragedy, *The Misunderstanding* is the story of a family and of terrible things that happen to it that have never before been related, as Maria says. But it is a modern tragedy of the absurd, for all that, with no Greek sense of an order with which one could be reconciled even through suffering and death.

The Stranger was written four years after *Caligula* and a year before *The Misunderstanding*. It is the novel which brought Camus fame, and in its economy and power is unsurpassed in his later works. It is also the novel which is taken most often as the illustration of the philosophy of the absurd which Camus sets forth in *The Myth of Sisyphus*. With the exception of the ending, however, its hero, Meursault, is anything but a philosopher. He lacks that awareness which gives even Caligula a philosophical touch. The sequence of events is very simple. His father deserted his mother when he was small. His mother, whom he has sent to an old folks' home, dies, and he comes to the funeral. He is unable to show any emotion or cry either while he sits by the body all night or at the funeral itself. But he is overcome by the sun and almost faints. The next day he meets a girl named Maria at a swimming pool. He takes her as his mistress the same night. When Maria asks him if he will marry her, he replies perhaps. When she asks him if he loves her, he says no. He makes friends with Raymond, a pimp who lives in his building, but with the same indifference as in his relation with Maria. He sees no reason not to be Raymond's friend, and later he sees no reason not to perjure himself when Raymond asks him to come to the police station with him to defend Raymond against the charge that he has beaten up his Arab girl friend. When Meursault and Maria go to the beach with Raymond and his girl and another couple, the Arab brothers of this girl show up and attack Raymond with a knife. Meursault takes away Raymond's revolver so he won't shoot the Arabs, and later himself goes for a walk on the beach. He sees one of the Arabs sitting by a rock in the shadow with a knife glinting in the sun, and now he reenacts what he had earlier thought when Raymond handed him the gun, namely, "that one might fire, or not fire—and it would come to absolutely the same thing." Although he knows he could turn around at any time, he keeps walking toward the rock and, when he gets near, kills the Arab with Raymond's revolver.

Why does Meursault commit this senseless murder? Not, certainly, because he is a fiend, as the jury later suggests on the basis of the fact that he did not weep at his mother's funeral. Nor was he looking for trouble when he went out. His original motive in walking to the shade of the rock is the opposite: "Anything to be rid of the glare, the sight of women in tears, the strain and effort—and to retrieve the pool of shadow by the rock and its cool silence!" The heat itself and the glare of the sun become the chief clue to why he goes forward knowingly to do something he has no wish to do. "It struck me that all I had to do was to turn, walk away, and think no more about it. But the whole beach, pulsing with heat, was pressing on my back." The heat becomes for him an unbearable pressure that leads him to shoot the Arab as a gesture of desperate revolt, a breaking of the unendurable tension.

> I was conscious only of the cymbals of the sun clashing on my skull, and, less distinctly, of the keen blade of light flashing up from the knife, scarring my eyelashes, and gouging into my eyeballs.
> Then everything began to reel before my eyes, a fiery gust came from the sea, while the sky cracked in two, from end to end, and a

great sheet of flame poured down through the rift. Every nerve in my
body was a steel spring, and my grip closed on the revolver.[24]

This apocalyptic breakthrough is something more than a solar agony
and ecstasy. The key to this "something more" is provided by Meursault's statement: "It was just the same sort of heat as at my mother's
funeral, and I had the same disagreeable sensations—especially in
my forehead, where all the veins seemed to be bursting through
the skin. I couldn't stand it any longer." What has happened here
is nothing other than Meursault's mourning for his mother. That he
did not weep at her funeral was not because of hardheartedness,
but because he identifies himself with her. Like her, he expects
nothing of the world; this lack of expectation is the clue to his seeming indifference to life. It is not that he wants nothing, but that—
aside from a few immediate physical sensations—he hopes for
nothing. He is a man who has schooled himself never to demand
anything of life, never to expect anything of it; therefore, he thinks
it a matter of no importance whether he marries Maria or whether
he perjures himself for Raymond. The one time he thinks of marrying Maria is when she is most like his mother as he knew her—
gossiping with other women—but it is also to escape the "women's
talk" which he finds so oppressive that he leaves the cabin. He identifies with his mother, but he does not really want her in the form
of marriage to Maria; for he expects nothing out of marriage either.

But why, we must ask, does a man who is so indifferent to matters
that closely concern him give way to an outburst of violence in a
matter that does not concern him at all? He explains it as shaking
off his sweat and the clinging veil of light, but he also knows that
the relief he finds is one that destroys him.

> I knew I'd shattered the balance of the day, the spacious calm of
> this beach on which I had been happy. But I fired four shots more into
> the inert body. . . . And each successive shot was another loud, fate-
> ful rap on the door of my undoing.[25]

What is this murder-suicide but the involuntary protest of the self
which has been pressed in on itself so far that it has no choice but
to explode? Like the rebel whom Camus describes in the book of
that title, "he confronts an order of things which oppresses him with
the insistence on a kind of right not to be oppressed beyond the
limit that he can tolerate." Only there is nothing conscious or aware
about Meursault's protest. It is the limit which the self sets to the
vast, indifferent nothingness which crushes it out of existence.

[24] Albert Camus, *The Stranger*, translated by Stuart Gilbert (N. Y.: Vintage Books,
1958), pp. 75–6.
[25] *Ibid.*, p. 76.

This same protest is the clue to the one other explosion which Meursault experiences, when the prison chaplain forces his way in on him and tries to bring him to confess before he is executed. Meursault has by no means been indifferent to the certainty of the guillotine. But he has schooled himself with considerable effort to a precarious balance, which the priest now upsets. When the priest asks to be called "Father" and insists that he is on Meursault's side and will pray for him even though his heart is hardened, something breaks in Meursault, and he starts yelling insults at the top of his voice. It is at this point that we discover the deepest ground of the indifference and hopelessness that he shares with his mother—his constant awareness that he will die and that he will die alone. It is better to burn than to disappear, he tells the priest, challenging the latter's ordered universe with the vision of the absurd. He has a certainty that the priest has not—the fact of his present life and of the death that is coming. This certainty makes it a matter of indifference whether he had done x or y, whether he has lived "authentically" or "inauthentically." In the face of the absurd, there can be no image of man, no image of a meaningful direction of personal existence, "nothing, nothing had the least importance, and I knew quite well why." A slow, persistent breeze had been blowing toward him from the years that were to come, *pendant toute cette vie absurde que j'avais menée*. This breeze—the awareness of his future death—has leveled out all the ideas of brotherhood and solidarity that people have tried to foist on him in the equally unreal years he was living through.

> What difference could they make to me, the deaths of others, or a mother's love, or his God; or the way a man decides to live, the fate he thinks he chooses, since one and the same fate was bound to "choose" not only me but thousands of millions of privileged people who, like him, called themselves my brothers. . . . All alike would be condemned to die one day. . . . And what difference could it make if, after being charged with murder, he were executed because he didn't weep at his mother's funeral, since it all came to the same thing in the end?[26]

This leveling down of everything to a common nothingness is reminiscent of Caligula, but in the end of The Stranger, Meursault achieves a transformation and even a sort of happiness which were altogether denied Caligula. His anger at the priest has washed him clean and emptied him of hope. Now he is able to understand why his mother took a fiancé at the end of her life.

[26] *Ibid.*, p. 152.

With death so near, Mother must have felt like someone on the brink of freedom, ready to start life all over again. No one, no one in the world had any right to weep for her. And I, too, felt ready to start life all over again.[27]

His identification with his mother now takes on a positive aspect. He lays his heart open for the very first time "to the benign indifference of the universe." So much farther along is he than the Modern Exile of the nineteenth century that he is not horror-struck by "the heartless voids and immensities of the universe," as is Melville's Ishmael in *Moby Dick*. Instead, he finds indifference a welcome relief from the even worse that he has expected, and he feels a partnership with the inhuman absurd that comforts him. "To feel it so like myself, indeed, so brotherly, made me realize that I'd been happy, and that I was happy still." This new feeling even gives him a tenuous bond to the society that has rejected him. The original exile of his indifference has been reinforced and doubled by the attitude of the jury. Threatened by the fact that Meursault's murder of the Arab was completely unmotivated and absurd, they converted him into a fiend. By so doing, they only widened the gap that separates Meursault from the society that judges and executes him. Now, however, Meursault feels that, just because he expects nothing of his fellowman, he will be less lonely if, on the day of his execution, there should be a huge crowd of spectators who would greet him with "howls of execration." This would be at least a minimal contact.

As *Caligula* and *The Stranger*, *The Myth of Sisyphus* deals with suicide, but this time as a philosophical problem pointing to what Camus calls the fundamental question of philosophy—"judging whether life is or is not worth living." What challenges the sense of meaning in life is the feeling of absurdity, and absurdity Camus defines here as the exile of man in the era of the "death of God."

> In a universe suddenly divested of illusions and lights, man feels an alien, a stranger. His exile is without remedy since he is deprived of the memory of a lost home or the hope of a promised land. This divorce between man and his life, the actor and his setting is properly the feeling of absurdity.[28]

The question which Camus wishes to focus on, therefore, is whether the absurdity of life requires one to escape it through hope or suicide. Man's fate in this unintelligible and limited universe, sur-

[27] *Ibid.*, p. 154.
[28] Albert Camus, *The Myth of Sisyphus and Other Essays*, translated by Justin O'Brien (N. Y.: Vintage Books, 1960), p. 5.

rounded by "a horde of irrationals," is to preserve a studied lucidity in which the feeling of the absurd becomes clear and definite. This lucidity recognizes that it is not the world that is absurd but our relation to it. The world in itself 'is not reasonable. "But what is absurd is the confrontation of this irrational and the wild longing for clarity whose call echoes in the human heart."

> Man stands face to face with the irrational. He feels within him his longing for happiness and for reason. The absurd is born of this confrontation between the human need and the unreasonable silence of the world.[29]

On the basis of this lucidity, Camus attacks the existentialists, whom he sees as using the absurd as a springboard into eternity. "To an absurd mind reason is useless and there is nothing beyond reason." In contrast to Kierkegaard's "leap of faith," Camus declares: "I want to know whether I can live with what I know and with that alone." For Kierkegaard, dread and despair lead to God. For Camus, they do not. "The absurd is sin without God." The absurd mind prefers to adopt despair fearlessly rather than feed on the roses of illusion. "Everything considered, a determined soul will always manage." The existentialists see reason as becoming confused and escaping by negating itself. "The absurd is lucid reason noting its limits." The real danger lies not in the leap itself, as Kierkegaard thinks, but in the moment before. "Being able to remain on that dizzying crest—that is integrity and the rest is subterfuge." Camus is only interested in "knowing whether or not one can live *without appeal*."

> I don't know whether this world has a meaning that transcends it. But I know that I do not know that meaning and that it is impossible for me just now to know it. What can a meaning outside my condition mean to me? I can understand only in human terms. What I touch, what resists me—that is what I understand. And these two certainties—my appetite for the absolute and for unity and the impossibility of reducing this world to a rational and reasonable principle—I also know that I cannot reconcile them. What other truth can I admit without lying, without bringing in a hope I lack and which means nothing within the limits of my condition?[30]

Having set forth the lucidity of absurd reason, Camus presents us with an image of the Absurd Man. The Absurd Man lives in time only. He does not negate the eternal, but he lives only in relation to his lifetime—*without appeal*, "assured of his temporally limited freedom, of his revolt devoid of future, and of his mortal conscious-

[29] *Ibid.*, p. 21.
[30] *Ibid.*, p. 38.

ness." The revolt is the affirmation which the Absurd Man makes *despite* the absurd, the purely subjective affirmation which enables him to continue living without illusion and without suicide. Like Caligula and Meursault, the Absurd Man sees the consequences of all actions as equivalent. He may be responsible, but he cannot be guilty. The absurd mind does not look for ethical rules, but for images of man, illustrations which have the breath of human life. The images of man that Camus chooses—Don Juan, the actor, the conqueror—are of men who expend themselves without getting excited because they know they live in time without hope. "In the absurd world the value of a notion or of a life is measured by its sterility."

It is sterility, the sterility of the absurd self imprisoned within itself, that Camus illustrates with his three images. He sees Don Juan as having to go from woman to woman because he knows that "there is no noble love but that which recognizes itself to be both short-lived and exceptional." In contrast to the mother or wife, whom Camus sees as having a closed heart to the rest of the world, Don Juan's heart has a love which brings with it all the faces in the world and at the same time knows itself to be mortal. "Don Juan has chosen to be nothing." We may question whether this choice to be nothing recognizes the true limitations of existence, the limitations which Pascal expressed when he said man is not everything nor is he nothing. Camus sees Don Juan as that insulting, great, mad, and wise man who transmutes "kindness to generosity, affection to virile silence, and communion to solitary courage." But Don Juan is less the image of Stoic lucidity than of the all-or-nothing Modern Promethean when Camus imagines him with his legendary bravado, "that mad laughter of the healthy man provoking a nonexistent God." Camus speaks of Don Juan's way of knowing as "loving and possessing, conquering and consuming" and refers in this connection to the Biblical use of "knowing" in connection with the carnal act. But for the Bible this word means mutuality, real mutual contact, and mutuality is the one thing that Don Juan entirely lacks as he goes from one woman to another. Nor does he even possess the wholeness that Camus ascribes to him when he eulogizes: "It is indeed because he loves them with the same passion and each time with his whole self that he must repeat his gift and his profound quest." If by "whole self" Camus means the person, then that self would change with each new love and would bring the past loves with it. And if Don Juan really lived in contact with the actual moment of passing time he would not live with "the same passion," but with a unique one which would respond to the uniqueness of each new woman he loves. But he does not meet them in their uniqueness, and his "wholeness" patently excludes that continuation of response and responsibility which such meeting with uniqueness entails.

In his discussion of the actor, Camus emphasizes the reality of the ephemeral, the fleeting, and suggests that "it directs our concerns toward what is most certain—that is, toward the immediate." The actor applies himself wholeheartedly to being nothing or to being several, Camus declares. In his three hours on the stages "he travels the whole course of the dead-end path that the man in the audience takes a lifetime to cover." If Camus were really concerned with the immediate and not with the passage of time, he could never have developed his "ethics of quantity" that sees time as the mere sum of passing moments, the flowering of life as a sheaf made up of disparate acts of love. Rather, he would need to understand the organic continuity and the concrete reality of presence and present-ness. A premature death is indeed irreparable, as Camus says and as his own early death shockingly illustrates. But this is because of the new meanings which the whole of one's past life takes on in each unique present and not because "nothing can make up for the sum of faces and centuries he would otherwise have traversed." Like Meursault, Camus uses the passing of time and the certainty of future death to negate the reality of the concrete present. The absurd here is not in one's actual relation to the world, but in the thought that detaches one from that relation. Despite his declaration that he is an integral part of history, even Camus' conqueror is not so much a man who gives himself to life as a man who has a fondness for lost causes. There is only one victory, and that is eternal; so he takes the role of the Modern Promethean, opposing in absurd defiance the order with which he cannot become reconciled:

> "Opposite the essential contradiction, I maintain my human contra-diction. I establish my lucidity in the midst of what negates it. I exalt man before what crushes him, and my freedom, my revolt, and my passion come together then in that tension, that lucidity, and that vast repetition."

Camus sums up his essay with the myth of Sisyphus, the Titan of ancient Greek legend condemned by the gods to roll an enormous stone up a hill in Tartarus only to recommence his terrible labor as soon as the stone has rolled back down again. Camus' Sisyphus is the Modern Promethean who "drives out of this world a god who had come into it with dissatisfaction and a preference for futile suf-ferings" and who "makes of fate a human matter, which must be settled among men." Camus insists that there is a silent joy, a tremendous affirmation in this image of the Absurd Man, whose fate belongs to him and who is the master of his days.

> In the universe suddenly restored to its silence, the myriad wondering little voices of the earth rise up. Unconscious, secret calls, invitations from all the faces. . . . There is no sun without shadow, and it is essential to know the night. The absurd man says yes and his effort will henceforth be unceasing. . . . A blind man eager to see who knows that the night has no end, he is still on the go. . . . The struggle itself toward the heights is enough to fill a man's heart. One must imagine Sisyphus happy.[31]

This image of the "higher fidelity that negates the gods and raises rocks," this conclusion "that all is well" and the universe no longer sterile or futile, is a moving one. But it is in complete contradiction with Camus' Absurd Man as he has pictured him. The going on of Sisyphus is painted in far brighter colors than that of Beckett's Unnamable, but that is not true of Caligula, Martha, Don Juan, or even, except at the very end, Meursault. Camus' Sisyphus lives in and accepts the present. None of his other characters does. In this very essay, Camus stresses that it has not been sufficiently pointed out that Ivan Karamazov's "everything is permitted," which follows his recognition of the death of God, "is not an outburst of relief or of joy, but rather a bitter acknowledgment of a fact." It is hard to escape the conclusion that Camus, in his insistence that one must imagine Sisyphus happy, has succumbed to romanticism. Certainly, there is no basis for happiness in the never-ending Sisyphic affirmation *despite* the absurd; for the absurd by Camus' definition is the absence of a meaningful relation to the world, and no amount of subjective rock pushing can change that fact. The Absurd Man of the early Camus, like the Absurd Man of Beckett, is imprisoned in the self.

[31] *Myth of Sisyphus, op. cit.*, p. 91.

18

THE DIALOGUE WITH THE ABSURD: THE LATER CAMUS AND FRANZ KAFKA; ELIE WIESEL AND THE MODERN JOB

IF THE Absurd Man were limited to Samuel Beckett and the early Camus, it would be impossible to assert that there is an image of man that shapes the crude material of the absurd into a direction of meaningful personal existence. At most we could speak of an invaluable criticism of whatever might be sentimental, moralizing, or idealistic in the contemporary images of man we have considered. In the later Camus, however, and in Franz Kafka, the absurd is shaped into a positive image of man, one that loses none of the shock of the confrontation with the absurd yet finds a way toward authentic existence through that very confrontation. We may call this positive image the Dialogue with the Absurd.[1]

Camus' book *The Rebel* is a continuation of the absurdist reasoning of *The Myth of Sisyphus*, but one that sets forth an image of man in revolt as the latter book does not. The connecting link between the two books is the affirmation which leads the Absurd Man *not* to commit suicide despite the irrational silence that he encounters. The step beyond *The Myth of Sisyphus* is the recognition that this protest against the absurd is already the affirmation of values—of something worthwhile in the individual who rebels, in man, in the solidarity of all men. The Absurd Man recognizes that life is good since only through life can he continue his desperate encounter with the absurd. If it is good for him, it is good for all men. Therefore, the Absurd Man rejects suicide and murder alike. He accepts the contradiction inherent in the experience of the absurd—the exclu-

[1] As I do in my interpretation of Kafka and the later Camus in "The Modern Job" section of *Problematic Rebel, op. cit.*

sion of all values in favor of life and the recognition that life itself is a value judgment and that living means choice. If he believes in nothing else, the Absurd Man must at least believe in his protest, his rebellion. In so doing, he is demanding "order in the midst of chaos, and unity in the very heart of the ephemeral." The problem which Camus sets for himself is whether all rebellion must end in the justification of universal murder, as it did with Caligula, or whether, without laying claim to an impossible innocence, it can establish a genuine responsibility.

The answer that Camus gives to his own question is that the no of rebellion already implies a yes. That yes is the identification with something in man on the basis of which he rebels. In contrast to Sartre's proclamation that we ourselves invent values, Camus declares that "analysis of rebellion leads at least to the suspicion that, contrary to the postulates of contemporary thought, a human nature does exist, as the Greeks believed." These values do not exist in the individual alone, however, but in the solidarity of all men. "Man's solidarity is founded upon rebellion, and rebellion, in its turn, can only find its justification in that solidarity." Rebellion which leads to acquiesence in murder is no longer true rebellion, for rebellion discovers limits within itself, the limits of human dialogue. "I rebel —therefore we exist." Rebellion, to Camus, offers the sole possibility of finding a rule of conduct outside the realm of religion and its absolute values. And rebellion corresponds to the reality of human existence in the present historical situation.

> Insurrection is certainly not the sum total of human experience. But history today, with all its storm and strife, compels us to say that Rebellion is one of the essential dimensions of man. It is our historic reality. Unless we choose to ignore reality, we must find our values in it.[2]

In his discussion of "Metaphysical Rebellion" in *The Rebel*, Camus forgets about the limits that rebellion discovers in itself and demands the all or nothing of the Modern Promethean who wants to destroy transcendence in order to recover his alienated freedom. But in his insistence on the dialogue between man and man which discovers the values of justice and liberty in the historical struggle, he reestablishes these limits and moves to the Modern Job, whose contending still includes the trust that meaning may be found in the Dialogue with the Absurd.

Camus' *Resistance, Rebellion, and Death* not only is a witness to the life of dialogue, as we have seen; it is also an honest recog-

[2] Albert Camus, *The Rebel, op. cit.*, p. 21.

nition of the inescapable reality of the absurd and a call to a courageous dialogue with it. "This world has at least the truth of man," Camus writes, "and our task is to provide its justifications against fate itself." This justification is not based on the eternal verities but upon witnessing and contending. "With all my being I shout to you that I mean not mutilating him and yet giving a chance to the justice that man alone can conceive." So far from the absurd leading to the acceptance of injustice, it must mean the insistence upon justice.

> Nothing is given to men, and the little they can conquer is paid for with unjust deaths. But man's greatness lies elsewhere. It lies in his decision to be stronger than his condition. And if his condition is unjust, he has only one way of overcoming it, which is to be just himself.[3]

Camus recognizes the problem that faces the man who combines a philosophy of negation with a positive morality. Unlike Nietzsche, who stresses the need for nihilism in order to make possible the creation of new values, Camus points *beyond* nihilism to the hard choice that faces us: creating a new civilization or perishing. At the same time, he will not fall back on those easier moralities which ignore the problematic of modern man. To create new values we must pass unflinchingly through the personal and historical experience of the absurd.

> The uneasiness that concerns us belongs to a whole epoch from which we do not want to dissociate ourselves. We want to think and live in our history. We believe that the truth of this age can be found only by living through the drama of it to the very end. If the epoch has suffered from nihilism, we cannot remain ignorant of this nihilism and still achieve the moral code we need. No, everything is not summed up in negation and absurdity. We know this. But we must first posit negation and absurdity because they are what our generation has encountered and what we must take into account.[4]

If we think of Camus as only positive, we miss him. "The world I live in is loathsome to me," he confesses. Yet this does not lead him to misanthropy, like Melville's *Confidence Man,* but to solidarity with the men who suffer in this world. Camus is able to agree with Freud as to the existence of a "death instinct, which at certain moments calls for the destruction of oneself and of others." In fact, he feels that this instinct is the only way of explaining perversions, such as alcoholism and drug addiction, which lead an individual to his death while he knows full well what is happening. The desire to live is

[3] *Ibid.,* p. 30.
[4] *Ibid.,* p. 45.

coupled with a desire to be nothing, a vertiginous attraction to death for its own sake. "Behind the most peaceful and familiar faces slumbers the impulse to torture and murder." Yet this recognition of a death instinct does not lead Camus to conclude, with Freud, that war and interhuman hostility is man's fate. No one could speak out more strongly than Camus against the guillotine and capital punishment in general, and he does so on the basis of the solidarity of all men—in guilt and in mortality.

Camus sees his art itself as a Dialogue with the Absurd, a dialogue from which emerges not only values but hope and joy. "The only certainty left to us is that of naked suffering, common to all, intermingling its roots with those of a stubborn hope." Camus ranges himself on the side of those obstinate men who in the battles of our time have never despaired of a certain honor. He declares himself "tired of criticism, of disparagement, of spitefulness—of nihilism, in short." What must be condemned should be condemned swiftly and shortly, but what can still be praised should be praised at length. "That is why I am an artist, because even the work that negates still affirms something and does homage to the wretched and magnificent life that is ours." The reason that Camus loathes "society's dreadful morality" is that "it results, exactly like absolute cynicism, in making men despair and in keeping them from taking responsibility for their own life with all its weight of errors and greatness." Europe has not yet emerged from fifty years of nihilism, but there is hope as soon as people reject the mystifications on which that nihilism is based. "We have nothing to lose except everything. So let's go ahead. This is the wager of our generation." Camus would like to go ahead in solidarity with all men, but he is willing, if necessary, to stand with those courageous few who will not surrender when societies plunge into nihilism, totalitarian or bourgeois.

> Personally, I have never wanted to stand apart. For the man of today there is a sort of solitude, which is certainly the harshest thing our era forces upon us. I feel its weight, believe me. But, nevertheless, I should not want to change eras, for I also know and respect the greatness of this one. Moreover, I have always thought that the maximum danger implied the maximum hope.[5]

"We stifle and yet survive, we think we are dying of grief and yet life wins out." Camus sees the gentle stirring of hope as "awakened, revived, nourished by millions of solitary individuals whose deeds and works every day negate frontiers and the crudest implications of history." Through the work of these solitary men "there shines forth

5 *Ibid.*, pp. 188–9.

fleetingly the ever threatened truth that each and every man, on the foundation of his own sufferings and joys, builds for all."

Camus' greatest portrayal of the Dialogue with the Absurd is his novel, *The Plague*. The plague that swallows up the city of Oran in the inescapable reality of collective death is experienced as a total exile that corresponds exactly to Camus' definition of the absurd in *The Myth of Sisyphus:* "that sensation of a void within which never left us, that irrational longing to hark back to the past or to speed up the march of time." "Each of us had to be content to live only for the day, alone under the vast indifference of the sky." Like Joseph K. in Kafka's *The Trial*, the people of Oran experience the absurdity of being "sentenced, for an unknown crime to an indeterminate period of punishment."

The chief characters of *The Plague* may all be understood in terms of how they encounter this absurd world of the plague. Father Paneloux, the city priest and intellectual, tries to bring it within a larger, objective order in terms of which he can give it meaning as the punishment of a sinful people. But his faith in the divine order is shattered by witnessing the death of an innocent child. He turns away from the world and dies of undiagnosed symptoms—"a doubtful case." He is the nostalgically rational man who cannot stand up to the reality of the absurd. In contrast to him stands Tarrou, the journalist, the godless saint who, having lost faith in any kind of objective order, tries, like Camus' Sisyphus, to posit meaning and value *in spite of* the absurd. He is an absurdist rebel who insists on being a victim rather than an executioner and who accepts the price of exile from history that this insistence implies. But Camus no longer advocates this type of rebel, as he did in *The Myth of Sisyphus* and in the early part of *The Rebel*. He sees that it has no ground to stand on, precisely because it wishes to discover values through the self alone, rather than the dialogue with the absurd which confronts us. After Tarrou has died, his friend, Doctor Rieux, sums up the futility of such rebellion:

> How hard it must be to live only with what one knows and what one remembers, cut off from what one hopes for! It was thus, most probably, that Tarrou had lived, and he realized the bleak sterility of a life without illusions. There can be no peace without hope, and Tarrou, denying as he did the right to condemn anyone whomsoever— though he knew well that no one can help condemning and it befalls even the victim sometimes to turn executioner—Tarrou had lived a life riddled with contradictions and had never known hope's solace.[6]

[6] Albert Camus, *The Plague*, translated by Stuart Gilbert (N. Y.: Alfred A. Knopf, 1948), pp. 262-3.

Camus presents a third alternative to the denial of the absurd in the name of objective order or the subjective affirmation of meaning *despite* the absurd. This is the Dialogue with the Absurd which finds meaning in this very encounter. Doctor Rieux, the narrator and central figure of *The Plague*, embodies this dialogue with unmistakable clarity. He is like Tarrou in that he is both an exile and a rebel, but unlike Tarrou he is not interested in being a saint, but in being a man. He does not want to know, but to cure, not to find salvation, but to restore health. He does not accept creation and the order of death as he finds it, but fights against it. The plague may help people rise above themselves, he says, but "when you see the misery it brings, you'd need to be a madman, or a coward, or stone blind, to give in tamely to the plague." Although a doctor, he has never got used to seeing people die, and he holds that even the religious man can serve God no better than by rebellion against "the order of death." The fact that his victories will not be lasting is no reason for giving up the struggle. Camus has stated that he is with Rieux the healer, not Tarrou the saint, and the healer, as Rieux himself pictures him at the end of *The Plague*, is the very image of the man who rebels within the Dialogue with the Absurd:

> He knew that the tale he had to tell could not be one of a final victory. It could be only the record of what had to be done, and what assuredly would have to be done again in the never ending fight against terror and its relentless onslaughts, despite their personal afflictions, by all who, while unable to be saints but refusing to bow down to pestilences, strive their utmost to be healers.[7]

The same thing which makes Rieux the exemplar of the Dialogue with the Absurd makes him a Modern Job. He both trusts and contends, even though this trust is the existential trust of the atheist who cannot believe in God, and his contending is a contending with an absurd which remains absurd to the last.

> It is Doctor Rieux who recognizes the plague, who organizes resistance to it, who patiently fights it. . . . It is through his unsentimental, day-by-day fight against the plague in a community of men pushed to the limits of their humanity that he is able at the end to "bear witness in favor of those plague-stricken people" and, while leaving a memorial "of the injustice and outrage done them," to "state quite simply what we learn in a time of pestilence: that there are more things to admire in men than to despise." . . . His affirmation at the end of the book . . . is a witness to humanity wrested from the heart of the inhuman, meaning wrested from the absurd. Rieux's dialogue

[7] *Ibid.*, p. 278.

with the absurd implies a trust that, though the absurd will never be anything but absurd, meaning may emerge from man's meeting with it.[8]

Rieux's trust in the meaning that arises from contending with the absurd is clearly expressed in his final statement. The plague has disappeared entirely from Oran, but Rieux knows that the plague bacillus has not died. It is lying dormant in "bedrooms, cellars, trunks, and bookshelves," biding its time until "the day would come when, for the bane and enlightening of men, it would rouse up its rats again and send them forth to die in a happy city." Thus, while Rieux accepts the unremitting, never-ending struggle with "the plague" as the inescapable human condition, he also affirms that meaning and value may arise from that struggle—if one stands one's ground and meets the absurd rather than refusing to see it, as Father Paneloux, or retreating into subjective affirmation of values, as Sartre and Tarrou.[9]

Camus' last novel, *The Fall*, seems at first glance to be a throwback to his earlier Absurd Man. Certainly, it contains no positive image of man within itself. Yet in a negative way it, too, points to the Dialogue with the Absurd.

The hero of the fall bears the ironic name of Jean-Baptiste Clamence. He does not say, as Eliot's Prufrock, that though he has seen his head (grown slightly bald) brought in upon a platter, he is no prophet and this is no great matter. He *is* a prophet, and one who makes as much of the matter at hand as he can. But he tells us flatly that he is a false prophet, one who, unlike his namesake John the Baptist, heralds the coming of no savior. If his head is put upon a platter, he will utilize even this situation to continue his domination of others in that closed little universe in which he is the pope, the king, and the judge. The key to this "universe" is that he has come up against the absurd and has been unable to withstand it. He was a respected lawyer who contributed his services to worthy causes, loved many women, and felt secure in the approval of the world, until his image of himself is shattered by a single event. A young woman whom he sees leaning against a bridge on the Seine jumps in after he passes by. Though he hears the splash and her cries for help, he does not try to save her. This act of withholding himself so undermines his faith in his own motivation that he leaves his work and the society of those he knows and becomes a "judge penitent," confessing to others in order to get them to confess to him. Unable to assert his own innocence, he takes refuge in the common guilt. He retires from

[8] Maurice Friedman, *Problematic Rebel, op. cit.*, p. 437f.
[9] For a fuller interpretation of *The Plague*, see *Problematic Rebel*, pp. 432–8.

a world which he has found insupportable into a hell of nonexistence
—a world without reality and without grace into which he tries to
attract others. At first glance, this may seem a commendable honesty.
But actually it is the deepest form of dishonesty, the sheerest inauthenticity. In his very acceptance of the gap between what he once
pretended to be and what he is, he surrenders that tension which
might have led him back to some form of real existence.

Clamence has none of the three responses to the absurd that we
have seen in *The Plague*—the objective, the subjective, or the dialogical. Instead, he gives up any attempt to live with the absurd at all
and, with it, any hope of real existence. The absurd that he has discovered and cannot bear is not the absurd in the world, or in his
relation to it, but in his own self. He is an excellent example of Buber's
"seeming man," a man whose confirmation is based on appearing to
others to be a person that he is not. But his "seeming" is so thoroughgoing that he is unaware of it himself. When he fails to risk himself
to save the young woman, he can no longer confirm himself. He
knows, on the contrary, that when a call comes to *him* rather than to
the social role that he plays—when he is claimed in all his being and
at the possible cost of his own comfort and safety—he will not answer.
Thus, it is his rejection of the call to his real self that is the basis of
his retreat from the common world to his private hell. The girl's attempt to commit suicide was probably motivated by her own encounter with the absurd, and so was her cry to be saved, once she hit the
water. Yet if Clamence had tried to save her, he would have wrested
meaning from the absurd—for her and for him. Instead, he suggests
at the end of the book that neither he nor you would take on the risk
of this Dialogue with the Absurd even were this event to happen
again:

> O young woman, throw yourself into the water again so that I may
> a second time have the chance of saving both of us! A second time, eh,
> what a risky suggestion! Suppose, *cher maître*, that we should be taken
> literally? We'd have to go through with it. Brr . . . ! The water's so
> cold! But let's not worry! It's too late now. It will always be too late.
> Fortunately![10]

In *Problematic Rebel* I join Franz Kafka to the later Camus as one
who points to the Dialogue with the Absurd.

> What is at stake in the question of the image of modern man is
> nothing less than the very meaning of human existence face to face
> with the absurd. No one puts this question before us so compellingly

[10] Albert Camus, *The Fall*, translated by Justin O'Brien (N. Y.: Alfred A. Knopf,
1957), p. 147.

as Franz Kafka. In every line that he has written, whether in finished stories, unfinished novels, notations in his diary, or letters, this is his central concern. . . .

The key to Kafka, perhaps, is that sense of caricature which is borne in on us again and again. If one feels that one recognizes reality in Kafka, one always feels at the same time that it is somehow caricatured. Though this caricature is of the nature of an abstraction from concrete reality, it does not point outward to some still more abstract concept but back to an altogether concrete way of seeing—a perception of reality that again and again lays bare the absurdity inherent in Kafka's particular relationship to it.[11]

The comprehensive interpretation of Kafka on the basis of which I claim him for the Dialogue with the Absurd, cannot be reproduced here, but only referred to.[12] Kafka's heroes move from self-sufficiency to ever more anxious isolation and exile. Some of them experience the world's breaking in on the self, destroying its security and calling it to account. Others are engaged in a hopeless and unceasing striving for a contact with reality that they can never attain, a call that they can never clearly hear, and an uncertain calling that will "answer" that call. The result is guilt and anxiety, the guilt of Joseph K. in *The Trial* or the endless going astray of the Country Doctor and of the Hunter Gracchus. The conclusion is that there is a goal, but there is no way; the "way" is only a hesitation or wavering. "The true way goes over a rope which is not stretched at any great height but just above the ground," reads a Kafka aphorism. "It seems more designed to make people stumble than to be walked upon."

As important as is the question of Joseph K.'s guilt in *The Trial*, is the frighteningly irregular and corrupt bureaucracy that has him in its clutches. This bureaucracy wraps its tentacles around the whole of Joseph K.'s reality until it finally crushes him to death—with his compliance! Most of the workings of the Law are removed from sight and understanding, while what can be seen offers a spectacle of disgusting dirt and disorder. The goddess of Justice is portrayed by the court painter as "a goddess of the Hunt in full cry." K. accepts his guilt in the end and reaches out at the same time for help. Yet neither of these attitudes saves him from dying grotesquely and cruelly, "like a dog!" All this may seem simply absurd, yet if we put it together with the problem of existential guilt that lies at the heart of *The Trial*, we discover that what Kafka is really pointing to is the Dialogue with the Absurd:

[11] *Problematic Rebel, op. cit.*, p. 130.
[12] See *Problematic Rebel*, pp. 130–72; 276–82; 317–27; 334–93; 419–31; 440–2; 459–64.

In *The Trial*, Kafka is clearly as concerned about the grotesque absurdity of the world that K. encounters as about K.'s existential guilt. But he is concerned most of all about the confrontation of these two, about what happens when the world breaks in on the self as it does on K. Although the world that confronts the self is absurd, it places a real demand on the self that the latter must meet. The self can find meaning in its existence neither through rationalizing away the absurdity of the world nor through rejecting the world's demand because of this absurdity, but through answering with its existence the demand that comes to it through the absurd and that can reach it in no other way. This is the ultimate meaning of the world breaking in on the self, as Kafka develops the theme.[13]

What is true of *The Trial* is also true of *The Castle*. So far from possessing some clear order and meaning, the Castle is "only a wretched-looking town, a huddle of village houses." The small windows of its tower glitter in the sun "with a somewhat maniacal glitter," and its battlements are "irregular, broken, fumbling, as if designed by the trembling or careless hand of a child." K. has to prove that he has been called by the Castle to be a land-surveyor before he can practice his calling and survey the land. To do this he must make contact with the Castle, which he cannot do. The paradox of his calling is that he can never know who calls or how to answer, yet he must establish his calling in order to exist as a person and is accountable for the inauthenticity of his personal existence if he does not. Confronted by an absurd reality which seems by its very nature to offer no personal meaning, he is, nonetheless, not free to turn away to any "higher" reality or to abandon his search as hopeless.

> The self finds meaning in its existence not through identifying society and social confirmation with the call nor through turning away from them to some pure call that one hears apart from the world. It finds meaning, rather, through answering with its existence the call that comes to it through the absurd—through the bigoted villagers and the endless, senseless hierarchies of Castle officials, the call that can reach it in no other way.[14]

Kafka does not stop with portraying the absurdity of modern man who seeks for immediacy by ways that insure against his ever reaching it. He presents us again and again with the question of whether there can be a positive way for the Absurd Man. Human existence, to Kafka, is the tension between "the sanctum" and "the sputum." "The road to love always goes through filth and misery." If one despises the road, one will miss the goal. Human existence means suffering,

[13] *Problematic Rebel, op. cit.*, p. 355.
[14] *Ibid.*, p. 391.

but suffering is the positive element in this world, the thornbush which has to catch fire if one wants to go farther on one's road. The message from the Emperor will never reach you, but you sit at your window and dream it to yourself. The first sign of nascent knowledge is the desire for death, the desire to be taken from this unendurable life—the cell one already hates—to the cell one has yet to hate. Yet there is "a vestige of faith that during the change the Master may chance to walk along the corridor, contemplate the prisoner, and say: 'You must not lock up this one again. He is to come to me.'"

Although Kafka speaks of a trust in the indestructible, he finds this trust only in existence itself and not in any ideal world of the good, the beautiful, and the true. Kafka is concerned with the world that breaks in on the self and judges it and the world that calls man to real existence.

> Both the judgment and the call come to man through the absurd. His task, therefore, is not to escape from the absurd into inward contemplation but to stand and withstand, to hear and contend. . . . Kafka *fights* against the transience of the world, not by leaving the world for some immutable, metaphysical realm but through perceiving and creating, hoping and despairing. It is in existence—his own and that which comes to meet him—that Kafka glimpses the indestructible and the eternal.[15]

Kafka possesses a trust in existence which not all the terror and conflict of his life can destroy. It is a trust that the world will come to you unsummoned. But it is no less a trust that the world calls you and that you can call the world. Life's splendor lies forever in wait, writes Kafka, veiled but not hostile, reluctant, or deaf. "If you summon it by the right word, by its right name, it will come."

Kafka's writings discover the human again and again in the very heart of the bewildering social hierarchy, personal meaning in the midst of the impersonal absurd. Kafka said of himself that he had vigorously absorbed the negative element of his age and in that sense had the right to represent his age. Exiled from the meaning that Kierkegaard found in Christianity and his fellow-Jews found in Zionism, he saw himself as "an end or a beginning." It is precisely in this tension between the end and the beginning that he points most clearly to the Dialogue with the Absurd.

> Kafka . . . is . . . the man who more than any other has sought the way forward through the very heart of the absurd. . . . If we see Kafka only in terms of his problematic, we shall join those who regard him as "an end"—a neurotic, a nihilist, an enemy of culture, or a

15 *Problematic Rebel*, p. 430.

desperate believer "fleeing humanity," in Camus' words, "in order to try to enter . . . the desert of divine grace." But if we see in Kafka the humor and the trust and the steady movement toward meaning in the teeth of contradiction and despair, we shall glimpse the sense in which Kafka is "a beginning" for modern man.[16]

From an intensive dialogue with Melville, Dostoyevsky, Kafka, and Camus, there emerges, as I have shown in *Problematic Rebel*, the figure of "the Modern Job." This figure makes possible a distinction between *two* types of modern rebels. A far more significant choice for alienated modern man than that between conformity and rebellion, adjustment and individualism, being an insider or an outsider, a "square" or a "beat," is the choice between postures which deepen our alienation and that posture which withstands and transforms it. It is the decision between ignoring, settling into, or romantically rebelling against our modern exile and taking that exile up into the dialogue of trust and contending that accepts the exile and gives it meaning.

From a surface, statistical point of view, the vast majority of modern men are not rebels. They either ignore or accept their alienation and exile. Those who can do neither revolt. In the first instance, this revolt is expressed in the attitude of the Modern Promethean who tries to recover the true existence from which he has been alienated by denying the reality of the independent other that confronts him. Unlike the Prometheus of Aeschylus, he does not rebel on the ground of an order that includes man, but against an "order" that seems hostile or indifferent to him. This "all or nothing" attitude of the Modern Promethean both reveals and intensifies his inner contradiction. Although his rebellion is neither dubious nor unreal, it is not a simple, heroic rebellion which can be glorified in the image of the romantic hero. A "depth image" of modern man shows him to be a *problematic* rebel, an uncertain and divided figure beneath whose romantic gestures are revealed a bewildering intermixture of personal freedom and psychological compulsion, a crisis of motives, and a problematic of guilt.

The most far-reaching consequence of the alienation of modern man and the deepest level of his problematic is the paradox of the person in the modern world. Unable to believe any longer in an objective absolute or order through which his personal destiny is determined or in a Biblical God who calls him, modern man nonetheless knows himself as a person face to face with a reality which transcends him.

---

[16] *Ibid.*, p. 461f.

His very existence as a person demands that he find a "vocation," a "calling" through which he can realize his unique possibilities in response to the task that he knows to be his. Yet that confirmation which could give him assurance as to what his calling is or how he is to answer it is lacking. He cannot, for all that, use his unsureness as an excuse for not responding to the call, for the very existence and continuity of his self depend on the personal meaning that only the discovery of personal and social vocation can give him.

If the "all or nothing" of the Modern Promethean brings us into the problematic of modern man, the "not everything yet not nothing" of the Modern Job helps us to go beyond it. The Modern Job is the second form in which modern man has rebelled against his situation as an exile. In him, the alienation of modern man is not deepened, as it is in the Modern Promethean. Rather, he helps us to take unto ourselves the problematic of modern man and shape from it an image of meaningful human existence, an image that neither leaves out this problematic, nor simply reflects it, but wrestles with it until it has found a new way forward.

The Modern Job is this way forward himself.

> In the world of "the plague" no room is left for . . . that anthropomorphic approach to the absurd which led the early Camus to a stoic rebellion against a world that will never again assume the appearance of rationality longed for by the lucidity of subjective consciousness from Descartes to Sartre . . . Camus' very definition of the reality we confront as absurd depends upon his *expectation* of rationality. . . . When we speak of dialogue with the absurd, it is not, therefore, the absurd of the early Camus that we mean—the product of a disappointed expectation born of a nostalgia for lucidity more characteristic of modern rationalism than of man as man. We mean, rather, the affirmation of a concrete reality that we can meet yet cannot comprehend as it is in itself apart from that meeting. This latter meaning of the absurd . . . Camus himself arrived at in *The Plague*.[17]

The Modern Job neither accepts evil nor cuts himself off from history to avoid it. The Modern Job faithfully affirms what confronts him as the "given" of his own existence, and at the same time contends with it, as the Biblical Job contends in his dialogue with God. This Dialogue with the Absurd does not mean *either* denial *or* affirmation on principle, but standing one's ground and meeting what comes with clear-sighted trust—in each new situation that confronts one affirming where one can affirm and withstanding where one must withstand. "The dialogical leads inevitably to Job's question to God," writes

[17] *Problematic Rebel,* p. 468f.

Buber. "My God will not allow to become silent in the mouth of his creature the complaint about the great injustice in the world."[18]

The most impassioned complaint, the most stubborn and faithful Dialogue with the Absurd, the most moving embodiment of the Modern Job is the work of the young novelist and writer Elie Wiesel. His slim volumes—one an autobiography and the others novels—form one unified outcry, one sustained protest, one sobbing and singing prayer. In the first, *Night*, Wiesel tells the story of how he was deported with his family from his Hungarian-Jewish village when he was a child of twelve, how his mother and sister were metamorphosed into the smoke above the crematories, how he and his father suffered through Auschwitz, Buchenwald, and forced winter marches until finally, just before liberation, his father died. For Wiesel, the "death of God" came all at once, without preparation—not as a stage in the history of culture, but as a terrifying event that turned the pious Hasidic Jew into a lifelong witness to "the great injustice in the world."

> Never shall I forget those flames which consumed my Faith forever. Never shall I forget that nocturnal silence which deprived me, for all eternity, of the desire to live. Never shall I forget those moments which murdered my God and my soul and turned my dreams to dust. Never shall I forget these things, even if I am condemned to live as long as God Himself. Never.[19]

On a later day when he watched the hanging of a child with the sad face of an angel, he heard someone behind him groan, "Where is God? Where is He? Where can He be now?" and a voice within him answered: "Where? Here He is—He has been hanged here, on these gallows." When, after the liberation of Buchenwald, he looked at himself in a mirror, a corpse gazed back at him. "The look in his eyes, as they stared into mine, has never left me."

Wiesel's novels are continuous with the autobiography. In *Dawn*, he places this same boy, now called Elisha, in the position of a Jewish terrorist, killing English soldiers in an effort to secure the independence of the Jewish state in Palestine. It is he himself who must execute the English hostage, Captain John Dawson, whom the Movement has sentenced to die as a reprisal for the hanging by the British of one of their number. He cannot rid himself of the impression that he

---

[18] Paul Arthur Schilpp and Maurice Friedman, editors, *The Philosophy of Martin Buber* volume of *The Library of Living Philosophers* (LaSalle, Ill.: The Open Court Publishing Co., 1966), "Responsa," translated by Maurice Friedman, Chap. VI.

[19] Elie Wiesel, *Night*, Foreword by François Mauriac, translated from the French by Stella Rodway (N. Y.: Hill & Wang, 1960), p. 43f.

has donned the fieldgray uniform of the Nazi S. S. officer. He redis-
covers the presence of God when he spends the last hour with the
hostage before shooting him. His victim-to-be is sorry for Elisha and
troubled by him—an eighteen-year-old turned terrorist—while Elisha
tries in vain to hate him. When he kills John Dawson, he feels that
he has killed himself, that he himself has become the night.[20]

In *The Accident*, this same child of *Night*, somewhat older and now
an Israeli correspondent at the United Nations, is almost killed by a
taxi, and in the course of a long and painful recovery confronts the
fact that he had seen the taxi, that he wanted to die, that he did not
fight to stay alive even in the hospital, but left the burden entirely on
the doctor. He is one of the "spiritual cripples" whom the world does
not dare to look in the eye, amputees who have lost not their legs or
their eyes, but their will and their taste for life.

The Hungarian painter Gyula, who visits the hospital room repeatedly to do his portrait, confronts his friend's will to death with
the silent offer of friendship—a proof that if God is dead, man is alive.
Man's duty is to make suffering cease not to increase it, Gyula tells
him. This means a rejection of the lucidity that exchanges the light
of hope for the clear darkness of the absurd.

> "Lucidity is fate's victory, not man's. It is an act of freedom that
> carries within itself the negation of freedom. Man must keep moving,
> searching, weighing, holding out his hand, offering himself, inventing
> himself." . . . "The dead, because they are no longer free, are no
> longer able to suffer. Only the living can. Kathleen is alive. I am alive.
> You must think of us. Not of them."[21]

Next to Camus' *The Plague*, the clearest presentation in literature
of the progression through the Modern Promethean to the Modern
Job is Wiesel's novel *The Town Beyond the Wall*. The plot of the
book is the return of Michael after the war to his native Hungarian
city. Entering by means of a Black Market organization that can get
through the "Iron Curtain," he is arrested by the police and forced to
say "prayers," i.e., to stand eight hours at a stretch before a wall without moving, eating, or drinking. The police hope to extract from him
a confession as to who helped him get into the country—a confession
that would condemn his friend Pedro to death or imprisonment—but
they have not reckoned with his tenacious loyalty to his friend and his
capacity to endure by going inward to the sources of memory.

After the war and the extermination camps, Michael goes to Paris

[20] Elie Wiesel, *Dawn*, translated from the French by Frances Frenaye (N. Y.:
Hill & Wang, 1961).
[21] Elie Wiesel, *The Accident*, translated from the French by Anne Borchardt
(N. Y.: Hill & Wang, 1962), p. 120.

and lives in utter solitude in order to seek his God, to track him down. Even in his determination not to give in so easily as Job, even in his insistence that he will be a match for God and will defy his inhuman Justice, he still remains within the dialogue with God. "He took my childhood; I have a right to ask Him what He did with it." Michael combines the Modern Promethean and the Modern Job, and he shows the link between them: in our time, man *has* to go through the first to reach the second, but he *may not* remain in the first. At the death of the "little Prince"—a Jewish boy pampered by the Nazis in the concentration camps only to die under a truck in Paris—Michael's suffering leads him to the verge of madness.

> An immense wrath, savage and destructive welled up suddenly in Michael. His eyes flashed. The little prince's death—this death—was too unjust, too absurd. He wanted to pit himself against the angel as Jacob had: fell him with a blow, trample him. One gesture, just one, but a gesture in proportion to his misery.[22]

But Michael recognizes that greater than the mad revolt of the Modern Promethean is the tension of the Modern Job who refuses to go mad. "The man who chooses death is following an impulse of liberation from the self; so is the man who chooses madness. . . . To keep our balance then is the most difficult and absurd struggle in human existence." Madness is an easy, comfortable escape, a once-for-all act of free will that destroys freedom. Like the existential psychoanalysts, Michael understands that madness represents a moral choice as well as a psychological compulsion.

Michael's friend Pedro, "a living rock" like Gyula, warns him against the mad revolt which tempts him.

> "You frighten me," Pedro said. "You want to eliminate suffering by pushing it to its extreme: to madness. To say 'I suffer, therefore I am' is to become the enemy of man. What you must say is 'I suffer, therefore you are.' Camus wrote somewhere that to protest against a universe of unhappiness you had to create happiness. That's an arrow pointing the way: it leads to another human being. And not via absurdity."[23]

These, of all Pedro's words, are the ones that later come to Michael's aid. The way does not lie via the early Camus' subjective affirmation despite the absurd, but via the Modern Job's Dialogue with the Absurd.

Only after he has already come back to his native city does Michael discover what has impelled him to return—the desire to find the man who watched impassively from the square above during the whole week in which the Jews of the "City of Luck" were gathered in the synagogue and deported to their deaths. In Michael's desperate need to understand and to confront this indifferent observer shines forth the trust and the contending of the Modern Job. The spectator's "presence is evasive, and commits him less than his absence might. . . . He is there, but he acts as if he were not. Worse: he acts as if the rest of us were not." He reduces himself and us to the level of objects. The man who insists that he felt nothing when he saw the Jews deported and who resolutely refuses to let himself be humiliated, nonetheless suffers visibly under Michael's contempt, under his refusal to dignify him with hatred. Realizing that this man has become human again, Michael realizes too that "down deep . . . man is not only an executioner, not only a victim, not only a spectator: he is all three at once." It is this man who reports Michael in order to force Michael to hate him rather than just despise him.

In the prison cell—Michael's last "prayer"—Michael comes closest of all to madness, to "a door opening onto a forest, onto the liberty in which anything is permitted, anything is possible." Michael is obsessed by King Lear "who preferred suffering at the hands of men to flight into a trackless desert," who faced treason and cowardice directly and said, "I am here and nowhere else!" Yet he berates him for not going mad as a way of spitting in their faces, protesting against pain and injustice, rejecting their life and their sanity. Like Ivan Karamazov, Michael wants "to turn his ticket in"—not to reject God but his world. Madness is, indeed, the way of the Modern Promethean —Melville's Captain Ahab and Dostoyevsky's Kirilov and Ivan. To resist it without glossing over *or* submitting to the suffering that gives rise to it is the way of the Modern Job. The Pedro whom Michael now imagines coming to speak with him in his cell points this latter way and shows it for the sober, courageous revolt that it is:

"The only valuable protest, or attitude, is one rooted in the uncertain soil of humanity. Remaining human—in spite of all temptations and humiliations—is the only way to hold your own against the Other, whatever it may be. . . . To see liberty only in madness is wrong: liberation, yes; liberty, no."[24]

Michael finds the alternative to going mad in making himself responsible for his prison cellmate, a young boy who is completely silent and, until he responds to Michael's heartbreaking efforts, completely out of touch. In bringing Eliezer back to dialogue, Michael brings

[24] *Ibid.*, p. 172.

himself back to humanity. Pedro has taught Michael and Michael teaches Eliezer the necessity of clinging to humanity. "It's in humanity itself that we find both our question and the strength to keep it within limits." To flee to a Nirvana through a considered indifference or a sick apathy "is to oppose humanity in the most absurd, useless, and comfortable manner possible." Like Doctor Rieux in *The Plague*, Michael recognizes that "It's harder to remain human than to try to leap beyond humanity." The real heights and the real depths of humanity are found "at your own level, in simple and honest conversation, in glances heavy with existence." Man asks the question within himself ever more deeply, he feels ever more intimately the existence of an unknowable answer, and he brings both of these into the Dialogue with the Absurd.

Malach, the Hebrew word that is usually translated as "angel," actually means "messenger." *The Gates of the Forest*, Wiesel's major novel to date, is the story of the lasting effect of two "messengers" on the life of the young Jewish refugee Gregor. Gavriel, the nameless messenger to whom he gives his own Hebrew name, is an archetype of Jewish suffering; Leib the Lion is an archetype of heroic Jewish resistance against oppression from Judah Maccabee to the present. Gavriel and Leib accompany Gregor—in person or in memory— through spring when he hides from the Nazis in a cave in the forest, through summer when he plays the role of a feeble-minded mute in the village where Maria, the former family servant, passes him off as her nephew, through autumn when he joins the partisans fighting under the leadership of his childhood friend Leib the Lion, and through winter when he seeks a way forward in postwar New York.

Gavriel teaches Gregor that all that is left is to learn to laugh in the face of the horror—a laugh of terrible, bitter defiance of the absurd. It is the laugh of a man poised midway between the Modern Promethean and the Modern Job and holding the tension of both. The message which this messenger brings Gregor is that of the "final solution," the unsuspected extermination of the Jews. "I tell you, Gregor," says Gavriel, "that hope is no longer possible nor permitted: . . . the Messiah has come and the world has remained what it was: an immense butchery."

Gregor makes the Promethean laughter of Gavriel and the Job-ian courage of Leib his own, and they sustain him and give him strength until that distant day in postwar New York when he is confronted by a Hasidic rabbi who recognizes both his suffering and his pride. When Gregor admits that what he wants is that the Rebbe cease to pray and that he howl instead, the Rebbe, with a movement of revolt, says to him: "Who has told you that force comes from a cry and not from prayer, from anger and not from compassion?" The dancing, the singing, the joy of the Hasid is *in spite of* the fact that all reason for dancing, singing and joy has been taken from him. The revolt of the Modern Promethean is unmasked by the Rebbe as only a romantic gesture. It still leaves the question of what to do, of how to live, of the direction from which salvation and hope must come.

It does not matter whether or not the Messiah comes, Gregor realizes, or the fact that he is too late. If we will be sincere, humble, and strong, the Messiah will come—every day, a thousand times a day —for he is not a single man but all men. Gregor's last *kaddish* is for Leib the Lion, his old comrade in battle, who, while alive, incarnated in himself what is immortal in man, that which "enriched hope by placing it in a context of simplicity and humility."[25] This prayer for the dead is also a prayer for life—a prayer that, despite their loyalty to the past, Eliezer, Elisha, the "I" of *The Accident*, Michael, Gregor, and Elie Wiesel himself will be able to live for the living and not for the dead. It is a prayer for all of us—for we are all the inheritors of Auschwitz and Hiroshima—that we work our way through to the trust and contending of the Modern Job who meets the living present, including the absurd, with the courage that these "messengers on high" have bequeathed.

God and man exchanged places, the legend at the end of *The Town Beyond the Wall* tells us, and remained so for centuries, perhaps eternities—until the drama quickened and the past for one, and the present for the other, were too heavy to be borne. This interchange of God and man is hinted at throughout the novel: "In prison, under torture, man becomes powerful, omnipotent. He becomes God. That's the secret: God is imprisoned." God suffers with man, and in him. The Modern Job does not contend with an entirely alien Other, hostile and indifferent, such as Captain Ahab's White Whale or Caligula's absurd. Even the absurd reality over against us has a meaning—a meaning which can only be revealed in our trusting and contending. The dialogue, or duel, between man and his God does not end in nothingness: "As the liberation of the one was bound to the liberation of the other, they renewed the ancient dialogue whose echoes come to us in the night, charged with hatred, with remorse, and most of all, with infinite yearning."

The Absurd Man confronts us with the question of whether we can shape the raw material of contemporary existence into a meaningful

25 Elie Wiesel, *The Gates of the Forest*, trans. by Frances Frenaye (New York: Holt, Rinehart & Winston, 1966). I have based my interpretation upon the original: *Les Portes de la Forêt* (Paris: Éditions du Seuil, 1964).

image of man. With full respect for the honesty and seriousness of both Samuel Beckett and the early Camus, we cannot say that either succeeds in molding the resistant clay of contradiction and absurdity into a figure of genuine humanity. Instead, they provide a challenge to the very concept of meaningful or authentic existence. In the Dialogue with the Absurd, on the other hand, this challenge is met and a positive image of man emerges which does not gloss over the absurd and yet does not settle down in it or abandon itself to a defiant subjectivism. "Today," I have written in *Problematic Rebel*, "meaning can be found, if at all, only through the attitude of the man who is willing to *live* with the absurd, to remain open to the mystery which he can never hope to pin down." This dialogue means an open-minded and courageous standing one's ground before the absurdity of a world that one cannot image, of an otherness that one cannot grasp—not even in the meeting with one's fellowman—and of the self within that one cannot fathom. The Dialogue with the Absurd thus represents a unique fusion of the Existentialist of Dialogue and the Absurd Man.

[26]After this book went to print, Dr. Rollo May, my friend and colleague on the Council of Existential Psychology and Psychiatry, pointed out to me that my two references to his view of existential guilt are seriously misleading, especially since I link him with Erich Fromm and Medard Boss. The sentence in *Existence* in which Rollo May speaks of existential guilt as failure to realize one's potentialities can only be understood in the context of the whole section on "ontological guilt." In this section, Rollo May holds that guilt is a universal existential reality, present in every human being. It is involved in consciousness as such and is a part of the limitation of our finite existence. Our failure to realize our potentialities is only one aspect on expression of this deeper structure.

XI

CONCLUSION

19

THE IMAGE
OF MAN AND
MORAL PHILOSOPHY

IN DEALING with types of contemporary images of man and with particular thinkers within those types, we have criticized those images which seem inadequate because of insufficient concreteness, insufficient humanity or uniqueness, insufficient concern with the direction in which one must realize one's potentialities, or undue abstraction from the interhuman and social contexts in which this realization must take place. Despite these criticisms, there can be no question that each type of image contributes an essential element to an adequate contemporary image of man. We cannot do without the awareness of the social dimension of the Modern Socialist; the emphasis on creativity and life energy of the Modern Vitalist; the search for presentness and timelessness of the Modern Mystic; the dedication to personal holiness of the Modern "Saint"; the Modern Gnostic's concern with overcoming the effects of the dehumanized social world through individuation and fulfillment of the self; the awareness of personal dynamics of the Psychological Man; the emphasis upon concrete, personal reality and authentic human existence of the Existentialist; and the unresolvable cacophonies of the Absurd Man that set limits to our search for authenticity yet do not preclude the immediate, day-by-day meaning that may be found in the Dialogue with the Absurd. Each of these elements is of importance, in one degree or another, to every man who seriously engages himself in the search for a meaningful and still modern contemporary image of man.

A temptation that many fall into in our age is the attempt to choose one or two of these types of images to the exclusion of the indispensable elements of all the rest. The equal and opposite temptation is the loose eclecticism which, regardless of issues and contradictions, makes a patchwork quilt out of every possible contemporary image without any real personal integration that would give them meaning. All of these images are "live options," to use William James' phrase. But an option implies the necessity of decision. One cannot go on forever trying to take all paths at once. It is one thing, therefore, to say that vital elements of each of the types must be included in any adequate contemporary image of man. It is quite another to pretend to follow several different directions simultaneously as if there were no real differences among them.

The interrelation of the types that are discussed here can also be understood in terms of an organic development. Many of the men of our age have carried on a dialogue with each of these images at successive stages, building on what went before and retaining the vital elements in each. In almost the same order as the parts of this book, the writer has made his own way by turn through the Modern Socialist, the Modern Vitalist, the Modern Mystic, the Modern "Saint," the Modern Gnostic, Psychological Man, Pragmatic Man, the Existentialist, and the "Life of Dialogue." If the Dialogue with the Absurd is the terminal point of this book, it is only as the author's unique personal integration over more than a quarter of a century of all the contemporary images in this book. As such, the organic form of this book represents one more contemporary image of man to which the reader may bring his unique response, understanding it, criticizing it, and, where it speaks to his condition, making it his own.

The reader who opens himself to the "live options" we have considered can reach a personal conclusion, even though one that is never definitive or final. Our choice is not between a hopelessly broad relativism and a rigidly narrow exclusivism. Every real confrontation with a contemporary image of man is of inestimable value if we bring ourselves to it in sufficient seriousness and depth. The value of our confrontations with particular images of man can be greatly enhanced, moreover, by an understanding of the *problem* of a contemporary image of man. Such an understanding is essential for those of us who tend to bog down in the quicksand of despair, on the one side, or in the marsh of sentimental idealism, on the other. It can give us a surer footing on the difficult path in between. It can point us toward that direction of personal existence which grows out of the confrontation of reality and possibility. It can help us shape the absurd into an image of authentic humanity.

Whatever may be the case with "religion," the religious man has always been aware of the central importance of the image of man.

This is because the religious life is not in the first instance philosophy or gnosis—an attempt to know *about* the world or God—but a way that man walks *with* God, a flowing with the Tao, a discovery of "the action that is in inaction, the inaction that is in action." For the religious man, it is not enough to have a "philosophy of life": one must live one's philosophy. Rabbi Leib, son of Sara, went to the Maggid of Mezritch not to hear him say Torah but to watch him lace and unlace his felt boots. "Not to say Torah but to be, Torah"—this is the existential demand that all religion ultimately places on man. Philosophies of religion are ultimately meaningless abstractions if one divorces them from the living Buddha, Lao-tze, Confucius, Jesus, Mohammed, Moses, St. Francis, and the Baal-Shem-Tov. When Swami Prabhavananda and Christopher Isherwood claim in their introduction to the *Bhagavad-Gita* that it does not matter whether Christ or Krishna really lived since we have their teachings and they are universal, they miss the central reality from which all religious teachings spring and to which they again and again point back: the image of man.

The true teacher, too, has always been aware that, above all, he is confronting his students with images of man and that it is precisely through this confrontation that he *educates* the student. The unique response of every student to the image of man is that which draws out of him the potentialities of becoming and makes him at last into an "educated" man—one who has made tradition his own and thereby become more uniquely himself. In moral philosophy and the moral life, on the other hand, this is not so evident. Regardless of how people actually reach moral decisions, most people *imagine* that they proceed from a set of abstract values or universal principles and apply these in everyday life. In our present intellectual climate, as a result, the image of man represents a radically new approach to moral philosophy. My own absorption in the image of man grew in important measure out of a profound dissatisfaction with the notions of academic moral philosophers as to how genuine ethical decisions actually take place.

Today, the question of the source of moral authority has been taken up and taken over by fields that would never have been considered moral philosophy in the past—psychology and psychoanalysis, the social sciences, logical positivism, and linguistic analysis. One of the most bewildering contemporary trends is cultural relativism, which accepts all moralities as descriptions of the culture of this or that group or subgroup while removing their normative status as values with any binding force from without or any existential reality from within. Moral relativism of the popular sort must be unmasked as not

being a moral position at all. It tries to reduce the normative "ought"
to a purely descriptive "is" and substitute a statement of what people
do value for real valuing from within. But this does not mean that
we can act as if its challenge does not exist. The appeal to unanimity
and universality is a thing of the past; for, like it or not, we live in
dialogue with other individuals and peoples with different cultures
and values from our own. We should welcome, rather than bewail,
this phenomenon. It forces us to a deeper searching for a basis for
morality which we can really believe and live—with all our heart,
and not just "as if."

The ethical can be defined, at its simplest, as the tension between
"is" and "ought"—between the given of a situation and the direction
of movement which we choose in response to a moral demand. A
moral problem cannot be grasped adequately from without; it must
be seen from within the situation of the man confronted with the
necessity of moral decision and moral action. The question is not,
What ought *one* do in this situation? but What ought *I* do? No two
men are ever in the *same* situation. Despite all similarities between
situations, every genuine moral decision is unique. The situation's
claim on you cannot be sidestepped through general precepts concerning what "they" would do under similar circumstances. Yet neither is
the moral claim a subjective or arbitrary one. The image of man, with
its combination of the demand placed on one by what is other than
oneself and one's unique response to that demand, finds the narrow
way between the impersonal objective and the arbitrary subjective
to the heart of moral decision and moral action.

Moral philosophy is invariably grounded in a concept of human
nature; yet this concept usually remains an empty abstraction, and
the conclusions of moral philosophy all too often consist of ideals or
values so general as to offer little guidance in any specific moral
dilemma. What is more, ethics all too often remains on the level of
rational thought and conscious moral choice, rather than reaching
those inner springs which enable one to decide and to act as a whole
person. The greatest contribution that Plato has made to the lived
moral life of mankind is not his idea of the Good or the subtleties of
his dialectic, but his image of Socrates in the *Apology*, the man who
showed in his life and death what it means to say that "an unexamined life is not worth living."

Moral decision does not take place through the application of already existing universal values or of the conclusions of a dialectic,
but through the response of the whole person in particular situations.
Into this response enter attitudes that he may not be aware of, yet
ones that shape his decision even in new and unique situations. One

does not go directly from a conscious precept to a moral action, for no action in which a person involves himself merely on a conscious level could really be moral in a meaningful sense of the term. Rather one goes from deep-seated attitudes, themselves the product of one's meetings with past situations, to the response to the present situation which produces the moral action. Our image of man—our *images* of man—enter into this response more deeply and fully than any general principle ever could. What is more, one cannot really apply a general principle except by way of an image of man. Moral terms and precepts, such as humility, considerateness, generosity, loving one's neighbor, take on meaning only when embodied in concrete individuals. The loving humility of St. Francis may be an image of man for countless people throughout the ages, but not the masochistic humility of Marmeladov in *Crime and Punishment,* or the hypocritical humility of Blake's "A Human Abstract."

In *Fundamental Principles of the Metaphysic of Morals,* Kant bases his categorical imperative on the universality of law: "So act that the maxim behind your action could be a universal law." But this is to make the essence of morality a universal reality, of which the particular moral action is only a concrete application or illustration. It is to assume that men confronted by the necessity of moral choice find themselves in essentially the same situation. Kant recognizes, in his reformulation of the categorical imperative in terms of maxims rather than actions, that one cannot tie the unconditional ought of the universal to particular actions. But he imagines that one can find maxims that will serve as an adequate link between the realm of the universal and that of the empirical. One ought not commit suicide, he says, for if everyone did so, that would violate the purpose of nature, which is to preserve and maintain life. In our post-Darwinian, nuclear-holocaust age, these "universal principles" of the eighteenth-century Enlightenment no longer seem self-evident. Even apart from that, such impersonal reasoning can hardly appear to the man contemplating suicide as a *moral* demand that he not do so. He may be quite sure that most people will not follow his example as individuals, however close the threat of nuclear war may bring us to "the technically perfect suicide of mankind." His real question cannot be, "Shall we all commit suicide?" but the much more lonely and individualized question, "Shall *I* commit suicide?"

Even Kant's strongest illustration of his point, that of lying, is hardly convincing. While it is true enough that a liar depends on the general currency of honesty for the effectiveness of his lie, this is not itself a *moral* but merely a practical deterrent. It is, in Kant's own language, a "hypothetical," or conditional, imperative which says, "If you do not want to be ineffective in your desire to put things over on other people, you had better not overdo the undermining of the general trust."

Kant does not give a single convincing illustration of his categorical imperative, nor could he. The bridge between the universal realm of law and the particular realm of action cannot be made by maxims; for they lack the force of real moral law, on the one hand, and of real personal claim, on the other. Maxims, moreover, can lead to the illusion of acting out of "good will" precisely at the point where I am betraying the person who needs me or the cause that calls me. The "I" with which Kant is concerned is not the actual person who must make a moral decision, but only the universal, rational element which he defines as the dignity of the person. Kant insists on "moral autonomy," yet as the final judge of value he refers to universal reason and to the "kingdom of ends," to which one belongs as a rational being.[1]

Beginning with the question of why Kant's categorical imperative has so little power of moral suasion, Bergson implicitly reverses this valuation of the universal over the unique. In his contrast between universal morality and morality of example, Bergson points to the way in which we make the image of the other our own and incorporate our relationship to him into our innermost attitudes:

> Only those who have come into touch with a great moral personality have fully realized the nature of this appeal. But we all, at those momentous hours when our usual maxims of conduct strike us as inadequate, have wondered what such or such a one would have expected of us under the circumstances. It might have been a relation or a friend whom we thus evoked in thought. But it might quite as well have been a man we had never met, whose life-story had merely

[1] This critique applies only to Immanuel Kant, *Fundamental Principles of the Metaphysic of Morals,* translated by Thomas K. Abbott, with an Introduction by Marvin Fox (New York: The Liberal Arts Press, 1949). To Kant goes the credit of being the first philosopher to insist on the unconditional character of the moral "ought" if it is to be truly moral. We owe to him too the understanding that prior to the moral situation there are formal principles which are the necessary presupposition of an actual morality. In both these senses, the image of man follows Kant in its approach to moral philosophy. It cannot follow him, however, in his insistence that the ontological basis of morality can be discovered for "any rational being" and need not take into consideration man's existence as man. Nor can it follow him in the *source* of moral obligation that he sees as binding the rational "ought" to the empirical "is." The "I" of the *person* who must decide whether or not to commit suicide cannot be identified with the "I" of the *rational being* free only in the metaphysical realm of universal law. For a further discussion of Kant's moral autonomy, see Maurice Friedman, *Martin Buber: The Life of Dialogue, op. cit.,* pp. 198–200.

been told us, and to whose judgment we in imagination submitted our conduct, fearful of his censure, proud of his approval.[2]

Bergson understands well that this is not a matter of an objective relationship to an object, but of a personal response to a person. Our "imitation" and "internalization" of that person do not make us identical with him. Rather, his voice becomes part of us and enters into our responses to unforeseen situations that he himself never had to encounter.

> It might even be a personality brought up from the depths of the soul into the light of consciousness, stirring into life within us, which we felt might completely pervade us later, and to which we wished to attach ourselves for the time being, as the disciple to his teacher. As a matter of fact this personality takes shape as soon as we adopt a model; the longing to resemble, which ideally generates the form, is an incipient resemblance; *the word which we shall make our own is the word whose echo we have heard within ourselves.*[3]

The word which we make our own is the product of the dialogue which each of us has with his own image of man.

Bergson does not follow through on this insight into the source of morality; for his image of man, as we have seen, is really a synthetic combination of his philosophy of creativity with the saints and mystics whom he somewhat arbitrarily selects as examples of it. Buber, unlike Bergson, does not deal explicitly with the image of man as a source of moral values. Yet in his essay, "The Education of Character," he points to the image of man as the answer to the moral relativism of our time. The moral relativist denies that values are anything other than the subjective needs of groups. This denial is not a product of reason, but of the sickness of our age; hence, it is futile to meet it with arguments.

> It is an idle undertaking to call out, . . . "Look! the eternal values!" Today host upon host of men have everywhere sunk into the slavery of collectives, and each collective is the supreme authority for its own slaves; there is no longer, superior to the collectives, any universal sovereignty in idea, faith, or spirit. . . . This is true, not only for the totalitarian countries, but also for the parties and party-like groups in the so-called democracies.[4]

All that the teacher can do in the face of this situation is to help keep awake in the pupil the pain which he suffers through his distorted relation to his own self and thus awaken his desire to become a real

[2] Henri Bergson, *The Two Sources of Morality and Religion, op. cit.,* p. 34f.
[3] *Ibid.,* pp. 34–5; italics added.
[4] Martin Buber, *Between Man and Man, op. cit.,* p. 110f.

and whole person. He can awaken in him the desire to shoulder responsibility again by bringing before him "the image of a great character who denies no answer to life and the world, but accepts responsibility for everything essential that he meets."

What neither Bergson nor Buber has done, this book has attempted to do: to bring out in a thoroughgoing way the implications of the image of man for moral philosophy. Ethics we have defined as the tension between "is" and "ought." Similarly, we have said of the image of man that it is neither an ideal nor a mere description but the tension between the two. The image of man is no moral standard imposed from without or universal "ought" that need only be applied. Yet it is concerned with the moral in the most profound sense of the term. The sickness of moral relativism is at the same time a sickness of our image of man. The "ought" of modern man tends to be a mere aspect of the "is": instead of giving genuine direction to the ever-expanding "is," it tends passively to reflect it. Sexual "morality," for example, is thought of more often in terms of what "one" does or of the statistics of the Kinsey reports than in terms of any genuine moral claim!

Many of our criticisms of contemporary images of man have been at the same time and by the same token statements of their inadequacy as moral philosophies. With the problem of the *source* of moral values and moral decision—the problem of how I discover what I *ought* to do in this concrete situation—Bergson, as we have seen, cannot really help us. Jung has posited the unconscious as the source of moral values and has thereby relativized good and evil to mere functions of wholeness. He puts aside the conscience that distinguishes right from wrong in concrete situations in favor of an "individuation" which has no reference, check, or court other than itself. Freud, on the other hand, grounds conscience and morality in the Oedipus complex and thereby reduces all sense of "ought" to the "is," all sense of the normative to the purely descriptive. There is moral fervor behind Freud's plea that the individual and the society be freed from the murderous cruelty of the ruthless super-ego. But morality itself he robs of any intrinsic meaning.

William James recognizes the uniqueness of every real moral dilemma, yet he rests his morality on pragmatic consequences without adequate concern for the task of making a moral decision *in the present*. Dewey's ethics of potentiality, in contrast, makes all things serve the purpose of releasing and fulfilling potentiality, but leaves "potentiality" itself a vague, neutral term without any value direction of its own. Even in Dewey's *Theory of Valuation*, with its "means-ends continuum" and its distinction between "prizing" and "appraising," valuation is purely technical and descriptive. No real moral conflict is ever envisaged; no situation is ever imagined more complex than the breaking down or stalling of a machine whose functions are already defined by its nature. The fallacy of deriving the "ought" from the "is," the "desirable" from the "desired," that has plagued empiricist moralists from the time of David Hume and John Stuart Mill is not resolved by Dewey either.

Erich Fromm heightens the Modern Pragmatist to an ethic of "self-realization," but he does not thereby escape from the pragmatist's dilemma of defining values in terms of a functioning which itself implies other, assumed values. The good for Fromm is what contributes to "the mature and integrated personality," while vice is what destroys this "truly human self." The values Fromm makes explicit are instrumental ones; the others remain hidden and unclear, vacillating between human relationships seen as of value in themselves and as mere means to the end of self-realization. As a result, the interpersonal is always in danger of becoming, in practice, a secondary factor rather than a primary one, as Fromm would have it. It is not enough to tell me that my relations to people and work will help me to become mature, integrated, creative, and productive. If I have a genuine ethical concern, I may not reduce the situation to a function of my becoming; for I am concerned about whether a certain action *toward others* is right or wrong.

To Sartre, there is no longer any basis for values; values are something we ourselves invent. The great significance of Sartre for our purposes is that he recognizes, as Dewey and Fromm do not, that there are real, inescapable consequences of "the death of God," that we cannot cling to the same old values when that relationship to reality that undergirded and informed them has atrophied or disappeared. Yet this does not mean that Sartre's "invention" of values is a satisfactory moral philosophy. Sartre claims that it is absurd to charge him with arbitrariness since he defines man in relationship to involvement. But what enables Sartre's existentialist to avoid arbitrariness in the way he *responds* to that situation? To leave as the ultimate criterion of values the minimizing of self-deception, as Sartre does, is to leave values primarily a relationship to oneself alone and only secondarily to the world in which one is called upon to act and decide. It is to divest one's relationship to what is not oneself of full moral seriousness, and in this sense at least it appears arbitrary.

The Existentialist of Dialogue denies Sartre's claim that subjectivity is the only alternative to the belief in universal, objective values. For him, moral values are neither already there in some Platonic world of Ideas nor are they his own "project," the product of his own invention. He *discovers* them in his meeting with the world, with other men, with being. Hence, he discovers them *with* others and *in re-sponse to* the situation. For Albert Camus, moral values come into being in the concrete situations of life, in the dialogue between man and man. Rebellion, to Camus, opens "the way to a morality which, far from obeying abstract principles, discovers them only in the heart of battle and in the incessant movement of contradiction." Because the other person has not only ears but a mouth, as Franz Rosenzweig puts it, and may say something that will surprise you, the ethics of "the Life of Dialogue" cannot anticipate the need or claim of the other and cannot have a set moral response. Moral codes may be useful rules of thumb, but they cannot claim universal, objective validity in advance of the claim of the present. We cannot live with-out ethical norms, but the "true norm" is not the moral standard im-posed from above which one must submit to or rebel against. It is that command which calls forth our most personal response, our re-sponse as the whole and unique persons that we are. It is never a maxim which applies to everybody and nobody, but an attitude—a command that remains latent in your being until you hear the address of the unforeseen situation as a claim on *you* to which you must re-spond with all your force. Only the command which addresses the particular Thou that you are in the very situation in which you find yourself is one which can call forth a response of the whole person. Otherwise you must suppress your unique response to the present situation in favor of some abstract and timeless formula of "responsi-bility."

One of the most easily misunderstood aspects of this approach to moral philosophy is its rejection of a universal ethic that need only be *applied* in each new situation. This even includes, as we have seen, any moral principle that might dictate that one *ought* to have an I-Thou relationship in every situation. One can perhaps speak of one's willingness to respond according to one's resources and accord-ing to one's situation as a universal ought. Yet this means precisely giving up the pretense to know the answer to the situation before one has heard the question and has met it from the ground of one's per-sonal uniqueness. It is, of course, essential for an ethic of personal relations that there be a continuity of being responsible *for* a Thou as well as responding *to* him. Otherwise continuing, committed rela-tionships, such as friendship, love and marriage, would be unthink-able, not to mention the helping relationships of teacher and student, therapist and patient, pastor and congregant. Spontaneity does not mean gratuitous, arbitrary action; for response with the whole being involves all that one has been, including one's past relationships with this person and others and one's image or images of man.

It is only in a direct, mutual relationship that I grasp concretely the unique value of the other, experience his side of the relationship, and know what can help him. Yet I do not necessarily cease to deal lovingly, or at least respectfully, with him even when he is no longer Thou for me in any but a formal, or potential, sense. I carry from one moment of meeting to another the form of relationship. I carry the other with me, as it were, as one for whom I am responsible, one to whom I am ready to respond when I meet him again. But when I meet him again he will not be the same as he was before, and very often I must meet someone with whom I have had no previous real relationship. It is the image of man and not any universal precept that enables me to say, "Nothing human is alien to me." The image of man enters into and forms that attitude which makes me ready to meet and respond to any man whatever as a human being with human dignity, someone I stand open to know, to respect, perhaps even to love. Thus, the image of man plays an essential role in linking one moment of realized dialogue with another. It is, often, the very form in which dialogue remains potential, awaiting its actualization.

The image of man is neither "is" nor "ought," nor the combination of the two. It is man's becoming in the truest sense of the word, i.e., his becoming as a person and as a man. In this becoming, what we call the "is" is not a static given. It is a dynamic, constantly changing material that is continually being shaped and given form—not merely by inner and outer conditioning but by the directions that one takes as a person. What we call the "ought," similarly, is not some abstract ideal but a constantly changing, flowing direction of movement that is at one and the same time a response to the present, a choice between possibilities in a given situation, and a line of advance into the future.

Moral philosophy, we have stated, is invariably grounded in a concept of human nature. Very often this concept is expressed in terms of the issue of whether man is fundamentally "good" or "evil." The contemporary images of man that we have discussed sharpen this issue. Freud, in *Civilization and Its Discontents*, leaves no doubt about his opinion that man is hostile and aggressive, not as a secondary product of frustrated instinct, but as an expression of a basic, inborn "death instinct." Jung criticizes Freud for seeing man as basically evil, and he himself characterizes the "evil" side of the self as the "shadow," the complement of the good. If it is not suppressed, this "evil" can be brought as such into that very integration which Jung calls the "self," thus achieving a type of Modern Gnostic wholeness in which the individual knowingly succumbs to evil "in part." Fromm criticizes Freud for seeing man as antisocial by nature and only secondarily in relationship, whereas Fromm holds, as Sullivan, that man becomes destructive only when his neurosis turns him aside from a creative relationship with other people and with his work. For Fromm, man is potentially good or evil, with health on the side of good. For Carl Rogers, in contrast, man is unqualifiedly good. Rogers' theory of the complete acceptance of the "client" by the therapist is based on the assumption that the client is "good" in his depths, that he is by nature social and constructive, that all he needs is to be accepted by the therapist so that he may accept himself and he will make manifest the socially good person that he really is. Martin Buber's reply to Rogers on this point suggests that there is a third alternative to seeing man as "evil," to be controlled, or "good," to be trusted, and that is seeing him as "polar" and in need of personal direction:

> What you say may be trusted, I would say stands in polar relation to what can least be trusted in this man. . . . The poles are not good and evil, but rather yes and no, acceptance and refusal.[5]

A second problem of moral philosophy that the image of man elucidates is that of "motivation." Motives which in the past might be accepted at their face value—humility, love, friendship—must now be looked at more critically. For, as Nietzsche and Dostoyevsky saw even before Freud, they may, in fact, mask resentment, hatred, or hostility. Positive conscious motives are now regularly unmasked as the sublimation or repression of one or another negative emotion in the unconscious.[6] We need only recall Nietzsche's astonishing psychological acuteness in unmasking unworthy motivations behind Christian virtues. "How nicely can doggish lust beg for a piece of spirit when a piece of flesh is denied it!" says Nietzsche's Zarathustra. "Hath not your lust just disguised itself and taken the name of fellow-suffering?"

This unmasking begins in the service of truth—what Philip Rieff calls Freud's "ethic of honesty." Yet it ends, paradoxically, by making all truth questionable and by undermining the foundations of existence between men. "One no longer fears that the other will voluntarily dissemble," writes Martin Buber in a statement on "existential mistrust." "One simply takes it for granted that he cannot do otherwise."

> I do not really take cognizance of his communication as knowledge. . . . Rather I listen for what drives the other to say what he says, for an unconscious motive, say, or a "complex." . . . My main task in my

[5] "Dialogue between Carl Rogers and Martin Buber. Moderated by Maurice Friedman," in Buber, *The Knowledge of Man, loc. cit.,* p. 179f.
[6] For a fuller treatment of this subject see my discussion of "The Crisis of Motives" in *Problematic Rebel, op. cit.,* pp. 328–32.

intercourse with my fellow-man becomes more and more, whether in terms of individual psychology or of sociology, to see through and unmask him. In the classical case this in no wise means a mask he has put on to deceive me, but a mask that has, without his knowing it, been put on him, indeed positively imprinted on him, so that what is really deceived is his own consciousness.[7]

As an alternative to "unmasking and seeing through," Buber offers a "greater realism," a clear-sighted trust that sees the person in his concrete wholeness and not in terms of our own already established categories of analysis:

> Man is not to be seen through, but to be perceived ever more completely in his openness and his hiddenness and in the relation of the two to each other. We wish to trust him, not blindly indeed but clearsightedly. We wish to perceive his manifoldness and his wholeness, his proper character, without any preconceptions about this or that background, and with the intention of accepting, accrediting and confirming him to the extent that this perception will allow.[8]

The question which Buber poses for us here is whether it is possible, without going back behind Psychological Man, to go forward beyond psychologism—beyond the removal of human existence into the psyche, which itself is transformed from a flowing stream of happenings to frozen psychic entities subject to objective analysis.

Another moral problem that is illuminated by the image of man is that of adjustment. As a creative alternative to shallow conformity and sterile rebellion, the image of man offers a new and more fruitful way to look at the problem. The choice is not between submitting oneself to society and being an individual, but between an unfree relation to other selves and to social groupings, whether it be one of submission *or* rebellion, and a free and spontaneous response to the values of others. At times, this may mean acceptance of those values and at times rejection, but in any case it means a unique personal relation to them that does not involve the suppression of one part of the self at the dictates of another. In contrast to such a response, all "adjustment" is merely a conditioned and partial reaction.

One of the most important and problematic aspects of any morality is guilt. The image of man distinguishes between two types of guilt: the impersonal and the personal. Certainly, there is purely social and even neurotic guilt derived from a set of mores and taboos imposed upon the individual by parents and society and incorporated into an

[7] Martin Buber, *Pointing the Way, op. cit.*, p. 223f.
[8] *Ibid.*, p. 227.

internalized "super-ego." But there is also real personal guilt, guilt which has to do with one's actual stance in the world and the way in which one goes out to relate to other people from that stance. This real personal guilt is an essential ontological aspect of the image of man as we have discussed it. If there is such a thing as real, or existential, guilt, then it cannot be merely additive and atomistic, as Helen Merrell Lynd has held, but must be grounded in the whole self and never entirely detachable from it. To speak of existential guilt is not to agree with those existentialists, such as Rollo May and Medard Boss, who see real guilt as arising from the failure to realize one's potentialities. One's potential uniqueness may be given, but the direction in which one authenticates one's existence is not. One discovers it in constantly renewed decisions in response to the demand of concrete situations. When we are guilty, it is not because we have failed to realize our potentialities, which we cannot know in the abstract, but because we have failed to bring the resources we find available to us at a given moment into our response to a particular situation that calls us out. Our potentialities cannot be divorced from the discovery of our personal direction, and this comes not in the meeting of man with himself, but with other men and with the image of man that he acquires through such meeting.

Personal guilt is neither objective nor subjective. It is dialogical—the inseparable corollary of one's personal responsibility, one's being answerable for authenticating one's own existence and, by the same token, for responding to the partners of one's existence, the other persons with whom one lives. Where there is personal responsibility, there must also be the possibility of real guilt—guilt for failing to respond, for responding inadequately or too late, or without one's whole self. Such guilt is neither inner nor outer, nor is one answerable in it either to oneself alone or to society apart from oneself, but to that very bond between oneself and others through which one again and again discovers the direction in which one can authenticate one's existence.

Real personal guilt is not only an essential corollary of the image of man. It is also one of the most important and illuminating links between the image of man and ethics. As Hans Trüb has pointed out, real guilt is the beginning of *ethos*, or responsibility. Just as it arises from the failure to respond to the legitimate claim and address of the world, so it leads one to desire to set one's relations to other persons right. True guilt, in contrast to neurotic guilt, takes place *between* man and man, as Buber states. It is an ontological, interhuman reality of which the *feeling* of guilt is only the subjective and psychological counterpart. It is a real event between men—a rupture of dialogue and an injury of the interhuman order that we have built up in common. As such, it must not only be recognized, but repaired—through the re-establishment of dialogue.

This approach to guilt can be applied to social problems, such as capital punishment, through Dostoyevsky's formula, "Each is responsible for all." To remove a man's responsibility for his actions because of the conditioning influence of his environment is to deny his existence as a person. To place all the responsibility on the individual criminal by executing him is to deny the equally real responsibility that other persons and society have for what he has become. The most realistic approach is that which affirms that each is responsible for what he does and at the same time that each is responsible for all. This approach is incompatible with capital punishment.

Another way of understanding guilt and the image of man is the dialectic of the call and the calling to account. The world calls a man to become himself through fulfilling his "calling," that to which he is called, and it calls him to account when he does not do so. This guilt is existential: one is accountable as a person and not just as someone who fulfills a social role. Every man stands, whether he knows it or not, in a continuous personal accountability so long as he lives. No man achieves a plane where he may not only approve of all he has been but may take for granted his responses to the new, unforeseen situation that awaits him. Our existence in time is characterized above all else by just this necessity of meeting the new face that the moment wears. The question of whether one's existence is authentic or inauthentic cannot be answered by the sum of one's actions, or by any objective standard that detaches guilt from one's personal existence itself. Neither is it merely a subjective or arbitrary matter, but the responsibility of the self in relation to the world. This responsibility cannot be judged from the standpoint of the world alone or of the self alone or of any third party looking at the world and the self, but only within the relationship itself.

At the same time, since guilt is not just a matter of specific acts, there is no point where one can accurately draw a line and say, "These acts were avoidable and these not; these acts are a subject for guilt and these for shame." We are accountable for our existence in a way that eludes our rational grasp of guilt and innocence. We are guilty for not answering or answering in the wrong way the call that we could never clearly hear. "Only those fear to be put to the proof who have a bad conscience," says Kafka. "They are the ones who do not fulfill the tasks of the present. Yet who knows precisely what his task is? No one. So that every one of us has a bad conscience."⁹ Although the world that confronts the self may be absurd, it places a real demand on the self that the latter must answer with its existence. This demand is both the call and the calling to account.

Tarrou's question in *The Plague*, "Can I be a saint without God?" may be rephrased, "Can I be moral after the 'death of God,' after the disappearance of any universal, objective source of morality?" What is essential to this question is not, "Do I *believe* in God?" but "Is there any connection with reality or being, any existential trust, that makes a moral life possible today?" What is decisive for ethical decision and action is not the profession of belief but the life attitude. Insofar as religion may be described at its deepest level as a basic *attitude* or relationship arising in the encounter with the whole reality directly given to one in one's existence, one can say that the life attitude which underlies any ethics must ultimately be of a religious depth. But one need not say so; for the reality to which the image of man points lies deeper than the articulations of belief and nonbelief. It does not have to do with metaphysical essences or theological creeds, but with that existential trust which enables one to stand one's ground before what confronts one and to meet it in a way faithful to its otherness and one's own uniqueness. To the Modern Job, as I have written in *Problematic Rebel*, it need not matter whether this is expressed in terms of the "atheism" of the later Camus or the "theism" of Buber. The basic attitude in both is essentially the same: the readiness to meet what is essentially other and hold one's ground when one meets it, the Dialogue with the Absurd in which trust and contending are inseparably conjoined.

Whether he sees himself as religious or not, modern man cannot be ethical in the way that the religious man of former times was, before the "death of God." Two possibilities remain open for modern man. The first is being ethical within given, inherited structures—the family, the church, the culture, the state—ordinary living which, because it *is* within these structures and because it rests on some genuine interhuman contact, is ethical in practice, whatever the names by which its source is called or miscalled. The second is the vastly more difficult and painful discovery of the ethical in limit situations, in the "absurd," in the "eclipse of God." Both of these alternatives are a necessary part of any authentic life. Essential to them both is the continually renewed discovery of the ethical through the openness and response of one's whole personal existence. Essential to this openness,

⁹ See the interpretation of Kafka in Maurice Friedman, *Problematic Rebel, op. cit.*, pp. 130–72; 276–82; 317–27; 334–93; 419–31, out of which this dialectic of the call and the calling to account emerges.

in turn, is the image of man that we encounter and make our own and that enters thereafter into our free response from the ground of our personal uniqueness and of our unique situation. Moral values are not verified by abstract knowledge: they are authenticated in our lives— by our withstanding and being true in the situations that confront us. Nothing can so effectively point to what such withstanding and being true means as can the image of man. The image of man is concrete and particular rather than abstract and general. Yet it rejects all imitation of the way of others in favor of that open, free dialogue that calls us and calls us to account.

While there are, as we have seen, objective criteria for judging the adequacy of one or another contemporary image of man, in the end each of us must decide through his unique personal response which image of man, if any, possesses for him the right tension between the "is" and the "ought," which possesses the most meaningful combination of a call from without and a response from within, of the concrete and the universal, the human and the unique. In this sense, we shall inevitably emerge not with one, but with many different images of man. Yet the fact that our unique personal responses will constitute in every case a judgment as to which is the right tension, which is the most meaningful combination, gives our variegated images of man a formal unity, even if not a unity of content.

The image of man is not only a *new* approach to moral philosophy. It is also, I am convinced, a helpful one. While the interest theory of ethics derives the "ought" from the "is" and states, in effect, that because a thing is desired it is desirable, the logical positivist tends to proceed in the opposite direction and turn a normative statement into a purely descriptive one: to say a thing is desirable really means only that it is desired by the person who says it is, and that he would like others to desire it too. The result is the same—the reduction of values to objective, descriptive, "handle-able" dimensions for which one claims scientific warrant without personal involvement, decision, and risk. Such procedures ignore the real meaning of moral valuation— the ultimate choice of what personal or social way of life is meaningful, what is authentic, what embodies real values. They destroy the very essence of moral philosophy by obliterating the distinction between sheer objective description of what takes place when man values and his own inner decision in response to the question: "What ought I to do in this situation?" The image of man cannot offer the precision of linguistic analysis or the inspiration of idealism. But it can set us once more on the road toward a moral philosophy that is both honest and genuine—one that does not reduce the "ought" to the "is" nor displace the "ought" from the actual to the ideal.

Huxley's *Island* and Sartre's *Absurd Friendship*

I N his last novel, *Island*, Aldous Huxley insists on a combination of upward and sideward transcendence quite absent in *The Devils of
Loudun*. The Mynah birds on this island paradise are trained to say
two words: "attention" and "karuna," or compassion. The yoga of death
and the yoga of "suchness," or the "Clear Light of the Void," are coupled throughout with the yoga of love. Huxley's earlier emphasis on
contemplation as the final goal and good is replaced by the Mahayana
Buddhist's insistence that "nirvana is samsara," that the One cannot be
found apart from the ten thousand things.

When Will Farnaby, the cynical journalist from England who has
found his way to the island, finally takes the psychedelic *"moksha-
medicine,"* he is so overcome by his vision of unity with God that
Susila, who administers it to him, has to insist that he come back from
the Absolute and relate to her and to the world around him. In criticism
of Huxley's counsel to use mescalin in order to take "chemical holidays,"
Martin Buber charged that people on mescalin see the world transfig-
ured into sheer glory of color but do not want to look at or touch others.[1]
In *Island* Huxley himself is aware of and warns against this danger by
way of Susila, who brings Will back to "reality" through a mutuality of
touching—a "dialogue of touchstones" such as I myself point to in
Touchstones of Reality.[2]

> ". . . One touches and, in the act of touching, one's touched. Complete
> communication, but nothing communicated. Just an exchange of life,
> that's all." Then, after a pause, "Do you realize, Will," she went on,
> "that in all these hours we've been sitting here—all these centuries in
> your case, all these eternities—you haven't looked at me once? Not once.
> Are you afraid of what you might see?"
>
> He thought over the question and finally nodded his head. "Maybe
> that's what it was," he said. "Afraid of seeing something I'd have to be
> involved with, something I might have to do something about."
>
> "So you stuck to Bach and landscapes and the Clear Light of the
> Void."

[1] Martin Buber, *The Knowledge of Man: The Philosophy of the Interhuman*,
ed. Maurice Friedman, trans. Maurice Friedman and R. G. Smith (N. Y.:
Harper Torchbooks, 1966), "What Is Common to All."
[2] Maurice Friedman, *Touchstones of Reality: Existential Trust and the Community of Peace* (N. Y.: Dutton Books, 1974), pp. 26–29.

"Which you wouldn't let me go on looking at," he complained.

"Because the Void won't do you much good unless you can see its light . . . in people . . . Which is sometimes considerably more difficult. . . . *Sunyata* implies *karuna*. The Void is light but it's also compassion. Greedy contemplatives want to possess themselves of the light without bothering about compassion. Merely good people try to be compassionate and refuse to bother about the light. As usual, it's a question of making the best of both worlds. And now," she added, "it's time for you to open your eyes and see what a human being really looks like."[3]

How far this novel, written shortly before Huxley's death, is from Huxley's statement in *Heaven and Hell* that "color is our touchstone of reality"![4] And Will understands this insoluble wedding of the paradox of opposites:

"It isn't the sun," he said at last, "and it isn't Chartres. Nor the infernal bargain basement, thank God. It's all of them together, and you're recognizably you, and I'm recognizably me—though needless to say, we're both completely different. You and me by Rembrandt, but Rembrandt about five thousand times more so."[5]

Though by no means so great a novel as *The Devils of Loudun*, *Island* attains an image of human wholeness that the former does not approach.

Jean-Paul Sartre's most impressive image of authentic human existence is his portrayal of Brunet in the two published fragments of the projected but never completed fourth novel of *The Roads of Freedom*, *Drole D'Amitié* (*Absurd Friendship*). Here in a Nazi prisoner-of-war camp Brunet develops from the rock-solid Communist Party leader that he was before into a person who takes it upon himself to give some life and hope to his fellow prisoners. When he is called to account by Chalais, the hard-line Party intellectual who arrives in camp with the latest Party line, Brunet gives up his life in an assertion of friendship that places him in the previously unthinkable position of going against the Party and rejecting its abstract truths for simple human ones.

Before the coming of Chalais, Brunet taught his comrades that the U.S.S.R. would enter the war against Hitler. After Chalais' arrival he admitted his "errors" and conformed to the Party line that the U.S.S.R. would never enter an imperialist war. Yet in his heart of hearts he continued to believe that the Soviet Union would be attacked and would

[3] Aldous Huxley, *Island* (N. Y.: Harper & Row, 1962; Perennial Classic, 1972), p. 326 f.
[4] Aldous Huxley, *Heaven and Hell* (N. Y.: Harper & Row, 1971). When a student brought this sentence to my attention two years after the publication of *Touchstones of Reality*, I was surprised and pleased to discover that Huxley too had used the phrase "touchstone of reality."
[5] Huxley, *Island*, p. 327.

have to enter the war. This seemed to him a hopeless "truth" since it would make the Party wrong and thereby condemn all men to everlasting isolation and solitude. But when his coworker and friend Schneider turns out to be Vicarios, a former Party member who has been formally accused by the Party of giving information to the Algerian government, Brunet is not willing to expose him. When he discovers that Chalais has informed the men about Vicarios and that two of them have set out to kill him, Brunet runs to defend him, thus walking knowingly into a trap that Chalais has set for him in order to get rid of the man who still has the loyalty of the rank and file. After beating off Vicarios' attackers, Brunet (who continues to think of him as Schneider) voluntarily joins him in escaping from the camp. It is, as he himself says at the end, a gesture of friendship, one made to a man who confesses he hated Brunet as a leader of the Party that had been steadily persecuting him, a man with whom Brunet himself had thought he could never again be friends.

When they get outside the barbed wire, they discover that someone has given them away to the Germans. They run in a hail of bullets, one of which hits Vicarios, making it impossible for them to go on any further. It is at this point that Brunet completes the merger of the "in-itself" and the "for-itself" and becomes the sole hero in Sartre's fiction to show meaningful personal and social direction and to demonstrate what freedom coupled with responsibility can mean. While Brunet pleads in vain with Vicarios for a recognition of their friendship and a hope for a new life, Vicarios bitterly announces that he is dying, that it is the Party that has driven him to his death, and that everything is Brunet's fault. Brunet no longer cares about the Germans, Chalais, or even the Party, only about his overwhelming wish that Vicarios not die.

> This absolute of suffering, no human victory will be able to efface it: it is the Party which drove him to his death; even if the U.S.S.R. gains, men are alone. Brunet . . . plunged his hand into the soiled hair of Vicarios. He cried out as if he could still save him from the horror, as if two lost men might be able, at the last minute, to conquer solitude:
> "—The hell with the Party! You are my only friend."

Vicarios does not hear for he is already dead, but Brunet cries again into the wind: "My only friend!" Staring fascinated into the empty visage in front of him and realizing that it is to *him* that this death has arrived, he rises and marches to meet the Germans advancing toward him through the trees: *his* death has only just begun.[6] It is a pity that this impressive novel was never completed and that what was written has not been published in English translation. It shows a warmth and humanity that one looks for in vain in Sartre's other literary works.

[6] Jean-Paul Sartre, *"Drole D'Amitié," Les Temps Modernes,* Vol. 5, Part I, Nos. 49 and 50 (November and December, 1949), pp. 769–806 and 1009–39. My translation from the French.

INDEX